AUSSIES wanna KISS

AUSSIES wanna KISS

Rachel Emmes

A copy of this publication can be found in the National Library of Australia.

ISBN: 978-1-921791-00-0 (pbk.)

Animation: Brett Bower – brett@brettbower.com.au
Logo: Leon Goltsman
Website: www.crewmark.com.au

Second Edition 2010

AUSSIES wanna KISS

To order additional copies of this book, contact:
Xlibris Corporation
1-800-618-969
www.xlibris.com.au
orders@www.xlibris.com.au
500366

Contents

AUSSIES wanna KISS™

Edward de Bono said: *"Dealing with complexity is an inefficient and unnecessary waste of time, attention and mental energy. There is never any justification for things being complex when they could be simple."*

I would add: *Complexity creates confusion and often is the catalyst of contrived fraud.* Contrived fraud by politicians has enabled the gradual sabotage of the Australian Federal & State's Constitutions with the instigation of adverse legislations in reducing the rights of Australian citizens to suppression, to where politicians are no longer the *servants but the masters.*

Government by the people for the people is democracy but government by the party for the party, is Communism. When voting is no longer based on who will do the best for the country but rather who will do the least damage, we're sitting on a time bomb.

Rachel Emmes

Acknowledgement and thanks

MY HUSBAND JOE has always given me unconditional love and the space I've needed to *learn to grow*, develop and fully appreciate life. And our daughter Ellie, who lights up our lives every minute of the day, we have the privilege of being her parents and as her Mum, I have been presented with the most important purpose I could ever have wanted to aspire to, and that which no business or career could ever satisfy. Because I have these two wonderful people and other than a fair go for all Australians – I want for nothing.

There is no such thing as our own success. Success is only successful when it's shared with and by others. I would like to thank some very important people for their help, their contributions, their friendship and support. My very dear parents and family have always been there for me through thick and thin, together with so many exemplary people who live in our midst. Good friends are a blessing and I am grateful for so many, particularly Anne, Grant, Natalie, Nathan, Chayah, Gaye, Sue, Kevin, Richard, Renzo, Matt, Richard and so many others. Exemplary people don't need rules and red tape to recognise real people in need, nor do they shun away from an opportunity to help others. Helmut is such a person. He heard from his friend that I needed help. I didn't know him, we had never met, but he gave me a demonstration of the highest level of goodness, kindness and trust that I have ever encountered. Helmut is a very humble and learned man and I will never turn away from any opportunity to deal with others in the way he dealt with me, in trying to repay his virtuous deed.

Daniel, Ulysses, Les, Pino and Bill – are dedicated and highly skilled professionals. Their caring and compassion towards others, especially in their time of distress saw them forge on unaided and unsupported by any (complacent) government agency, setting them at a level we should all want to aspire to. Their attitude of putting "people before profits" in being prepared to take risks to help others kindles a faith and trust in humanity second to none. Robert and Michoel are both highly skilled, people passionate life teachers whose wealth of knowledge they devotedly share with so many people in finding the true meaning of happiness, understanding of ourselves and in what success really means, they have helped me find and understand me.

This book has been a moving work for me and whilst I am the author, there have been many contributions from my fellow Australians – this is our (Australian owned) book, looking at our very serious problems with very sensible solutions. I would like to thank you for taking the time to read this book, for thinking about the concepts to change all of our lives and hopefully joining in improving the direction of our wonderful country, which can initially be done by participating in the Petition at our website <www.aussieswannakiss.com> and supporting the draft proposed reforms, as covered. It has been said that the majority of Australians don't care for politics, and who could blame them, but if we do not wake up to government impositions on us, we will get what we deserve for our complacency. Please discuss the book with your family and friends, as it is in all of our interest, *pre-warned is pre-armed*!

Inspiration

ALL DECENT AUSTRALIANS need and deserve a fair go, and this is the best inspiration for anyone, particularly for me. I have seen many injustices at all levels of our society, in my personal and in my business life. I am compelled to do my bit in trying to make a difference to all of our lives. In particular for our children, to ensure they have every door wide open to them and that they never get slammed up against the *"blank walls of incompetence, complacency and unfounded encumbrances"* or that they should lose any opportunity. This is paramount to every loving parent and decent person.

I have come to the realisation that we must all delve deeply into our intellectual and emotional selves to awaken our enormous individual and collective potential, in doing some very serious soul searching. Most of us ignore or don't know how to access this potential. It's like having all of the ingredients and recipe for our favourite chocolate cake but not being able to find our glasses to read the recipe. If we can access the recipe for life then we are able to access our true potential and reap the rewards for all of us collectively.

We have all been blessed with limitless potential and the ability to be passionate about issues important to every single one of us. The only thing that can stop us is ourselves, our lack of inspiration and therefore lack of motivation. We have a moral and ethical responsibility to become proactive whenever the opportunity presents itself, particularly in the fight against injustices and inequality, at all levels of society. I hope this book will inspire others to become proactive in helping to grow and develop themselves and to instil this culture into others, for the benefit of our collective improved quality of life now and for the benefit of the generations to come. If we are not advancing forward, we are going backwards and those who fail to become proactive get stuck with the scraps of life, doing what they've always done and getting what they've always got!

We are fortunate in Australia to have so many good people, who go out of their way to give freely of their time and resources for the benefit of others and for no obvious rewards for themselves, just because the opportunity to make a difference to someone else presents itself. The fact is that many small acts of kindness are measured on par with the large earth-shattering contributions made by those fortunate enough to have been given those opportunities.

One of the most empowering things I have heard is that *"If I have changed but one life, I have changed the world"* and, in this sense, many small acts of kindness do change individuals' worlds enormously and thus our own greater world, in a small but tangible way. One of the greatest wonders is that we never know just how desperately our kindness has been needed by others in giving them hope, security and self worth without an ego.

The only true form of success comes from our personal growth and refined self development and then in our ability to help others grow and maximise their own potential, thus can we benefit personally. No matter who we are, our acts of caring and kindness may seem irrelevant or trivial, but they can be life-changing for ourselves and others in making the most profound difference to our whole world. What comes around goes around in the strangest way and if you have any doubt just remember the following story if ever you're thinking of turning away from an opportunity to help another:

Fleming was a poor Scottish farmer. One day, while trying to scratch out a living for his family, he heard a cry for help coming from a nearby bog. He dropped his tools and ran to see who needed help and there up to his waist in thick black mulch, was a terrified boy, screaming and struggling to free himself. Farmer Fleming saved the boy from what could have been a slow and terrifying death.

The very next day, a fancy horse-drawn carriage pulled up at the Scotsman's poor farm house and an elegantly dressed nobleman stepped out of the carriage and introduced himself as the father of the boy farmer Fleming had saved the previous day. "I want to repay you, you saved my son's life," said the nobleman. "No, I can't accept payment for what I did," the Scottish farmer insisted.

At that moment, the farmer's own son came to the door of the family hovel. "Is that your son?" the nobleman asked. "Yes," the farmer replied proudly. "I'll make you a deal. Let me take him and give him a good education. If the lad is anything like his father he'll grow to be a fine man you will be proud of." And that he did.

In time, farmer Fleming's son graduated from St. Mary's Hospital Medical School in London and went on to become known throughout the world as the noted Sir Alexander Fleming, who discovered penicillin. Years later, the nobleman's son was stricken with pneumonia, and what saved him? Penicillin. The name of the nobleman was Lord Randolph Churchill and his son's name? Sir Winston Churchill.

What goes around comes around. Neither the farmer nor Lord Randolph foresaw the impact of their deeds to themselves and the benefits reaped by humanity forever.

This story may be an urban legend, but like any good story, those who quote it, do so with increasing confidence that it is accurate. Yet its central message is still valuable, that random acts of kindness can be repaid with many unexpected dividends.

Eventually most of us reach a point in our lives where we realise that irrespective of how much we own, all of our worldly possessions are worth nothing in the great scheme of things. In the cemetery the bodies of those, who achieved no financial wealth in their lifetime lay next to those who have achieved great financial success, yet only a good name and our good deeds are our legacy when we leave this world.

It is only when this realisation hits us that we gain the wisdom of humility, which comes with the acceptance of our mortality and the realisation that kindness and caring for others are the essence of a good and meaningful life. If we are fortunate enough to attain this level in our early years, we have a greater head start than most in providing ourselves with the opportunity to live happier lives. We are then able to be a positive inspiration to others in helping them reach that level.

Australians, old and new, of all ages, of all faiths and backgrounds continually put their hand up to give their valuable time and resources (rightfully belonging to their families) for no financial gain to themselves, just to lend a hand. Many volunteers – selflessly risk their lives to save others. There are also those who fundraise for so many worthy causes in our communities, all working without fanfare or recognition. Numerous people and organisations contribute money so generously to help thousands of Australians in so many plights, make such a difference to each and everyone of us and their legacy lives as a tribute to their benevolence. Aussies find time, have skills and a natural spirit of generosity, we truly care, even though we joke that we don't.

It would be a crime not to acknowledge the special people in our community who perform the most difficult jobs, while contending with bureaucratic and financial constraints and difficult conditions. These are our police, doctors, nurses, paramedics, teachers, defence forces, emergency services, etc. those who look after *our* welfare. These vital service providers want and need better resources and conditions, to enable them to get the job of looking after us done well, and in turn, we can provide them with the job satisfaction and good conditions and resources they rightfully deserve.

Some special people are hard to see or remember. These are the "whistleblowers" at every level of our society, bringing crimes against us all to the fore. Crimes that would go unapprehended and we would wear greater corruption and greed than currently, without these selfless people, many risking their employment, condemnation and character assassination. Whistleblowers are rarely recognised, but are appreciated. May your numbers grow with pride and with the certain knowledge that what you do is the right thing for all of us and you are both acknowledged and greatly appreciated.

Perhaps one of the greatest injustices is this:

We treat the famous, the celebrities, as "Special People",
When it's the "Special People" living among us
who we should treat as Famous!

Introduction

OTHER THAN OUR indigenous brothers and sisters, we were all, at sometime in the not so distant past, a migrant or born to migrants who chose to live here. We are either a first or a 10th generation or somewhere in between, but we're an Australian.

Over the past 220 years since first settlement we have developed our own caring culture which we are proud of, and want to share with others. We want to continue to develop this cultural attitude towards all mankind, regardless of race or creed. We need, more than ever, to extend our positive personal attitude to the preservation and enhancement of our country and our environment with innovative conservational methods and alternative fuels, while maximising our primary and secondary industries, ensuring every Australian benefits.

Aussies appreciate and desperately want to grasp opportunities to advance Australia for the benefit of every Australian, now and for the future. However, we are aware of the systemic drawbacks, blockades, hindrances and perversions to constructive progress, causing tremendous losses in time, money, resources and opportunities.

Progress and improvements are impeded by governments over-regulating in inappropriate areas, while failing to regulate in areas needing regulation. Wasted financial and human resources are expended in an abundance of cumbersome procedures, rather than effectively achieving the objectives. We have wrongfully accepted unaccountable mismanagement as the norm; including wilful and systemic corruption; poor priorities and alternative agendas at all levels of business and government. This has been allowed to cultivate under a barrage of bureaucracy, impractical and unfair constitutions which are generally attributed to profits before the interests of the people. Millions of individual Australians have lodged complaints with governments but most complaints are not acted on and most go unreported. This is relied on by governments to conceal their failures and their obligations to the people. Unfortunately, politicians create problems as they do not have the solutions. Privacy laws and confidentiality rights are nothing more than a non-transparent cloak to conceal Government failures and political parties ulterior motives.

Almost every government office and agency receives complaints from thousands of Australians each year. There are more than 40,000 complaints received each year by the Australian Securities and Investment Commission "ASIC" Example:

More than 10 individuals complained to ASIC regarding a fraudulent counterfeit operation, involving more than A$15million. The matter and the complaints were ignored, or dismissed by ASIC under the cloak of *"barter schemes were deregulated by ASIC in 1999"*. In addition to the counterfeit, the complaints related to numerous breaches of the corporations act, including – trading while insolvent, trading while deregistered, trading while in liquidation, false misleading and deceptive conduct by de facto directors and trading under a Phoenix operation, but nothing stirred ASIC to investigate. The matter was then referred to the under resourced NSW Police, who referred and recommended the matter [back] to ASIC, as the police stated are the Australian government's corporate regulator and the most appropriate authority to conduct this investigation, but ASIC refused the police.

There have been no less than 6 companies placed into liquidation due to this counterfeit operation, together with the many other complainants and creditors, who all suffered extensive loss and damage. These complaints, and the complacency of ASIC was referred to the highest level of both sides of State and Federal government, all falling on deaf ears. That is, the matter was fobbed off by government and oppositions, to pursue any other agenda and leaving a liquidator to fund investigations and prosecutions. Death threats were made against several of the complainants, with one suffering his business being burnt to the ground, but still no intervention or assistance was provided by any government authority. The Minister for Corporations, the Hon Nick Sherry 24 Jan 2009 advises *"I have no jurisdiction over ASIC . . . ."* while Bob Debus, Home Secretary *"I have no ability to instruct the Australian Federal Police.* Nathan Rees' office advised ". . . *don't worry, Mr Rees will get to the bottom of this I can assure you* . . . . Nothing. Malcolm Turnbull was provided with extensive documentation and prima facie evidence . . . . Nothing. On 14 Sept 2009 the NSW Parliamentary Secretary for Police, Angela D'Amore advised *"the matter has been thoroughly investigated and there is no evidence to support your fraud allegations"* yet the liquidator advises that no one from the police or any government agency has ever attended his office to inspect the volumes of evidence! Ms Keneally's office advised in Jan 2010 that they would be onto the matter but 9 months later . . . . Nothing.

The complacency by government towards individuals and groups is contemptuously tolerated and should not be acceptable, yet it appears there is very little any individual or group can do to overcome those who burden our society. The only available opportunity to demonstrate distain for government is in our 3 yearly voting, otherwise there is certainly no incentive by any government "party" system to seek changes. A hung government was the result of the 2010 election where almost one million people did not vote or rather their vote was invalid because of their contempt for a defective party system. Then there are those who use and abuse their privileged positions to hide behind their status, and those in the business sector who ride high on the inequality of bargaining power, not afforded to the average person.

In October 2009 after completing his findings into whether we need a Charter or Bill of Human Rights, **Father Frank Brennan states that what we really need** is to *"turn back the tide of criminal behaviour in powerful governments"*. Those who benefit by sheer deception and abuse of power who inflict financial and emotional losses and destruction on the lives of their innocent victims, Australians. Those who go un-apprehended in their privileged government positions, who have curiously avoided giving themselves the power to intervene in adverse conditions imposed by government through to the corporate world, yet curiously granting themselves powers they are not entitled to, in making the people subjective and in forging off the growing awareness of this political system's redundancy.

The landscape of democracy as we have known has changed, not just here but in the countries of our allies. We are witnessing disgruntled people power movements such as the US Tea Party Movement. Patriotic Americans are fed up with the same abuses to their Constitution as we are fed up with government conflicts of interest between big business and the people, fed up with international treaties impositions which give greater consideration to those in other countries than their own and to those who illegally enter their country and receive greater support than to their own. Look up this movement on the internet, it is a revolution and becoming less peaceful everyday.

Aussies are just as fed up trying to conform with or maintain untenable systems, especially over-governing and over-regulating, while under-productive bureaucracy is propped up by a failing judicial system. We contend with illogical, near-sighted "political correctness" as a means of providing excuses, rather than solutions. Change for the sake of political correctness is not change; it is wallpapering over the cracks, compounding our problems. If change is to take place, it starts with each and every person striving to achieve individual and thus, collective improvements to every facet of our lives. I must emphasise how our own individual attitudes, behaviour and standards impacts on the whole scheme of things, starting in our own homes.

We all have the ability to implement changes for ourselves and, by example, to champion change in those closest to us. However, for overall changes to take place in Australian business and political arenas there are uncompromising bureaucratic hurdles and ingrained inflexibility to any change, which can only be overcome by the majority of us, working together to direct government in a fresh government process and not accepting vote gaining, flash-in-the-pan policies which are dropped after elections.

If we want to see improvements in our country, we need to redirect our "employee" government, to achieving "our objectives" (it's our government, after all) rather than government "party's" prioritising their party's objectives and the survival of the party, over everything else. We need to ensure every facet of our lives, from ourselves to the top government office is addressed, ensuring a KISS (Keep It Simple Stupid) formula in grasping change with enthusiasm, and implementation of improvements is taken on efficiently.

If it's not simple, it just won't happen. Mistakes will be made and they will be rectified, but inaction, procrastination and mismanagement can only prolong misery, allow disenfranchised members of society to degenerate further, allow crime to flourish, lives to be forsaken and it will be near impossible to reverse if we are not proactive now.

As you read on you will observe some reiterations and I make no apology for this, as most of the issues and proposed changes cross collateralise, horizontally and vertically, between personal, business, community and government issues, for the consolidation and development of all of our country's resources and insulating us from adverse international conditions.

This book is not intended as a statistical reference book, but statistics have been gathered from the Australian Bureau of Statistics, other government agencies and sources, to demonstrate issues and impacts. There are many clichés used as a means of saying much with few, but meaningful words, easily recalled. This book is based on both generalisations and specifics and although it is not my autobiography, it does encompass many of my unique and not so unique experiences, gathered in the course of my business and personal life.

You may well be enlightened by generalities and comments and in these circumstances, it is your responsibility to assess your direction and priorities in life, in passing your strong moral and caring philosophy onto those who have not yet grown or developed into the people Australia needs. People who may need your help to find the will and the way of striving to produce a happy balance in their lives and then onto those they influence.

I have attempted to write this book in a fashion which ensures the concepts are understood by all ages and all levels of educational standards with ease, ensuring every person can evaluate the opportunities presented and to be inspired to participate in change, particularly our young people who stand to be the greatest benefactors of change.

Many of the concepts and ideas are not unique and are in fact timeless, proven methods. Some people may consider these concepts to be outlandish or old-fashioned, but they are based on a common-sense approach to what I believe the majority of Australians want to see implemented and achieved. Concepts may need to be refined and further developed for the 21st century by experts and you may be one of them in your respective field, so grab the opportunity to go forward.

As a nation we have a remarkable head-start. Per capita Australia produces the greatest results in all fields from sports to music; from the arts to medical research; from innovation to ingenuity. We are creative and resourceful and our thirst is for more opportunities to excel and to project Australia into new and existing world markets. However, to get the process moving we need to establish a solid foundation in getting our "house", metaphorically speaking, our country, in order first and to resurrect what is not so common these days – "Common Sense". I share this obituary which you may have read, but many may not have:

The Sad Passing of "Common Sense"

Today we mourn the passing of a beloved old friend, Common Sense, who has been with us for many years. No one knows for sure how old he was since his birth records were long ago lost in bureaucratic red tape. He will be remembered as having cultivated such valuable lessons as knowing when to come in out of the rain, why the early bird gets the worm, that life isn't always fair, and maybe it was my fault.

Common Sense lived by simple, sound financial policies of don't spend more than you earn and reliable parenting strategies of having adults, not children, in charge.

His health began to deteriorate rapidly when well-intentioned but overbearing regulations were set in place, particularly when he was no longer able to take photos of his children and their friends at the beach or at a picnic or in school concerts. Reports of a six-year-old boy charged with sexual harassment for kissing a classmate; teens suspended from school for using mouthwash after lunch; and a teacher fired for reprimanding an unruly student, only worsened his condition.

Common Sense lost ground when parents attacked teachers for doing the job they themselves failed to do in disciplining their unruly children.

It declined even further when schools were required to get parental consent to administer Panadol, sun lotion or a band aid to a student, but could not inform the parents when a student became pregnant and wanted to have an abortion. Common Sense began to lose the will to live as the Ten Commandments became contraband; churches became big businesses and criminals received better treatment than their victims.

Common Sense took a beating when you couldn't defend yourself from a burglar in your own home and the burglar could sue you for assault.

Common Sense gave up the will to live after a woman failed to realise that a steaming cup of coffee was hot, she spilled a little in her lap and was promptly awarded a huge settlement. His heart finally failed when Santa was no longer allowed to 'HO HO HO' as it might scare small children, although it did them no harm for centuries gone by.

Common Sense was preceded in death by his parents, Truth and Trust and by his wife, Discretion; while his daughter, Responsibility; and his son, Reason are all feeling the pain suffered by Common Sense. He is survived by three stepbrothers – "I Know My Rights", "Someone Else is to Blame", and "I'm A Victim".

Not many attended his funeral because so few realised he was gone. If you still remember him, we ask you to pay tribute by giving him consideration when dealing with others and to make sure we remember him in every facet of our daily lives and to accept nothing less than common sense at all levels of our society.

**Common sense only comes to those who practise
common sense practices and standards.**

Some readers will applaud my comments, some will be appalled and then there are those who have no opinion at all. But one thing is for sure, thank God in

Australia we have the freedom to have and share our opinions and we trust almost implicitly that we do not denigrate the rights of others or allow them to denigrate ours. In sharing my opinions, I hope to inspire others to speak up about injustices and continuously look for opportunities to help each other in building Australia to the greatest heights, where we can improve our quality of life and opportunities for all Australians.

I am not a political or legal expert and many may doubt my literary skills. I am more than certain that this book will not be considered for the Prime Minister's or the Premier's Literary Award, but I write this book with experience and great passion for my fellow Australians. At the time of writing, the details contained are correct, but may have changed by the time the book is distributed or it is read, and there are some wonderful contributions from my fellow Australians, some of which have been gathered from their passionate public domain efforts.

I thank God in the truest sense and not in the way this phrase indicates a sense of relief. Many of us acknowledge a Higher Power is at work in our lives, either directly and powerfully or haunting the periphery of their future. Australia has an excellent, but sadly not unblemished record of having different faiths, living tolerantly and harmoniously together. This can only improve with education, tolerance and equality, but only for those who are tolerant.

If faith helps us find comfort and direction, it is often something more which is needed to claim our political rights. **People Power, is the only way we can collectively address urgent changes to fundamental community issues; redress our decaying democracy; rectify our eroded National Constitution from those who have not been empowered to sabotage the true intention of this document or transgress from providing a true justice system and equality.** These are the basic fundamentals as to why we have been contending with an ailing system of running our country and preventing us all being able to enjoy "life, liberty and the pursuit of happiness". That, at least, is what the American constitution promises and we know whatever the Yanks can do, Aussies can do better!

After reading this book, I would ask that you go to our website: <www.aussieswannakiss.com> and go to the "Petition" page to consider participating, as the objective of this book is not to have a good *"whinge."* Its objective is, firstly, to acknowledge our social, political and economic shortcomings and problems, pose reform based on equality and then refine the initial draft plans as covered in this book with viable amendments, to be produced by experts in all respective fields, and – with your support of the Petition – to proceed in seeking to implement changes expeditiously through a referendum to the High Court of Australia and through a cohesive movement to **Advance Australia** fairly. The survey at the website gives the participant the opportunity to have a say, which until now may very well be our first opportunity to vote for and achieve **what we want** rather than based on a principle of "whoever promises **whatever it takes to get themselves into *POWER!*"**

SECTION 1

"The State of Aussie Politics"

The Backbone of Australia

Acknowledging problems is half of the solution . . . .

AUSTRALIA'S BIRTH RATE increased by a record 296,600 babies born in 2008 which was up by 11,400 over 2007 Coupled with immigration (currently 300,000 pa) and then reduced by deaths and migration to other countries, we have now exceeded the 22 million mark in a country which is more than 4 times the size of our nearest neighbour, Indonesia. Indonesia's population exceeds 230 million. Our national population is less than that of Los Angeles or Moscow and geographically we are approximately the same size as the United States of America (without Alaska) with their more than 310 million people, the legal and statistical population, anyway. The US has approx 20% or 62 million living on 20% of the country yet we are concerned about sustaining 50 million on the same 20% of the space in another 40 odd years. To determine a long term **"Sustainable Population"** we must first be able to sustain our current population and then ensure the future population will be sustainable. We have the space and resources to grow and the greatest opportunities to develop. Inland, we tend to lack only two things, trace minerals in our soil and reliable access to water. Australia is no doubt the envy of our over populated neighbours, who celebrate the disparity at times by fishing in our Exclusive Economic Zone.

Like most western societies, we are experiencing massive disparities in our national birth rates. In France, Germany, England, Canada, Greece and The Netherlands the birth rate is down to less than 1.6% with Italy achieving 1.3% despite baby bonus packages of US$17,000 Meanwhile, Australia, overall, now sits at 1.97% (2007-08) but it has been suggested that 2.11% is what is required as a minimum to sustain a national culture.

Bird life and bird procreation requires a sustainable environment and we like most animals, are subject to our environment and food supply. We are no different. Take away our ability to feed and house our young and you take away the incentive to have more children or sustain society's overall needs and the ability to provide opportunities for more young Australians for the longevity of our nation. This is the primary undermining factor effecting and destroying many functional families in Western society and thus the country.

Some observers suggest that at 1.3% it is impossible to reverse the long term consequences of decaying population levels. In Japan, people, particularly women (who have always had a culture of subservience to their men), have sought careers over marriage and in countries, such as China (and Spain) where families suffered the torment and often torture of failing to adhere to a one child family policy, are now having to deal with further suffering from the ill effects of that short-sighted policy. Except in several of China's exclusive economic zones, such as Shanghai, where restrictions have been lifted, women have become the valued gender.

This policy has produced societies of men without women, as it was the female baby who was commonly sacrificed – often effectively slaughtered by parents, through murder or calculated neglect, in order to have a male able to work harder and continue the family name, while conforming to this policy. Now, these sad and sorry single blokes must support their aging population, with one young person required to support three aged people. To the contrary, in Muslim societies, where men can have many wives, they can produce many children and the opposite is apparent. For example, Osama Bin Laden and his father alone have reportedly fathered 80 kids between them.

With the disparity in cultural birth rates, it is estimated that by 2025 the population of France will be 50% Muslim and by 2050 Germany will be a Muslim State. A one-child system whether by official policy or by individual choice, would see a society reduced by 75% in just 3 generations, eg four grandparents producing two parents, producing one child. If the world wanted to maintain a static population of 6 billion this could only be achieved if every couple throughout the world agreed to have only 2 kids, ie a zero population growth in only replacing the previous generation. There would be as much interest and co-operation from 100% of all nations to such a proposal, peacefully, as there would be in conforming 100% to emissions reductions by all nations!

In Western society, the first and most crucial sign of a failing economy is the downturn in the birth rate. Yet it is slow retail sales, which attracts the attention of government, as retail trends portray an immediate short-term impact, not dissimilar to the tenure of the government of the day. But retail sales are a false gauge, fluctuating in the short-term while our birth rate is for the very long-term. The reason governments like to rely on retail trends and make efforts to influence retail trends is that they can be performed during the life of the government. It can also be used as a lever to increase interest once it appears that there has been an increase in spending.

The figures below aren't some daft appeal to "populate or perish". Rather, it is that we need to **acknowledge what is needed to "Sustain the Population" and just as important for many of us, is to "Sustain the Culture" we enjoy**. As a nation, we need to have a real debate about what constitutes a sustainable population and culture for Australia. The inconsistencies in government polities have seen the Howard government introduce incentives to populate with A$3,000 baby bonus payments, while the Rudd Labor government was concerned for our inability to provide schools, care for the aged and for the pressure on all resources and infrastructure from increasing our population. The Labor government seeks to terminate these incentives to slow the population growth, yet it fails to deter breaches of our boarders and the massive immigration into a country while we cannot sustain all of our people. We have made the laughing stock of those seeking "Economic Asylum". We have massive contradiction in policy objectives in such short periods based on no proven formula, or rather there is just no real foresight or long-term planning from either political party for their short term tenure.

Our longest standing and most similar ally in western society in many respects is the USA and if we were to compare population growth and trends, much can be learnt.

Year	USA	Australia
1908	75,994,575	4,232,278
1958	150,697,361	9,947,358
2008	281,421,906	21,542,500
	Almost double every 50 yrs	1 Oct 2009 – 22 million (Project 50 million in 2058)

By 2009 we were less than 10% of the population of the USA which kicked off in 1620 giving America a head start of some 168 years over Australia, first settled by the Poms in 1788 but lifestyle choices, values, music and many fundamentals of our society are on par with our mates, the Yanks. Based on our relatively short history, we have a distinct advantage over the US in our ability to see and learn from their historical developments and mistakes. We are witnessing the failings of a Republic but the sound decisions of a solid Constitution which Americans cherish, while most Aussies wouldn't have a clue about ours.

Many lives were lost by both England and America in the fight for US independence, while we will not "appear" to lose one dear soul if we choose to cut our umbilical cord with the UK. It would only take the determination of the majority through a national referendum and with a stroke of the pen, amend away our Constitutional protection and dependence on England, if we no longer wanted to be a part of the British Commonwealth. Yet, government legislation has already reduced the Queen's sovereign powers to intervene into our affairs and thus demonstrates a contrived existence of the diminishing Royal powers, but I would dare say that Her relevant is perhaps more important these days than it may have been in days gone by.

Wars and civil unrest with native American Indians and those who were brought over against their will from Africa, as slaves, who suffered generations of persecution from their fellow Americans for no other reason but for the colour of their skin. Then to a Civil War between the North and the South and, now, to have as the 44th President of the USA, an African American man, is nothing short of sensational. It is truly a demonstration to people from all walks of life as to humanity's ability to love and respect each other and outgrow past unfounded bigotry and biases.

Australia like so many other nations has also been guilty of segregation, discrimination and cruelty in our short past: from our "White Australia Policy" regarding immigration to the treatment of Australian Aborigines. The white European conquerors of Australia were so haughty that on seeing the different culture of the Australian Aborigines, they immediately deemed it inferior to their own and set about changing their lives. Should they instead have observed this culture and put aside prejudices, perhaps they might have learned valuable lessons from a people still in tune with nature and the land today.

Perhaps instead of removing Aboriginal children from their families and causing generations of pain and anguish, lessons ought to have been learned from these people to have better enriched the lives of their own families. Policies imposed on "black fellas" demanding they conform to what was claimed to be "civilised standards of living," included "our values" purported to be superior to theirs. These once innocent people have been introduced to alcohol, petrol sniffing and white-fella diseases, destroying their once serene way of life and for many, their survival skills and cultural knowledge in an ill-conceived attempt at creating some sort of illusion of a white "supremacist standard." This is no different to any other supremacist (power crazy) "party" of the past or those who continue to roam the earth today, under different banners.

In 1788, Captain Arthur Phillip brought the first convict settlers to Botany Bay and over the following years colonies were set up around the country with State lines or boarders flexing, based on no rhyme or reason. New South Wales originally extended to Melbourne. Each State established its own constitution and judiciary system which were run by free white land owners who saw the opportunities in a new country and who vested in themselves the supreme power of government as they adopted the Westminster system of government in 1854.

Ultimately in 1901 we formed a National Federation with its own Constitution and the independent State judicial systems. The States agreed to work together with a small national (Federal) government. Government positions were held tightly by the very few educated aristocratic land owners. Today most (fortunate) Aussies are land owners, are educated, are able to make educated decisions and we no longer need to rely on aristocrats and academics to hold portfolios they are not skilled in, and thus are a liability to governing this country efficiently. We have tens of thousands of educators, medical practitioners, qualified tradespersons and professionals in all fields, all forming part of the millions of educated Australians who possess good intellect, stable emotions and who have access to all forms of information. Those who are capable of conducting votes daily on issues of concern, if there were to be a need.

As a society we must learn from both the arrogant mistakes of our predecessors and their tried and true 'good life practises and skills' if we want to save ourselves the grief of preventable continuity of mistakes and losses. To be able to accelerate positive growth, we must not be hindered by obstacles or the indulgences of those with poor priorities or those who purport to have the skills to handle specific requirements of society, but do not!

The government and judicial systems governing us today were founded on the knowledge and resources available prior to 1901 and while we have grown and developed technologically and in every facet of life over the past 109 years, Federal and States constitutions have but transgressed away from what the people had accepted then. Although those constitutional designers are dead, many would consider that they appear to be "ruling from the grave" but I dare say that they would indeed be turning over in their graves, if they were to witness the abuses to the Constitution with adverse Federal and States legislations by politicians and their parties. Many Constitutional references appear obsolete, as many of our most imperative Constitutional safe-guards have been violated by crafty politicians. Politicians, particularly since the end of WW2 have over-ridden our Constitution with adverse, and thus, defective legislations which are then upheld by a no longer "independent judiciary" seeking to interpret the variations.

Then the privatisation, or rather flogging off, of our most imperative assets and utilities to private corporations to maximise profits, while deregulating industries have enabled governments to move away from the real job of government. This has enabled governments to achieve their political party's ulterior agendas, while their "opposition party" watched on, never demanding referendums be put to the people, as prescribed in our Constitution. Legislations have provided the mechanisms for hindrances to efficient and truly effective governance which no longer prevails, but enables governments to pursue their "party's philosophies and agendas" and the agendas of those who are bank-rolling them.

Maintaining an abused Constitution only serves to reward and protect the positions of power our politicians have rewarded themselves, those who could still be considered to be primarily "aristocratic academics". Political academics who have studied politics but have never worked outside of the legal or political field, in the real world, many would consider unemployable. Yet it is their concepts, theories and philosophies which work on paper or in their minds, which are more than often implemented and then found not to be practical, realistic for a common sense application. Therefore, many "theories are proven to be equitable or fair" in the long term to encompass the needs of any diverse community.

When impractical theories are implemented they are eventually proven not only ineffective but, worse, counterproductive. Flawed theories and short term objectives cause us to lose years of valuable time, money and opportunities, which can take decades and even centuries to undo the damage, if ever and often it's easier and more effective to adapt to new ways.

Technocrats are a class of people who must be recognised for their great intellect and contributions and while we cannot live without them, they should not be solely relied on as the sole arbiters in choosing a nation's direction. It is only when we can use the skills of academics together with the appropriate amalgamation of collective practical skilled persons that we can make up a functional society, producing maximum results for the benefit of every person and not only for a select, elite few. While we have some of the best academic minds in the world (also blessed with common sense) these minds are more than often hindered or prevented from initiating their very best and logical efforts for Australia's benefit. All too often, skilled academics are intercepted or prevented by political "parties" who have their higher agenda to protect and strive to achieve, irrespective of adverse results in other countries, or the lack of any proven practise – be it the Liberal Conservatives at one end of the spectrum, though the intermediary minorities, to the far end of the spectrum in the Labor Socialist philosophies. Both major parties and their collaborators have instigated a barrage of adverse protocols and procedures to deflect our attention away from their true motifs and we have all been too busy making ends meet day to day to see the "Cause" yet individually and collectively, we suffer the "Effects". How did this happen?

Political parties have their masters, that is, their financial backers and the Fabian Society is the primary master of our Labor government. These sorts of organizations have always been considered to be part of conspiracy theories, but they do exist, and they do impact on our society, much more than we would care that they do. Their membership is passed from generation to generation of those who have a need or an insatiable ego to belong to, or to be a part of, a powerful immortal entity with its ideologies that tantalizes and gives some sort of satisfaction which they do not have, or cannot achieve in their lives. This belonging compensates for the short length of a persons natural life, in that the "society" or entity is ongoing and the individual's part gives them some deluded sense of immortality and purpose. Wealth accumulates from the wealthy members who set their long term agendas, which are supported by massive compounded financial resources, thus enabling their creative exploitation of the poorer in society to achieve their long term manipulative objectives.

The **Fabian Society** was founded on 4 January 1884 in London as an offshoot of a society founded in 1883 called, *The Fellowship of the New Life*. They wanted to transform society by setting an example of clean simplified living for others to follow, but when some members also wanted to become politically involved to aid society's transformation, it was decided that a separate society was to be set up, thus The Fabian Society. The Fabian Society additionally advocated renewal of Western European Renaissance ideas and their promulgation or spreading throughout the rest of the world. Immediately upon its inception, the Fabian Society began attracting many prominent contemporary figures drawn to its socialist cause, including George Bernard Shaw, H. G. Wells, Annie Besant, Graham Wallas, Hubert Bland, Edith Nesbit, Sydney Olivier, Oliver Lodge, Leonard Woolf and Virginia Woolf, Ramsay MacDonald and Emmeline Pankhurst.

It is best known for its initial ground-breaking work beginning late in the 19th century and continuing up to World War I. The society laid many of the foundations of the Labor Party and subsequently affected the policies of States emerging from the de-colonization of the British Empire. Today, the society exist in Australia (the Australian Fabian Society), Canada (the Douglas-Coldwell Foundation and in past the League for Social Reconstruction) and New Zealand.

The group, which favoured gradual incremental change rather than revolutionary change, was named – at the suggestion of Frank Podmore – in honor of the Roman general Quintus Fabius Maximus (nicknamed "Cunctator", meaning "the Delayer"). His **Fabian strategy advocated tactics of harassment and attrition rather than head-on battles** against the Carthaginian army under the renowned general Hannibal Barca.

At the core of the Fabian Society were Sidney and Beatrice Webb. **Together, they wrote numerous studies of industrial Britain** (based on philosophical academic theories, that is**), including alternative co-operative economics that applied to ownership of capital as well as land.** Fabian socialists were in favour of an imperialist foreign policy as a conduit for internationalist reform and a welfare State modelled on the Bismarckian German model; they criticized Gladstonian liberalism both for its individualism at home and its internationalism abroad. The Fabians favoured the nationalization of land, believing that rents collected by landowners were unearned, an idea from the work of American economist, Henry George.

Many Fabians participated in the formation of the Labor Party in 1900 and the group's Constitution, written by Sidney Webb, borrowed heavily from the founding documents of the Fabian Society. At the Labor Party Foundation Conference in 1900, the Fabian Society claimed 861 members. It was at this time that many of the future leaders of the Third World were exposed to Fabian thought, most notably India's Jawaharlal Nehru, who subsequently framed economic policy for India on Fabian social-democratic lines, to now where more than 400 million are starving. Obafemi Awolowo who later became the premier of Nigeria's defunct Western Region was also a Fabian member in the late 1940s. It was the Fabian ideology that Awolowo used to run the Western Region but was prevented from using it on a national level in Nigeria. It is a little-known fact that the founder of Pakistan, Barrister Muhammad Ali Jinnah, was an avid member of the Fabian Society in the early 1930s. Lee Kuan Yew, the first Prime Minister of Singapore, stated in his memoirs that his initial political philosophy was strongly influenced by the Fabian Society.

The founders of the Fabian Society went on to found the London School of Economics, specifically to further the plans of the Society. It was funded in part by Sir Edward Cassel, who stated . . . *"Our object is to make this institution a place to raise and train the bureaucracy of the future Socialist State."* The influence of this School cannot be underestimated. Major government bodies around the world carry a high proportion of alumni, including the economic and banking sectors of the USA, the United Nations and the new European Union. Australian connections include Kevin

Rudd, William McMahon former PM, Graham Hill an Australian Federal Court Judge.

Another member of the Fabian Society, Cecil Rhodes, funded the Rhodes Scholarship with the express intention of raising up promising young graduates to establish a secret society in order to *"take the government of the whole world".* Foundation members were all Fabian Society members who worked very closely with the London School of Economics. Although the recipients and members had very heavy American connections, Australian connections include Bob Hawke, former PM. From this spawned the Royal Institute on International Affairs, Council of Foreign Relations and the Institute of Pacific Relations.

It must be understood that the over-whelming intention of this 'family tree' of societies & institutes was always to support, further and activate the "world government" aims of the Fabian Society. George Bernard Shaw, an original member stated . . . . *"the Society made it possible for respectable citizens to support socialism without suspicion of lawless desire to overturn the existing order."* He also stated: *"Fabianism feeds on Capitalism, but excretes Communism."* And again: *"Our propaganda is one of permeating – we urged our members to join the Liberal & Radical Associations in their district, or if they preferred it, the Conservative Associations – we permeated the party organisations and pulled all the strings we could lay our hands on with the utmost adroitness and energy, and we succeeded so well we gained the solid advantage of a Progressive majority full of ideas that would never have come into their heads had not the Fabians put them there."*

To understand how this works, look at The Australian Labor Party: Formed in 1891 approximately 30 years older than the Country Party and more than 50 years older than the Liberal Party. The Australian Labor Party entered Federal politics at the first Commonwealth elections of 1901 when 16 Labor members were elected to the House of Representatives and eight to the Senate. They met before the first sitting of Parliament on 8 May 1901 and agreed to form a Federal Labor Party. Chris Watson, a Sydney printer and former member of the New South Wales Parliament was elected the first leader of the Party. It was at the 1908 Interstate (Federal) Conference that the name 'Australian Labor Party' was adopted.

During the first decade of the Commonwealth, when the Australian Parliament was divided on the tariff issue between Free Traders, Protectionists and the Labor Party, that the ALP gradually increased its numbers and influence. In the following years, the Labor Party mostly supported the Liberal protectionist policies of Alfred Deakin. In October 1907 Watson was succeeded as leader by Andrew Fisher, a miner from Gympie in Queensland. Fisher formed the second Labor Government in October 1908, a minority Government which, with Deakin's support, lasted until 1909 At the elections of April 1910 Labor won a majority in both Houses and for the first time was able to embark on a program of reform and innovation. It founded a Commonwealth Bank, introduced a maternity allowance, established the Australian Navy, brought more employees within the scope of Federal Industrial law, took over the issuing of bank notes and introduced a per capita system of payments to the States. The Government was defeated in May 1913 but won a subsequent double dissolution election in September 1914.

A weakened Labor Party struggled through the next ten years trying to re-establish the political supremacy it had lost in the conscription split. The Party did not recover until 1929 when the National-Country Party Coalition was defeated after it tried to impose punitive industrial legislation (sounds like Workchoices?). The ALP won the election of October 1929 and its leader, James Scullin became Prime Minister. The Scullin Government was soon engulfed in a world-wide depression that hit Australia hard. Under such trying economic times the ALP proved incapable of devising the policies needed to maintain living standards and social services. The Scullin Government was defeated by the new Lyons group in the Parliament in November 1931 and lost the subsequent election. Discontentment which had simmered between the industrial and political wings of the labor movement broke out into open factional warfare during the 1930s A number of Labor politicians at both Federal and State levels were expelled and splinter parties were formed. Labor stayed out of government for 23 years after the defeat of the Chifley Government, largely due to 'the split' of the Democratic Labor Party (DLP) from the ALP.

During the 1940s and early 1950s strong pressures had built up within the labor movement over the activities of communists in the trade unions. The Communist Party was then a united and coherent political unit and a number of its members reached prominent positions in trade unions. This created problems for the ALP because it meant that part of its affiliated membership was under the leadership and influence of another political party.

In 1945 the ALP had set up Industrial Groups in some States to oppose Communists in Union elections. 'The Movement', which operated as a secret organization led by B.A. (Bob) Santamaria, dominated many of the Industrial Groups and built up increasing influence within the party itself. In a protracted struggle between 1954 and 1957 supporters of The Movement and the Industrial Groups were forced out of the ALP, which tactfully gave up any claim to intervene directly in union affairs.

In the following years, the Communist Party split into three competing factions and from that time, most Labor members are members of **the Fabian Society. The British intellectual socialist movement, whose purpose is to advance the principles of social democracy via gradualist and reformist, rather than revolutionary means.**

From its years of struggle, the Labor party turned to and established the **Australian Fabian Society** in 1947 dedicated to Fabianism with its focus on the advancement of socialist ideas through gradual influence and patiently promoting socialist ideals to intellectual circles and groups with power. The Australian Fabian Society's close historical ties with the Australian Labor Party is evidenced in the number of past Australian Labor Party Prime Ministers, Federal Ministers and State

Premiers who were, and are, active members of the Australian Fabian Society. The current President of the Australian Fabian Society is former Australian Prime Minister Gough Whitlam. The Australian Fabian Society has had a more than significant influence on public policy development in Australia since the Second World War, with many of its members having held the highest levels of political power and influence in our land.

After WW2 "The League of Nations" was established, appearing to be acting in the best interest of all nations. This became "The United Nations" or better known to many today as "The House of Lies" and so governments, many with their common Fabian and other Societies backing, pursued achieving their single World Government objectives.

The **Bilderberg Group**, which holds unofficial conferences annually by invitation-only to around 130 guests, most of whom are people of influence in the fields of politics, banking, business, the military and media, with conferences closed to the public. Historically, attendee lists have been weighted towards politicians and heads of State, including Juan Carlos I and Queen Sofia of Spain, Queen Beatrix of the Netherlands, Greek prime minister Kostas Karamanlis, Finnish prime minister Matti Vanhanen, Sweden foreign minister Carl Bildt, U.S. State Department James Steinberg and U.S. Treasury Secretary Timothy Geithner, World Bank president Robert Zoellick, European Commission head José Manuel Barroso etc. Board members include those from many large publicly-traded corporations including IBM, Xerox, Royal Dutch Shell, Nokia and Daimler.

It is these people and those organizations who determine the objectives of the UN and its offshoots, for example, the World Trade Organization who impose policies on UN members, without much media or other attention. They go about quietly destroying nation's assets, infrastructure and society while, supposedly democratic governments comply. Dictating, for example, who we can import apples and meat from, where and how much of what produce we can export, hence the depletion of our manufacturing industry with fast and furious advances on the destruction of our farming industries.

The UN runs programs such as "Planned Parenthood" to curb population growth. Bill Gate's friend contributed US$37 billion towards "Controlled Population" while the UN creates mass hysteria and division between people using sensitive issues such as the environmental as scare tactics, with contrived science to support and cloak their real agenda of taking land ownership by the corporate elite and with the introduction of adverse government legislation in meeting UN Treaties objectives, and we sit quietly coping it all.

Deceptive infiltrative methods used by "parties" based on the ideologies of their bankers and backers (who control them), is why ordinary Australians have had to endure hardships now requiring two incomes just to sustain the family, is why families become dysfunctional, is why crime destroys communities, is why we witness the demise of industry, stand over tactics by unions, the loss of jobs, over taxing, high interest due to fictitious inflation, adverse legislative encumbrances, selling Commonwealth assets, detrimental international treaties and agreements etc. We are now embarking on the final blows of lowering our individual and national wealth and democratic rights which will result in, communism, that is dog eat dog.

I hope after you read the next pages, you will appreciate that it is time we act cohesively with the greatest show of people power this country has ever seen and as a matter of urgency to take back our sovereignty, our country, our rights and to dismiss all adverse legislations which supports any International Treaties which are detrimental to the objectives of the Australian people. This can happen in the creation of a movement above the party system, starting with your support at our petition and a reformed political system.

It is interesting to note, that while Gough Whitlam has been widely acknowledged as the grand "master" of the Fabian Society in Australia, it is not so widely known that Sir John Kerr is also a Fabian and as it appears so was Malcolm Fraser. This would answer the question many Australians ask at the poling both *"who do you vote for Liberal or Labor, they are almost the same"* **and so they are.** When Kerr, the Governor-General sacked the Whitlam government and replaced it with the Fraser government, were they using the Fabian Society tactics as outlined in the previous comments by G. B. Shaw? How is it that the Whitlam Labor government was sacked for far less damage than the Rudd Labor government, yet there is no intervention by the Queen, her representative (Rudd's friend) Quentin Bryce or the Opposition party?

Of particular interest is the fact that Fraser held a major post under the McMahon government, McMahon being a graduate of the London School of Economics. Although not confirmed, it is rumoured that a young John Howard, is also a Fabian. *Notable Australian Members*: **Gough Whitlam** (**ALP** Prime Minister 1972-75): **Bob Hawke** (**ALP** Prime Minister 1983-1991): **Paul Keating** (**ALP** Prime Minister 1991-1996): **John Cain** (**ALP** Premier of Victoria): **Jim Cairns** (**ALP** Deputy Prime Minister): **Don Dunstan** (**ALP** Premier of South Australia): **Geoff Gallop** (**ALP** Premier of Western Australia): **Neville Wran** (**ALP** Premier of NSW 1976-86): **Frank Crean** (**ALP** Deputy Prime Minister): **Arthur Calwell** (**ALP** Former Leader): **John Faulkner** (**ALP** Senator and National President): **Julia Gillard** (**ALP** Deputy & now Prime Minister): Kevin Rudd (**ALP** Prime Minister): **John Lenders** (**ALP** Treasurer of Victoria): **Henry Hyde Champion** (Journalist): **John Percy Jones** (Businessman): **Nettie Palmer** (Writer): **Ernest Besant-Scott** (Historian): **Lucy Morice** (Feminist): **Charles Strong** (Clergyman): **William Henry Archer** (Statistician): **Edward Shann** (Economist): **Charles Marson** (Clergyman): **David Charleston** (Trade Unionist): **John Howlett Ross** (Teacher): **Bernard O'Dowd** (Writer): **Phillip Adams** (Broadcaster)and many others, eg **Barack Hussein Obama** (US President).

Australians have reached an age where it is detrimental to rely on likeminded philosophy driven academic politicians in groups or "parties" to make major fundamental decisions for us in achieving eg Socialist objectives, having failed in most Communist countries and proving to be harmful, other than the World Governments testing ground – China.

We are able to research and access information on whatever we are looking for and then cast an educated vote on every social issue pertinent to achieving the most complex of decisions. There is little need for the continual spending of hundreds of millions of hard earned and limited taxpayer dollars on official "inquiries" and on electioneering and the costs of holding elections for parties, not dissimilar to each other. Money and resources are squandered every time we hold an election under the current system. This wasted money could better be spent on affordable housing and on our ailing infrastructures and on creating new business and work opportunities.

In early 2008 we had our first inkling of what was called a "World Recession" but was rather it is a "Global Financial Crisis" with the knowledge of the demise of sub-prime lenders around the world but primarily in the USA. With losses sustained by many Australian investors into overseas investments, particularly by Superannuation Fund Managers who invested poorly and negligently their investor/workers hard earned money from compulsory government required superannuation investments. Up until about that time no worker had a choice as to where their superannuation was invested. In hindsight, I'm sure all would agree that super funds would have been better invested into the workers own home mortgages.

There were many losses sustained by Australians and Australian institutions, including Local Governments in overcharging Council rates which provided surplus funds. Money which ought to have been invested into their respective community where it was purported to be spent on improvements, lost through overseas investments. No doubt, without community consultation or reason, rates will be increased to build up those banks for investment again, at the cost to the rate payer of course, unless changes are adapted! We suffer dictated rates, taxes and impositions but for little accountability from any level of government, more later . . . .

Government Enabled Banks To Create "Recession" and we pay for it!

"*RECESSION*" AND "*DEPRESSION*" are not natural (financial) phenomenon – they are created by banks in pulling back money, crippling business and a nations economy, thus holding governments to ransom.

As housing prices rose over the past few decades, US mortgage originators, brokers and lenders created and promoted ever more deceptive products to extract further profits from current and aspiring middle class families. This was exacerbated by irresponsible investors and fund mangers who failed to do their own due diligence into the financial products offered, before dealing with irresponsible lenders, who greedily lent to naïve family borrowers. Novice borrowers who could ill afford the tricks and exploitation tactics of expert double dealers, perceived as "cheap loans" but for their sole purpose of achieving "money" greedily and ruthlessly at any cost and from anyone who believed or needed to rely on them.

It was poor and fraudulent *underwriting*, allowed to be conducted in a deregulated industry, not irresponsible *borrowers*, who were the primary cause of the foreclosure crisis. Distorted salaries and incentives paid throughout the deregulated industry where government failed to ensure adequate trade practices were imposed and making it possible and profitable to aggressively market loans to families who never had a prayer of paying back. But the idea was to suck them in, jack up the rates and create the illusion of a profitable portfolio of investments which could then be sold off for more profit.

Prepayment penalties and imposed fees on home owners for paying mortgage debt early on adjustable or variable rate mortgages resulted in payment shock when low teaser rates skyrocketed to exorbitant levels. Borrowers with interest only loans found that their loan principal increased as they paid back their mortgage. "No-doc" loans locked unsuspecting borrowers into mortgages they could not afford. Deals were done with little or no paperwork and often under-secured.

This overview gives the picture of some of the points – the formula is simple. Many brokerage firms participated but let's focus on the biggest, Goldman Sachs – positions itself in the middle of a speculative bubble, selling investments, many known to be rubbish. They suck up vast sums of investments from the middle and lower levels of society, aided by a governmental system which facilitated this, by its failure to regulate or then intervene to rewrite the rules. Why? For the relatively few pennies the banks throw at them as political donations (Obama received US$981,000 in donations from Goldman Sachs employees for his political campaign) and government relishes in the high taxes they achieve, including those paid by overpaid employees.

Goldman used two methods to hide the mess they were selling. First, they bundled hundreds of different mortgages into instruments called **Collateralized Debt Obligations "CDO"**. Then they sold investors on the idea that, because a bunch of those mortgages would turn out to be OK, there was no reason to worry so much about the bad ones: That is, the CDO as a whole was sound. Thus, junk rated mortgages were turned into AAA rated investments. Second, to hedge its own bets, Goldman got companies like AIG to provide insurance – known as credit default swaps. The swaps were essentially a racetrack bet between AIG and Goldman: Goldman is betting the Excons will default, AIG is betting they won't, and we all know who won. It led directly to the collapse of Bear Stearns, Lehman Brothers, Freddy Mac, Fanny May and AIG, whose toxic portfolio of credit swaps was in significant part composed of the insurance that banks like Goldman bought against their own housing portfolios. In fact, rather than government suing the crooks for fraud and taking their assets to repay investors, at least US$13 billion of taxpayers money which was given to AIG in the bailout ultimately went to Goldman, meaning that the bank made out on the housing bubble twice: It screwed the investors who bought their rubbish CDOs and then by betting against its own rubbish product, it has now been turned around to where taxpayers are paying off those same bets, after the government bailed out. A massive win on the round-about as well as on the swings, from selling and insuring defective loans, fraud on a scale the world has never seen, all under the watch of Government "Experts"!

Finally, when it all goes bust leaving millions of ordinary citizens broke and starving, they begin the entire process over again, riding in to rescue us all by lending us back our own money. Greedy, smart guys in the Central Banking industry keep the cogs oiled. They've been pulling stunts like this over and over for centuries and now they're preparing to do it again, creating what may be the biggest and most audacious, bubble yet, a Carbon Credit Trading Scam, see how this is to impact on democratic countries under the Emissions Trading Scheme section.

The move by mortgagees to take possession of defaulting mortgagor's homes was the next mistake the US government made. Was it a mistake or contrived to reward those who caused financial ruin. When people lose their homes someone else wins them for a faction of the value. All government needed to do to prevent this catastrophe, initially, was to ensure lenders relied on fair trading and fair banking policies in a regulated system, but having failed this basic fundamental of good governance, they then failed to intervene by promptly instigating a moratorium to hold-off foreclosures, pending resolution of disparities in loans to the benefit of investors, home buyers and taxpayers.

Why did the US government come to the aid of the banks and not their taxpaying citizens? Governments have colluded with the Central World Banks for centuries which is generally concealed and detrimental to taxpayers. They have allowed and thus participated in the methods of **fraudulent Fractional Reserve and Fractional Interest**. This conspiracy against borrowers, including government borrowers, is for the banks financial benefits and have enabled banks to create and lend at 9 times more (worthless monitory notes and primarily, computer transactions) than the actual assets/gold value that they hold and are supposedly restricted or limited to in lending against. If you or I did it, we would end up in jail quick and lively. Example: 1 onz of gold today can create say A$1200 not 9 times more at A$10,800 in Fractional Reserves. Then this $10,800 is loaned out to governments and taxpayers for interest. The fact is, there is nothing of value behind the difference of A$9,600 not gold or any asset of value to support the creation of this money. Interest is then charged on worthless computer transactions, what a business for an elite minority and what hardship for the abused majority in "Usury" – the illegal charging of exorbitant interest – especially when money is created out of nothing. Government's for allowing and participating in this scheme would have been exposed if the banks would have been allowed to collapse during this or any future, Global Financial Crisis.

Had the US government allowed those banks to collapse, nothing negative would have happen to any of us – bank bankruptcies layers would have produced at least 10% of the value of the loans and that would have been sufficient to pay back the investors of real money. The Central Banks defeated and a real monitory system started up. Responsible government could have taken back their sovereign power of creating their own money, although the US might have had a problem in that the Fort Knox Gold Bullion depository is empty!

Money is created out of debt, not gold or value.
"MONEY = DEBT – Fools Gold"

There was a court case in the US where a mortgagor (borrower) challenged his bank which was suing him for the repayment of a mortgage loan. The home owner proved that what was lent was not real money and therefore the "loan" transaction was set aside by the court and the debt forgiven.

We are constantly misled by government through the media into believing that the *"cost of money is dictated by overseas lenders"* and this may be partly so, because our governments have allowed us to be dictated to by the money changers or the Central World Banks. Perhaps if we manage to change our political system from the party system to honest independent members, we could take the lead from Abraham Lincoln who in 1861 wanted to kill the Central Bank's hold over the country. Lincoln needed money to fund the US Civil War and he went to his Secretary of Treasury to apply for the necessary loans. The European bankers were afraid that the US, if they were to be one block or one nation, would attain economic and financial independence, which would upset their financial domination over the world. They wished the Union to fail and so offered loans to Lincoln at 24% to 36% which he declined to accept. Lincoln sought the advice of Colonel Dick Taylor of Chicago who offered the solution *"Just get Congress to pass a bill authorizing the printing of full legal tender treasury notes and pay your soldiers with them and go ahead and win your war with them"* and *"if you make them full legal tender they will have the full sanction of the government and be just as good as any money."* Lincoln produced 450 million worth of the new bills using green ink on the back to distinguish them from other notes, hence **"The Greenback"**. The result for Lincoln was a victory but his assassination.

In 1913 the **US Federal Reserve**, which **is a privately owned bank and is not owned by the US government** as we would believe, was created by an act of the US Congress. The US Federal Reserve is more powerful than the US Government which is the largest creditor of the Federal Reserve and it is guaranteed by the people and their taxes. Read the book *"The New Economic Disorder"* and Google *"The Money Masters"* to see how the Central Banks control everything eg a retraction of money by banks cause "Recession" and "Depression" and is a great tool to make governments subservient to them in *"Rowing the Economy"* with wars being the greatest money spinner. Monetary monopoly affects every national interest, it can and will plunge the world into chaos – watch and see when more governments cannot or will no longer repay their debts, wars will be contrived where these greedy grubs will become even wealthier and the people of the world will suffer.

We are in a system where money is created out of nothing, where greedy bankers and those who consider themselves to be elite of mankind in determining our future, those who developed the bubble that burst in 2008 will create an even bigger bubble with the debts of democratic countries. George Bush borrowed more money than every president before him all put together and Obama has borrowed more than Bush. Trillions of US dollars and billions of Aussie dollars to appease their masters in throwing money into anything (eg maybe paying building mates double the cost for new school buildings in a purported "Education Revolution") that gets a country into their clutches and as a double edged sword, appearing to be a positive initiative of the (Labor) government in fighting off a non existent "Recession in Australia", but for the creation of the largest deficit this country will have to endure. The current bubble in the making will have catastrophic consequences to any country which goes forward with a large deficit and this is why *I am advocating for the insulation or quarantining of Australia*, plus the creation of our own *Bank of Australia*, covered further in this book.

The abandoning of International Treaties which are not in our direct best interests is imperative as they will totally destroy our society, our culture, our way of life, our future. If you have doubts as to what you are reading, just take a good, long hard look at the **"Effects and the Causes"** – the loss of our manufacturing industry, the sale of our assets to international entities with profits taken overseas, the demise of our farming industry, growing government impositions, growing government debts compounded by interest and thus excessive taxes will rise (with a Carbon tax to be the cherry on top) with governments always bailing out the banks, not the taxpayers, even after banks post A$6 billion in profits. These are the "Effects" you now know the "Causes" it's not just inept governments or rocket science.

It is imperative that every government issue and circulate all of the currency and credit needed to satisfy the spending power of the government and the buying power of their consumers, without cost to the government to carry on its own commerce and infrastructural development. The privilege of creating and issuing money is not only the supreme prerogative of government but it is the government's greatest opportunity – the government can save the taxpayer immense sums of interest, providing less financial stress on families so as they can not just survive but thrive, and it will allow our country to grow regionally – it is a matter of practical administration where money ceases to be the master and become the servant of humanity to where democracy will rise superior to the money power brokers. This cannot happen when political parties must answer to their money masters.

We can repay our hundreds of billions in national debt now in "Australian Legal Tender" just as Abraham Lincoln did. America and all nations can get out of financial jail in the international courts in seeking the discounting of Fractional Funds back down to the substantiated value of held assets ie writing off about 90% of the debts. Failure to do this will see the fulfillment of the greatest contrived Depression and manipulation of mankind and all of the world's assets, never able to be remedied – sounds like some agenda?

Government intervention by instigating equality in fair trading practises would have ensured that the home owners and investors would have been provided with rewritten loans, preventing the realisation of massive losses but now you see that there were no losses to the banks. The home owner could have received a revised loan with equitable terms, perhaps extended terms, at least until rates came down to an affordable level, which would have kept them in their homes to minimise losses to all and sundry.

An attrition of interest rates did transpire due to adverse market conditions, rather than a national (or even international) rethinking of greed, but to no relief or benefit and to the demise of the 1.5 million US citizens who have lost their homes due to sub-prime foreclosure, which could have been prevented. Currently there are 2 million US mortgage holders who are delinquent in their repayments and a further 20% of home owners have mortgages which are of greater value than their home is worth. Intervention with regulated "shared risk for shared spoils" that is, fair and affordable interest, rates and terms would have prevented most losses, but for crook panic stricken fund managers on behalf of mortgagees wanting to cash out quickly. This just added further fuel to the fire of losses by both the investors and the millions of Americans left bankrupt due to "*economic conditions*" and the destruction or revaluation of property values caused by an over supply from mortgagee foreclosures. Home owners consequently left to live in their cars and caravan parks.

This transpires everywhere where skilled authorities do not or cannot step in quickly to impose moratoriums on repossessions with the view of resolving both inequalities and in establishing fair trading terms to save the homes and losses to all parties. Regulating banks with sound trade practises is just as important as ensuring jobs are secure and all of this adversity could have been avoided had governments done their job of regulating to protect its citizens.

What Capitalism has produced and caused to flourish, is organised greed, which will always defeat disorganised, over encumbered bureaucratic governments. Capitalism, is the Moral & Legal Dilemma of the 21st Century, where Company Directors have a conflict of interest between their shareholders and their client/customers.

Even with the lowest bench mark level of interest in 50 years there are no stringent government regulations imposed on banks, no ability to direct banks in how much of any interest savings are to be passed on to customers or when savings are to be passed on. Irresponsible governments have fobbed off responsibility in the adverse "deregulation of the banks". This has been coupled with the selling off of our government owned banks and thus there is no real ability for competitiveness or in *"keeping them honest"* but who keeps governments honest?

The US government granted US$700 billion in taxpayer money to bolster up failing banks, lending institutions and publicly listed companies with no guarantee that these entities can trade out of their difficulties. In making these advance, there were no government demanded for any changes to lending institution policies of mismanagement, only considering slashing the exorbitant hundreds of million of dollars from the wage packages of executives who created the financial rack and ruin. No talk of recompense from them for their wilful and negligent damages.

The joke is, in light of the above, is that the US government in granting US$250 billion to the ailing American International Group Inc "AIG" (not to be confused with the Australian Industry Group, also called AIG) was made by expert US economists, yet there was no foresight or determination made by the very best US financial experts as to government stipulation on spending of their taxpayers funds. Billions of dollars shelled out by experts to those who caused such negligent losses and who were allowed to continue their lack of performance, who then rewarded themselves with executive (bonus) salaries of a further US$250 million. *After* these dumb payments by the US government were exposed, the government had to "rethink" and find a remedy for undoing their short-sighted failure. Then, as a means of fixing their incompetence and getting the money back, the US government imposed a 90% income tax on those executive bonuses. The punch-line to this joke is, that it is this need for experts to "rethink" (most policies and decisions) when the horse has bolted that is of the greatest concern to our people regarding how our governments operate, or rather fail to achieve good governance.

It was revealed on 23 Jan 2010 that Goldman Sachs in accepting US$11 billion from US taxpayers' during the financial crisis awarded its banker/employees a 57% pay rise, after its annual profits skyrocketed almost six-fold last year to US$12.2 billion. Their bank/employees were the best-paid bankers on Wall Street for 2009 and that the average employee at the bank pocked US$554,000 in salary and bonuses in 2009 – an increase of US$202,000 on the previous year. They paid out a total US$17.83 billion in compensation and benefits to its approx 32,500 staff across the globe. These windfalls were reported as US President Obama unveiled plans to cut the size and the risk-taking of the banking sector, saying: *"Never again will the American taxpayer be held hostage by a bank that is too big to fail,"* Mr Obama has introduced a tax, dubbed *"Spank the Banks",* which will net US$125 billion over a decade, in a bid to curb the *"obscene"* bonus culture.

Obama's stance implies regulations. But how does any political party impose regulations on the very institutions they are so dependent on for political campaigning? Will these moves be transparent, or will there be but another smoke screen in appearing to be doing the right thing towards the people but firstly protecting the corporate giants and thus themselves under new loophole legislations? Will Australia follow suit and impose regulation on corporations to bring about commons sense salaries and fair trading?

Deregulation was falsely sold to Australians as *"creating competition"* but this has now been proven to be false, it does not work and could never work, as greedy people always consider their best (financial) interests, this is unaccountable exploitation. Those representations by our government ministers were but false, misleading and damaging and created the loss of millions of Australian's homes, farms, business' and thus marriages and bankruptcies due to "Economic Conditions!" Competition can only be created by creating competition and the best competition will be with the creation of an Australian owned bank as this is the only true means of *"keeping them honest".*

The banking industry merely highlights that most of the financial problems our societies are suffering with are due to the lack of government expertise and the arrogant failure to rely on real experts. Powerless experts who are ignored for the pursuit of political parties agendas and their accountability to the World Banks, with their more than often illogical and inconceivable policies and priorities.

Money thrown at banks that would have been better secured and invested back into the mortgages of citizens by government to enable mortgagors to repay their banks and able to provide citizens with the ability to keep spending or stimulating their economy. Money better used in preventing evictions and preventing the creation of dysfunctional families who become bankrupt liabilities, reliant on social welfare with many turning to crime. Effectively this failure, which has yielded more than 2 million Americans homeless, can destabilise the entire American economy further.

Not to mention the 45 million and growing, Americans living below the poverty line, in a country once considered the greatest Super Power on Earth. Globally, no one is out of the "Global Financial Crisis Woods" yet!

Crime is a symptom of poverty and making the way back from a poverty stricken economy is harder for everyone as these effects are now international, rather than localised. The option of government intervention and rewriting as government loans would have then provided the bank lenders with replenished funds for investment into new regulated business loans and business growth rather than the need for more stimulus packages, which will see the country into deficit for many decades to come and possibly it is out of the ability to repay, without negating assets.

As taxpayers money was given to the banks (the culprit) rather than to citizens (victim) and government is now required to bolster the economy with more taxpayer stimulus schemes into industries to save jobs while putting their citizens further behind the eight-ball. Governments dumped billions into the failing car industry. An industry suffering from greatly reduced consumer demand due to the lack of affordability and other financial constraints of citizens. Incentives are given to entice those who cannot afford a new car, to over extend themselves financially. A massive injection of funds going into an industry reliant on what we would all like to see as redundant fossil fuels but alas an excessive investment into temporary short term saving of jobs. Offering nothing more than a wish and a foolhardy hope that "things" will improve and get back to where they were once again. If this plan fails, there will be thousand of new cars to give away or for recycling and then, no jobs! This is not long term sustainable planning.

The cycle of boom and bust will continue while the practice of greed is maintained and where governments give consideration to business before its people, to where the then British PM Gordon Brown stated that *"there is a new world order emerging"* and it will be one of just two scenarios: One where the people realize who and what is behind this emergence and demand change to their system of government, or they do nothing and let a single world government rule them and destroying our countries and our lives.

There are now real concerns for the US (and others) regarding the ability to service these loans or worse, defaulting on the trillions of dollars in loans. Default for financial reasons could end up as political reasons and this would ensure global catastrophic consequences. Remember: It is the banks who cause "Recession" and "Depression" and war causes the greatest windfall for them and their corporate allies.

On 9 Feb 2010 Barnaby Joyce, the then Shadow Minister for Finance and Debt Reduction, Leader of the Nationals in the Senate, LNP Senator for Queensland stated that *"Rudd is rattled by debt. Mr Rudd appears to be excessively sensitive about the Labor Party debt. One of the reasons for his sensitivity could be the unrelenting rise in our nation's gross debt and the Australian public's understandable concern about this. Australian Commonwealth Government Securities outstanding, as of the 8th December,*

2009 was A$115.71 billion. By the 5th January, 2010 the amount had risen to A$117.31 billion outstanding. By the start of February, it had risen again to A$120.61 billion. Now, not even midway through February, it has risen again to A$122.01 billion. Mr Rudd, Mr Swan and Mr Tanner concern themselves about where A$3.2 billion for the Coalition's environmental plan will come from, but their debt has gone up by almost double that amount in approximately two months. The interest bill on the current debt would be approximately double what the Coalition requires for their environmental plan. Mr Rudd does not want to tell the Australian people about the pain that will come because of this debt and the interest expense that will have to be financed. Mr Rudd does not want to talk about the pressure this debt will place on basic services – health, education, aid, and roads. Mr Rudd wants to close his eyes and hope it all goes away, very similar to his approach to the public hospital problem.

The last time the Labor Party was ousted from government they left Australia with a A$96 billion debt. It took ten years to pay off this episode of Labor's bad management." A country with insurmountable debts from wasted expenditure remains answerable and accountable to aggressive foreign lenders, with little concern and lies to those who will have to pay back, us. This coupled with all holds removed from international buyers of property and business will prove to be part of an objective not in our interest. Australians must stop these buyouts and become self sufficient once more.

A customer complaint is a free warning of a business flaw, while a down-turn in business is a wake-up call from the whole economy. Right here, right now, and on a golden platter is an opportunity to revitalise and to establish new industries: eg a new car industry based on renewable energy; expand renewable energies for domestic, commercial and industry through Geothermal energy; new agricultural and processed food industries all the while reducing pollutants and in providing long term employment and affordable housing in semi rural areas. For example in the Hy-wire car: General Motors introduced it in 2002 and it runs on hydrogen fuel cells capable of producing 94 kilowatts of power continuously (without refuelling) running on a *saltwater* (no fossil fuels) solution and at 129 kilowatts for short periods. It is envisaged that the cells will be capable of powering your house as well, imagine no electricity bills, no pollution and less cost which will not be popular with profit government and their backers.

General Motors were confident that they could produce a commercially viable Hy-wire model by 2010 although in light of bankruptcy terms imposed by the new 60% shareholder, the US government, for the US$50 billion invested, the future is unknown. GM's owed billions of dollars to creditors but with the bankruptcy this is written off, sending creditors to the wall with little if any consideration by their government, the major shareholder as well as the bankruptcy administrator. However, with just part of this US stimulus package or the A$200 million (as secretly provided by the Australian government to Holden) alternative initiatives could be guaranteed, if not for the lack of will to digress from fossil fuels and the very lucrative taxes it provides.

There is also the huge potential for an **Australian Ethanol and bi-products industry which, if owned by Australian Farmers can provide them with a lucrative industry, replacing environmentally hazardous industries which do not provide a return to Australia and it can increase agricultural jobs while encouraging decentralisation.** Currently this lateral thinking will only be allowed to be taken on by government appointed corporate monopolies, rather than them being prepared to let go to the benefit of Australians, ensuring the country and its citizens will be allowed to prosper and without depleting natural resources or rather selling us out, see section on Environment.

Green initiatives could ensure governments would never have a need to bolster up the car industry in meeting further short term injections to maintain jobs or impose new taxes but rather comfortably afford to reduce tax. If government were to provide subsidies to buyers of these eco friendly vehicles for their old car trade-ins, it would provide millions of long term home grown jobs. It would also produce a massive reduction in pollutants as an environmental bonus, coupled with recycling mentals from old car components. So why isn't this happening as a matter of urgency as it is the most obvious avenue forward, except for the loss of the massive fuel taxes.

Eventually there will be more than US$14 trillion invested by the US government into stimulus packages, including billions into the growing welfare payment system. Welfare payments which are rejected by many US State governors; Massachusetts, Gov Deval Patrick asked, *"What happens when the stimulus bill runs out if we take the unemployment reform package . . . it would cause us to raise taxes on employment and business when the money runs out and it will . . ."* This was supported by the governors of Idaho, Alaska, Texas and Southern California. Money expended by any government from a deficit for the sake of welfare and infrastructure must eventually be repaid from other sources.

US experts predict that the cost of their aging population dependant on welfare and Medicare will see the entire annual US budget expended on nothing else within the next 40 years if changes to the way of life do not happen now. This coupled with a growing principle and interest deficit could see the US having completed their "wheel of fortune" from the bottom to the top and back to the bottom, God forbid!

In spite of A$300 billion stimulus package the Australian *full-time* employment rate is not growing (28,000 full time jobs were lost in the last quarter of 2009) and this debt will increase with increased welfare and the interest cost on top of those borrowed funds. It will require taxes and interest rates to rise, creating a disastrous effect on business and therefore long term employment in a country currently suffering with the reducing ability to sustain itself, particularly the farming sector. While we must help our unemployed with welfare until we can put them on their feet again, the amount provided does not come close to their crossing the poverty line. This in itself causes mental illness and crime to rise for mere survival, pushing up the costs of maintaining a growing dysfunctional society. As business shrinks the ability to maintain current unemployment benefits also shrinks, let-alone provide for the increased unemployed. In this vein government approved taxpayers funded therapy for our politicians, poor buggers!

The Australian Federal Labor government in releasing more than A$15 billion in surplus from the previous Liberal government's over-taxing methods are taxing methods maintained by the current Labor government, with higher taxes, higher utilities costs and interest to be imposed. The "achievement" of a tax surplus was accompanied by a negligent lack of reinvestment by Federal government into States maintenance and improvements to infrastructure over the past decades and wrongly perceived as good Federal governance. Had reasonable taxes been imposed and consistent qualified investment into maintenance and new business been upheld nationally, we may have always shown a deficit which now transpires but with now with limited and reducing sources to repay.

An unknown end principle debt plus interest will encumber our very existence to our lenders. How grave this situation has become was evidenced when the leaders of nearly all the world's central banks converged upon Australia to "*write the final epitaph*" for the current Global Banking System. A **"Secret Summit"** of top bankers was held in Sydney on 6 February 2010 regarding concerns as to renewed fears about the global economic recovery. Representatives from 24 central banks and monetary authorities including the US Federal Reserve and European Central Bank attended. The two-day talks were shrouded in secrecy with high-level security believed to have been invoked by law enforcement agencies. The event was dominated by Asian delegations including governors of the Peoples Bank of China, the Bank of Japan and the Reserve Bank of India.

The arrival of the high-powered gathering coincided with a fresh meltdown on world share-markets, with renewed concerns about global growth and Sovereign debt. There are real fears that countries including Greece, Portugal, Spain and Dubai could default on debt repayments. This combined with disappointing US jobs data would seem to put the US on very shaky grounds also. As international stock markets are falling again and fears for security of international debts rise, "*This does feel like '08 and '07 all over again whereby we had these sort of little fires pop up and they are supposedly contained, but in reality they are not quite contained,*" said Global Advisors chief executive Andrew Kaleel. "*Dubai should have been an isolated incident but now we are seeing issues with Greece, Portugal and Spain*"

We are kidding ourselves if we think the world is out of serious financial difficulties and that we are safe. The worst maybe yet to come and unfortunately we are no longer deficit free. We are a country which has allowed billions to be wasted on defective scams and must now back step to focus on our best interest, in thinking and planning nationally firstly, not internationally to our demise eg the European Union and this should give US citizens great concern with plans for a similar Union.

The moneymen gathering also came at an important time of a contemplated overhaul of the global banking system which is to include new capital rules applying to banks and more stringent standards regulating executive pay, neither dissimilar to the new Obama stance. A key part of the talkfest was to be a special meeting of Asian central bankers chaired by the governor of the Central Bank of Malaysia, Dr Zeti Akhtar Aziz, but little attention to this "Summit" was reported in our major media, and what further security for repayment or debt reduction will we offer to our lenders – NSW and California or just our coal mines so that they do not even need to trade with us? Of course they can build and live in Chinese provinces in Queensland and WA. Don't worry about the Labor government letting in a few thousand in boats breaking our border, when tens of thousands can be let in with Australian issued work permits, who are paid at their country's rates of pay to work at their country's owned businesses, while Australian rates of pay forbid us being competitive on the world market. Increasing mining taxes for these entities is just to keep us quiet and get a few extra dollars, when we should own these interests with all profits remaining and working here.

The other major error, by irresponsible government has been in the privatization of (our) government assets and utilities, which can never be overturned, unless our Constitution and political system is revisited. Perhaps the only benefit and probably the motivation for privatisation was that it has given governments the opportunity to get out of the day to day clutches of succumbing to over demanding Unions. Unfortunately for those corporations who have not left for other countries, including the few government interests remaining, they must still contend with Unions demanding more than can be provided from business income. Unions must also be regulated sensibly to co operate in what are the right wages and conditions for all jobs. Unions must be limited in their abilities to hold to ransom any person, industry or the nation.

Australian workers and industry have endured a very vicious circle, from suppression of workers to over awarding workers, to the point where large corporations have replaced people with automatic facilities wherever and whenever possible, irrespective of adverse results. For example: Shoddy automatic phone answering recordings to direct calls. The greatest waste of everyone's time and money is preferred by corporations who would rather escape union's impositions forced on them, than employing by default the union, when they employ a young telephone operator for example. Systems that are defective, time consuming and costly are better than a dictatorial employee's union.

Turn the Tide

T HE MAY 2009 Australian Federal budget failed to provide any credible projections or business incentives – relying on some unknown fix-it remedy or if you like, a miracle, coming about sometime between 2013 to 2023. This will be at a time when the current politicians will be off the hook and no longer accountable for the situation but very comfy for life on their government ongoing handouts and pensions. Meanwhile with a little string and sealing wax, projections and promises or policies shot from the hip without any overall structured planning, will alter with every successive budget, with every successive election campaign and every successive political party. In other words, all we will get will be just unsubstantiated and unaccountable rhetoric from election to election, from party to party, from decade to decade.

By no means is "debt (always) bad", especially when it is spent on well overdue infrastructure but infrastructure improvements are only short term job opportunities. Once these projects are completed there will be the long term cost of maintenance together with the principle debt (borrowed) and interest to repay, unless the then government once again short-changes the maintenance requirements. Many infrastructure initiatives can only be afforded if they are supporting long term viable business, producing secure, long term full time employment and both yielding increased taxes. **Better infrastructure only improves the economy where it creates better business opportunity.** If new business is stillborn, no amount of infrastructure can improve it and thus more infrastructure, is only more debt. The short term government initiator will have completed their relatively short term tenure and leave the next administration to clean up the financial mess of short term planning. It is urgent as a responsible and patriotic nation to:

◆ **THINK AND PLAN NATIONALLY** and expeditiously to establish long term jobs by developing existing and creating new Australian owned and operated industries. Taking back internationally outsourced call centre work for job creation here and also as a security priority. This will require a competitive labour component be determined based on demographic sustainability, supported by increased tariffs on imported goods versus increased unemployment, welfare, poverty and crime and ensuring all profits remain here as is done in many countries. This will create breaches of many United Nations Treaties.

◆ Terminate or amend those UN Treaties that are not in our national interests, see further as to why.

◆ Ensure infrastructure improvements aid new, expanding and relocating industry and residential areas, firstly. This will assist in decentralising to ailing towns and provide for a sustainable population growth and quality of life.

What we have been experiencing is the result of 40 years of over-inflated values and prices, over-inflated personal and corporate egos, over-capitalising into areas of governance, duplication, excessiveness and pure greed affecting all of our lives. In other words – individually and collectively many of us have been living way beyond our means and needs while others reap greater rewards for unaccountable incompetence. What is needed is a return for Australia to a government providing for the best interests of its people in a solid and cohesive overall plan rather than one of policies by each party trying to outdo the other at election time. Over a reasonable period of time, the acceptance and implementation of this overall sure fix-it plan will create the readjustment of our values, priorities, political and judicial systems and a change in our mindsets towards what is required for our individual and national maintenance and affordability to reasonable and sustainable levels.

What we have done over the past 40 years is to make Australia less competitive and thus buy more goods from overseas, from countries which have reinvested in better manufacturing equipment to beat our industries on price and whose employees can live on a pittance. That is, developing countries achieve more value for their currency than we do!

Although our labour laws have been a factor, as have been "free trade" with almost non existent tariffs, it is mother earth that continues to pay the dearest price because our mineral resources are rapidly depleting while some of our trading partners have low or non-existent environmental laws. One of the quickest ways to stimulate some Aussie industries would be to impose environmental sanctions on these countries, sanctions equivalent in effect to higher tariffs.

It is imperative that while government invests into short term infrastructure projects for job creation, that this be overcompensated with long term industry investment. This overcompensation is of paramount need just to balance the costs of infrastructure, unless more taxes and costs are intended to be charged and applied to the new roads, bridges and rail systems – with history as our greatest witness as to this exploitation.

While our national home building industry and supporting infrastructures are vital, re-establishing Australian primary and secondary industries ought to be seen as a great priority in making us less dependent on imports, increasing exports, reducing national debt and making Australia self sustaining. This does not appear to be high on either the Liberal or Labor government's agenda or their cronies, with more and more manufacturing going overseas, while we import more and more of what we used to grow and make here.

The most unfortunate part of our new deficit is that much of these funds are borrowed from overseas lenders, rather than from Australians having invested their superannuation and savings into Australian Bonds, through the Bank of Australia. See the section on the proposed re-establishment of an Australian government owned bank where funds would be invested by Australians into new business and developments in providing a return to Australian investors rather than see our profits going overseas.

What a change! Investments from Australians going into improving Australian industry, particularly agricultural and manufacturing which has been forced out of business by governments incompetence. Business which was held to ransom by unions and bureaucratic concocted demands, left Australia for their inability to maximise profits and who could no longer tolerate the abundance of red tape and burocractical hurdles.

Only with strong and decisive positive attitudes and expertise can we individually and collectively plan and determine what we want to achieve as our desired results. Australia has not been in a "Recession", but we have felt the ripples of the overseas "Global Financial Crisis" here particularly with the loss of investments funds and in making everyone pull back to caution.

As a nation, we have developed strong allegiances with many countries – we have an ANZUS Treaty with the US and New Zealand but this does not commit the USA in any way to defending Australia. We cannot afford to assume that the defence relationship would be strong enough to maintain ties with the USA in the long term if the US allegiances were to change for any reason of, say, a stronger relationship with another country for motives such as "oil" or UN Treaties. Australia has an open door policy with many countries and while agreements are intended to serve both sides, we must maintain an international position of **non subservience** to any country or any agreement in maintaining our freedom to express and to adopt a position of neutrality, whenever the occasion arises and to protect the interest of every Australian, firstly. This is not to be misconstrued as any anti-any other nation proposition, but to the contrary, it is a pro-Australia policy in giving priority to Australia in achieving greater competitiveness, self sufficiency and self-reliance in every facet of our lives.

Our Free Trade Agreement with the USA (or with any other country) has not been to our benefit. The US government heavily subsidises their farmers and we would be better equipped commercially, if the Australian government matched the US farming subsidies to our farmers to enable not just an equal but perhaps a more competitive edge to our farmers in supplying both our local and world export markets. It is not, and never has been, a level playing field in economic terms for Australia or Australian farming. In fact, if the ACCC ensured maximum mark-up margins and fair trading terms, farmers would appreciate a better return and there would be less reliance on government subsidies.

On one hand government imposes taxes and water restrictions on the limited water supply to farmers and on the other hand, it gives farmers meagre subsidies, welfare and drought relief – that is, giving with one hand [welfare and relief] but taking with the other [water taxes] with the only jobs created not being from working on the land or in building our economy, but in the paper double shuffling of excessive staff in bureaucratic government offices and agencies.

Providing adequate **FREE WATER** supplies to our farming industry would reinvigorate our dying river systems and it would create new agricultural and secondary farming industries, while alleviating non productive "white collar waste". The benefit would be the ability for the farming community to repay the cost of new water from the fair taxes on their profits which many are currently denied being able to make. It is the farmer, the primary and secondary manufacturer who will be our financial salvation, not some "white collar taker" or some multinational conglomerate. Water is not a commodity, it belongs to all Australians and the responsibility for distribution has been vested in government, to provide this and other services. Water is not government property to deal with, or sell rights to.

We are truly living in the most interesting of times in world history with religious faith and atheism both growing in all realms – from religious fanaticism right through to no belief or faith whatsoever. Massive advancements in resources and technology over the past 100 years have not protected us from corporate and government incompetence and corruption rather accelerated these problems, to what we continue to witness as the cycle of fortune and opportunity continuing to turn. From the extreme wealth of once buoyant and dominant Western world markets, to countries such as Japan now diving into a "Recession" shaping up to be worse than that of 80 years ago; to Russia and China awakening to becoming new market leaders.

The following chapters are not to be taken as isolated issues but in the context of a concerted culmination of every *major* facet of our individual lives, our economic and business world and the critical part which only responsible government can play. Addressing and amending areas crucial to every person on this planet starts with a major consolidation, with prioritising of people with the environment firstly and before profit and if there be a deficit for our kids, it will be one they can easily trade out of.

From The Sheep's Back To Where?

GOVERNMENT STATISTICS (ABS published 2005) based on the total population from the 2005 Census reveals:

ESTIMATED RESIDENT POPULATION, Age Groups as at 30 June 2005

State		0 to 4	5 to 9	10 to 14	15 to 19	20 to 24	25 to 34	35 to 49
NSW	Male	218,313	224,767	234,791	232,970	237,390	484,507	736,826
	Female	205,760	213,249	222,570	221,482	226,933	482,651	737,896
	State Total	424,073	438,016	457,361	454,452	464,323	967,158	1,474,722
	% of state	6.26%	6.47%	6.75%	6.71%	6.85%	14.28%	21.77%
Vic	Male	156,774	162,925	171,564	171,089	181,272	360,089	549,620
	Female	149,576	154,557	163,200	164,376	175,646	363,746	561,926
	State Total	306,350	317,482	334,764	335,465	356,918	723,835	1,111,546
	% of state	6.10%	6.32%	6.67%	6.68%	7.11%	14.41%	22.13%
Qld	Male	123,712	130,748	138,362	135,214	138,894	277,160	437,270
	Female	123,712	130,748	138,362	135,214	138,894	277,160	437,270
	State Total	247,424	261,496	276,724	270,428	277,788	554,320	874,540
	% of state	6.24%	6.59%	6.98%	6.82%	7.00%	13.98%	22.05%
SA	Male	44,931	48,479	51,854	52,931	53,985	101,196	168,318
	Female	42,889	46,248	49,199	50,147	50,629	96,426	168,657
	State Total	87,820	94,727	101,053	103,078	104,614	197,622	336,975
	% of state	5.70%	6.14%	6.55%	6.68%	6.78%	12.82%	21.85%
WA	Male	63,703	68,477	72,452	74,469	74,144	142,550	226,755
	Female	60,610	64,930	69,102	70,639	69,951	138,788	226,043
	State Total	124,313	133,407	141,554	145,108	144,095	281,338	452,798
	% of state	6.18%	6.64%	7.04%	7.22%	7.17%	14.00%	22.53%
TAS	Male	15,440	16,299	17,749	17,473	16,018	27,811	51,460
	Female	14,632	15,606	16,790	16,603	14,970	29,148	53,353
	State Total	30,072	31,905	34,539	34,076	30,988	56,959	104,813
	% of state	6.20%	6.57%	7.12%	7.02%	6.39%	11.74%	21.60%
NT	Male	8,992	8,527	8,551	7,773	8,888	18,002	24,891
	Female	8,507	8,000	7,944	6,998	7,411	17,108	22,483
	State Total	17,499	16,527	16,495	14,771	16,299	35,110	47,374
	% of state	8.63%	8.15%	8.13%	7.28%	8.04%	17.31%	23.36%
ACT	Male	10,322	10,533	11,230	11,976	14,612	25,633	35,317
	Female	9,863	10,131	10,580	11,628	13,674	25,370	37,131
	State Total	20,185	20,664	21,810	23,604	28,286	51,003	72,448
	% of state	6.20%	6.35%	6.70%	7.25%	8.69%	15.68%	22.27%

NB Population per state indicates almost 50/50 male and female with a slight edge in favor of females

ESTIMATED RESIDENT POPULATION, Age Groups as at 30 June 2005

State	0 to 4	5 to 9	10 to 14	15 to 19	20 to 24	25 to 34	35 to 49
NSW	424,073	438,016	457,361	454,452	464,323	967,158	1,474,722
Vic	306,350	317,482	334,764	335,465	356,918	723,835	1,111,546
Qld	247,424	261,496	276,724	270,428	277,788	554,320	874,540
SA	87,820	94,727	101,053	103,078	104,614	197,622	336,975
WA	124,313	133,407	141,554	145,108	144,095	281,338	452,798
TAS	30,072	31,905	34,539	34,076	30,988	56,959	104,813
NT	17,499	16,527	16,495	14,771	16,299	35,110	47,374
ACT	20,185	20,664	21,810	23,604	28,286	51,003	72,448
	1,257,736	1,314,224	1,384,300	1,380,972	1,423,311	2,867,345	4,475,216
	6.19%	6.46%	6.81%	6.79%	7.00%	14.11%	22.01%

(as publised by Aust Bureau of Statistics 30 June 2005)

50 to 64	65 to 74	75 to 84	over 85	Total 2005	% Total Populat.	Total 2008	% incr fr 2007
585,862	233,506	144,919	35,740	3,369,591	16.58%		
582,212	246,703	190,164	75,038	3,404,658	16.75%		
1,168,074	480,209	335,083	110,778	6,774,249	33.3%	7,019,100	1.30%
17.24%	7.09%	4.95%	1.64%	100.00%			
424,776	169,270	105,645	25,846	2,478,870	12.19%		
432,974	182,248	140,044	55,174	2,543,467	12.51%		
857,750	351,518	245,689	81,020	5,022,337	24.7%	5,340,300	1.80%
17.08%	7.00%	4.89%	1.61%	100.00%			
342,438	129,919	92,371	36,016	1,982,104	9.75%		
342,438	129,919	92,371	38,020	1,984,108	9.76%		
684,876	259,838	184,742	74,036	3,966,212	19.5%	4,320,100	2.50%
17.27%	6.55%	4.66%	1.87%	100.00%			
139,347	56,016	37,719	9,462	764,238	3.76%		
142,032	60,823	50,292	20,443	777,785	3.83%		
281,379	116,839	88,011	29,905	1,542,023	7.6%	1,607,700	1.10%
18.25%	7.58%	5.71%	1.94%	100.00%			
177,139	63,732	35,768	8,609	1,007,798	4.96%		
172,821	65,866	45,357	18,208	1,002,315	4.93%		
349,960	129,598	81,125	26,817	2,010,113	9.9%	2,188,500	2.90%
17.41%	6.45%	4.04%	1.33%	100.00%			
45,569	18,374	10,773	2,482	239,448	1.18%		
45,917	19,140	14,023	5,633	245,815	1.21%		
91,486	37,514	24,796	8,115	485,263	2.4%	498,900	0.90%
18.85%	7.73%	5.11%	1.67%	100.00%			
15,986	3,535	1,269	281	106,695	0.52%		
13,329	2,710	1,202	406	96,098	0.47%		
29,315	6,245	2,471	687	202,793	1.0%	221,100	2.20%
14.46%	3.08%	1.22%	0.34%	100.00%			
27,522	8,300	4,681	1,024	161,150	0.79%		
28,547	8,923	6,110	2,265	164,222	0.81%		
56,069	17,223	10,791	3,289	325,372	1.6%	346,800	0.40%
17.23%	5.29%	3.32%	1.01%	100.00%			

50 to 64	65 to 74	75 to 84	over 85	TOTAL			
1,168,074	480,209	335,083	110,778	6,774,249	33%		
857,750	351,518	245,689	81,020	5,022,337	25%		
684,876	259,838	184,742	74,036	3,966,212	20%		
281,379	116,839	88,011	29,905	1,542,023	8%		
349,960	129,598	81,125	26,817	2,010,113	10%		
91,486	37,514	24,796	8,115	485,263	2%		
29,315	6,245	2,471	687	202,793	1%		
56,069	17,223	10,791	3,289	325,372	2%		
3,518,909	1,398,984	972,708	334,647	20,328,362	100%	21,542,500	1.76%
17.31%	6.88%	4.78%	1.65%	100.00%			

With a 10% increase and some variations since these statistics, we are fortunate to have almost equal the number of men to women in all States, unlike say China. Note the population of Western Australia, the largest sized State has 9.9%; the Northern Territory has 1% and South Australia's 7.6% – there is a total of 18.5% 3,764,929 of the population living on two thirds of the continent, and 81.5% are living on one third, the eastern States. Based on statistics, it would be reasonable to estimate the Australian population, due to natural attrition, not continuing with 300,000 migrants per year, to reach 50 million over the next 50 odd years but on our current unplanned development path, this is unsustainable – no debate or research required, but diligent planning is. Now is the perfect time to address all of our facilities, infrastructures, regional development, governance, personal and corporate attitudes and social directions.

These statistics have been included as an indicative point of reference for the following chapters and note that at 1ˢᵗ October 2009 our population stood at 22 million (see Bureau of Statistics for more information). Accurate statistics are vital to enable government to plan and project requirements of health, education, security, transport and all other major infrastructure and development needs. With the problems we suffer in many portfolios particularly health, it would seem very few government departments or ministers rely on these statistics or consultants reports or plan according for current and future needs, as many national initiatives are confronted with the hurdles of dealing with the State's bureaucracies.

Unfortunately our needs are dependent on the ability to alleviate variances between Federal and State Governments priorities. The disparity of population versus size of the States and the inequality of State government brains and agendas makes it difficult for, say, a larger sized State with a smaller population to be able to obtain Federal government assistance on par with smaller States, that is, without a national planning approach. But if the larger States have what to offer in affordable housing, work and resources, decentralisation can be achieved easily and this will reduce the over demand on infrastructure in major cities and over-crowded States to manageable levels.

This country "grew up on the sheep's back", that is, we grew and prospered on the land, from our primary resources of wool, wheat and natural produces and we wore Australian grown and manufactured woollies; socks, jumpers and good quality clothing. You only needed to own two good quality woollen jumpers which lasted for years, and could then be handed down, with a few more years left in them. Compare this to the many cheap imports that only last for a few washes and need more spending on replacements, this makes these items expensive rubbish.

We ate and drank local produce and we even manufactured our own car. Everyone who owned an FJ Holden took great pride in it. That's how Australia became the lucky country that everyone wanted to flock to. Growing, producing and making our own. Today our choices of local produce are limited and our choice of locally manufactured goods is almost nonexistent, as we rely on cheap inferior imports, based on world competitive pricing from countries seeking to attain a greater share of the market and who do not share our high labour and tax components.

Progressively, we have reduced our own ability to be competitive and we have compromised our individual and national physical and mental health by tolerating cheaply produced imported goods, see section on Health Standards. We have developed some sort of pride in driving a German car and drinking Belgian beer, sitting on Swedish furniture and watching American TV shows on our Japanese TV, in our made in China acrylic PJs and slippers. We may have free trade with many countries but *free trade* has been very expensive, as it has priced much of Australian produce and most of Australia's manufactured goods out of our own market, regardless of being competitive on the world market, with the full impact not fully realised and may it never be.

Think of it this way. A kingdom exists in a wide brown land. Let's called it Pacifica – For years Pacifica has grown wheat, sheep and cattle and sold that produce at home and overseas and its people prospered and were very happy. One of the winning allies in the Great War, Pacifica had a great manufacturing base, but it's kings then let this become old and decrepit, not encouraging or supporting business and farm owners to be better and smarter or helping them but penalising them and allowing monopolies to come into the country, buy up and to exploit them, all for the gain of **fools gold.** *"Pacifica is rich!"* its kings say, *"There's so much wealth underground that we can't dig it up or package it fast enough.* ***Let's squeeze the farmers out, starve'em off if the pollution from mining doesn't kill'em first, and then flick'em off like flies, one by one, they'll never know what hit'em and we'll feed the rest of the country food we import cheaper!*** *In fact if we bring in cheap (dodgy) beef it could destroy our beef industry so the beef farmers will close down pretty quickly and we can meet our quota of imports from developing countries and get out of paying a small fortune in emissions fines for cow farts. The States will help if we sling'em a few bucks, then we get the land off'em cheap and dig the hell out of it!"*

And so they did. Pacifica used to make clothing and footwear for its own people, including some famous brands of durable products well suited to its climate and terrain. But now it is easier to buy that stuff from the Middle Kingdoms than to do it themselves. Pacifica now has a vast government employee base, stock-brokers; merchant bankers, insurance salesmen and a whole bunch of people who mine and export gas and minerals, including plutonium for nuclear weapons. But it doesn't have anyone who makes anything, or damn few, and those left are all dying off. And if ever Pacifica sells its mining industries due to bad debts or pressure from "trading partners" or in conforming to adverse treaties or just because it's "kings" want to cash out quickly, there'll be nothing around to pay for all the stuff thought to be needed, no jobs and no skills. The land will be barren and the people will be very unhappy as they have no future, because they let their kings sell them out and the new kings may not be kind.

The Chinese state-owned corporation Sinochem has bid A$2.8 million for the Australia's farm chemical group Nufarm. It's the second time Nufarm has received an approach from a Chinese firm in two years. Communist China, the country we are heavily in debt to, wants to buy up farms in Gunnedah to coalmine. China no longer appears to be happy to be a "trading partner" but rather own or conquer Australia and employ their own staff on their labour terms (NB Last year 2,600 miners died in China). Shenhua Watermark, is a subsidiary of the Chinese minerals giant Shenhua Group which is moving to buy six more farms in the Liverpool Plains district near Gunnedah. This buy up has been cleared by our Federal Government's Foreign Investment Review Board, but their Australian representative, Joe Clayton, said two more farms were under contract and another 17 were being negotiated. Mr Clayton said Shenhua would not be mining under the richest food-producing agricultural land on the plains.

The Shenhua coal exploration area is next to an area where a coalition of local farmers has maintained a year-long blockade against BHP Billiton, which is also planning a series of coalmines. Sales of coal and iron to China went up from A$16 billion to A$89 billion and obviously this is why the farming industry is being destroyed and how it is falsely purported that *our export sales are up*. Farmers on the blockade in the BHP Billiton area next to Shenhua's zone, said they had written to the Treasurer, Wayne Swan, asking him to consider that they were pursuing a court case against the NSW Primary Industries Minister, Ian Macdonald, over his approval of the BHP Billiton license. Lawyers acting for the Caroona Coal Action Group wrote that should the validity of the BHP Billiton license be called into question it could trigger an investigation into the Shenhua exploration area. Mr Swan declined to comment about the review board decision. Swan said, *"I always act, and the Government always acts, in the national interest,"* but this is both false and misleading. Both the NSW State and the Federal governments are selling us up, exploiting and destroying our assets, blinded by short term profits for long term economic and environmental destruction in support of adverse agendas and treaties. Farmers and residents in the Hunter Valley of NSW are suffering serious health problems; **cancers and Aasphyxiation from the cocktail of toxic contaminants, not Bronchitis or Asthma but slow and painful murder**, known to Environment Ministries but there is no intervention or protection, rather resistance to any inquiry (www.abc. net/4corners Mon 12 Apr 2010) to protect the people, their farming produce (eaten by the world) or to their properties. The winds blowing poison over the Hunter Valley don't stop there, in more ways than one.

According to: *The Australian* 28 Aug 2010 Anthony Klan, Amos Aikman: *"Independent MP Tony Windsor **was paid three times more for land sold to a mining company than others nearby**. The sale of election winning MP Tony Windsor's farm to a coalminer delivered the king-making MP a windfall about three times greater than nearby farmers who sold to the company. Mr Windsor's family was paid A$4.625 million by Werris Creek Coal in February for the sale of 376ha Cintra, south of Tamworth, reaping about A$12,300 a hectare. According to lands titles searches, the three other farms of substantial sizes to be sold to the mining company changed hands in the past 18 months for between A$2,767 a hectare and A$5,128 a hectare. A 351ha nearby property was sold to the coal group for A$1.8m in 2008 – representing A$5,128 a hectare – and another 317ha parcel changed hands for A$2,767 a hectare in April this year. Mr Windsor, who has long been critical of mining in the nearby fertile Liverpool Plains because of its impact on underlying ground water, yesterday repeated his claim that the mining of that property was legitimate because it was "completely different country". "Overall, I am not opposed to mining. In fact, in several instances I have pushed for it, but I am very much opposed to mining where there is an interface with the ground water, as is the case with Liverpool Plains," Mr Windsor said. When asked about the differences in the sale prices between his property and those of his neighbours, he said, "I think we should terminate this conversation".*

Selling off of Australian farming lands can never be of national interest and mining in the NSW food bowl will destroy the water-table, destroy agriculture and is a direct contradiction to the governments concerns regarding Greenhouse pollution and thus the government created need for an emissions trading tax. Revenue from short term government pursuits to sell off our assets gives the perception of a strong economy but long term it will destroy our economy, with no more assets to sell, no more natural resources to extract and little revenue to meet the cost of high welfare.

Compared to many people throughout the world, Australians certainly live in the very luckiest country but there are millions of Aussies feeling they must be living in a different country as they are not afforded the opportunities this great country can and is able to offer us all. Our government pays A$500,000 a year in tax free wages to several employees, to give away hundreds of millions of dollars to those in other countries, while our own are struggling, this is beyond sanity or comprehension. For many Australians, frustrations come from the inability to find and procure the balance between our "wants" and our "needs" individually, and how much more so, as a nation. This is the challenge of each of us individually and collectively.

In this vein, don't take for granted our freedom of speech, freedom of choice and every other conceivable freedom and basic luxury, and protect it. While we appreciate that every home has hot and cold running water and at least one inside dunny and we enjoy drinking clean healthy water, as we walk on paved footpaths and drive our cars on sealed roads, these are things we deserve but should not taken for granted, as they are not afforded in so many countries. We love our lifestyle, our flag, our unique form of the English language and a fair go. But, we have bowed to "Political Correctness" and detrimental party politics, which has lead to the demise of our social and political standards, thus a lack of respect and contempt for authority has evolved.

Geographically, Australia is the largest island but the smallest continent and economically it is perhaps one of the youngest nations. Just 221 years since the first settlement and 108 years since Federation, we are still enduring teething problems in a rapidly and ever changing technological environment, and we have a long way to go to ensure equality and a system able to produce positive results expeditiously, but our existing structure does not tolerate a fair balance for change and great resistance.

What Do We Learn From Anzac Day? Contribution from the Ausbuy Team:

"ANZAC Day has passed for another year, but to acknowledge its meaning one day a year with public outpouring is not what Australians have worked, fought and died for. Although I have heard the messages for many years only this year did I truly appreciate the meaning of the four words which define the Spirit of ANZAC: Courage, Endurance, Sacrifice and Mateship. These characteristics define the essence of Australia. It is a land which tests

its people. *Indigenous Australians instinctively understood how to live in harmony with the land, and immigrants in the past two centuries have* **embraced this Spirit to create a nation that is productive, innovative and clever.** *But we seem to have forgotten how to develop these skills.*

Despite our relatively small population size and isolation, Australians have made significant contributions worldwide to innovations in engineering, mining, agriculture, medicine and much more. Australians invented refrigeration, revolutionised mining, created the combine harvester, the cochlear ear, the pacemaker, the Hills hoist, the Victa mower and much more borne of ingenuity, identifying and fixing a problem. These difficult times glaringly show that we have been duped into forgetting the very foundations of our nation in the grab for immediate gratification, selling off our most productive assets, exporting jobs and creating debt that will take generations to pay back, or see ourselves ruled by foreign States because we have simply sold out. We do not want to be tenants in our own country.

AUSBUY's Corporate Members and Friends of AUSBUY support the ANZAC spirit. These businesses are clever, productive and innovative. They employ thousands of Australians and keep the decisions, the profits and jobs here. But in our grab to be good global citizens, we have forgotten that home is where it all starts. The concept of a "fair go" has been forgotten. Vision and hard work built this country. All we ask is that we take time to really consider what it means to be Australian and to honour the legacy of the ANZAC spirit."

It was not in the ANZAC spirit that the Prime Minister gave every child A$1,000 and pensioners A$1,400 for Christmas in 2008 If not wasted on poker machines (NSW poker machine turnover increased 500% after the payments) but spent at K-Mart or on useless "things" the money went to China; if spent on petrol it went to the Arabs; if we bought a computer it went to Taiwan; if we purchased fruit and vegetables it went to Mexico, Honduras and Guatemala and if we bought a new car it went to Japan. Very little of this money other than the wage component went to improve Aussie productivity or help to grow and develop the Australian economy, bail out the ailing hospitals or provide dental assistance to those desperately needing this help. If giving A$1,000+ to each person wasn't enough, a further A$900 went out in April 2009 – not towards ongoing tax reductions which give long term benefits but a "great government public relations ploy" in giving with one hand and continue taking back double with the other, in creating the illusion that the Labor government are generous good guys, giving us gifts. This was a contrived and dishonest payoff as Australians know "there's no such thing as a free lunch" but unfortunately many get sucked into this propaganda.

Money to **SPEND, SPEND AND SPEND SOME MORE** (on imported products, because there's nothing else to buy), when just one year ago interest was increased on home loans to punish us and to make us **STOP SPENDING** because the economy was "*too strong*". Now we will pay for this propaganda and inconsistency with huge interest increases and new and higher taxes on everything to punish us for changing the world climate or whatever excuse fits. Then fuel prices increase and push up the cost of living appear as if we are spending more. The inept decisions to privatise our water, power facilities, vital roads and utilities, that is, the costs of essential services to sustain life have risen and are now set to skyrocket. Increased costs "appear" as if consumers are spending more, enabling government agencies and the Reserve Bank of Australia to justify higher interest rates to slug us with, while purporting to "keep inflation down". This is a deceitful smoke and mirrors act par excellence, in playing Australians for fools in extorting money, much of which is put to pure waste. This is no different to the "skilled" US government's money men giving the crooks behind the sub-prime scams the ability to give themselves pay rises, and then having to rethink their dumbness in how to get the money back.

In the 1950s, fewer than 10 years after Japan was hit with atomic bombs on Hiroshima and Nagasaki, the Japanese pulled their socks up and produced an abundance of cheap commodities. We lapped it up although we considered it to be *"Jap Crap"* and as their technology improved, so did the quality and price of Japanese goods, which are hardly considered cheap by any standards any more. No different to Germany, who also lost WW2 then excelled in the automotive and electronics industries.

Japan was labelled "the sausage" as it imported just about everything – particularly primary produce – and it manufactured and produced secondary goods sold to the world, cars, electrical and electronic goods. By the 1970s wealthy Japanese were over here buying up every piece of property they wanted from condos and golf courses on the Gold Coast, to major developments nationally. From 1950 till 2009 some 60 years on, we have seen Japan economically rise and then dive deep, due to the demise of the world's want for Japans goods due to China and other Asian countries now being more competitive. Japanese suicides are running at 30,000 a year and there are more than 125 million people living on just 377,727 sq kilometres of mostly uninhabitable land. The Japanese government is faced with perhaps the most difficult of tasks in finding solutions to turning their economy around, compared to any other country.

As with Japan, from humble post war beginnings and poor wages to their workers we now see China dominating world markets, ranking number one and able to boast a US$480 billion surplus while most western countries have a deficit. China's annual growth was approximately 30% a year and this was "unsustainable", slowing to about 9% a figure that would rate as an overcooked economy in Australia, in need of cooling! The Chinese government realises that as long as they have world demand for their inexpensively manufactured goods, they will have market domination. With that comes the ability to increase the price of their goods at a time when demand increases again. This is particularly so when they have total dependence on them from countries unable to compete for their own lack of any manufacturing industry remaining, let alone having a competitive labour component, which unfortunately we in "Pacifica" have become.

Then China can produce less and charge more, to earn more as Japan did, providing a greater return with less investment into primary products for the manufacture of goods. This would secure their citizens; provide a healthy growth for their economy and could then "appear" to assist them in meeting pollution reduction targets! As Japan had, China has the ability to purchase properties, businesses and any remaining business in any country and see us heavily in their debt from loans. As the wheel-of-fortune continues to turn China is at a distinct advantage, it is a country born out of a strength that only Russia can partially appreciate. It maintains Communism where its government enjoys the dependence of its citizens on their government as an absolute power while government and a few elite business owners reap the benefits of capitalism, which can only be the envy of every Fabian-backed western government.

In the meantime, Chinese businesses face few controls and maintain many poor standards. This has been witnessed in scandals, such as the dilution of milk products, adding a melamine derivative (known to cause kidney stones) just so it could fool Chinese milk protein assessments and the repeated discovery of lead paint in children's toys and using human faeces in growing vegetables and fed to the world, see section on Health Standards.

If world markets demand for Chinese goods drops, we may see increases in prices sooner rather than later. China and other East Asian manufacturers are suffering major unemployment and their monetary investments in the US (particularly) are in jeopardy. They may have no choice but to increase their prices and we will have no choice but to pay inflated prices for Asian goods, unless we strive to change our direction. Going back to where our strength was derived "on the sheep's back" and in becoming more self-sufficient, more self-reliant and dependant on our own primary and secondary goods. Alternatively on its current course we could find that every primary agricultural and manufactured product in Australia, is either owned by international interests or imported, and we will no longer have the ability, skills, financial resources or initiatives to reconstruct these industries, which have been greatly depleted since the 1960s.

If you were either born here or arrived here before 1950 you would have lived in Australia for at least 25% of the entire period Australia has been settled (by the British in 1788) and you would have seen so many changes in this very short period of time. In the past 50 years mankind has experienced the most aggressive industrial and technological advancements, more than any 500 plus year period has ever experienced. Falling into this bucket, I was born when there were just over 8,700,000 Australians. We had a "White Australia Policy"; milkmen delivered milk every night with no additives or preservatives, there were home bread and fruit vendors with horse drawn carts until the late 1950s. We got a black and white TV when I was 8 years old with programs for about 8 hours a day. TV programmes had no violence or profanity allowed, censorship was common decency, a car was a luxury, as was the phone and I can say, people were happier with less, things!

It has taken 50 odd years to get our population from 6.7 million to 22 million and now with a multitude of nationalities, our horizons and opportunities have broadened, particularly with communications and technology. Our population may well more than double over the next 50 years but unless we are able to plan a solid direction for our personal, through to our social needs nationally through skilled government, our kids, grandkids and great grandkids will suffer. They will suffer mentally and physically from the worsening ill effects of further denigration to our most basic needs of health, quality of food, education, work opportunities, personal and national security and good government and they will bear the burden of a far more intolerable debt level than we are contemplating today.

The world economic downturn can be considered a disaster if we do not learn from it and treat it as we should, as a wake-up call to address and rectify excessive indulgences and waste at every level of society. These times can provide new opportunities for a self sustaining economy and a fairer, more transparent system of governance, where no Australian would be left out in the cold or be considered a minority, or live in fear or anxiety. But if we approach the situation with complacency to these crucial issues, we could slide into a Depression both individually and as a nation which would be disastrous.

Remember: **Everything in this country started with OUR FARMERS and everything will finish in our country with our farmers.** Adversity towards them, is adversity to all of us, they are the Backbone of this country – teach this to your children!

Perception Becomes Reality

WHEN OUR ECONOMY is strong, our morale, our perception and our attitude are also strong and vibrant, but in just the past 40 years we have seen the greatest demise in our overall social standard of virtues, morals and attitude towards decency and equality in every level of society. We have become more and more tolerant of obscenity and more acceptable of crime and mismanagement, not for our common good. Contempt has flourished for police and authority; bank managers, lawyers and particularly politicians who have imposed many adverse laws which have undermined our constitutional rights eg the Fines Act of 1996 allows State government to impose fines without any referendum by the people while local government enforce more than 30,000 plus bi-laws to where your dog can be booked for parking illegally and you can be fined A$1 million for cutting down a tree which is destroying your plumbing. Not so long ago these public officials were held in the highest regard. A bank manager was once considered the pillar of the community but today he or she is resented as a representative of his or her exploiting employer, the bank – the "rip-off merchant" and politicians have become laughable and proving that they cannot resolve problems, rather they create them.

The main reasons fall on governments in their fobbing off responsibilities for administering the country, imposing many harsh taxes, deregulating big business, purported as competition but this has failed to ensure adherence to decent standards of trading. Thus authority is frowned upon by most sectors of the community. Deregulation has allows government ministers to escape accountability while oligopolies, duopolies and monopolies exercise their might. When banks adopt the same policies and there is price fixing in various industries particularly the petroleum industry, there is no real competition, only the inequality of bargaining power between big business and the little customer.

Individually we are helpless when a bank takes undue fees out of our account, although we would be at the police station quick and lively if someone grabbed 20 bucks out of our pocket, yet when banks help themselves to our money, is this any different? It is claimed that there is more than A$300 million a year overcharged to customers, most going unrecognised or unchallenged, why? Because they can get away with it! Banks know that most people will not waste their time, which is costly in pursuing what appears as small overcharges and fees. From a banks perspective the worst that can happen is the bank reluctantly and only as a cost cutting factor, will pay back the few complainants who yell loud and long enough. A few dollars here and a few dollars there taken from customer's accounts amounts to more than A\$300 million a year and this is fraud. That is, banks have the best computer facilities to ensure overcharging does not take place, certainly not in favour of the customer. So where is the ACCC or the Department of Fair Trading in this unfair trading, or rather theft?

◆ If legislation were to be passed imposing a 100% of the overcharge as a fine to be paid to the customer, watch how quickly bank and utility providers accuracy would improve.

Individually and collectively we have become too tolerant of injustices within the community, although holding resentment for authority and those who represent it, particularly those who allow others to take advantage of us. Resentment is the festering of "anger" which culminates in disenfranchising sectors of the community. This hapless resentment of authority for personal circumstances can create a need for escapism, far too often to alcohol and drugs, which turns into drunken violence. This creates a dysfunctional society with crime from drug and alcohol abuse resulting in domestic and civil violence, destroying lives and marriages through anger and frustrations for poverty and inequality.

As with bank managers, lawyer jokes are synonymous with our contempt and disrespect for that profession. The Judicial system has made lawyers indispensable officers of the court and a law unto themselves. The judiciary relies on antiquated mechanics and procedures preventing the average person representing himself in pursuit of justice. With many wonderful, talented and selfless exceptions to the rule, some of whom I am very privileged to know – legal practitioners have also gained a general reputation as rip-off merchants. Many solicitors are ill equipped to attend to the broad variety of legal requirements and types of litigation they claim to be able to. Many are unable to comprehend the facts of a matter over the intricacies of the procedures. In many instances this proves to be to the financial benefit of a solicitor but at the peril of the client. That is, they are paid whether they win or lose from good representation or not! The courts are overflowing with cases that run for year after year, for hundreds and thousands of dollars that at the end of the day neither party wins – just the lawyers. There is no accountability to taxpayers for maintaining the costs of running the courts and the judicial system is not based on productivity, rather an endless stream of government funds in supporting this protected species of elite bureaucracy.

Over the past 40 years, government has shed responsibility by both selling off assets and particularly in distancing itself from responsibility by appointing "independent" agencies. Yet with so many "independent agencies" government still needed to create a hugely cumbersome and intricate departmental infrastructure. Set up to relieve the pressure on politicians while attempting to appear as if work is actually happening, but what has transpired is that there is less accountability and reduced responsibility for more than triple the costs to taxpayers. The development of more departments, more agencies, more associations and group which has created a very intricate system in the spreading of work but this provides a greater inability to be efficient. By "work" I mean real work as against the fake-work that multiplies exponentially as bureaucracy expands. You know what I mean: planning meetings to facilitate strategic developments meetings and then in selecting and empanelling team members tasked to do real work after extensive research and many more meeting. It's the old three people required to change one light globe and then two more to give reports to all levels of management above.

The creation of "independent" agencies does nothing but remove the onus of performance away from government Ministers to unaccountable agencies. This also creates the illusion of having created more employment in administrative "white collar" jobs. This appearance of creating new jobs looks good if a government were trying to demonstrate sound economic practices and "appear" to be reducing unemployment as an election stunt. But this only drains society's financial resources and provides counterproductive, unsustainable waste in a system of duplication both in the many States constitutions and nationally, while politicians and bureaucrats are freed to pursue their agendas.

It has resulted in our being over-regulated in the most inappropriate areas while we are not governed to acceptable standards in business or government, nor does it allow government to produce positive results expeditiously. Out of sheer financial mismanagement and as a result of growing community awareness we hear of the NSW State government wanting to appease the community by reducing government employment but unfortunately the positions made redundant are in the most inappropriate areas, for example, sacking nurses when the need is for more nurses, as well as doctors and so forth. Then due to the lack of providing adequate financial assistance into educating our young people to be doctors, we entice Indian doctors to come here to fill urgent positions, while they leave their country short. The NSW government would suggests slashing A\$26 million from the front line of the already under resourced NSW police resources, while State Rail authorities increase the number of bureaucrats jobs and their pay packets by increasing fares on public transport while providing a very poor service. These are wrong decisions made by the wrong people. To spite governments mismanagement, waste and high taxes, overall, Australia has seen exceptional growth over the past 10 years (primarily due to mining the hell out of the country) yet so many sectors of the community are poverty stricken, bankrupt or verging on bankruptcy with more than 40% of bankruptcies as a direct result of "Economy Conditions". There are hundreds of thousands of homeless children and their parents who need to access the Supported Accommodation Program (Aust Institute of Health and Welfare report). Statistics over the past year indicate that 600 people a month are becoming homeless, which is synonymous with poor government budgetary determination and the lack of skilled human resources to fix this problem of immediate and long term planning. **In 1987 the then Labor Prime Minister, Bob Hawke promised that *"no child would live in poverty by 1990"*.** Having had billions of dollars in government surplus funds raked in since then, there is just no good or reasonable excuse for there to be any homelessness, let-alone a greater homelessness in Australia now than under Hawke, other than it not being a government priority by either party when in government or in opposition.

Hundreds of families are losing their homes every week due to their inability to maintain the "Australian Dream" of owning their own home. Wanting to own a home is not a crime but failure by government to secure a balance to every sector of the community, is the crime. A survey was carried out about 2 years ago and it was determined that more than 70% of Australians surveyed are "unhappy". The primary cause being financial problems, regardless of full time employment. This leads to the root cause of the creation of dysfunctional families, where 50% end up in divorce. As the needs of society continue to break-down, this is the crime of unaccountable governance for which our politicians of the past 50 years are guilty of.

To compound the serious housing problems by stupid short term governments for the long term of Australia: The Federal government has opened up the flood gates to overseas investors in buying up houses in Australia. This has increased the demand for the seriously short supply and therefore housing prices have disproportionately increased, while reducing available rental accommodation. More than A$20 billion has been spent by overseas purchasers in the last financial year, pushing up the average home price to a level that most Australians will never be able to afford their own home. Many of these houses were bought and just sit empty, not rented out but left empty, just appreciating the capital gains, while putting a roof over an Australians family is becoming more impossible and new comers are given greater consideration and assistance than Australians. Where was the community consultation? Where are the skilled authorities? Where is the cohesiveness of what a party ought to be able to co-ordinate? Who makes rash decisions based on adlib conflicting policies and where are those who ought to be opposing poor governance?

Knowing all too well the dire problems with the housing situation, the Federal government in their infinitely stupid May 2009 budget, amongst other irrational spending, spent A$3 billion plus (the cost of more than 15,000 semi rural houses) on a defective Roof Batts Scheme. A Risk Analysis was commissioned by the Government and presented in April 2009. The report wanted the implementation of the scheme delayed as the Scheme was not ready to be rolled out. The report repeatedly warned of the risk of fraud, 'major fall-out' and ominously for the Government, the risk of litigation. It also repeatedly warned of the risk of "early termination' of the scheme. The 'Risk Register' was part of a broader Minter Ellison report which warned that the scheme could cause house fires, deaths and injury, poor quality installations and rorting by the industry. It would appear that **Mr Rudd ignored all reports and any advice which was negative of this wilful waste of taxpayer's money. If it** is ever allowed to be proven, it may produce a very serious case of not just fraud to be appropriately answered to, but one tantamount to involuntary manslaughter in relation to the instigation and then the continuity of the programme with the deaths of 4 men and the safety issues treated with lesser importance. There was no "Cost Risk Analysis" of this project or any project or plan by the Rudd Labor government and he certainly made Whitlam look like an angel, yet many Australians were dismayed by his termination as PM?

Another free lunch (get your free batts) cross promotion (spend up with China) propaganda deal, caused fires in more than 200 roofs (at the time of writing); the loss of four young men's lives installing the batts; then a billion dollars to check and rectify thousands of jobs and chase up installers who fraudulently claimed money for installations that were never carried out. This also caused an environmental hazard from dumping old batts – when that money could have provided the hand-up needed by many families (at least 15,000) **not an ongoing pittance of a welfare hand-out, but a real hand-up** – a job in a new or expanding industry (with working capital of A\$3 billion, to say the building and associated industries), a home with an affordable mortgage, the real purpose of good government. Peter Garrett, Minister for the Environment never had the skills or the experience to have made such an irrational decision or participate in it, nor do any of his cohort ministers, yet he took the fall for his PM and was rewarded with a new ministry by Ms Gillard. Expert knowledge or advice highlighted the problems associated with this "free lunch Labor propaganda" but arrogance does not take experts advice and Mr Rudd maintained his commitment that "*the buck stops with me*" and so it did, with this debacle and every other dumb initiative the government had made. Rudd might be gone as PM but the damages we enabled him to get away with will live on through his then second in command Ms Gillard in a party system which rewards adverse philosophies, poor policies and those who pursue their own and their party's agendas. Rudd will remain one of the ongoing well rewarded with PM entitlements, a protected species, sheltered from accountability and recourse for the loss of life, abuse of power and mass destruction he created in his short reign.

Very few individual Australians are able to get government support or help regarding issues or complaints, many of which are of grave concern not just to the complainant but pertinent to us all. It is all too easy for government employees and Ministers to disregard any one single personal complaint or even a group of complainants, particularly about government departments or ministers – conveniently forgetting who is employed by whom. There are many disadvantaged people and groups in so many facets of our society with problems ranging from fair access to the legal system; to inequality of bargaining power between large and small business and individual customer, due to adverse legislation; to access to a hospital bed; to care for the elderly and disabled; to those who do not know how to or do not want to be integrated into our society; to many who are prepared to work for lesser pay, as their financial commitments are less, but they cannot take this work due to those jobs being shipped off overseas; to small and medium sized business being penalised by adverse bureaucratic encumbrances making their business and lives non viable and intolerable etc.

There is now an organisation to help Australians with government acts of corruption: The Australian Civil Authority (the "Authority") which was created in June 2008 by a group of Citizens concerned with the mounting corruption within Governments and associated Corporations. The Authority is independent and created within the Sovereignty of the People and totally outside of Government legislation and control. The Sovereignty of the People is paramount over their Parliament and those within are subservient to the People. Therefore, the Authority acts under Sovereignty with an inherent right under its charter to investigate malpractice, corruption and or treason within Government(s) as termed within the Commonwealth of Australia Constitution Act 1900 (UK).

The Australian Civil Authority is the Authority of the People and affording them a protection from corruption within the powers that be, that have continually remove their rights for a self ordained power to do at their Will. People should always report corruption to the Australian Civil Authority regardless of their complaint, to a statute body for the purpose of record and should it be necessary to be later investigated by a Sovereign Body.

The Authority will only consider matters relating to Governments or any Corporation involved with Government dealings. However some people may consider a situation that may relate to Government that they should report it and allow the Authority to decide. Contact with the Authority is by written form posted to the central address: Australian Civil Authority. PO Box 65, WERRIS CREEK NSW 2341 AUSTRALIA

Resentment sets in when those who are suffering or are disadvantaged from their inability to get a fair go, then rebel in many forms adverse to a cohesive society. Not many people are prepared to band together or spend many years fighting a system or institution especially when the life span of the institution or system exceeds our own. Years and years can be spent fighting for an issue to help ourselves and others, but to be slammed up against blank walls and to be confronted with the deaf ears of bureaucrats, those who should be eager to support and help. Issues that may include amending constitutional legislation in tune with the needs and wants of a progressive and fair minded society, which continues to daunt us due to the adverse legislations which have effectively killed our Constitution. Unless you are filthy rich and creative, Australians have a deliberately inaccessible and cumbersome legal system that as a democracy we can only be ashamed of. The judicial system protects "its peoples" rights to continue distancing their system from the people's right to justice.

The judiciary was established to be independent of government, yet government legislations have successfully infiltrated the judiciary with politicians now able to delegate to the judiciary with amended laws and new legislation and the judiciary, to the distain of many good people in that field, must conform. The result: the judiciary is no longer independent, this is a fallacy. In this vein, it is ludicrous and inconceivable that the legal system, the very backbone of peaceful society claims autonomy, and remains unaccountable to the people, while it facilitates legislation adverse to the people and their Commonwealth Constitutional rights. The judicial system is such an integral part of our infrastructure and its function is so desperately in need of fresh ideas to reflect the values of varying generations. There is an urgent national need to overhaul the judiciary to becoming a healthy and accessible system, with various affordable methods of recourse for all of the people.

Although originally based on sound and solid legal fundamentals, the judicial system or procedures were also designed by academics aristocrats of a by-gone era. Today we would call them "big business" and the judiciary, by default, facilitate and protect "big business" by default. Old rules and systems are mechanically applied despite the existence of new and changed circumstances by the few who do not want to negate their autonomy for external accountability, while the members of the legal fraternity or judiciary remain protected species.

If you have the need to lodge a complaint about a solicitor through the respective State's Law Society or Institute you will find that this is a biased department which protects the interests of its members, before the interests of any individual and therefore our community. Siding or finding favourable determination against its members (legal practitioner) costs its insurer Law Cover and this is defended at all costs with every loophole in the book relied on, particularly the financial inability to pursue a matter by many a complainant.

◆   A truly unbiased independent national legal complaints body, instigated by the Senate with State representation is imperative in seeking amendments to the complaints process against a new National Judicial System, see that section.

Countless innocent individuals and business people who "cannot afford their day in court" end up bankrupt, while the financially secure often "Big Business" operators, rely on the fact that there is little if any legal remedy for their prey. Any level headed, fair minded person must ask how any government professing to have the community's interest as a priority (be it from either side of the political arena) can for so many decades stand back and not contest and rectify this gross miscarriage of justice. The only logical answer is that it suits the government of the day's political and or financial agenda in supporting their decision to deregulate big business and the way it conducts its affairs. Then for the judiciary to protect its own nest, while the average person suffers the greatest adversities from inequality with no bargaining power or ability to seek recourse whatsoever. This is not just a crime against an individual but against all Australians and humanity.

This contributes to rising bankruptcies, as a direct result of *poor* "Economic Conditions" and high interest; see section on Bankruptcies and breach of privacy laws by credit reporting agencies. The reiterated point is that **people have suffered, are**

still suffering and will continue to suffer bankruptcies and liquidations due to poor government administrative decisions made by many poorly skilled political persons' with their poor ulterior motifs, who hold government positions or work within government delegated agencies. Those who need to spend hundreds of millions of dollars on consultants to tell them what they should know in holding down specific ministries, but then continue to fail to action the advice provided.

The backbone of any country is only as strong as its healthy non arthritic parts all working in unison. This means that all components need to be perfectly aligned with no pinched nerves and with healthy blood flowing from a strong and infallible heart. This is mandatory for achieving maximum systemic function able to produce maximum benefits to every facet of its physical and mental existence. If any organ has a defect or an infection the entire body suffers pain and cannot perform to its optimum, it cannot focus on anything other than its ailments or worse, cancer. If life saving surgery is required to remove cancer, that is what we do, without delay. Each and every one of us, the jobs we do and our environment, make up every tissue, every cell, every bone, every organ and the blood (water) of our 'national body' – with ego, our greatest mental illness. Our personal, corporate and governmental choices and behaviour affect both the physical and mental health of the entire national body. MM Schneerson said, *"Cancer to the body is as ego to the soul"* perverting and preventing a wise mind governing a good and kind heart. It's a wise government which is intended to delegate real priorities and lead by good examples and ensure skilled people make good decisions in the interest of the majority, and it is our responsibility to ensure we are governed by individuals able to pursue our best interests.

The Best Country In The World Is Getting Stuffed

"We are firstly a society not an economy, albeit a society reliant on a solid economy"

WITH ACCESS TO so many forms of media from radio, TV, newspapers and the internet, Australians are far more in tuned with social and political issues than ever before in the history of mankind and are also demanding more accountability than ever before. Political parties have been riding on the general slogan and the consensus that, *"It's time for a change"* and *"moving forward"* as they are aware that society hold deep rooted contempt for politicians, particularly those who have been found to be corrupt or lie to gain office.

To date politicians have not been held accountable for their representations and promises. A promise is a person's word and a *"man or woman is only as good as their word"* and a representation, which is not factual, is a lie! These are the primary reasons politicians are ridiculed in a feast by the few unbiased media and why we as a society have developed resentment and contempt for government authority. With history continuing as our witness, one broken promise or lie continues not just from within the government but it transcends from one government to the next. It really is time to change who and how we are governed, and particularly, to where our national priorities lie. Readdress what we expect from those we appoint to carry on "the business of the country" and what is fair and equitable for all Australians who are tired; **Tired of excuses, broken promises and misrepresentations; tired of complacency; tired of wasted and sacrificed resources; tired of lost opportunities for improvements; tired of calling on the deaf ears of individuals and collective politicians whose priorities are not "ours"; tired of relying on those with a lack of respective skills for specific functions; tired of redundant and adverse legislature, and worse, tired of paying for political party's spin doctors who facilitate the pursuit of ego driven ideals and agendas of others.**

Today with extensive consumer awareness through the media's talk back radio and if news worthy enough for current affairs programs, we are able to make a hell of a racket and protest vigilantly to get overwhelming media and public support. If you can name and shame and hit the raw nerve of a minister, or his party, especially before an election there is a hope or at least a "promise" that issues may be addressed some time down the track or as part of the next election propaganda, but no guarantee of performance during the term.

Early in the 20th century "proactive" governments with very limited technology and limited alternative agendas (due to limited financial market scope) took the interests of the country as their foremost priorities. With less than a third of the population who paid less than a quarter of the taxes we are encumbered with today, and thus a fraction of the current annual tax revenue, those governments who endured two major world wars and the Great Depression were responsible for building solid infrastructures of roads, rail, defence forces, health and education. They built a strong common wealth asset base which we as citizens collectively owned. We owned our roads, banks and utilities with community assets worth more than five times what we are left with today, or rather has not been sold off. Today our country is run by "reactive" academic politicians, whose only accountability is in succumbing to the public oppositional shaming by their political opponents and this is "crisis management", not good government. Issues are not well-prioritised and there is no cost-effective long-term planning by those who are unskilled to hold the portfolios they do, resulting in reactive, crisis management.

The losses through crisis management by unskilled bureaucratic bunglers, together with maintaining the priorities of "party politics" has led to the continual selling off of our community assets, then diverting these funds and taxes to accommodate the hefty, counter-productive bureaucracy. Bills and legislation have enabled governments to operates the way they want, pushed through Parliament, never put to the people and now our financial future has been compromised by an indiscriminately wasteful **Prime Minister who did not run a Democracy but what can only be considered an "Oligarchy"** (government controlled by a small group of people as opposed to a democracy). The A$130 billion plus in wasted resources and counterproductive measures are directly responsible for reducing, to a critical levels, the maintenance of our hospitals, education facilities, water and sewerage systems, transport and all fundamental infrastructures while reducing productivity and that which only skilled "proactive" Australians are able to fix.

There are many good politicians with common sense who start out dedicated and full of determination to be proactive and who want to make a difference and who are willing to take a limited risk in speaking up – not just to protect their backside but to get things done. But they too slam into party constitutional bureaucratic obstacles. They themselves cannot combat the system and eventually their selfless motivation falls by the wayside or they are brought to conform to their party's policies, or move on. Anyone can be a politician if they have the "gift of the gab" and "the bucks to back them" in getting support for their political ideologies or that of their party – but if, like most of us, we don't have the resources or the inclination we can always be a "Whingeing Aussie!"

Aussies are known for being a bit laid-back and easy going so how did we get the label of – "Whingeing Aussies?" Maybe because we're fed up with those we trusted to care for our best interests but who have pursued interests which are not for the common benefit of all Australians. Interests which are as a result of corruption, mismanagement and poor priorities affecting each and every one of us in our daily lives. Duplication, procrastination and the poor distribution of funds due to the lack of co-operation and compromise between the States and Federal governments has contributed greatly to the poor decisions being made by those ill equipped to make them.

Then watch the bickering and blame-storming! Independent Clover Moore rightly sums it up, *". . . petty party political point scoring or baseless personal attacks* [is why] *people are becoming increasingly cynical about the political process, and increasingly alienated by a style of politics which elevates personal attacks over substantial programs and services, for the public benefit"*. We constantly witness the "ugly face of party politics" in our parliamentary sessions and yet this is currently considered our best attempt at getting results and accountability! Of course there is a better way and maybe we're not such whingers after all! Just maybe our concerns, our opinions and ideas are valid and we have an obligation to right the wrongs and change the way government issues are handled and who handles them.

Locally, State by State and nationally for many decades we have sustained thousands upon thousands of examples of governments wasting financial and physical resources and losing opportunities which only emphasises the lack of care, and lack of skills, and lack of understanding for real priorities in the pursuit of ulterior motives. Lies and distractive issues are used as concealment of absolute corruption through all levels of government. This includes nonsense issues, such the Queensland Labor State government together with their State Health and Education Departments spending a small fortune in determining if "red pens" should be removed from schools. Hundreds of thousands of taxpayer dollars wasted, time lost which ought to have been directed to issues of real concern particularly improving agriculture, the standard of education and fighting corruption in that State, but no! *"Red pens used by teachers"* are the sort of issues deployed to merely divert the focus away from major issues such as the governments very own corruption with their involvement in the Heiner Affair and issues such as Brigalow Corporation and the proposed referendum to severe land ownership and value from individuals.

It is now suggested that there is to be a debate to determine whether biblical stories are offensive to children's development, and if they should be removed from schools to appease atheists or perhaps Communists who do not hold religious affiliations, but who would allow fictitious fairy tales or Shakespeare (misguided then) to be taught, sounds like a dangerous agenda? Where are we heading?

Whether you think stories of moral fibre that cannot be disproved are possibly to be removed from schools without determining the cost to society, if these stories – which have nurtured hundreds of generations before us – are to be considered for removal "for fear of offending the offenders' is sheer lunacy. Stories preserving morals and virtues are the essential nature and history of a culture. If we don't tell those stories that have been central to our society, we simply empty the field for other stronger and more coherent cultures and traditions to sow their seeds on the fallow ground we have prepared for them.

Mere diversions from the very serious issues of Queensland government as covered by a Sydney journalist who is not prepared to stay quiet on the corrupt activities of our most senior government ministers: 18 Mar 2009 [sic]: **Colin Dillon, a former police inspector, a whistleblower to the Fitzgerald Inquiry, which exposed corruption at the highest levels of the Queensland Police accused the current Queensland Labor Government of corruption and stated, *'I want to make it crystal clear, things are shocking in this State, corruption still exists and it permeates right through the whole government'.***

The Heiner Affair – 'Shreddergate'

– *A blight on the Australian Democracy*

O N 9 OCTOBER 2007 during the height of the historic 2007 Federal election which saw Mr Kevin Rudd elected as Prime Minister of Australia, Queensland whistleblower, Kevin Lindeberg spoke to a packed audience in the New South Wales Parliament's Theatrette about the Heiner Affair. He recounted the following words which he had earlier put to then Queensland Governor, Her Excellency Quentin Bryce in 2005 when she was making a decision about what to do regarding the unresolved Heiner Affair which was showing that Her Government was persisting in acting outside the law.

"*. . . The criminal law only carries a moral and constitutional basis of authority and respect in a democracy if it is applied equally by government against all citizens who transfers it. This is government by the rule of law. If, however, the law becomes an instrument of sectional application by government for government, such conduct is unfair and oppressive and sets government in conflict with democracy itself and the rule of law. That is tyranny.*"

After examining all the relevant evidence including a confidential report from the Beattie Government concerning its handling of the affair which she had requested some 18 months prior, Governor Bryce resolved to take no action.

Most recently, on 24 November 2008 Lindeberg appeared by invitation before the Tasmanian Select Joint Committee on Ethical Conduct to speak about the Heiner Affair as part of Tasmania's decision on whether to establish an integrity tribunal like ICAC, CMC and CCC. He spoke to the core point of the Heiner Affair thus: "*. . . I suggest that there are two issues of concern which justify my appearance here today. Their function under the overarching democratic principle of equality before the law for all was described by the 18th century attorney, Sir Thomas Fuller, and later by Lord Denning. Lord Denning put the principle most succinctly during his 1989 interview when he said:* **There is not supposed to be one law for the rich and powerful and another for the poor and oppressed, so next time anyone should come along and say to you, "Do you know who**

I am?", I hope you would find Fuller's words useful: Be you never so high, the law is above you."

He further states: ".... *The second issue stems from the accepted democratic principle that the prosecutorial and public interest discretion must be exercised by crown decision makers consistently and predictably in materially similar circumstances. It is: 'Be it monarch, president, politician or public official, what good is an oath of office if a breach does not invite appropriate punishment?'* [1]

The Heiner Affair is the longest-running political corruption scandal in Australian political history. As the years have gone by, the scandal has grown. Arguably, it is the nation's most serious. It is not going away. Out of its 20-year history, it now embodies all the fundamental democratic values which hold this nation together as both civilised and harmonious, and poses the key democratic question of whether or not we are all equal before the law. That is, are politicians and public officials, "the Governors", permitted to live by different standards and claim ignorance of the law as an excuse for their wrongdoing, while we the people, "the Governed", have no such privilege when breaking the law?

What is known about what was covered up and what was going on behind government doors, including the door to the Queensland Cabinet, can only be told now through the sheer persistence of one man, Kevin Lindeberg and a growing national band and international supporters, from High and Supreme Court Chief Judges, judges, QCs, academics, archivists, journalists, radio presenters, whistleblowers, teachers to ordinary people who have come to realise that unless this scandal is properly resolved Australia simply cannot claim to be a nation governed by the rule of law but instead by men (and women) who are prepared to abuse their positions of power and trust for self-serving and political reasons, and can get away with it.

The Heiner Affair demonstrates that unless corruption is nipped in the bud immediately, especially high-level corruption, without fear or favour, any subsequent cover-up can ultimately reduce an entire system of government to chaos.

In recounting this scandal now in such limited space, a certain licence of brevity has been necessary so that the essential elements can be told which may encourage a more detailed investigation later on by readers. This is a huge scandal with many limbs to it.

In September 1989 a meeting occurred between the Department of Family Services and Ms Janine Walker, Queensland State Services Union Director of Industrial Relations on behalf of youth workers from the John Oxley Youth Centre (JOYC) about Mr Peter Coyne's management of the Centre. The Director-General Mr Alan

---

[1]   Joint Select Committee on Ethical Conduct, Brisbane 24/11/08 (Lindeberg) Tasmanian Parliament's Hansard, page 54.

Pettigrew insisted complaints were to be put in writing before any investigation could be undertaken.

On 1st October 1989, ALP Shadow Families Spokesperson Ms Anne Warner told The Sunday Sun (page 18) that she had knowledge of children being handcuffed to fences, and being sedated with drugs having been told of the incidents by the Centre staff. She called for a review of management practices.

On 2 November 1989, the Department of Family Services appointed retired Stipendiary Magistrate, Mr. Noel Heiner, to conduct a Ministerial Inquiry. Heiner was provided with specific terms of reference and required to investigate and report back on the specific written complaints against Coyne, and on other matters relating to the Centre's security and treatment of detainees. Original complaints remained in the possession of the Department, and photocopies were provided to Heiner. His appointment was approved of by Families Minister, the Hon Mrs Beryce Nelson. She expected him to investigate allegations of sexual abuse over and above physical abuse. The Heiner Inquiry was set up under the *Public Service Management and Employment Act 1988.*

Later that month, Heiner began taping evidence from the Centre staff and had it transcribed into evidence on computer discs and hard copies. This became what is now commonly known as "the Heiner Inquiry documents." There is no doubt that the Heiner Inquiry investigated allegations of abuse of children at the Centre, including an incident in 1989, when two girls aged 12 and 16 and a boy aged 14, were unlawfully handcuffed to a tennis court fence all night on Coyne's orders because of their "alleged disruptive behaviour". It was later discovered, in 2001, that Heiner also took evidence about the alleged cover-up of the sexual assault of a 14 year old Aboriginal girl – known only as Annette – which occurred during a supervised bush outing to Mt Barney by other male inmates of the JOYC.

A whistleblower confirmed in 2001 and later in evidence before the 2003/04 House of Representatives Standing Committee on Legal and Constitutional Affairs, chaired by the Hon Bronwyn Bishop MP, that Heiner asked him questions about the pack-rape incident during the course of his inquiry. [2]

On 27 November 1989, Coyne approached Pettigrew seeking:

◆ a copy of all the written complaints;
◆ written advice on the process of how the complaints were going to be investigated;
◆ the opportunity to organise and conduct a defence against the complaints lay.

---

[2] http://www.aph.gov.au/house/committee/laca/crimeinthecommunity/report/vol2chapter2.pdf

Coyne also indicated that it was impossible for him to defend himself without knowing what the specific complaints were. (These requests were later refused). He approached Departmental staff assigned to assist Heiner and registered his concerns as put to Pettigrew. Coyne was given a brief one-page outline of written complaints. One complaint listed alleged abuse of children. He was refused access to specific written complaints handed to the Department on 10 October 1989.

The ALP won office in Queensland for the first time in 32 years in early December 1989. Wayne Goss, a solicitor, became Premier and Minister responsible for State Archives. Kevin Rudd became his Chief-of-staff and Principal Adviser. Warner became the Minister for Department of Family Services and Aboriginal and Islander Affairs (DFSAIA). She was always aware of the possible serious illegal activities inside JOYC. Ms Ruth Matchett was immediately elevated to the position of acting Departmental Director-General, replacing Pettigrew.

Coyne officially requested from Matchett copies of the original complaints and transcript of evidence gathered by Heiner in order to defend himself. He questioned the legal validity of the inquiry. He also informed her that he would sue for defamation if his career suffered as a consequence of the Inquiry. She claimed that she could not find any such complaints despite having been informed in a memorandum by her Deputy DFSAIA Director-General, Mr. Ian Peers, that the original complaints against Coyne were held on an official file in the Department's possession, created by Mr George Nix. It was described as *". . . a file compiled by Mr Nix including the original letters of complaint."*

On 11 January 1990, Heiner confirmed to Coyne that allegations of criminal conduct had been made against him. Coyne gave evidence to Heiner for the entire day. By an extraordinary lapse in memory after 14 years of imposed silence, in 2004, when the Bishop Legal and Constitution Affairs Committee had summoned him to appear before the committee after refusing an invitation to attend, Heiner could not recall interviewing Coyne. His memory about the child abuse was oddly vague. Heiner died in 2008.

Coyne was also accused of having an affair with the Centre's Deputy Manager, Ms Anne Dutney which he denied. He was told by Heiner that he (Heiner) only held copies of the original complaints, and that the original complaints were in the Department's possession. Coyne therefore sought access to the original complaints in a memorandum dated 15 January 1990 to Matchett, pursuant to **Public Service Management and Employment Regulation (PSME) 65** *which permitted such access.*

Two days later, **Matchett asserted that there were no complaints on Coyne's personal file while knowing that they were held on another separate file.** In January and February 1990, Coyne contacted his union organiser, Lindeberg. He had worked for the Queensland Professional Officers Association as its senior organiser for some 6 years. Coyne wanted union assistance in gaining access the Heiner Inquiry documents under **PSME 65**. As the documents were about him,

Coyne also indicated that he might take defamation action. Lindeberg saw his task as Coyne's industrial interests.

Significantly, Coyne's solicitors and two trade Unions placed the Queensland Government on notice of foreshadowed court proceedings on 8, 14, 15 and 23 February and 1 March 1990. This was done by letters, phone calls and meetings. The Queensland Government was told not to destroy the evidence, and that if access was not granted "out of court", then the matter would be settled "in court." Unbeknown to Coyne, his solicitors and Lindeberg, the Families Department had meanwhile secretly transferred the documents to the Office of Cabinet in a desire to gain access exemption under "Cabinet Confidentiality" or "Crown Privilege."

In legal circles this is known as the obstructionist tactic of "warehousing." It obstructs discovery. It was notoriously condemned in the 2002 *McCabe* tobacco smoking case of Victoria.

The relevant February/March 1990 Cabinet submissions (which are now held by Lindeberg) unquestionably reveal that all Cabinet members in attendance at the 5 March 1990 Cabinet Meeting, together with certain senior bureaucrats who aided in the shredding-decision process, were aware that the documents were required as evidence in the foreshadowed judicial proceeding when they were ordered destroyed to prevent to use as evidence.

Crown Law advice of 16 February 1990 reveals that the Queensland Cabinet, and Crown Law, knew that the records would be discoverable evidence upon the serving of the anticipated writ. By other evidence spoken in the media and in parliament, it was known that at least three Goss Ministers, if not all, were also aware that those public records contained evidence about the known or suspected abuse of children at the Centre before they ordered their destruction.

As each layer of this extraordinary cover-up has been peeled away over the years, the presence of child abuse at the Centre surfaced after being concealed from the beginning by those in the system and in government. It was primarily through the investigative journalistic skills of Bruce Grundy, Journalist-in-Residence, School of Journalism and Communication at the University of Queensland that this factor became known while working with Lindeberg.

Grundy resolutely reported on Lindeberg's fight for justice after he had been suddenly sacked by his union in May 1990 after challenging the Queensland Government's plans to destroy the Heiner evidence. Lindeberg had inadvertently learnt about the plan during a phone conversation with Minister Warner's private secretary. Lindeberg had been previously assured by Matchett that the Heiner Inquiry documents were safe.

The Goss Government closed the Heiner Inquiry, secretly transferred the documents into the Cabinet Room, indemnified all the witnesses and then secretly shredded all the material on 23 March 1990 while knowing that it was required for court. At the time, Goss's Chief-of-staff, Kevin Rudd – later to be known throughout Queensland politics as Dr Death or Mr Fix-it – became the strict gatekeeper of all Cabinet submissions going into Cabinet. Since this matter has recently flared, Rudd has made contradictory statements about his role in and knowledge of it, despite it going to Cabinet on three separate occasions at the time.

On Channel Nine's Sunday Program *"Queensland's Secret Shame"* on 21 February 1999, Goss Cabinet Minister, the Hon Pat Comben, publicly admitted that at the time, the destruction of the documents was ordered *"in broad terms we were all made aware that there was material about child abuse. Individual members of the Cabinet were increasingly concerned about whether or not the right decision had been taken* (with regard to the shredding)."

On *Sunday, Warner claimed that she had no knowledge of the incidents or that evidence of them was contained in the Heiner Inquiry documents when the Goss Cabinet ordered the material destroyed despite publicly revealing her knowledge of it in The Sunday Sun before becoming the responsible minister.*

Sunday also has former Queensland Police Commissioner, Noel Newnham saying "... *Some complaints concerned the handcuffing of children . . . . Allegations the children had been sedated inappropriately to cope with a management problem, and of course there were allegations of bad management practice in general. Those things were all known in 1989 Quite high up in the department."*

In 2005 Lindeberg obtained advice on the shredding from former Chief Justice of the High Court of Australia, the **Hon Sir Harry Gibbs, then President of the Samuel Griffith Society. He advised that sufficient inculpatory evidence existed to warrant charges under Section 129 of the Queensland Code. Section 129 of the** *Criminal Code* **(Queensland) – destruction of evidence – provides that:** *"Any person who, knowing that any book, document, or other thing of any kind, is or may be required in evidence in a judicial proceeding, wilfully destroys it or renders it illegible or undecipherable or incapable of identification, with intent thereby to prevent it from being used in evidence, is guilty of a misdemeanour, and is liable to imprisonment with hard Labor for three years."*

This advice was all the more poignant because the Queensland authorities, in 2004 had successfully charged and prosecuted a lowly Baptist Pastor for similar shredding conduct pursuant to section 129. This case confirmed what Lindeberg and others had said about section 129 for years. Relevantly, the Queensland Court of Appeal in *R v Ensbey; ex parte A-G (Queensland)* [2004] QCA 335 of 17 September 2004 said: *"... Now, here, members of the jury, the words, 'might be required', those words mean a realistic possibility. Also, members of the jury, I direct you, there does not have to be a judicial proceeding actually on foot for a person to be guilty of this offence. There does not have to be something going on in this courtroom for someone to be guilty of this offence. If there is a realistic possibility that evidence might be required in a judicial proceeding, if the other elements are made out to your satisfaction, then a person can be guilty of that offence."*

Lindeberg took his initial complaint to the Criminal Justice Commission (CJC) in 1990. It was treated in a highly perfunctory manner. In January 1993 the CJC cleared the Goss Cabinet (and senior bureaucrats) of any wrongdoing but in doing so misinterpreted section 129. The CJC claimed that judicial proceedings had to be on foot before section 129 could be triggered. Lindeberg declared that the interpretation was nonsense and persisted with this view for years in the face of ridicule from the CJC and others. Other aspects of the CJC clearance saw the facts incorrectly presented and the law both misquoted and misinterpreted, including **PSME Regulation 65**.

In 1995, when appearing before the Senate Select Committee on Unresolved Whistleblower Cases, Lindeberg's senior counsel, Mr. Ian Callinan QC said this: *". . . The real point about the matter is that it does not matter when, in technical terms, justice begins to run. What is critical is that a party in possession of documents knows that those documents might be required for the purposes of litigation and consciously takes a decision to destroy them. That is unthinkable. If one had commercial litigation between two corporations and it emerged that one of the corporations knowing or believing that there was even a chance that it might be sued, took a decision to destroy evidence, that would be regarded as conduct of the greater seriousness – and much more serious, might I suggest, if done by a government."*[3]

Did the CJC itself have a conflict of interest in going above the law to preserve those who think they are, those who are also legal practitioners who hold positions in government? **Solicitors and barristers making laws and holding political positions, is a conflict of interest. They continue to weasel their way around the law, while causing others to break the law:**

In April 2003, former Queensland Appeal and Supreme Court Justice, the Hon James Thomas, informed the University of Queensland's student newspaper that while many laws were arguable, section 129 was not. It was unambiguous in its intent and meaning. It embraced "futurity." He advised that those involved the shredding wrongdoing were still open to charges.

Relevantly, in his evidence before the Tasmanian Parliamentary Committee on 24 November 2008 Lindeberg said this about the CJC's investigation: *". . . It was conducted by a contracted barrister, Mr Noel Nunan. Unbeknown to me at the time he was an ALP member, activist, a former work colleague of Premier Wayne Goss before Mr Goss entered politics. Mr Nunan was a member of the Queensland Association of Labor Lawyers as was the CJC official, Mr Michael Barnes, who recommended him for the review purposes. They were mates investigating a mate . . . Both Mr Nunan and Mr Barnes have since been elevated to the bench as magistrates. Mr. Barnes is our State Coroner. Some of the CJC-CMC barristers, officials who concurred with this*

3   Senate Select Committee on Unresolved Whistleblower Cases in <<Brisbane>> on23 February 1995 Senate Hansard p3.

unprecedented and absurd view of the law which prevented charges being laid and which utterly undermined the administration of justice and the right to a fair trial, now sit on the Queensland bench dispensing justice in the name of the Crown."

The interpretation of section 129 was so profoundly wrong that it would have positively led parties involved in litigation to be able to destroy all known and relevant evidence up to the moment of a writ being lodged and served to prevent its use in those proceeding without breaking the law. As Professor Camille Cameron of the Law Faculty at Melbourne University later declared, such a view would inevitably lead to "a world without evidence." Put simply, chaos.

Despite its so-called "nth degree" investigation, the CJC never interviewed any Cabinet Ministers, senior bureaucrats, JOYC staff or inmates, Heiner, Crown Law, or the State Archivist. Indeed, so misconceived was the CJC's view about the archivist's role in the matter, that it caused an international storm of outrage in the world community of archivists which exists to this day and has grown and grown in notoriety.

In the *Ensbey* case, the counsel for Pastor Ensbey made an application to the Queensland Office of the Director of Public Prosecutions in October 2003 seeking to have the destruction-of-evidence charge under section 129 struck out because of its interpretation used by in the Heiner Affair. The application was refused. He was ordered to stand trial because the DPP said that section 129 did cover 'futurity" (citing *R v Rogerson*) and that it was in the public interest to place the matter before the court because the alleged offence was an attack on the administration of justice. While he was rightly tried and found guilty, it is quite clear that the authorities concurrently knew that the Goss Cabinet and certain senior bureaucrats had escaped justice for their shredding conduct in the Heiner Affair – in far worse and more clear factual circumstances – by section 129 being interpreted incorrectly.

In 2002, a major academic book *"Archives and the Public Good – Accountability and Records in Modern Society"* was published by the Universities of Pittsburgh and Michigan citing the Heiner Affair as one of the 14 great shredding scandals of the 20th century. It is now the subject of lectures on record keeping and good governance in major universities across Australia and throughout the world. Another academic book on recordkeeping was published in August 2009 in Austin Texas sponsored by the American Society of Archivists featuring the Heiner Affair as a prominent scandal.

In the meantime, 'Annette' who wanted the alleged rapists charged in 1988 but was threatened out of proceeding then, lodged a fresh complaint with the Queensland Police Service in 2007 in respect of her 24 May 1988 sexual assault at Mt Barney. The outcome is yet to be made public.

In August 2007, a two-year audit of the Heiner Affair was completed by leading Sydney barrister David Rofe QC with the assistance of Lindeberg and his lawyers. The 3,000 page, 9 volume audit found 68 alleged *prima facie* criminal offences capable of being made against those involved, either by initial (shredding and related) acts, or in their subsequent handling of the Lindeberg allegations at relevant times, which purportedly involved *inter alia* six sitting Queensland judicial officers (before their elevation to the Bench), Prime Minister Rudd and Governor-General Quentin Bryce when they held public office in Queensland at relevant times.

A raft of superior court judges issued an unprecedented public Judges' Statement of Concern on the Heiner Affair to Premier Peter Beattie in August 2007. They believed that the issues involved struck at the very heart of the administration of justice. They strongly urged him to appoint a Special Prosecutor to investigate the entire Heiner Affair: Mr Beattie ignored the letter, and resigned some 2 weeks later. Premier Bligh has ignored their plea also.

<http://www.heineraffair.info/site_pages/legal_opinions.html#judge>

The ALP prevented Senator Barnaby Joyce from tabling the Rofe Audit in the Federal Senate on 19 September 2007. One might reasonably suspect that the ALP never wanted the Audit's contents brought into the cold light of day under parliamentary privilege as it may have been detrimental to Kevin Rudd and the ALP in the lead up to the 2007 Federal election.

The Australian Prudential Regulatory Authority (APRA) in 2008 publicly cited the Heiner Affair as a *"high profile corruption scandal"* capable of standing alongside notorious corruption associated with Enron and HIH.

In February 2008, Lindeberg's legal team lodged a complaint with the bipartisan Queensland Parliamentary Crime and Misconduct Committee (PCMC) seeking a review of the CJC/CMC's handling of Lindeberg's allegations. The Rofe Audit was provided as evidence.

Then, in April 2008 after PM Rudd nominated Queensland Governor Bryce to be Australia's next Governor-General, Lindeberg became concerned that the integrity of the Office of Governor-General may be compromised if the swearing-in were to proceed while the PCMC investigation was on-going. He was concerned as to avoid another Hollingworth scenario and harm to the highest Office in the land. On legal advice, on 30 May 2008, he wrote to Her Majesty Queen Elizabeth II and sent a copy to then Governor-General Major-General Michael Jeffrey pointing out the relevant facts.

On 11 June 2008, Governor-General Jeffrey, on behalf of the Queen, sought an investigation into and advice on the Heiner Affair from Prime Minister Kevin Rudd before the swearing-in of the Hon Quentin Bryce as Governor-General on 5 September 2008, and later, in November 2008, the Queen further requested Premier Bligh to *"give consideration to the Heiner Affair allegations"*. Both requests were ignored. This highlights contempt

for the Crown, the Constitution, and in turn the Australian people, severely punishable crimes. It also clearly demonstrates the complacency of the Queen to intervene and thus questions must be raised as to what has happened to her relevance to the Australia political landscape, who changed this and why without any referendum by the people. It also draws attention to the inadequacy or just plain futility of the oppositional party style of government, in their failure to pull those responsible over the coals to accountability.

In response to a question in a newspaper blog, Mr Abbott stated, *"You know I think that the Heiner affair stinks. The problem is that half the Queensland establishment is implicated. If one person does the wrong thing he is in trouble. If dozens do the wrong thing they often get away with it because it's hard to pinpoint who, precisely, is to blame and it might not be fair to blame all. That's the difficulty with the Heiner Affair"*.

That's not the difficulty – the difficulty is ineffective government opposition, which fosters corruption by not calling for a Royal Commission. **The buck stop right there, at the Queensland Premier's Office and those who ran that show!**

Lindeberg told the Tasmanian Parliamentary Committee that should the PCMC recommend an inquiry into the Heiner Affair the following might inevitably happen: *"Such an enquiry, however would not only rock Queensland to its foundations but the nation itself because it is known that the Prime Minister Rudd and Her Excellency Governor General Quentin Bryce, are adversely named in the audit."* [4]

On 7 January 2009, the 'majority" ALP/PCMC members used their numbers to prevent the Rofe QC Audit being independently examined by an acting Parliamentary Commission. This decision was made in contravention of Section 295 of the *Crime and Misconduct Act 2001 which required bipartisanship to have a lawful outcome regarding finality. The breach is potentially so serious that it undermines the entire Fitzgerald reform process in the fight against corruption in Queensland because it relies on a bipartisan approach, ethically, morally and legally.*

As if to rub salt into the wound of abuse of power, those same ALP/PCMC members when appearing before the Tasmanian Parliamentary Committee on 24 November 2008, publicly assured everyone that the PCMC could not make "majority" decisions. Six weeks later, they did precisely that with the Heiner Affair.

Underpinning this claim, in 2009 at the CMC/ICAC/CCC Anti-Corruption Brisbane Conference, former Supreme Court Justice and ICAC Commissioner, the Hon Barry O'Keefe QC, informed the audience that the Heiner Affair represented serious unfinished (corruption) business for Queensland, yet there is no voice from the Queensland Liberal Party Leader.

---

[4]   Joint Select Committee on Ethical Conduct, <<Brisbane>> 24/11/2008. Kevin Lindeberg, Tasmanian Parliament's Hansard, Page 54.

In mid 2009 for the first time, under the authorisation of the Queensland Education Department, senior Years 11 and 12 students in all Queensland secondary schools now study the Heiner Affair in the Business Communications and Technologies course. The revised textbook, entitled "Business Communication and Technologies in a Changing World" (published by MacMillan), asks students to investigate and discuss the Heiner Affair in class.

At the time of writing, Lindeberg continues his tireless quest to expose the corruption and cover ups behind the Heiner Affair. The website <http://www.heineraffair.info/> His fight is our fight.

Media Integrity – This case also questions the integrity of sections of the media. When he was chosen as ALP leader in December 2007, Rudd flew to New York to meet Rupert Murdoch (NB Murdoch's comments regarding the Queen, further . . .), the CEO of News Limited whose family owns *The Courier Mail* and *The Australian*.

In the 1990s, Chris Mitchell was Editor at *The Courier Mail* (a Murdoch publication) that reported very little to discredit the Beattie Government. In 2004 he was promoted by Murdoch to the position of Editor-in-chief of *The Australian*. In the lead up to the 2007 election, *The Australian* ran articles describing Lindeberg as "obsessive" and being backed by 'extremists, anti-Semites and racists'. In a Statutory Declaration to the Australian Press Council, Lindeberg exposed the falsity of those claims and showed that he was running his own race and had nothing to do with extremists and abhorred anti-Semitism.

In February 2008 the Australian Press Council upheld a complaint by Scott Balson against *The Australian* over claims that he was 'extreme right wing, racist and anti-Semitic'. *The Australian* article was aimed at destroying Lindeberg's reputation by associating him with Balson (the so-called "right wing extremist" messenger).[5]

The timing of the attack was interesting, if not revealing. It was just before the 2007 Federal election at a time *Daily Telegraph* reporter Piers Akerman was exposing Rudd's involvement in the shredding of the Heiner Inquiry documents. If the law had been applied equally years before, Rudd might never have become Prime Minister. The politicised attack on Balson and Lindeberg by *The Australian* is one of the most crystallised and clear cut examples of the real power lurking behind Australian politics.

Kevin Rudd is reported to be the Godfather of Mitchell's and Christine Jackman's baby.[6] You can draw your own conclusions. Others to fall foul of the Heiner Affair are ABC reporter, Andrew Carroll and the University of Queensland's Head of Journalism, Associate Professor Bruce Grundy.

---

[5] http://www.gwb.com.au/gwb/news/goss/response.htm
[6] http://www.gwb.com.au/gwb/news/goss/jackman.htm

This is only a brief synopsis of the Heiner Affair – there have been books, reports, articles, interviews and textbooks written on the subject. For further information as well as the many other sites dedicated to this blight on Australian political history go to <http://www.heineraffair.info/index.html>

The Goss, Rudd 'Comradeship" continues, unapprehended and in Feb 2010 Goss and Rudd met with the three commercial television stations and extended to them A$250 million (was this in Swan's 2009 May budget?). The terms of this very favourable consideration have not been disclosed to the taxpayers (ie secret). What's the deal for Goss? Is he now employed by Federal government? What's expected from these private entities may become obvious in the coming election advertising, perhaps biases towards Labor?

Mr Rudd has deliberately avoided telling the truth, when inconvenient – false claims about the Sunrise Anzac Day ceremony, his meetings with disgraced former WA Premier Brian Burke, his hell bent intention to obtain a temporary seat on the UN Security Council, his A$10 million in donations to corrupt African nations and it becomes crystal clear, **Mr Rudd's credibility seems as shredded as the Heiner documents and as legitimate as a Carbon Credits (ETS cap-and-trade tax) Scheme in being able to change world climate**. If not, why wouldn't the PM call for an independent inquiry into this affair?

From Kevin Rudd's website (at May 2010): *"On 4 December 2006 Mr Rudd was elected as the 19th leader of the Australian Labor Party and over the following twelve months he travelled extensively throughout Australia, campaigning on a policy platform focused on **education reforms, climate change, health care, reforming Australia's Federal system of government** (which appears has already been done without any referendum by the people) **and restoring fairness to Australian industrial relations laws . . . . Mr Rudd has written extensively on Chinese politics, Chinese foreign policy, Australia-Asia relations and globalisation"* (the agenda of the Fabians and their allies).

In the first 2 years in office and in spite of billions of dollars wasted, including A$1 billion on consultants, Rudd achieved no positive policies or reforms as he had promised – nothing to improve education or health. He dismissed the Liberal Governments industrial relations laws, offering worse options eg you can't work less than 3 hrs which puts a lot of part time or under-employed workers (remember many people are no longer employed full time) and their employers in breach of new policies. The hospital systems have gotten worse under the Rudd Labor government and the only **assistance to farmers** has been through Centrelink in helping them **to leave their land**. He adversely changed our boarder protection policies to see more than 150 boats arrive in our waters during his tenure. He showed great resistance and distain in not accepting Mr Abbott's challenge for a debate on the ETS tax, because he knew he would lose with no solid evidence of man-made climate change, but for misrepresentations to achieve a carbon tax that could destroy our entire economy, making for an easy manipulative subservience of all Australians who want, food. Adverse legislation since 1973 has provided him with the liberty to reduce our democracy (etching towards "Communist Chinese Politics?")

A cleaver ploy of government is just to rely on the short term memory of the people, who are caught up in their day to day lives and survival. That is, when government is caught out for incompetence or corrupt acts they divert our attention to other issues. For example; **From the ETS, the roof batts fiasco, bad boarder security policies and rip-off faulty schools projects, our attention is diverted to a proposed new national health system** (another fiasco in the making). Excellent public relations and propaganda to take the heat off in achieving "*long term, slow attrition*" the objective of globalisation, a single world order and for Australians to (unwittingly) become subservient and play ball whether we agree to this, or not.

I believe, in an election year, the Labor government knew they had very few cards to play as their only opportunity to turn public opinion around and take the negative heat off the government, so they: 1. Put the blame on Rudd and this would have rightfully been so if this were a Republic run by a President, but the party and the Opposition allowed Rudd to run an Oligarchy and therefore the Labor party and Opposition are responsible for all of the mismanagement, but to escape this, Labor gave Rudd the boot and 2. Labor installed Julia Gillard as the first female PM in an attempt to turn the public opinion around in what they perceived as a positive move for the "party".

Rudd was not voted in by the people of Australia but only by those in his electorate and he was voted Prime Minister by his party who then ousted him for his and their poor policies and wasteful mismanagement and therefore the entire Labor government from his second in command down bears as much guilt as Rudd. For Rudd to have been elected by the majority of Australians we would be a Republic voting for a President and his party and that we are not, officially that is.

Different Rules for Different Australians

THE MAJORITY OF Australians are witty and clever, expecting nothing less than honesty, common sense, fairness and a no nonsense approach to achieving positive results for ourselves, our families, our communities and our country. We can demand all we like that our politicians be above reproach and corruption but this is not always what we have achieved under our current diluted Democratic system of unaccountable party politics. A Royal Commission must be sought to question why Mr Rudd did not want to ensure Ms Bryce was beyond reproach before she was appointed to the position as Governor-General, what was Rudd & Goss's part in the destruction of documents and the part of Noel Nunan. This is deception, demonstrating the oppression and corruption of democracy by high-handed dictators running an autocratic system of government.

Yet those who might save us face the stigma attached to a "Dobber" – by those with much to hide, in their ill portrayal of a "Whistleblower". But if it were not for these people, whose absolute concern is for the public, those in power would abuse their positions even further and continue unapprehended on a grander scale, greater than we currently know.

Whistleblowers, rather than being frowned upon, ought to be commended and rewarded. The Australian Law Reform Commission inquiry into whether more than 500 secrecy provisions in Federal Law are effective, or if they go too far, see public servants acting nervously to requests for information. They feel they have a conflict of interest because *"we're employees of the government, but we work for the public and there should be a culture of disclosure"* rather than *"if in doubt, over-classify or deny, that's the rule".* The law must be changed to reflect that:

Unless documents are classified as national security issues and protected under the strictest defence requirements, all documents and information should be freely available to any member of the public, without limitation. Government documents withheld from the public clearly demonstrate a government having something to hide and therefore there is something to be answerable for, no secrets!

While all levels of governments have grown disproportionately and into defiant complexities, they remain estranged from each other and from the people. Federal, States and local governments do not co operate or function cohesively and thus the people are no longer able to function effectively or efficiently. We have allowed them to fund issues that ought never make, the list of secondary priorities, let alone outrank major issues. We have afforded ministers and court officers to be above reproach and accountability for lies, deception and adverse dealings, see further the case of John Walsh.

A society can only function when the majority of workers are productive "blue collar" workers. That is, at the end of each day we can all see the result of what has been produced, be it a product or service. But since the advent and development of the industrial revolution we have experienced an exponential growth in administrative "white collar" workers and from this, our society has developed two serious liabilities:

1.   We suffer the encumbrances or having more "white collar workers" in legal, accounting, government and administrative roles **getting paid by the hour irrespective of productivity, versus paid on results.**

The **"blue collar worker"** – the farmer, the builder, the teacher, the plumber, the doctor, the labourer, the mother and so on, all skilled and unskilled labour who actually produce a product, commodity or a service. They are supporting the excessive numbers of "white collar" (particularly government) workers in having to charge inflated prices to meet higher interest and taxes to cover the excessive administrative costs. Our labour costs have had to become inflated to provide our ability to pay for this encumbrance on society and therefore we are not competitive here or on the world market.

When **we have a disproportionate amount of blue collar makers to the national white collar takers**, it is no different to having too many white blood cells in the body resulting in Leukaemia and killing the body. With our "Blue Collar" shortage in sustaining society the only way we can overcome these problems and provide a viable future is to:

a)   Import more blue collar workers and/or

b)   Slug the current blue collar workers with increased interest and more taxes. Strangling him until he falls over and then there is one less blue collar worker who becomes yet another bankrupt statistic with the cause being *"economic conditions"*. Together with his family he becomes dependant on welfare, suffers stress and depression from the lack of work, his inability to feed and house himself and his family and for the loss of his self esteem. This causes friction in the home and again, adds to the 50% divorce rate and proliferates insecure kids and a dysfunctional society, or

c)   The most viable option is to consolidate government to what is really required and then retrain "white collar takers" into "blue collar makers" filling the skills shortages and reducing administrative costs thus reducing taxes etc and this could be done with proficient planning over the next five years.

2. Over burdened with administrative hurdles and demands in doing all business. Culling and streamlining systems unilaterally nationally, will bring about simplicity and savings in all dealings. Equality of bargaining power or a level playing field between large and small business, will bring about less loss, waste and a fair go in expanding opportunities. Taxation reform together with reforming the legal system is what is overdue in bringing about a true balance of fair trading. Consolidation of the cumbersome and costly bureaucracy will remedy many forms of inefficiency and waste and with skilled persons, provide governmental management by objectives as opposed to crisis management and affording long term reduced taxes.

The most prominent example of both of the above liabilities coming from too many white collar workers, in too many levels of government relates to the hospital system. There was a time when the most senior nurses, matrons, had a key responsibility for running and administering hospitals. Not just providing nursing care and training staff and there were very few problems in what were better run hospitals. Since those days, more and more administrative tasks have gone into the hands of "professional administrators" who have limited, if any, knowledge of the hospital system and its specialised requirements. As a result, mishaps have seen courts awarding negligence claims (for what should be against hospital administrators) but this only results in government increasing the number of checks and balances and therefore hiring more administrators, rather than put the dollars on the front line and into the hands of those who are specialist, blue collar workers. More administration results in placing even less emphasis on medical care and more emphasis on avoiding negligence and legal liability. Consequently, staff numbers on the medical side (doctors and nurses) are often run on the cliff edge of critical minimums, with temporary nursing staff taking up the slack and patients having to wait up to eight hours for emergency attention. When this is not enough, staff must work double shifts at double rates creating exactly the sort of risks that may result in litigation and hospital expenditure costs running over projections!

If hospitals were allowed to spend money on their primary resources, their medical staff and equipment, they would provide better care with fewer errors and fewer legal claims, a no brainer! But if you thought hospitals existed to provide quality care, you'd be wrong. Hospitals are bloated bureaucracies tasked by government to minimise embarrassing errors for which Ministers might be held accountable. These are the very Ministers who, of course, would rather fund the current blame-and-butt-cover system rather than adequately fund hospitals. These are the "white collar government ministers" who require "white collar professional administrators" versus skilled hospital administration, to account to them for the validity and efficiency of every white collar barnacle in the hospital rather than providing **the real job** of a streamlined medical care facility.

In every ant colony or bee hive there is a strict delegation of responsibilities and everyone has to produce. A very strict proportion of workers are dedicated to every facet and function of the colony or hives' existence. Every worker is skilled in its specific field and each ant has self imposed responsibilities for its fair share of the work. The ants are totally patriotic and dedicated to the colony and hold no self interests. They do not form self interest parties, but work cohesively. If there are too many of any specific skill eg nurse bees or queen bees, they're killed off so as not to impede or be a liability to the community. Sounds like a good communist agenda but people are above that of ants or bees, yet we have a society overgrown with bureaucratic white collar workers, a situation which has brought us to our knees, while we suffer from the lack of skilled and unskilled blue collar workers. Now we could "kill'em (excess white collar workers) off" or we could retrain them into areas where they would be productive and no longer be a liability to our country. If this remedial action is not taken on expeditiously, we stand to suffer the same demise as the Great Roman Empire.

If we are to learn only one thing from history, it must be from the results of adverse indulgences of governments (and personally) and no matter how strong a society or empire is, it can implode. **The decline of the Great Roman Empire was attributed to several factors: It maintained a massive army (or today a burocracy) and thus the empire was forced to raise taxes frequently causing inflation to skyrocket.** This in turn caused major economic stress, attributing to Rome's decline. Roman historian A.H.M. Jones' says, *"There was a decline in agriculture and land was withdrawn from cultivation* (not dissimilar to restricted farm land-use in meeting the Kyoto Protocol), *in some cases on a very large scale, sometimes as a direct result of barbarian invasions* (or today, international buyouts). *However, the chief cause of the agricultural decline was high taxation* (eg with an Emissions Trading tax to add to the pile of taxes) *on the marginal land, driving it out of cultivation."* According to Rostovtzeff and Mises regarding Rome, *". . . Despite laws passed to prevent migration from the cities to the countryside, urban areas gradually became depopulated and many Roman citizens abandoned their specialized trades in order to practice subsistence agriculture. This, coupled with increasingly oppressive and arbitrary taxation, led to a severe net decrease in trade, technical innovation and the overall wealth of the empire".*

In his book *"The Collapse of Complex Societies"* Joseph Tainter presents the view that for given technological levels, there are implicit complexities in which systems deplete their resource base beyond sustainability. Tainter suggests that, **societies become more complex as they try to solve problems. Social complexity produces analysts who are not involved in primary resource production.** Such complexity requires a substantial "energy" subsidy, meaning extensive resources or other forms of wealth are required to be invested. When a society confronts a "problem," such as a shortage of or difficulty in gaining access to energy, it tends to create new layers of bureaucracy, infrastructure, or social classes to address the challenge. In Tainter's view, while invasions, crop failures, disease or environmental degradation may be the *apparent* causes of societal collapse, the ultimate cause is *"diminishing returns on investments in social complexity"*.

Australia (as America and others) has become just as complex a burocracy as the great empires of by-gone days with our governments supporting philosophies, both to the far left and the far right, but neither of our two major political parties have forged towards a long term balance of equality or focused on the root of successful governance, the basic needs of all citizens. Rather on over indulgences of governments into less appropriate areas, particularly international treaties, and thus there is no transparency. Transparency would reveal not just non productive servants of the people, but destructive. Without immediate redress, the great empire of Australia may find itself in the same scenario as the great Roman Empire, with the takeovers and buyouts by international consortiums, the under development of our primary and secondary resources and the massive taxes to support the massive army of white collar workers.

Over indulgences in bureaucratic numbers is coupled with major disparities in regards to relevant wages and salaries pertinent to job results, not just turning up and being there. You'd be pretty mean if you denied a Prime Minister or any productive Ministers earning anything less than the most senior company executive within reason, anything from $200,000 to $500,000 a year. But in the normal commercial wage scheme and subject to the same tax rulings, the same superannuation benefits and the same pension scheme as all Australians. Repay genuine government business travel and other costs but not allowing politicians to receive a low wage attracting low taxation with massive tax free benefits during and after the cessation of their government employment.

Untaxed benefits which can be read about in many articles, but to demonstrate that this is an issue that has been going on for decades while politicians numbers and costs have grown – Reader's Digest story by Paul Raffaele in August 1999 issue: "Outrageous Perks" – full story on the internet – some pertinent quotes: *". . . with very few checks and balances, our 822 State and Federal parliamentarians have awarded themselves a range of benefits that according to one study, are three times more expensive than those of their counterparts in Britain and New Zealand. The cost to the nation is staggering . . . In Federal parliament alone, the budget to support each of our 224 MPs in the past financial year was over A$1,500,000 – more than a third of a billion dollars in total . . ."* This article is 10 years old and thus proving that things have only gotten worse, never resolved but with the lurks and the perks having only escalated and serves to make the hair of underpaid, over worked blue collar makers, stand on end.

*". . . In two months following his elections loss in 1996, Paul Keating billed the taxpayer close to A$94,000 for perks to aid his transition into private life. According to a government document released under the Freedom of Information Act, in the **68 days** following his election defeat, Keating, a millionaire business consultant, spent A$47,855 on travel alone, for himself, his wife and staff. In his first year out of office, up until July 1997 he billed the taxpayer more than A$620,000. This included $156,602 for chauffeured limousines . . ."* and *". . . The most recent Federal Department of Finance and Administration annual report*

shows that VIP transport for politicians, ex-politicians and High Court judges cost us well over A$14 million in the 1997-98 fiscal year . . . . they use them to go shopping or into town for dinner, keeping drivers waiting about, sometimes for hours", says Mr Black" and "In some States, overseas travel is offered via carefully structured schemes. Victorian MPs can each pay A$20 a year to become a member of the Commonwealth Parliamentary Association. This gives them the opportunity to join one of eight international tours annually, funded by taxpayers . . . . Life time access to limousines and drivers . . . . and the three-yearly "study trips" for Federal members should be scrapped . . ."

How do our MPs acquire such extravagant benefits? Simple, they award it to themselves, just pushed through parliament as part of "unrelated legislation", where they remain well hidden. **If politicians and remuneration tribunals can't or won't bring MPs benefits into line with community standards, only the Australian public can apply the pressure necessary to effect real change. This cannot happen under our current political system.** Allowing politicians to award themselves is no different to giving the key to the chocolate shop to a chocoholic.

With politicians tax free benefits, many ongoing after the job, why wouldn't you want to be a politician and spin every yarn you could to get and then keep the job no matter what you have to say? And why would the government only match us dollar for dollar for our superannuation investment, to be reduced by the people's Labor government, when they wouldn't be satisfied with that. You'll never hear of politicians going on strike for unfair pay or poor conditions, they just unaccountably and without conscience up their own benefits, while pensioners are expected to survive on A$200 odd per week. Pensioners had to fight aggressively for an extra A$33 per week while their elected representatives line their pockets and while many employees agreed to wage reductions and shared work to be able to hold onto their jobs and to ensure others could earn some income. While there was such contention about increases to pensions, in the first quarter of 2009 government awarded its members an extra $90 a week and in Sept 2009 an additional 3%.

New Industry standards of wages and benefits need to be defined across all industries and demographics in line with other industries. They must be implemented and enforced. All benefits to current and future government employees must be capped, which must also apply to publicly owned banks and corporations. The current industry standards have allowed executives to pay themselves ridiculous salary packages which are not subject to any reasonable standard of performance, no different to the aristocratic land owners of colonial days.

National wages and benefits for all industries need to be adjusted and fall in line with proposed amendments in meeting a minimum standard of living. For example, if a $150,000 gross income is acceptable for a proposed Local government Minister or a Federal Minister it would be taxed in accordance with the overall National taxing structure, see section on Taxation Reform, plus reimbursed for out of pocket expenses as demonstrably incurred from performing the job.

No perks to be provided after cessation of the job. Superannuation and pensions to be in line with industry standards not applicable after termination of the job rather at the appropriate age of retirement like every other Australian. Termination of all non conforming pension and benefits plans, to be brought into line with current aged pensions, that is once means tested.

Times are tough and the world remains financially unstable, to say the very least, but Mr. Rudd's found the money for his entourage of 114 people to go to Copenhagen. The carbon footprint for 114 personnel travelling business class to Denmark and back equals 1817 tonnes of emissions, equivalent to the annual output of 2500 people in Malawi – one of the countries at greatest risk from climate change. Rudd sent 114 people for our 22 million people while India with a billion people sent 55. Why? So he could feather his cap on the world stage where he wants to be the lead singer. Spend, spend and spend some more, it's not coming out of his pocket!

Mr Rudd revamped embassies overseas; builds a A\$14 million "War Room" opposite his office in Parliament House to handle daily emergencies (the reactive crisis management ones); **spent A\$600 million to build new ASIO headquarters, and in a paddock 35km from Canberra near Bungendore, builds "Headquarters Joint Operations Command" for A\$300 million (which could have been 1,000 new regional homes and infrastructure). Then he spent more than A\$1 billion to obtain consultants advice and in pursuing Asian Pacific agendas, which are not wanted by those member countries, and then from borrowed money he pledged to donate A\$50 million a year to Afghanistan** (while our charities warehouses are empty), **all to appease one man who for a short period in time held the position as our Prime Minister.** Even if the country were in surplus this wasteful spending still could not be justified, highlighting the lack of economic skills held by Government Ministers, yet very little effective Opposition!

None of the above expenditures were necessary nor should any of it have been given any priority by the Labor "party" with little if any opposition from the Liberal "party", powerless to put a stop to all this reckless spending. This A\$2 billion alone, would have seen pensioner able to achieve a decent standard of living, amongst other vital national needs. This behaviour is both immoral and reflective of an inadequate system of governance.

With the greatest of respect for our many upright exceptions who already know this – politicians and officers of the court are people expected to have impeccable living, business, educational and moral standards. They are expected to be pillars of society, above reproach, above any potential for improper behaviour or accepting any unfair advantage of one person over another or having ulterior motives, agendas or dealings. These standards are not too much to expect from empowered politicians and legal representatives but unfortunately when a system is cumbersome and if a person suffers with an inflated ego or is weak of character, the opportunity to succumb to corruption or his or her ultra ego can be irresistible and very overwhelming.

Corruption can be by participation or merely by looking the other way, thus fostering corruption. It can be by supporting inequality or egocentricity and through omissions, the result, our entire society falls apart and we witness the demise of our society, with chaos as our inheritance.

What politicians do in their personal lives, providing they do not break the law or act immorally should never be reported in the media. Being in positions of power, the consequences of their actions must reflect their position. Well rewarded for a job well done but penalised and dismissed for breaking the law with more severity than the average person. There have been reports of the serious crimes by politicians employed by Canberra including; 36 have been accused of spousal abuse; 7 arrested for fraud; 117 have been directly or indirectly bankrupted, more than once; 71 cannot get a credit card due to bad credit; 14 have been arrested on drug-related charges; 8 arrested for shoplifting and 84 have been arrested for drunk driving in the last few years. These are only the reported matters, rarely bringing the full thrust of the law upon them, with perpetrators certainly not fit to hold the positions of power that they do.

Our leaders and those they employ are entrusted with the greatest responsibilities and they are the examples our kids (need to be able to) aspire to. Respect is earned not bought and kids either respect their parents and authority, or they don't. This is based on what we see, what we hear, how we are treated and what is produced. It is also the reason we are experiencing disrespect and rebellion from the younger generations and why education standards are down. Kids see that it is the tail that is ruling the snake and not the head.

Loopholes, Lies and Abuse of Power

NATIONALLY WE ARE suffering with hindrances to almost every positive aspect and initiative required by a progressive society. Bureaucratic legislative encumbrances are imposed State by State, locality by locality and nationally. We have endured politicians instigating legislations which have effectively transgressed from our constitutional rights, and now we need to readdress for rectification in conforming to the best interests of the people. These amended constitutional changes (without referendum) demonstrate a conflict of interest between government, the courts, corporations and the people, creating disparities in the many State constitutions and every State's judicial constitution and this is inflicted on every Australian individually (flicked off one by one!). On its current course, amendment, without radical change, cannot be achieved. Our Constitution stipulates that only through referendums supported by the majority of the people can changes be made, but according to **Mark Dreyfus QC and Federal Labor Member for Isaacs and Chair of the House of Representatives Standing Committee on Legal and Constitutional Affairs** (Geelong Advertiser 12 Nov 2008): *"Constitutional reform is important in Australia because we believe strongly in the rule of law. The Australian Constitution provides the framework for our political systems; it is the agreed framework within which we develop solutions to common problems, resolve disputes over distribution of resources and settle questions of power and liberty . . ."*

Since Federation, 44 proposals for constitutional amendments have been placed before the Australian people, with only 8 passed (8 since 1901). It is now 31 years since we have amended the Constitution. It is nine years since the republic referendum, 20 years since the referendum prior to that and this seems likely to be the first decade since Federation to have passed without a single referendum being placed before the Australian people.

*Our Constitution remains very much as it was originally drafted. Constitutional reform is a two stage process; first, initiation by the Parliament and then approved or rejected by the people. The 1988 bicentennial referendum proposals concerned what many would view as an expansion of basic rights including fair and democratic parliamentary elections, recognition of local government and an expanded right to trial by jury. **There is a critical lesson to be learned: the process leading up to the referendum was composed solely of politicians, academics, judges and lawyers and what was left out of these processes? The direct involvement of the Australian people! This has been a consistent mistake throughout the history of attempts at constitutional reform."***

One idea to come out of the "2020 Summit" was the re-establishment of a Constitutional commission or convention. I support establishing regularly scheduled Constitutional conventions. I also propose that a permanent Constitutional Review Commission be established, along the lines of the Productivity Commission and the Australian Law Reform Commission. That is, to conduct public consultations along the lines of that conducted in Victoria which led to the Charter of Rights enacted by the Victorian parliament in 2006. This process showed that it is possible to "engage the community on fundamental rights and law reform issues" and "Leadership is about creating an environment in which reform can be countenanced, in which public engagement can occur, in which bipartisanship can lead to improved constitutional arrangements".

And here lies the loophole for the many governments to-date in preventing change, for and by the people but to facilitate greater government powers. That is, there are no *". . . initiations by the Parliament* [of any referendums] *and then approved or rejected by the people"* – little if anything is put to the people in a referendum vote but **Bills are negotiated, then accepted or rejected by politicians within the realm of a hijacked Constitution and pushed through parliament.**

Example: **Without a supportive referendum by Australians, the Australia Acts passed in 1986** severed the constitutional links that still remained between Australia and the United Kingdom. In 1987, as a consequence of the Australia Acts, **the Parliament of NSW amended the NSW Constitution Act of 1902.** The Governor remains the Queen's representative and exercises her powers, but the appointment and dismissal of the Governor is on the advice of the Premier. **All bills passed by the Parliament of NSW become Acts when assented to by the Governor in the name of and on behalf of the Queen.** There is no division of powers when the position of Governor is dependant on the Premier! **In March 2010 Kevin Rudd banned the holding of State Labor government's annual party conferences unless they are approved by the Prime Minister.** There is no division of powers between State and Federal Government when Labor holds government in both realms!

Our only vote is in determining which of the two parties is to enjoy the perks while having the ability to change the powers of government without the consultation of the people.

The Federal Liberal Opposition Leader, Tony Abbott in his book *"Battlelines"* advocates for a change to the Federal Constitution:

Section 51A *"The Parliament shall, subject to this Constitution, have power to make laws for the peace, order and good government of the Commonwealth with respect to any other matters . . . ."* and:

Section 111A *"The Parliament of a State may also surrender any power of the State to the Commonwealth . . ."* and Mr Abbott says, *"Australia in the twenty-first century is handicapped by nineteenth century judgments regarding which matters could be dealt with at a State level. The inter-colonial tensions of the 1890s are no longer a relevant rationale*

*for those safeguards built into the Constitution to protect the autonomy of the States . . . .
the Commonwealth parliament needs to be able to legislate more efficiently to ensure that
Australia is competitive in a global economy".*

**Broadening the powers to maximise the potential of every relevant
portfolio pertaining to our country to Federal government is a sensible
move, but NOT without changing the structure of the current political
system of government, as it will serve and further facilitate the Rudd style
of government and every successors on both sides.**

In seeking to broaden executive powers Mr Abbott has failed to acknowledge
how easily these powers can and have been abused by both sides of this, (no longer
preferred) two party system. Rather I would have thought that he would seek greater
safeguards to carry out the will of the people and in protecting them, by installing
and maintaining a Charter of Rights. Also, for overturning treaties and adverse
legislations imposed on agricultural and other industries. Currently as government
powers grow, the democratic rights of the people are increasingly in jeopardy and
are diminishing further. These two parties are so closely aligned that Mr Abbott's
amendments to the constitution would be a very appetising meal and serve both
sides in this two party system, very well.

Mr Abbott in his book shows an unshakable level of loyalty to the Liberal party
and in November 2009 he clearly demonstrated this allegiance to his party. He
initially showed no hesitation in supporting Malcolm Turnbull's adamant stance on
supporting an amended ETS even though personally Mr Abbott shared the concerns
of the majority of Australians for the Emissions Trading Scam and then he does
an about-face in opposing the ETS. Was this a ploy, an opportunity to gain the
leadership and a strong hold for Liberal who recognised that Labor were losing
ground as the number of people opposing the ETS were increasing? On 1 December
Mr Abbott succumbed to the will of the people in opposing Mr Turnbull and took
the leadership of the Liberal Party by one vote (42 to 41). As he moves forward
Liberal's popularity may increase but we will see where his true allegiances lie – with
the party or the people!

In addition to the Federal issues of incompetent bureaucracy – we have a
second level of government to contend with in the States bureaucracy. With 33%
of all Australians living in NSW we are suffering from the demise of all essential
infrastructures due to the lack of investment in maintenance and improvements. This
is demonstrated in commuters riding on trains more than 40 years old which break
down constantly on poorly maintained rail track systems. Hospital beds are closing
down while the demand for elective surgery has not slackened. Overall demands are
growing, from amongst other causes, the increased need created by drug and alcohol
related illness and poor food standards. No solid solutions are offered by the NSW
or Federal government.

Maintenance funding which the NSW State government has failed to accurately
administer, are funds that have been negligently allocated, commonly referred to

as misappropriation of (government) money. Funds that with due diligence would have provided efficient systems and administration. If rail systems would have been a priority over the past 12 years, commuters could have been enticed into relying on the public system and spending less on owning or running fossil fuelled transport. Defective planning has seen new residential areas opening while no decent road or rails systems have been included in the planning process. Spending a minimal on maintenance and failing to upgrade infrastructure, assumed by the NSW government wouldn't be noticed by the taxpayer if diverted to areas on the agenda of the State government and not to where we want it vested. But poor spending on transport systems have been more than noticed and promises from one Premier to the next have resulted in the latest promises of Ms Keneally but most not to come to fruition until 2017 while over A$500 million (the cost of 2,000 new semi-rural homes with repayable mortgages from newly created jobs) will have been added to the State's losses due to the now terminated CBD Metro plans of previous, obstinate Premiers. But wait, it will cost an extra A$30pa on NSW car registrations to pay for a rail system that will not be to the benefit of anyone living outside of Sydney or those who use private transport, fair? Good government?

There are so many instances of misleading and deceptive representations and just plain mismanagement from ministers with a lack of fiscal and management skills. Let's start with one very small example: When NSW held the "International Youth Day" which was a great public relations success, but it cost the taxpayers six times more than the State government projected it would cost. Was this poor accounting skills or the inability to manage the project, or both? Yet no one accepts responsibility, not the then Premier or any Minister, particularly the Treasurer of the day. Irresponsible spending and blowing out budgets by government demonstrates incompetence and that our money is in the wrong hands. There are few New South Welshmen calling for accountability because there is no effective means for any individual to challenge the government, certainly little from the opposition; no constitutional mechanism to dismiss an incompetent government and the cost would be insurmountable for any average person, so government gets away with concealment under "Commercially Sensitive Information" eg colluding with the Federal government to rip off land owners with new vegetation laws.

The NSW State Labor government installed the *Fines Act of 1996* where the people of NSW must now pay whatever the government deems in their "dash for cash". Constitutionally I believe a class action by those in NSW who have had harsh fines imposed on them, would provide a victory and overturning this corrupt legislation.

If you were to pursue government information under the Freedom of Information Act you would be denied access to sensitive information cloaked under this *"Commercially Sensitive Information that could prejudice business"* or under *"Cabinet deliberation"* which are the two areas Nathan Rees sought to retain as confidential and restricted from any amendments to the Freedom of Information Act. That should just about cover any minister from true transparency or public access to information as to where funds are truly being spent and adverse dealings with other governments or corporations or that funds designated to one project or function are diverted to "other costs".

Was the matter of the Ryde to Chatswood rail line just another case of poor or faulty projections or just more mismanagement? How is it possible that a rail line of just 12 lousy kilometres is three years late and one billion dollars above the projected cost? Is someone looking into every invoice and who got what payments, or are we "sheep" just accepting this as our new acceptable standard? Is this any different to the excessive rail maintenance contracts given out at inflated rates to mates? This fraud was uncovered, but we haven't heard the outcome as to any prosecution of those who participated, particularly any accountability for the Ministers who approved of those contracts and payments.

After 10 years of what has been considered to be national economic boom times, from digging up the earth, the NSW government has produced a State in near bankruptcy, yet government ministers fight and conspire for the "leadership". **If the NSW government were a company the directors (Ministers) would be charged with trading while insolvent.** So what chance has NSW got with unemployment growing higher than in any other State? Running hospitals without paying doctors, staff and creditor suppliers and flogging off our assets to meet the cost of their mismanagement. Currently we are only assuming the sales prices of our assets sold by government, are sold at true market values and not to mates at mate's rates and deals and it's highly unlikely that ICAC or ACCC, under their current mandate, would investigate.

It's only at election time do we get promises of improvements from those with much to lose in their comfy jobs. Reader's Digest *"Australia's Outrageous Parliamentary Pensions"* article by Paul Raffaele, he states, *"The NSW Legislative Assembly Members' Handbook, the 60-page manual that lists members' entitlements . . ."* Promises by politicians we know will be broken or at best we may get some sort of very expensive band aid remedy. There is no real foresight or solid planning from either side of the (arguably) two party system and the choices of governments in NSW are almost nil. Barry O'Farrell, the current NSW Opposition Leader states that he seeks to amend the Constitution to dismiss a non performing government or a government who mismanages the affairs of the State. However could or would his government be any better or is he just being the aggressive opponent in seeking to achieve his and his party's agenda? You be the judge!

It's a toss up between the State Labor government in Queensland and that in NSW, as to which one wins the award for providing the greatest mismanagement and corruption a State has ever had to endure. The Heiner Affair, Native Vegetation Laws amongst other adverse matters versus just about every NSW minister running his or her ministry by crisis management, rather than by objectives – reactive versus proactive. Once again, it is over governance, mismanagement and overstepping legal and moral boundaries, by those ill equipped to hold specialised positions which has resulted in the financial drain on the State and National resources and that which had led to the demise in the standards of infrastructure and assets. The myriad of Federal and State's hefty taxes including but certainly not limited to; income tax, GST, land tax, stamp duties on every conceivable transaction but this did not alleviate the more than A$140 million owed to hospital suppliers, while nurses have been privately paying for provisions for their patients. Now, there a new tax, a "*Congestion Tax*" which, by rights, should be imposed on State Ministers for their failure to ensure adequate planning and thus preventing the congestion created by their very own incompetence over the past 12 years.

The NSW State government cannot make ends meet nor can it move forward – it's a very troubled and confused head on a very sick and failing body. There can be no denial that Ministers and their employees are in crisis with an urgent need to defend and protect their positions and create an illusion of progress for the voting public of NSW for the 2011 election. Unfortunately the opposition are no better, offering little if anything different. With this track record would you invest in NSW Government bonds, as suggested by Mr Rees when he was Premier of NSW?

With some legitimate advertising costs A$100 million was spent on advertising by government leading up to the last NSW State election. Much of it promoted the "great initiatives" of the NSW Labor party while men like Carl Scully are sacked and Milton Orkopoulos, Minister of Aboriginal Affairs was sentenced for child sexual assault and drug charges and John Della Bosca left the NSW Health Ministry for his inability to remain faithful (or fix the ailing heath system), David Campbell for living a lie and Ian McDonald for his fingers in the till (same and the British MPs) Penrith's Labor member, Paul McLeay for watching porn and gambling on the job etc. etc. and these are only the ones which come to light. Over 200 changes of Labor State Ministers in 5 years at insurmountable loses to the taxpayer that cannot be calculated in lost money and lost opportunities. Concerns continue for ill equipped Ministers commissioning more consultants for more research, more inquiries, attend more meetings and international seminars yet achieving nothing constructive – rather, destructive. Our politicians are in denial as to their failings and the people of NSW continue to struggle with the frustration and losses, while Liberal appears to offer nothing better.

Ministers are not selected based on their experience or extensive skills in a specifically required area, they are chosen by their Premier and often they hold down several portfolios which they have little if any background in. For example and only to demonstrate an inept system relevant to all levels of government; The Hon Frank Sartor was the Minister for Planning; Minister for Redfern; Minister for Waterloo; Minister for Science & Medical Research and Minister assisting the Minister for Health (Cancer). We have been complacent in not asking him, what qualifications does he profess to have to hold down any, let alone all of these portfolios? And how can anyone with more than one portfolio give proper attention to it, let-alone to so many diverse portfolios. Therefore and based on what skills is Mr Sartor able to go about amending planning legislation, in accommodating his decisions? Unskilled decisions which will greatly impact on our future when he is long gone from his relatively short tenure. Our system of government allows for a Minister to be appointed to say, transport on one day and then be reassigned to be the Treasurer the next, yet have no experience in either portfolio.

In spending A$100 million to assist with campaigning for the State election it gave the Labor party greater exposure and a greater unfair advantage over any other political contenders, irrespective of the worthiness of other contenders. Money spent to provide the government of the day with an inequality of exposure, as against all odds and irrespective of a horrendous track record, a Labor victory!

If State government ministers did their jobs properly we would all see positive and constructive results in all portfolios and there would be no need to waste our money on their own public 'back patting exercises' or in providing us with pacifiers of more promises to forget the past. We would be satisfied with the results. Former premier Bob Carr was named the most disliked Premier ever with a 29% support rating. He was the lowest achiever we have ever known in NSW yet Bob won the last NSW State election as he appeared to be the best of a bad lot! It's a poor excuse for voting for him but there didn't seem to be a better alternative "party!" Jeff Kennett turned Victoria from a State almost bankrupt to achieving an AAA rating in six years. So why didn't the NSW Labor party enrol Bob Carr, Morris Iemma, Nathan Rees and now Kristina Keneally (4 Premiers in 4 years) into "Jeff's College for good Premiers". This is no mystery, it is sheer arrogance. That is, why didn't the NSW government ask Mr Kennett to consult to them, if they really wanted to do their jobs well, but we must first consider what are the real personal and party objectives.

"On Sale Cheap" – Aussie Assets

MR CARR AND Mr Egan left a hell of a legacy for NSW – a State in financial and infrastructure dilemma but for the sale of the remaining public assets – police stations, public schools, roads, water, power, jails, with plans to sell anything else they can get their hands on including one of our best money spinners the NSW State Lotteries Office. Every Premier and his government to succeed Carr including Morris Iemma, Nathan Rees and now Kristina Keneally, three premiers in 4 years are left to go down the same track. This over encumbered system of government is not doomed to failure, it has failed and so will every successive NSW State government irrespective of it being Liberal or Labor. The system overall and in each individual State does not work. The cost of mismanagement is being paid for dearly by every single one of us, financially and with disdain, negativity and the lack of respect to those who also suffer as a direct result of poor government. The police force who every day have to contend with their inability to carry out their jobs effectively and thus have no real happiness or job satisfaction. They suffer with depleted moral and so resignations from the police force continue to increase while crime flourishes.

Alan Jones (top rating talkback host, 2GB Sydney) held a phone poll one morning which produced 29,000 callers in favour of the people of NSW keeping our Snowy River Hydro Scheme. The Premier, Morris Iemma at 7.20am on Fri 2 June 2006 remained adamant that he would sell "The Snowy River Hydro Scheme". Prime Minister John Howard called 2GB advising that the Federal government would not sell its (our) shares in the scheme – resulting in Iemma having no choice but to back down on that same day. What a victory for "people power" against our government which unfortunately is what it took. It was a very loud, vigilantly proactive demonstration of solidarity by the people in protesting against the sale of a key asset, not just an asset but a major power infrastructure which generations previous and future are dependant. But this does not stop the sale of the electricity grids, merely deferred until after the election and State government proceeded to sell off our most valuable and most dependant infrastructures, although poorly maintained.

Then – after two major blackouts in Sydney in less than a week and a third shortly after the State government expressed *"dissatisfaction"* – the standard ministerial comment *"this is just not acceptable"* but not directed at their very own failure to maintain and upgrade the system – hypocrisy.

The initial reaction and support of the 29,000 people to the 2GB phone poll was outstanding, with a halt to this massive and destructive blunder. But how is it that we have to or we need to have a voice "against our government" and a need to demonstrate our strong determination to hold onto our assets? These assets were built, developed and fought for by our forebears for our common wealth today. These assets deemed by government to be free for ministers to deal with, contrary to the will of the majority of people!

How is it possible that we can allow any one government party for their relatively very short term of office, in the scheme of things, to have the ability to make decisions that can provide catastrophic consequences for every generation to follow? Selling off our assets; our institutions, our police stations, our schools, our roads, our most vital utilities and facilities to fill the financial deficit created by mismanagement. What will we do when we have to service further massive deficits but have no assets left to rely on and then have to contend with unregulated power providers, ripping us off? Electricity prices are now set to spiral with suppliers posting very healthy projected profits, thanks to inept State governments – but no ACCC to stop the exploitation of Australians with fixed maximum margins in determining fair market prices for use.

This people power victory was short lived with the re-election of Labor to the NSW State Government. Bob just paved the way for Morris who then paved the way for Nathan Rees to hive off our electrical facilities. Nathan Reese assigned Joe Tripodi in 2008 to the position of Minister for Finance, Infrastructure, Regulatory Reform, Ports and Waterways. Joe must have had a wow of a time spending A$290,000 on walkabout overseas in his attempts of achieving the adverse goal of getting rid of our vital public utility. No doubt Mr Rees was satisfied that Joe Tripodi was fit and proper to flog off our assets, but this extravagant waste for the adverse objective of flogging off, rather than retain for posterity is the best expertise the NSW government extends! Then after this investment Mr Rees in November 2009 dumps Mr Tripodi for another short term minister. In December the infighting for Rees' leadership, a great joke, resulted in Mr Rees being himself dumped, replaced by Kristina Keneally, who takes yet another short term direction and once again, she changes ministers and policies before it all happens again after the next election, if Liberal were to win. **Rather than resign for their inability to administer this key utility, the inept decision of the NSW Labor government in the privatisation of electrical supplies, may now see Australians vulnerable to sufferance with increases of more than 60% in electricity accounts, yet the ACCC does not step in and set maximum mark-up margins to protect consumers of this vital community utility.** This will cause thousands of people to go without either food or power. Ms Keneally stated *"there is no need for people to freeze to death in winter or die of heat stroke in summer because of 60% electricity price hikes"* as she will extend subsidies to those in need. But who will be providing these subsidies, certainly not the financially strapped NSW government! It will be the NSW taxpayer, again. In effect, those who will be paying an extra 60% on their own accounts, will also be paying to help subsidise those in need. While the warehouses of welfare agencies are struggling to meet community needs in an alarming increased demand for help, the worst is yet to come. Millions of people are struggling to pay their mortgages and put food on their tables, yet billions of tax dollars, which ought to have paid for the maintenance and improvement to power stations over the years, has been just wasted and Ms Keneally does not seek to justify why her government would spend A$20 million to improve the Sydney Fish Markets and other such activities that most people in NSW will not benefit from.

Selling off public assets and privatising utilities and government functions are a clear admission of government's inability to govern or administer. Government deregulating and privatising its obligation to administer public resources is no different to corporations out-sourcing productivity, the difference being one is a profit generator (a corporation) and one is a servant of the people (to meet community needs) – that is, neither are producing anything tangible. Anna Bligh the Premier of Queensland now seeks to sell off the assets of that State, and as in all States, without a referendum to the people.

At all levels of government, the "*adversarial party system*" primarily facilitates irrational emotive decision making, particularly regarding our assets. Without community consultation or a referendum for determination, the Howard Liberal government sold off Telstra. A major utility heavily reliant on and profitable to the country, as the communications industry continues to grow and provide a profit to its shareholders, but it was claimed by the Liberals, to be **too risky an asset to have taxpayer's money invested in.** After this event the Rudd Government would commit a huge investment of public funds back into establishing a new competitor to the telecommunications industry in a National Broadband Network. Telstra holds a major portion of our limited (compared to other countries) market in its very well established infrastructure**, yet the Labor government does feel that an investment of more than A$42 billion is risky for taxpayer**.

It is this very inconsistency between governments and within a relatively short period of time that is preventing the advancement of Australia, but with Telstra and a proposed new government competitor **there will now be a risk to both Telstra shareholders and particularly, the new taxpayer network, if this proceeds.** Whether the new entity can provide sufficient patronage to allow the capital cost to be repaid let alone make a profit, is a risk that never ought to have been conceived particularly in view of the Australian shareholders of Telstra, most having invested their hard earned income.

There will be hundreds of millions of dollars spent on reports as to whether cable to every home is necessary and if there is a need for government investment and if the borrowed cost of this new enterprise can be justified. It is certainly a firm response to the monopoly held by Telstra which also stands to face tougher regulation if the Government can achieve its ambitious plans for Australia's broadband. The proposal maybe absolutely brilliant but then we will witness competition able to destroy one communications provider, or the other. Rather than confront this: The Federal Government should give Telstra shareholders the opportunity to sell-back to the Federal Government (that is, the taxpayers) this well established infrastructure and invest into the improvements rather than invest excessive amounts into reinventing this business.

No private enterprise with a duty of care and an obligation to provide profits to its shareholders would buy our assets, if they were not profitable or had solid potential. Similarly, why would we sell viable assets particularly those we are so dependent on? Surely skilled long term Ministers can maintain a viable utility! Note the operative words here are *"skilled"* and *"long term"*.

It has been an age-old argument that private enterprise is more productive and efficient than government run facilities but this is not true. Private enterprise must produce a profit to its shareholders but government is supposed to provide services for the public (that is what we pay them to do) not seek a profit and so there is an absolute conflict of interest in relation to the best interests of the public. If private enterprise can make a profit and produce an efficient, say, road or rail system or provide water and power or a telecommunication service why can't government provide the same for a lesser cost to the user.

If the structure of the business or government function is solid and operated by qualified persons to run that specific business or infrastructure for the government, or even have the management outsourced, there is no reason why any function cannot be maximised at minimum operational costs.

Common wealth assets and utilities when managed efficiently should not make a loss, yet as community assets they do not need to make a profit in providing affordable services. Public utilities are for the use and benefit of the public taxpayer firstly, that is, before profits. This is why we pay taxes and each user pays for their utilities in accordance with their usage. If State governments had it their way, every facet of government would be farmed out and if all utilities, institutions and agencies operated by government were to be privatised, there would be no job left for any government ministers, other than to collect the revenue – sounds like a government agenda and sounds like they have past their use by date. State governments have sold off vital water and power knowing that increased costs will be a burden on society and there is an opportunity to provide power with a minimal cost to the consumer and the environment but for the losses to the faceless, financial backers of party governments.

Among the very bad decisions to sell off our assets, I would dare say the deals done by the NSW State Labor Party, regarding the Sydney Cross City Tunnel would have to be the one of the highlight of an unconstitutional "conflict of interest". Where government negates its responsibility to the people and their property to the benefit of private enterprise and who imposes excessive tolls to their benefit. Profits derived from what ought to have been a community infrastructure now go into a private business entity whose mandate is without any doubt, to gain assets and to make a profit. Government's only interest is supposed to be to provide sustainable systems and improve all forms of infrastructure for the benefit of the public in a caretaking capacity, not as a liquidator to cash in the assets. These private road entities enjoy the benefit of the Fines Act of 1996 imposed by the State government, a conflict of interest?

Had there been community consultation or a vote from interested persons held, I believe there would never have been any joint venture entertained by the State government. Maybe we seriously need a buy back proposal to return ownership of all infrastructures to the rightful owners, us! Hopefully without very expensive litigation which at the end of the day would produce nothing more than legal and court costs, making it even more expensive than having initially built it by taxpayers. This tunnel, as any others, would be self funding by us over the years and could have been supported by the State Lotteries profit – Oh, we sold that too in the short term "dash for cash".

The Labor government, in their absolute contempt, locked the Liberal Party out of State Parliament, to defeat Liberals objections to the sale of the State's Lottery Office clearly demonstrating this government's contempt for any opposition to their "own" agenda. Liberal succumbed to the sale of that asset too, for what is sought by one is on the same agenda as the other, or used as a trade-off by the other.

The State government then worked in collusion with the (private entity) Cross City Tunnel operator in changing traffic directions giving a further advantage to the private entity over the interests and consideration of the people of NSW. This is not just a conflict of interest but with the imposition of harsh and unconscionable conditions enforced under the Fines Act of 1996 and other legislation, ought to be charged with unconscionable conduct and abuse of power. If these are not conflicts of interest, then what is and yet we continue to reward those responsible with lurks, perks and payments? If State government were a company, ASIC could (not necessarily would) take action for just about every breach of corporation's laws by those running the biggest business in this State.

The people of NSW, as in all States, expect to pay fair and competitive prices for the benefits of improved roads, schools, hospitals and community assets. Irrespective of cost, all roads and other infrastructures would continue to be paid for without dispute over the many decades to come by Australians, as Australians have always done and providing the price for usage is reasonably based on the cost, planned maintenance and further improvements.

There was a time when your annual car registration paid for the costs of new roads and the maintenance and this included the ability to park on our roads. With many decades passing since then and ten times more cars, hence ten times more annual registrations which have increased regularly, but car registrations no longer includes the ability to park cars on our roads, with the advent of the new windfall parking meters and the great revenue from these and the hefty fines.

During the 2006 election campaign, the then NSW Opposition Leader Peter Debnam is quoted as saying of the State Labor government, that it is *"rotten to the core"* this was recently reiterated by Barry O'Farrell. Who would know better, but when it comes to opposing changes which will benefit politicians, or issues adverse to the people of NSW, there is little if any opposition from the "opposition". Why? Because the two "parties" Liberal and Labor, State and Federal are so closely aligned that their objectives do not differentiate. Democrats MLC Arthur Chesterfield-Evans released figures that show the Opposition only voted against the Government three times in the upper house in the last State parliamentary session at that time. It was stated, *"The Coalition supported the Government with 91% of the votes on bills from May 2006 and at May 2009 Mr Debnam has failed to throw in one question over 900 days"* at this deadhead government, why not? What's the point!

If we want real progress or change, the only current option is to look towards alternative minor parties or fragmented independents to break the mould. Minor parties will never be able to gain government, nor will they ever under this unconstitutional duopoly. Then there are community concerns in taking a risk on change to an unknown minor party or person; will they be worse, will they be better, will they too aspire to self and party glory in pursing their own wants over our need. Some did get momentum – the Nationals, but they got sucked up by Liberal and the Greens appear to be no more than a subsidiary of the Labor government and probably with financially backed by the same sources. Yet one thing is for sure, most minor parties have a snow flakes hope in hell of succeeding due to political donations and the duopolies media propaganda machines.

Political donations or contributions from unions and many levels of business not only influences decisions in favour of the best interests of political party's allies, but can adversely destroy the best interests of the people. People are hammered with advertising to win their vote, paid for by political donations. These short term political advantages for short term *governments are regardless of the long term ramifications to the country.* **Discontinuing political contributions or donations will eliminate many of our problems. Eliminating the requirement for political funding will eliminate governments directing taxpayer funds into their political campaigns (misappropriation is theft, but who will be investigating?). Spending funds for electioneering is misleading and damaging conduct (a corporate crime), yet governments get away with it. Money given as donations can be construed as bribes, as political parties are not charities.**

If you have ever had the need to call on your Local, State or Federal Member for assistance with an issue of grave concern to you and or others, you would have been added to the 160,000 annual complaints against the Health system or the 40,000 annual complaints made to the Australian Securities and Investment Commission and countless other complaints to other government ministries. It is estimated that there are about one million complaints a year or that 5% of the population complain – to local, States and Federal government's ministers on both sides of parliament and to the various government appointed agencies.

These are complaints which most will not see the light of day or have any resolve to our individual and probably collective issues. At best if you write to your local member, he or she will perhaps write to the respective minister say, Police Minister and then the Police Minister will write back to your Minister and your local Minister's office will write back to you with the Police Ministers response. This can go back and forth for a very long time, never once does anyone appreciate the urgency of your matter nor do they have the practical facility to help or utility for accountability.

In this vein, Ministers, particularly Opposition ministers, have generally become glorified postmen. "White collar takers" who are unable to bargain with their opposition and are legless when it comes to helping the majority of their constituents. A non productive liability in a no-results-required job, with little accountability for the many lurks and perks of a job too good to toss in. In this current system very few individuals can achieve duly deserved attention from any government or their "at arm's length" government agency. If a constituent's Minister chooses not to react or cannot assist with a complaint, there is almost nothing that can be done and nowhere else to turn. A paper trail is created by office staff for their Minister which purports to demonstrate some sort of attempt at performance. But there is no accountability when Ministers are operating in such a structure.

The third bureaucratic tier or level of government – the Local government, has always been considered the weak servant of State governments. In *"Beyond Symbolism; Finding a Place for Local Government in Australia's Constitution"*, Dr Oliver Hartwich of the Centre for Independent Studies says, *"Local government is not clearly defined in any constitutional change. It has no guarantee of autonomy or having any tasks to warrant sufficient sources of revenue. Local government has always been unpopular with an image of being responsible for rates, roads, rubbish and being very protective in retaining authority for planning decisions (with many Councils providing undue delays in approvals) and enforcing excessive costs and procedural encumbrances in the approval process. Many Local governments are involved in cases of corruption".*

Efforts by State governments continue try to take away planning powers from Local government, for their lucrative financial rewards. Dr Harwich says: *"The constitution does not spell out the functions and fiscal structure nor does it allocate any specific function to local government, all left to specific acts of parliament, which can be repealed . . . Symbolic recognition of local government to the Australian constitution would be meaningless and the balance of power would not change, local governments would remain in the hands of their respective State governments. The only direct consequence of such recognition, would be that it becomes easier for the Commonwealth to deal with a single or a group of local government authorities which would make intergovernmental relations more complicated and the greatest danger could be that recognising Local government in the constitution, would eventually become a vehicle for central intervention"* and under the current political system, subordinate to the Federal government and its agencies.

Local government aggressively raises revenue along the same lines as State government, with every opportunity to collect money from inflated rates, services, fees and fines. Federal Stimulus, another opportunity for local government: A resident of Bondi Junction wrote in the local paper, *"Waverley Council likes to pride itself on being "green". However, a recent application for solar panels cost me a A$400 development application fee and then A$609 for a construction certificate. Of the A$609 there was a A$175 inspection fee. The inspector came, stayed five minutes and did not even see the solar power system. The Federal government gave me an A$8,000 subsidy to help out while the Council charges me more than A$1,000 . . . the sooner planning powers are removed from Waverley, the better. Letters to them are ignored".*

There are thousands of stories of corruption and incompetence in Councils approving substandard developments, including the Auburn Central development which exceeded the stipulated height restrictions and is a fire hazard to the 1,200 occupants but this project was provided with an Occupancy Certification by the local Council, regardless of the poor standards of construction. Why? Maybe it was the A$120,000 donation by the developer to the Labor government which helped facilitate the approval? Then there was the Wollongong sex for favours scandal – in spite of purported transparencies and over regulation.

We have corruption at every level of government, leaving us with one hand tied behind our back while the other hand tries to deal the cards. It is a long pig trough from which so many are feeding and the temptation is for honest men to do likewise.

Over the past few years, millions upon millions of rate payer dollars have been lost by Councils investing their rate payers money into sub-prime lending, a clear demonstration of overcharging rates. There is no reason Councils need to charge exorbitant rates that are then required to be invested (and lost). Fraud is a crime but unfortunately mismanagement isn't.

Local Councils must be restricted in what they can do and what they charge in our rates. That is, to cover the cost of the local administration, garbage collections and projected costs for improvements to local infrastructure.

If there is too much money in the council coffers, rates need to be reduced down and only by majority local vote can rates be increased to meet the majority of local constituent-approved improvements.

Overstepping Democratic Boundaries

EVERYTHING MOVES IN cycles, from the rise and fall of Communist "party" governments in Russia, China and many Eastern European block countries to Capitalism and God forbid, maybe back to Communism. In Russia, resentments built up ever so slowly from within the ranks of the despondent, deprived workers over the years against the Tsar and his greedy government. Socialism by definition is government ownership and government control over everything, including you. All controls are "people" controls. If the government controls everything it is exactly as Marx set out to do – destroy the right to private property, eliminate the family and wipe out religion (evidence today is obvious). It was the union of workers which lead to civil war and the overthrowing of the Russian aristocratic regime in 1917 with the Russian Revolution, the insurgence of the "have nots" (food) against those who "had" (wealth).

At its formation, Communism saw the majority of people patriotic to the motherland and to their comrades, proud of achieving equality, but slowly over the proceeding decades people became weary of never having any opportunity to improve their position, never having the freedom of any religious belief. Massive propaganda signs and billboards were placed around communist countries to reinforce patriotism and support for the communist regime. With no faith or ability to seek a higher level, together with living in fear of the KGB's tyrannous oppressive authority (responsible for the murder of millions of Russians particularly under the tyrant leader Stalin), there was just no purpose to life.

By the 1950s everyone lived in fear – always looking over their shoulder to make sure no-one was watching them. That and looking over the shoulder of others to make sure no other Russian had anything more than they had. Communism in Russia led to its own eventual demise for the division, resentment and unhappiness Communism had achieved. What was missing from what was initially conceived as a wonderful concept of equality, was the lack of a credible and compassionate authority in providing any programme to nurture the growth and development of individuals. Rather, Communism transformed from its founding philosophies of equality for all, into a regime that dealt in brute force by dictators who ruled with ruthless oppression and suppressing their people to reliance on basic survival, rather than towards higher aspirations. It is the suppression by communist rulers in China that sees only a few greatly benefit (financially), while the majority of its people work for scraps. China will have to raise the cost of its exports or it will only a matter of time before the Chinese people rise up for change, as has been the case in Russia and other eastern bloc countries.

World history is dominated not just by religious and national wars but with civil wars and uprisings based on philosophical "party politics" from Fascism, Nazism (NAZI is short for National Sozialistische Deutsche Arbeiter Partei – National Socialist Germany Workers Party) , Socialism, Communism, to Capitalism etc., all purporting to be working in the best interests of the people. All "party members" strongly holding and supporting philosophies based on (academic) theories and all eventually digressing to ulterior repressive motifs, generally by a dictator taking control. There have been too few government leaders who have been able to stay focused on the best equal interest of all of the people, all of the time. Unfortunately **the only thing we have truly learned from history, is that we have learned nothing from history!** Mankind makes and continues to make the same mistakes, generation after generation. As The Great Roman Empire imploded, so did most of the "great" empires and "parties" from high taxes, greed, corruption, mismanagements, inequality and the inability to nurture its citizens.

Conservative Liberal "party" policies were deemed to create an arena of tolerance and open minded reform, but in the long term it produced something else. It produced over bearing consideration towards big business, which fosters a greedy form of Capitalism, while Communist principals were the result of resentment which built up (to reiterate) *slowly from within the ranks of the despondent, deprived workers over the years,* creating division between people and between our national best interest and priorities. This can lead to penalising those who have worked and achieved, for those who may not have and in creating class differentiations, and conflict.

History has demonstrated some very fierce dictators and oppressive dictatorial governments, those who impose the worst atrocities against their own people, with many still continuing today. From Stalin, to Idi Amin's tyrannical ruling of Uganda to the recent situation in Sri Lanka, Sudan and many other countries to where the US invaded Iraq and we saw the demise of Saddam Hussein.

No doubt Iraqis want to appease the USA but Iraqis may not want to accommodate the establishment of the US desire for the creation of a democracy or, at worst, they may not want to maintain it after the cost and effort to implement it and after the US forces leave Iraq. Iraqis still prefer a "strong leader" rather than a democracy, in part because Iraqis don't like argumentative politics and would rather have a benign dictator that their neighbours feared. This fits with their patriarchal society. Democracy may not be the desire of the populace and it may not suit the mindset of the Afghani or Iraqi people and thus may be beyond their needs, or culture to retain a democracy. Thus the allied forces stay on as police officers and a substitute army against corruption and division between their own citizens versus their role of training those would-be government defence forces.

Saddam Hassain was certainly a tyrant but weapons of mass destruction have never been found, so what inspired an invasion by the US? Was it George W Bush seeing seventy eight billion barrels of oil as an incentive for his company "Arbusto" (Spanish for Bush) in bombing the hell out of Iraq and its people? While his Vice President Dick Cheney (previously CEO of Halliburton for 5 years at US$8.8 million pa) saw that Halliburton and others got the contract to rebuild Iraq costing billions of dollars to US citizens, why would Halliburton and other US government contractors want to leave in a hurry? Mysteriously thousands of Iraqi children have been born with major defects since Iraq was bombed, with what? One child was born with 3 heads, while 2 to 3 new cases of deformity are discovered each day and it maybe that US taxpayers will be paying for this war forever.

Neighbouring Iran has had three consecutive tyrants ruling it with the current leader posing the greatest threat, not just to its own people but to the world at large, as it comes closer to nuclear power. It's interesting to note that there has never been a tyrant woman ruler of any nation throughout the history of the world. Is this a male's predominant need to conquer and control versus the female's inherent ability to nurture and seek peace? Is this distain for women by some cultures, the acknowledgement by their men as to the peaceful power of a woman and thus their overindulgent need for suppressing and controlling women? Women who could destabilise an aggressive perverted agenda for the subservient domination of all mankind for political or fanatic philosophies? Iran is now a country the west is most fearful of, but gutless to do anything about.

For the above reasons "Globalisation" or a "Single World Order", is an ill conceived fantasy, as it is adverse to the interests of freedom fighting democratic people. This concept may have some philosophical merit as did Communism for world domination but with the governments of the world having such a vast diversification of attitudes and mindsets towards their own objectives, let alone towards each other, it would lead to the manipulation of the world's fair distribution of resources and subservience of all citizens. It can never provide the 'one size fits all' solution for everyone. The only equality it can bring is in bringing us all down to the level of developing countries. Anyone who would pursue this is either naïve or holds an alternative personal agenda to be a supreme elite ruler in achieving his or her backer's objectives. No one in their right mind could imagine why any developed country would willingly hand control over its citizens or resources to one world government, one government able to effect change on any country or sector of the globe without retaliation from the citizens of that country – particularly if a decision is considered adverse to the objectives of the citizens of that nation. This concept should not be anywhere on the US or Australian compass when we all have so much to contend with including equality and peace in our own very diverse societies yet unbeknown to most of us, it is the very essences of our governments objectives.

World governance is on the same scale as that which was sought by the Russia of old with its fearsome KGB. Any such conductor with those aspirations is no different to Hitler prior to WW2 who achieved astounding support by creating patriotism through propaganda in uniting the German people, but in pursuing his own holocaustic agenda. It certainly gives rise to questions as to why bunkers are being located in close proximity to Parliament House in Canberra, without any "Opposition". On its current course and another term with Labor, it will only be a matter of time before government powers legislate to censor anything anti-the Labor government or its nominee UN empowered authority. This seems currently afoot with the Minister for Communications seeking to block internet sites but adamant not to disclosure which site, just purporting that they will be pornographic sites.

With a vigorous pursuit for a nonsense carbon tax, imposed UN treaties and a passion for Fabian ideologies, World Government is around the corner. Rudd would have most certainly and prematurely achieved his goal of taking his signed off Emissions Trading Scheme to Copenhagen. With a signed document under his arm, he believed he would have been the "Copenhagen Hero" but he would have been the only one at the party to come in fancy dress. Then presented with the opportunity he would sign us to the Treaty in committing Australia to a "Single World Government". As a hero he would no doubt warrant a high command position in the rule of tyranny, because: *After Democracy comes Tyranny – Is it not the time to "turn back the tide of political corruption?"*

The Carbon Credit cap-and-trade scam will be recorded in history as the greatest attempt at fraudulent deception of all time, supported and fought for by governments. How did Australia get sucked into international treaties which are adverse to our local needs? How did this phenomenon come about without any referendum by the people?

Current "International Treaties and Agreements" are making modern history and how they will change our future is up every Australian to stand up here and now to stop this, or sit back and just let it happen. Read in the section on Wars of the 21st century how the Nazi's took over Germany, and understand the background of how this comes about in Australia. There has been a slow progression although accelerated since 1973. A progression based on unfounded science or propaganda which results in the effects of – The Lima Declaration, hence the Kyoto Protocol and the Emissions Trading Schemes sale of Carbon Credits. It flares from good intentions of equality for all of mankind and to cleaning up the world, but it gets lost in supremacies and theories. First comes societies elite groups or parties with concepts, support is gained for long term schemes to be developed and slowly implemented. These plans have not been for immediate gratification but long term, from decade to decade and from century to century with *gradualist reform and attrition, slowly eating away democracy, rather than revolutionary means or head-on battles.*

Deceptive infiltrative methods (such as government handouts) are used by "parties" with their ideologies, or rather by those who controls them and this is why ordinary Australians have had to endure hardships, and we are just about to embark on the harshest of abuses. Those who advocated for the "League of Nations' after

WW2 known to us today as "The United Nations" and I hope after you read the next few pages, you will appreciate that it is time we act urgently, to take back our sovereignty, our country which will only happen in the creation of a "party to end all parties" which is the objective of this book.

Australian governments have neglected and abused the interests of Australians to the benefit of other countries. We have the Lima Declaration, Agenda 21 and the Kyoto Protocol and many other agreements. The icing on the cake would be the Emissions Trading Scheme or Carbon Tax.

Those in power would dispel this as conspiracy theories in concealing their responsibility for participation, but where there's smoke, there is definitely smoke and a very strong probability of fire – in maintaining ignorance or apathy we facilitate the problem, do your own research, everything is available to you, just for the investigating, so you be the judge!

With non-transparency comes the ability to covertly implement treaties and agreements which are not based on solid fact and thus are to the detriment of those who have trusted and democratically elected those responsible, but to achieve their long term agendas. This has been achieved as there is no community education or approval sought and this has been taken to the absolute limit. Politician's loopholes have placed themselves above the law able to entertain and enter into long term treaties. No referendums to the Australians people, just Bills then legislation passed for philosophical reasons and wanting to appear as good neighbours, but we can never be a good neighbour if our house is burning.

Much of the following information on treaties and agreements has been prepared by Sue Maynes for who we should all be very grateful, particularly for her efforts to address our Constitutional abuses. Sue and others have gone above what most people will ever achieve, not just for herself but for every Australian. Our rights have been abused because most of us are not informed, while many people have chosen to ignore widespread injustices and the perverse objectives of government. You are reading this book because you care about Australia, our country, our heritage, our economy, our inheritance to our kids. You are informed, and want to improve your education because *"pre-warned is pre-armed"* but millions of Australians are not up to speed on these issues, and it is up to us all to help them understand and to be proactive in being protective. When reading the following please note the implications of Dr David Siminton comments: *". . . one of the rules of becoming a member of the United Nations is that you must be an independent sovereign nation. That means you cannot be ruled, regulated or influenced by any other sovereign nation, such as England."* Where does that leave our standing in the UN or with our 1901 Constitution and Queen Elizabeth II, perhaps derailed by the new Queen of Australia?

The Lima Declaration is an international trade agreement similar to the General Agreement on Trade and Tariffs "G.A.T.T." Australia signed the Lima Declaration in 1975 and it is just one of hundreds of international agreements we are signed up to. These agreements have been supported by all major political parties but no government has ever put these to the Australian people and therefore 99.9% of Australians do not know what these agreements and treaties are about, or how they affect our lives. We are just not told because if we knew, there would be rebellion, revolution and so we are kept in the dark and left to suffer the consequences. To achieve these ends, Federal governments have passed legislation that perverts our constitution and have collaborated with State governments. The result is that these legislations have placed government above the people, from servant to master.

The Lima Declaration is a blanket agreement of international treaties, constructed at the hand of the United Nations and it has been used by our governments to undermine Australian Sovereignty, destroy our agricultural and industrial industries, prevents desperately needed dams including the Franklin Dam in Tasmania and others. One example of how this works: The restricted use and development of water resources, restricts agriculture and makes us dependant on developing countries. This is oppression against Australia – the Lima Declaration, the Kyoto Protocol, Agenda 21 and the ETS are thus but government acts of *Treason (by suppression and betrayal) against Australians for the interests of International Nations and their Treaties in achieving our submission to a world government.* Sounds like conspiracy, maybe and maybe not – you're judging!

Through high taxes and harsh conditions, the Lima Declaration of 1975 has wound down Australian manufacturing making us dependant on importing from other preferred countries, particularly China, together with as much primary produce as we can consume – fruit, meat etc. **It was anticipated that the reduction would be 30% but current estimates are that 90% of our productivity has gone along with those jobs.** Unskilled, short term governments have never given consideration to what happens to these agreements when Australians have lost their jobs, their businesses and their farms. No jobs equals no money, equals no need to import, while default or failure to comply with these agreements comes with hefty penalties that would bankrupt the country, leaving us subservient to anyone who would feed us.

Our Asian neighbours are also signed up to The Lima Declaration. In fact, they will help you establish your business in their country with land, no tax for the first five years, and you can get interest rates between 0% and 4% and then you can take advantage of the Australian Governments incentives to importers from preferred countries and other financial advantages. It is estimated that 50% of our "blue collar" ie primary producers will become unemployed and taxes will be increased to sustain the unemployed. Because everyone's income will be less, we will buy cheaper products or go without and government will purport that unemployment is less than it is because if you work 10 hours a month, you are deemed employed. More government employees will be employed and to ensure they are busy new burocractical hurdles will be invented to make life no different to the full employment of Communist Russia and we will be totally dependant on developing nations for everything.

Whitlam, Frazer, Hawke, Keating, Hewson, Howard, Beasley, the Democrats, Greens and the Nationals all subscribe to this type of economic genocide, albeit under different names *"North South Dialogue" – "G.A.T.T." – "Internationalism" – "Inter-dependence" – "International Monetary Fund" (I.M.F) "World Bank"* or the newly uncovered *"New World Order".* All different names for the same plan of total control of the world through the money system – control by sick minds, treasonous politicians and bumbling academics and bureaucrats. The following are some of the recommendations of The Lima Declaration and enforced by UN agencies such as the World Trade Organisation with powers above any nations government:

Resolution 5 – Recognizing the urgent need to bring about the establishment of a New International Economic Order based on equity, Sovereign equity, Inter-dependence and co-operation as has been expressed in the declaration and program of action on the establishment of a New International Economic Order in order to transform the present structure of economic relations.

Resolution 27 – Developed Countries such as Australia should expand its imports from developing countries.

Resolution 28 – Requires that developing countries increase their Industrial growth by more than the 8% recommended in earlier United Nations meetings and increase their exports by 350% by year 2000 (a contradiction to the emissions or carbon reduction plan).

Resolution 35 – Developed Countries (including Australia) should transfer technical, financial, and capital goods to developing countries to accomplish resolution 28 above.

Resolution 59 – The developed countries should adopt the following measures:

a) Progressive elimination or reduction of tariff and non-tariff barriers and other obstacles to trade, taking into account the special characteristics of the trade of the developing countries, with a view to improving the international framework for the conduct of world trade. Adherence to the fullest extent possible to the principle of the "standstill" on imports from developing countries and recognition of the need for prior consultation where feasible and appropriate in the event that special circumstances warrant a modification of the "standstill".

b) Adoption of trade measures designed to ensure increased exports of manufactured and semi-manufactured products including processed agricultural products from the developing to the developed countries:

c) Facilitate development of new and strengthen existing policies, taking into account their economic structure and economic, social and security objectives, which would encourage their industries which are less competitive internationally to move progressively into more viable lines of production or into other sectors of the economy, thus leading to structural adjustments within the developed countries, and redeployment of the productive capacities of such industries to developing countries and promotion of a higher degree of utilization of natural resources and people in the latter.

d) Consideration by the developed countries of their policies with respect to processed and semi-processed forms of raw materials, taking full account of the interests of the developing countries in increasing their capacities and industrial potentials for processing raw materials which they export;

e) Increased financial contributions to international organizations and to government or credit institutions in the developing countries in order to facilitate the promotion or financing of industrial development. Such contributions must be completely free of any kind of political conditions and should involve no economic conditions other than those normally imposed on borrowers;

This is why it is imperative that we quarantine Australia now and become self sustaining once again. We do not need to import, particularly fresh produce to maintain our own market. The Lima Declaration and other such detrimental instruments are not about feeding and supporting Australians. It is about the creation of a new world order and establishing the benefits for its rulers. What is needed is a balance of trade between our imports and exports to survive and advance Australia, but the less we import, the less we need to export to affect a successful offset. We need our own money system, controlled by our Bank of Australia and we need to remain independent of any international treaty that is not to our mutual benefit, just as every country and its government has the first obligation to do. This would require us doing the opposite of what the Lima Declaration and the Kyoto Protocol are dictating.

The Lima Agreement mentions no less than 21 times, the "New Economic Order" and this is what it's all about! This is why Peter Spencer is but the "effect of the cause" and so will we all be, if we do not regain control over our governments, dispense with all of these adverse treaties, declarations and protocols. The Lima Agreement is all about locking us into new developing countries, into *"their"* economic trap and *"their"* plans, which would give the UN total world economic control (as the brokers, the controllers), while reducing developed countries to third world status by putting the shackles of international debt on every human being and through adverse legislation we are prohibited from legal recourse, while government powers and censorship grow from the abundance of treacherous acts against our constitution. Alternatively, only a revolution will bring back our lives from world slavery and the legally enforceable shackles of debt, chained to the slave master, under Capitalistic money power. It is up to each nation to think and act, responsibly and locally for what is best for their people and from a position of strength able to help developing countries.

"Every Australian is immediately required to make a decision between debt controlled slavery in perpetuity – or the age of prosperity. Both are eminently possible, one we will have! Which one? Now rely on your gut feeling, ignore the controlled media propaganda it's owned by your would be masters, but decide now between perpetual slavery or the age of prosperity" Joe Bryant said this in 1992

The Lima Declaration is obtainable from the department of Foreign Affairs in Canberra, by phoning the treaties support unit on (06) 261 3590 Kevin Rudd, our Minister for Foreign Affairs will not doubt oblige. While you're at it, ask them how many treaties, declarations, conventions, etc exist and ask for copies. Ask for the complete set including with The International Treaty on Civil & Political Rights, that is, our Bill of Rights, which we do not have.

From Lima came: **The Kyoto Protocol** which is a United Nations Framework Convention on Climate Change (UNFCCC or FCCC) purported to be aimed at combating global warming. The UNFCCC is an international environmental treaty with the goal of achieving *"stabilization of greenhouse gas concentrations in the atmosphere at a level that would prevent dangerous anthropogenic interference with the climate system."* Two years after the Lima Declaration this Protocol was initially adopted on 11 December 1997 in Kyoto, Japan and entered into force on 16 February 2005 and by November 2009 there were 187 states which have signed and ratified the protocol.

Under the Protocol, industrialized countries committed themselves to a reduction of four greenhouse gases (GHG) (carbon dioxide, methane, nitrous oxide, sulphur hexafluoride) and two groups of gases (hydrofluorocarbons and perfluorocarbons) produced by them, and all member countries gave general commitments. Some countries agreed to reduce their collective greenhouse gas emissions by 5.2% from the 1990 level. Emission limits do not include emissions by international aviation and shipping, but are in addition to the industrial gases, chlorofluorocarbons, or CFCs, which are dealt with under the 1987 Montreal Protocol on Substances that Deplete the Ozone Layer. The benchmark 1990 emission levels were accepted by the Conference of the Parties of UNFCCC (decision 2/CP.3) were the values of "global warming potential" calculated for the IPCC Second Assessment Report. These figures are used for converting the various greenhouse gas emissions into comparable CO_2 equivalents when computing overall sources and sinks.

The Protocol allows for several "flexible mechanisms", such as emissions trading, the clean development mechanism (CDM) and joint implementation to allow countries to meet their GHG emission limitations by purchasing GHG emission reductions credits from elsewhere, through financial exchanges, projects that reduce emissions with excess allowances. Each country is required to submit an annual report of inventories of all anthropogenic greenhouse gas emissions from sources and removals from sinks under UNFCCC and the Kyoto Protocol. These countries nominate a person (called a "designated national authority") to create and manage its greenhouse gas inventory. Countries including Japan, Canada, Italy, the Netherlands, Germany, France, Spain and others are actively promoting government carbon funds, supporting multilateral carbon funds intent on purchasing carbon credits from developing countries, and are working closely with their major utility, energy, oil and gas and chemicals conglomerates to acquire greenhouse gas certificates as cheaply as possible.] Virtually all participating countries have established a designated national authority to manage its Kyoto obligations, specifically the "CDM process" that determines which GHG projects they wish to propose for accreditation by the CDM Executive Board.

While all of the above sounds so good, so reliable, so credible but man-made global warming is not a proven science and leaked emails support scientist's involvement in enabling government to pursue this under their false reports. Without international treaties and fudged reports, we are capable of instigating our own renewable energy sources and thus reduce pollutants as necessary, but even if there were merit or facts to support it, we can never guarantee that other countries will adhere or cough up the fines. To even contemplate implementation of emissions controls is nothing but absurd, let alone can compliance be assured. China (the greatest polluter) has already demonstrated it will not be answerable to any outsiders in regulating them.

After the election in November 2007 Kevin Rudd immediately signed the ratified on 3 December 2007, just before the meeting of the UN Framework Convention on Climate Change which took effect in March, 2008. When he was in the opposition, Rudd commissioned Ross Garnaut to report on the economic effects of reducing greenhouse gas emissions. The report was submitted to the Australian government on 30 September 2008 The policy of the Rudd government contrasts with that of the former Australian government, which refused to ratify the agreement on the ground that following the protocol it would be costly for Australians and that countries like India and China with expanding economies and large population would not have any obligations. Furthermore, it was claimed that Australia was already doing enough to cut emissions, with a pledge of A$300 million to reduce greenhouse gas emissions over three years.

The greenhouse gas emissions in Australia from 2008 to 2012 were projected to be at 9% above the level in 1990, including the effects of land use, land-use change and forestry (LULUCF). The figure is slightly above the Kyoto Protocol limitation of 8%. In 2007 the UNFCCC reported that the greenhouse gas emissions in Australia in 2004 were at 25.6% above the level in 1990, without the LULUCF correction. The previous Australian government, along with the United States, agreed to sign the Asia Pacific Partnership on Clean Development and Climate at the ASEAN regional forum on 28 July 2005 Furthermore, the State of New South Wales (NSW) commenced the NSW greenhouse gas abatement scheme. This mandatory scheme of greenhouse gas emissions trading commenced on 1 January 2003 and is currently on trial by the State government in NSW alone. Notably, this scheme allows accredited certificate providers to trade emissions from households in the State. The scheme is still in place despite the outgoing Prime Minister Howard's clear dismissal of emissions trading as a credible solution to climate change. Following the example of NSW, the National Emissions Trading Scheme (ETS) has been sought to be established as an initiative of State and Territory governments of Australia, all of which have Labor Party governments, except Western Australia. The purpose of ETS is to establish an intra-Australian carbon trading scheme to coordinate policy among regions. As the Constitution of Australia does not refer specifically to environmental matters (apart from water), the allocation of responsibility is to be resolved at a political level, not by the people. In the later years of the Howard administration (1996-2007) the States governed by Labor governments took steps to establish an ETS:

(a) To take action in a field where there were few mandatory Federal steps, and
(b) As a means of facilitating ratification of the Kyoto Protocol by the Labor government.

We all know that something is very wrong. How have governments been able to reduce our democracy, pervert our Constitution and steal the assets of the people and what can we do?

From a speech given by **Sue Maynes to the Inverell Forum,** March 2008 at **<http://peopleofthecommonwealth.blogspot.com>** *"On approx the 29 January 1998 the leader of the National Party placed on the table of Parliament, a document seeking to move the Governor of the State of Queensland into the Constitution Act 1867 as a Parliamentary Secretary and a public official. This was done under the Imperial Acts Application Act 1954 section 15DA. This document was **not challenged by any member of any party or any independent member of the Queensland Parliament,** and therefore became official on 29 January 1999. See Constitution (Parliamentary Secretaries) Act © The State of Queensland 1996 On the same day the Queensland Constitution 1867 reprint was proclaimed, thus verifying the position of Parliamentary Secretary under its Constitution. From this day on, **the Governor of the State of Queensland was no longer a sworn representative of Her Majesty Queen Elizabeth II,** but was now inside the 1867 Constitution, conducting the daily business of the government and allocating "laws" applicable to each government department. **He was removed from his "no party allegiance" and had become, effectively, a part of the Queensland government and under the Premier's control.***

On 9 November 2001 the Premier of the State of Queensland, the Honourable Peter Beattie presented to Parliament the new Constitution of Queensland 2001 Bill. The elected Members for the people of Queensland, the Members of the Legislative Assembly, passed the Bill, said only to 'modernise' the Constitution of Queensland. This constitution was assented to by the Governor on 3rd December 2001 (no longer a separate power but under the ruling government) and upon assent, under section 95 of the new Constitution, Acts subject to the

Constitution Act 1867 were repealed. Section 92 immediately came into force which repealed parts of the Constitution Act Amendment Act 1922. This allowed the Parliament to move back prior to the removal of the Legislative Council at referendum in 1922 and 'recreate' the positions of that former Legislative Council.

Queensland then became, at the completion of these matters, without the assent of any of the laws by the Crown or Her Representative, an independent sovereign State and fractured the common law and the separation of powers in that State. Although the Governor was clearly now a public servant under the current Queensland State Government, he still held the Public Seal of the State and sealed all documents signed under the Hand of the Sovereign with the Public Seal of the State, therefore rendering void, any contracts, Acts, Laws, etc under the Hand of the Sovereign. In fact, on that day, 3 December 2001, the Governor of Queensland with the authority of the Entrenched Provisions contained in the Constitution Act 1867 (Reprint No 1), and the Commonwealth of Australia Constitution Act which in their manner and form hold the entrenched provision of "The Governor of Queensland" and exercising the delegated authority of "The Crown", did unilaterally 'Assent' to the 'Constitution of Queensland Parliament of Queensland Bill' without the consent of the People's of Queensland through the ultimate and absolute authority gained through a vote of 'Referenda' and in doing so, this Constitution of Queensland 2001 became the 'Fundamental Law of Queensland.' **Queen Elizabeth II has never raised this with her representative or the lack of a response to her request pertaining to an inquiry regarding the appointment of Ms Bryce as Governor General.**

As a progression, (again, you do some research): **The Brigalow Corporation** (of the State of Queensland) originated in the old Queensland Crowns Lands Act and came about through the Queensland Government borrowing from the Federal Government funds to develop what was termed the "Brigalow Belt" (about 4 million acres) out from Rockhampton during the 1960's. The old Crowns Lands Act (Queensland) has now been converted to the "Land Act 1994 (Queensland)" and this is where you can find the "Brigalow Corporation" today. In essence the government of Queensland has moved all the crowns land AND all crown land that was sold (fee simple) into the Brigalow Corporation through the Land Act, Land Title Act, Property Law Act, etc, etc, etc. Where the money went is yet another story! The "Brigalow Corporation" in not Listed as a "Public" company on the Stock Exchange, it is an "Exempt Public Authority" which is found by definition at s9 and 5A of the Corporations Act 2001 (C'wth) (in right of the Crown), except there is no "Crown" in Queensland just "the State". The term "The State" or as written in most modern Queensland statutes, "This Act binds the State". It is quite clear in the Second Reading Speech by Premier Beattie, that at the time the Legislative Assembly voted for the passing of the Parliament of Queensland Bill 2001 and the Constitution of Queensland 2001, they were allowing the use of Acts which had been framed but had not been passed by the Legislative Assembly and were, in fact, adjourned sine die going back to 1991. "Sine die" meaning to be Adjourned without giving any future date of meeting or hearing. Those Acts were proclaimed on 7 June 2002 and then reprinted as law of that Parliament.

By the passing of these Acts by the Parliament of Queensland, the subject citizens of Her Majesty have suffered the loss of their judicial relief at Common Law and all those rights which are originally entrenched in the Commonwealth of Australia Constitution Act at sects 109, 107, 108, 50, 51, 52, 53, 54, Chapter II, III, sects 75 and The Corporations (Q) Act 1990 (Q) Reprint No 3, was reprinted as in force immediately before 15 July 2001 ©State of Q 2006. At this time, the State of Queensland became a Corporation Government. Under the definition of 'person' in the Acts Interpretation Act 1901 (C'wth), section 22 (1)(a) expressions used to denote persons include a body politic or corporate as well as an individual. The Acts Interpretation Act 1954 (Q) defines a person as an 'individual and a corporation' and as such the once Sovereign People are now subject to the corporate government of the State of Queensland and as such are 'chattels' of the State of Queensland Corporation, while the governor is now an employee of the government, not Queen Elizabeth II.

I refer to the following Acts – the Reprints Act 1992, the Statutory Instruments Act 1992, the Legislative Standards Act 1992. These Acts were used in conjunction with the Constitution of Queensland 2001, section 92 to create the corporation Government of the State and then further to repeal those Acts under section 95 of that Constitution. Those Acts moved back in time, one may say like the Tardis, reprinting, removing the Crown out of all Acts as far back as the Magna Carta then reprinting back to the Australia Acts (Requests) Act 1985 and removing all the positions as cited in that Act. The only part of the Commonwealth of Australia Constitution Act which is recognized by Queensland is the Commonwealth Constitution commencing at section 9. The sections of the Commonwealth of Australia Constitution Act which are not recognized include the High Court and the Federal Court. By using the Australia Acts (Request) Act 1985 section 12 in conjunction with the other three State Acts, the Acts reprinted Queensland into a corporate State. In conjunction with the Acts Interpretation Act 1954 section 15DA(2) which allowed for the automatic commencement and assent of any Act that had been laying dormant for a period of twelve months, Acts which were framed to create the corporate State of Queensland in 1992, 1993 and 1994 were reprinted by the Reprints Act 1992 which is under the Department of the Premier. The elected Members of the Sovereign people of the State of Queensland have, since 29th January 1999 taken it upon themselves, (contrary to the Criminal Code Act 1995(C'wth) to which they are all subject under Chapter 7 – The proper administration of Government), to create for themselves, under the Constitution of Queensland 2001, a corporation Government in which the Sovereign people of Queensland and their property are mere chattels of the State. This surely is a breach of the trust and faith which the electors of Queensland placed in their elected members to uphold and respect the laws of the Commonwealth.

The State of Queensland Australia is registered with the US Securities and Exchange Commissions under No. 0001244818.**The Queensland Treasury Corp is registered under No. 0000852555** I have copies of their Annual Report for Foreign Governments & Political Subdivisions including the Queensland Treasury Corporation's 2006-07 Indicative borrowing program Update. I also have the Queensland State Accounts December 2006 which carries gross private information.

Government Tiers – All Government tiers, including local councils are now inside the Parliament of Queensland. The Members of the Legislative Assembly are clearly individuals and members of the corporation as defined in the Acts Interpretation Act 1954 sect 32 & 33. Members of the Legislative Assembly are paid by the Parliament of Queensland and are elected subject to the Election Act (Queensland) which is an Act enacted by the Parliament of Queensland.

All elections held in Queensland since 6th June 2002 are elections at common law but the Election Act of Queensland is subject to the Uniform Civil Procedures Rules 1999 of Queensland, therefore any vote given in any State, Federal or Council elections since that time are votes in name only. The Acts Interpretation (State Commercial Activities) Act 1994 amended the Acts Interpretation Act 1954 to define "the State" to mean the Executive government of the State of Queensland. Under the provisions of this Act, "the State" may carry out commercial activities 'without further statutory authority' and 'without prior appropriation from the public accounts' {s47C.(3)} Section 47C. defines 'commercial activities to include 'commercial activities that are not within the ordinary functions of the State' and these functions may be delegated by a Minister to an officer of the State who may sub-delegate delegated powers to another officer of the State. An 'officer of the State means a chief executive, or employee of the public sector or an officer of the public service'. The Second Reading Speech of the former Premier the Honourable Peter Beattie when he created the new Government of Queensland, placed inside the Parliament himself as Premier (President), the Ministers, the Governor as a parliamentary secretary, the judges and justices of the Supreme and District Courts, the Supreme and District Court, the Local Government Councils.

Kevin Rudd was head of the public service in Queensland when this disgrace was plotted. It was achieved by bringing the Governor of Queensland into the public service (as a parliamentary secretary) and thereby bringing him and then Ms Bryce under their control. This move is illegal without a referendum, but it has been largely ignored by the media who are gagged when it comes to issues detrimental to Labor governments. Government methodically removed the people's rights under common law, by going back through all the laws ever written (as far as the Magna Carta of 1215) and rewrote them for their own benefit. All private land and assets are now owned by the Brigalow Corporation, and can now be removed without the need for compensation. *The "separation of powers" has been removed, as has the presumption of innocence.* Read more at http://sosnews.org/newsfront/documents/brigalow.htm

The public officials are not public officials of "the Crown" but public officials of "the State" of Queensland. As all real property has now been taken back by the State and held under the State Corporation, the Brigalow Corporation, the public officials are in fact now working for the owners of the land, the State Government of Queensland. When the State of Queensland removed the land and placed it under the ownership of the State, they did so without compensation or without a referendum.

Judicial Results – Because this new Constitution was presented to, and passed by the Parliament of Queensland without respect of reference to the Commonwealth of Australia Constitution Act section 106, to the Queensland Constitution Act 1867 and without a referendum of the People as cited at section 53, this removed the Separation of Powers and recreated Queensland as an independent, sovereign, corporation government outside of and not, therefore, subject to the laws of the Commonwealth or other States & Territories, in contradiction of the Commonwealth of Australia Constitution Act. The Common Law has been repealed from the Supreme Court Act 1995 (Queensland), Reprint No. 2, reprinted as in force 2 March 2001 © State of Queensland 2001, by the omission of Part 9 – Division Heading 4 Common Law & Jurisdiction; Division Heading 5 Equitable Jurisdiction; Division Heading 6 Criminal Jurisdiction – Section 199 Laws of England to be applied in the administration of Justice; Section 200 Common Law and General Jurisdiction of the Court, Jurisdiction at common Law; Section 2001 Equitable Jurisdiction; Section 202 Criminal Jurisdiction. Courtesy of the Constitution of Queensland 2001 Chapter 4 – Courts – section 58 – Supreme Courts – the Supreme Court's jurisdiction is now of the State.

Queensland is now outside the Commonwealth of Australia as an independent sovereign State without common law, and the people are subject to civil and statute law only. The 'common law and general jurisdiction'; the 'Laws of England to be applied in the administration of justice' and 'equitable jurisdiction' have been removed under the Supreme Court Act 1995(Queensland) Reprint number 2A dated 2nd March, 2001 under Schedule 2 of the Constitution of Queensland 2001. All private equity and inheritance in the State is the property of "the State", see Corporations (Queensland) Act 1990 (Queensland), Reprint No 3, reprinted as in force immediately before 15 July 2001 © State of Queensland 2006. All courts, including the Magistrates Courts, are inside the Parliament of Queensland. The jurisdiction of the Supreme Court of Queensland is found in the Constitution of Queensland 2001, Part 5 – Powers of the State. Therefore it is assumed that the Judges of the Supreme and District Courts of Queensland must protect the 'assets' of the State of Queensland and find only in favour of the State, not in favour of the registered owners of private land who have lost, under the statute laws of Queensland, the rights to use their fee simple land as they see fit.

The Constitution of Queensland 2001 Chapter 3, Sections 51 & 27 are ultra vires to the Commonwealth of Australia Constitution Act at s109, s106, s107, s51 & s52 of the Referendum (Machinery Provisions) Act 1984 (C'wth). Ultra vires meaning:

Without authority, an act which is beyond the powers or authority of the person or organization which took it. The common law and references to the Crown have been removed out of the Supreme Court Act 1995 (Queensland). Civil law and statute law have a very different requirement for the committing of any offence, whether an indictable offence, a summary offence, a simple offence or an absolute offence such as a traffic offence where a guilty mind is not required to commit that offence. Under the civil law system, which is now subject to the Uniform Civil Procedures Rules of the Supreme Court Act 1991(Queensland), every person is guilty until they prove their innocence. The Supreme and District Court, other courts and the Judges and Justices of those Courts are now inside the corporation of the Government and not sworn representatives of the Crown. Under the Constitution of Queensland 2001, all documents are issued or signed under the Public Seal of the State. This would be any document appointing a politician, a Judge or any person who should swear an oath of allegiance to the Sovereign. The Governor now seals that document in accordance with the Constitution of Queensland 2001 section 37 with the Public Seal of the State therefore voiding the appointment of any of those people by the Sovereign but making those people in effect 'officers of the State' and subject to the 'Powers of the State' as cited in Part 5 of the Constitution of Queensland 2001.

Sovereign People – We are all subjects of Her Majesty under section 117 of the Commonwealth of Australia Constitution Act. The Parliament of Queensland does not recognize the rights of the sovereign people inside the State of Queensland. What now happens to people who have been prosecuted, fined, imprisoned etc. under the civil law of Queensland, which does not exist elsewhere in the Commonwealth of Australia?

The people of Queensland are still, under section 117 of the Commonwealth of Australia Constitution Act, subjects of Her Majesty Queen Elizabeth II and protected by Her laws as there has been no referendum under section 128 of the Commonwealth of Australia Constitution Act to allow the separation of Queensland from the Commonwealth of Australia.

Those who hold a Deed of Grant in fee simple in Queensland, now only hold a statutory title, and that title is upheld by the civil laws of the Supreme and District Courts of the corporate Government of Queensland and the Judges of the Supreme and District Courts who are inside the Government. Your common law estate in fee simple is now held by the corporate Government of the Sovereign State of Queensland. Under the definitions in the Acts Interpretation 1954 (Queensland), section 36, the definition of 'property' and 'land', the State of Queensland now owns all your property, which includes money, real and personal property from the past and any future property which includes your Will. I refer to the definition of 'land' under section 22 – Meaning of certain words (aa) 'individual' and (c) 'land' of the Acts Interpretation Act 1901(C'wth) and the definition of 'property' in section 130.1 of the Criminal Code Act 1995(C'wth) The Acts Interpretation Act 1954(Queensland) is ultra vires to the Commonwealth of Australia Constitution Act, Criminal Code

Act 1995(C'wth), Chapter 7 – The proper administration of Government; the Acts Interpretation Act 1901(C'wth). The Acts Interpretation Act 1954(Q) defines property both present and future, owned by you as an 'individual and a corporation' as subject to a statutory instrument only and that statutory instrument is not only applicable to your land, but all property that you, as a person in Queensland now own, as opposed to the previous common law indefeasible deed of grant in fee simple. All land, including private land held previously in the common law estate of inheritance in fee simple by private individuals, is now held by the corporation of the State of Queensland known as the Brigalow Corporation. The only tenure that any financial institutions hold in land in Queensland today, even though they may believe they hold an estate in fee simple, is in fact held by the corporation of the State, the Brigalow Corporation and is now the full property of the State. The lending institutions now only hold a statutory title and an interest only in the land by virtue of the Statutory Instruments Act 1992 under which the rules of the Supreme and District Courts are found under section 12 of that Act.

The owners of that property taken by the corporation can only hope that the corporation has not used your real property as an asset to borrow funds for the corporation for whatever purpose. If the independent State corporation fails or its borrowing is too extensive, it will again be the sovereign people who will bear the financial consequences. Your Deed of Grant in fee simple is now a statutory title only, and that title is upheld by the civil laws of the Supreme and District Courts of the corporate Government of Queensland and the Judges of the Supreme and District Courts who are inside the Government. Your land is now held by the Government of Queensland in the Brigalow Corporation with no compensation paid to you for that acquisition. For "Even though the King may not enter" (Plenty v. Dillon [1991] HCA 5; 171 CLR 635 F.C. 91/004 (7 March 1991) the Queensland Government and the delegated authorities thereof can, without fine or legal interference.

To have Queensland become an independent Sovereign State and to remove the common law, set up statutory civil law and have Queensland not recognize the Commonwealth of Australia Constitution Act but only that Act from section 9 onwards, a full referendum would have been required of the people of the Commonwealth of Australia to enact, validly, that Queensland, from 29th January 1999 was now independent of the Commonwealth of Australia and a State in its own right. **That did not happen as a pre-requisite.**

In the Second Reading Speech for the Constitution the Premier stated that the Constitution would be 'broadly accessible' to the people of Queensland. Considering that this Act has effectively removed all common law property rights from the people of Queensland it should, one would reasonably assume, have been put to a referendum of the people. The sovereign people of the Commonwealth of Australia have never been required at a referendum by virtue of section 128 of the Constitution of the Commonwealth of Australia to vote to allow "the State" of Queensland to fracture the Commonwealth and become an independent sovereign state.

Assets of the Corporation – As the corporation of Queensland, when it was formed, had no assets, it had to acquire assets if they wished to borrow. Under the Queensland Government (Land Holding) Amendment Act 1992, they immediately took all the Crown land and estates in fee simple registered under the Property Law Act 1974 as equity for the corporation without compensation to the registered owners of the property whether they live in Queensland or anywhere else and converted that property for their own use, contrary to Chapter 7 of the Criminal Code Act 1995(C'wth) – The proper administration of Government. The Queensland Government Land Holding Amendment Act 1992 was reprinted into law through the Parliament of Queensland Act 2001 whereupon all Crown land, assets and infrastructure on that land including schools, hospitals, roads, etc became subject to and responsible to the Ministers of the State of Queensland as cited at Chapter III of the Queensland Constitution 2001.

The Acts Interpretation (State Commercial Activities) Act 1994 amended the Acts Interpretation Act 1954 to define "the State" to mean the Executive government of the State of Queensland. Under the provisions of this Act, "the State" may carry out commercial activities 'without further statutory authority' and 'without prior appropriation from the public accounts' {s47C.(3)} Section 47C. defines 'commercial activities to include 'commercial activities that are not within the ordinary functions of the State' and these functions may be delegated by a Minister to an officer of the State who may sub-delegate delegated powers to another officer of the State. An 'officer of the State means a chief executive, or employee of the public sector or an officer of the public service'.

Under the Lands Legislation Amendment Act No. 64 of 1992 © The State of Queensland and further now in the corporation of the State known as the Brigalow Corporation and further by amendment of the Constitution Act 1867 Reprint 2A which clearly defines that any estate or interest in the land to be acquired from any other person, the definition of land clearly does not include any estate, therefore the only land held has been transferred from the Real Property Acts of 1861; 1877; 1952 and 1956 into the Land Title Act 1994(Queensland) Reprint 7 © State of Queensland 2003 and you hold your land in a statutory title only, without any further element of tenure of the Crown and the Courts are inside the Government and subject to the rules of the Court as found in the Statutory Instruments Act 1992© The State of Queensland.

Recent newspaper articles have shown the next steps in this "Legal Land Theft". The Queensland Government plans to determine Land valuation via the Improved Capital Value, which would allow their asset base to rise extraordinarily, as well as increase the amount of rates to be increased to the land owners. *A second article states regarding the* Queensland **Urban Land Development** – *"Both the authority and a developer will be able to write their own by-laws, open and close roads, levy their own rates, enter buildings without a warrant and cut councils out of the planning process in designated areas, all without being elected"* Dare we ask, where's the referendum?

What is Behind This – It is quite clear that those who have been put in power by the sovereign people of the State have, since 1992 when the original Acts were being framed, had a full intention in time, to bring about their own personal agendas and their financial backers, regardless of the wishes of the sovereign people who have, in good and open faith and intention, by secret ballot at elections, voted these people into positions of power and of trust. Those who must Swear or Affirm an oath of allegiance to Her Majesty that they will uphold Her laws for the benefit of the people of the State of Queensland. That power has turned from the power granted by the people to the Legislative Assembly to make laws for 'peace welfare and good government' on behalf of the sovereign people of Queensland using funds from taxes paid by the citizens of Queensland and all of Australia, into a totalitarian system of Government, whereby we the people are subject to the corporation Government of the State. The ramifications caused by these actions carried out over a long period of time by the Members of the body politic dating back as far as 1992 are so vast and wide spread it will take a long time to remedy and repair the whole system of government in Queensland. The Parliament can make any laws they wish but I do not believe that under a democratic system of Government they are elected to Parliament to make draconian laws which remove the rights of the sovereign people to their use of their land without fair and just compensation.

Under the Constitution of Queensland 2001, by the removal of common law in the State of Queensland, the public officials of this State can acquire an interest in private registered land without compensation, for the benefit of the State Government's corporation. This also includes the property owned now and in the future as the sovereign people are in fact "an individual and a corporation" and therefore subject to the corporation Government of the State of Queensland. It is very clear from the time line of events that this was a well-planned manoeuvre to remove Queensland from the Federation of Australia and through that action from the protection of the Australian Constitution and Common Law & Equity.

The former Premier said in the Second Reading Speech for the constitution, *'we all look forward to the day when we are a republic'.* The people of the Commonwealth of Australia at referendum in 1999 voted against a republic but wished to retain the present system of Government with a clear separation of powers under common law and for the Commonwealth of Australia to remain exactly the same with a combined Federation of States as was created in 1901. Mr Beattie also stated, *". . . but this Act is much more, it is the fundamental law of Queensland that underpins our system of government. The entities it provides for include this Parliament, the Supreme and District Courts of this State and the system of local government that we know in Queensland. The office holders under this Act include the Governor of Queensland, the Ministers of the Crown and the judges of the Supreme and District Courts. This law is of supreme importance."* *Further in the speech, the Premier stated "Our entity as a Sovereign State, the democratic ideals on which our State is built, rest on our Constitution".*

Is it Legal? May I first say – that as this matter covered almost 30 years, there can be no doubt that every major Queensland politician must have been aware of this plan, particularly Kevin Rudd. There is also no doubt that every major Federal politician should have been aware of the plan including both John Howard and Kim Beasley. And finally there can be no doubt that the Governor-General of Australia was complicit in this plan. *Commonwealth of Australia Constitution Act, Chapter II* **The Executive Government,** *Section 61: The executive power of the Commonwealth is vested in the Queen and is exercisable by the Governor-General, as the Queen's representative and extends, to the execution and maintenance of this Constitution and of the laws of the Commonwealth.*

The primary fact that all these changes and manoeuvres were done without a referendum of the People clearly shows that the politicians involved knew they would not succeed if the people were asked for their approval (don't ask the question if you don't like the answer). There in lies the major area of illegality.

McHugh J in Kable v Director of Public Prosecutions (NSW) stated *"That there is a common law of Australia as opposed to a common law of individual States is clear".* Lipohar v R [1999] HCA 65; 200 CLR 485; 168 ALR 8; 74 ALJR 282 (9 December 1999) At 53 . . . . If the common law were fragmented, it would be necessary to spell out of the Australian constitutional structure principles to resolve conflicts or variances between, in particular, "federal common law" and that of the particular State in which the executive government of the Commonwealth conducted its activities . . . Lipohar v the Queen is still law and subject to the section 77M of the Judiciary Act 1903 (Cth). It is only the High Court of Australia who can remove the common law from the State of Queensland, not the elected members of the Legislative Assembly.

A referendum of the Queensland people was to be sought in July 2010 by the Qld Labor government (currently abandoned). This referendum was to ask the people of Qld to (NOW) approve the 2001 Queensland Constitution. As this Constitution has been clearly operating since 2001 this belated referendum raised alarm bells. What were the people truly being asked to approve, given that it has been legislation for over 9 years? Can this be retrospective? Has any legislation under this Constitution been lawful given the people did not approve it in 2001? Meanwhile the government's reliance is on the ongoing ignorance of the people of Queensland and perhaps Ms Bligh should be providing answers. Where is the Queensland Liberal Party or any other person or party on this grave matter? Why was the referendum dropped like a hot potato and not pursued? Because this corruption would have been exposed with unanswerable questions.

Is this happening in other states? Yes. *New South Wales removed the Governor in 1987 under the Consolidated Amendment Act 1987.* WA is almost in the same situation as Queensland. The State Govt, the World Wildlife Fund and the Real Estate Institute of WA have combined to sell Bush Blocks. All Governors of each

State now obey the Premier's in each state. See their websites. Native Vegetation Laws have been introduced to prohibit farming activities and destroying the value of properties without recompense to the "owners" – *". . . flick'em off like flies, one by one, they'll never know what happened".*

Then, NSW Native Vegetation Laws: In wanting to covet private property, but not wanting to pay for it, how did the Federal government get away with it in NSW? They got the State to take it instead! Unlike the Federal Constitution, the State Constitutions (except one) contain no provision for the payment of fair compensation for the taking of property. NSW legislation requires it, but the NSW State simply overrode that with *ordinary legislation*, smacking of "Rule by Decree" and with no objection from State or Federal government Oppositions, why? Perhaps the interest, objectives and accountability of both parties lie with the same masters?

As a further level of control over the people, the Federal government created the 'grand-daddy' of all the environmental acts in the Environmental Conservation and Protection Biodiversity Act 1999 – so important it has its own web-site. Section 3 states that the objects of this act are to provide for the protection of the environment. Section 528 Definitions states that environment includes people and communities. In clear words, this means that the government have given themselves control OVER the people and their communities under the definition of environment and the guise of 'protection'. And of course, this includes their assets. You no longer have the right to make your own decisions in opposition to government 'thought processes.' Hence, fluoride in the water over the massive community protests, the removal of councils despite the people's protests, etc.

In 1983, the full bench of the High Court ruled in a case commonly called the 'Tasmania Dams case'. Their ruling opened the door for government theft of all ownership rights, by making the decision that unless the deeds changed hands there had been no acquisition, therefore no compensation was required. Completely contrary to previous decisions where ownership rights had been expressed as going well beyond the actual title deed, encompassing both the physical and non-physical elements of ownership, particularly of land. The Hawke government were elated at this decision and the door was open to massive 'land ownership rights' theft which is escalating.

This scam was at the hand of the Federal government, the Howard Liberal government who masterminded this scheme through the State governments, to achieve their goal. It was the passing of the Native Vegetation Act (NVA) laws which restricted farmer's use-rights for clearing their land and it locked up 109 million hectares of private property. The Federal government paid the States to make these unjust acquisitions which saved the Federal government tens of billions of dollars in UN Climate Change Compliance penalties, as well as saving 83.7 million tones of carbon credits from private landowners.

Similarly, the Federal government used the Commonwealth Natural Heritage Trust of Australia Act where the Commonwealth gave NSW A$1.2 billion that it got from the sale of Telstra, for their part in stealing billions of dollars worth of other people's property. When there is the mighty buck involved, you will never find resistance from State governments.

Ian Henke, Executive Director Institute of Constitution & Research says: *"It appears that the validity of the Constitution does not reside in law, but in history and acceptance .... Are we Young and Free?"* and *"We now have a system of law in which the system has been rigged to assure that the citizen can't beat the government. Is our Constitution valid? Are we really the people of the Constitution?"* Ian Henke says, "Australians in their thousands are battling the massive impost of government charges, legislations, fines and levies. We are seeing our ownership rights removed daily through the frightening growth of government regulations. Ask yourself why Federal and State government need to form a body such as COAG, if they already govern as a Federation? Understand the words *"peak intergovernmental forum"*. Doesn't that mean the main body? Isn't Parliament the main body under our Constitution? Doesn't this mean we no longer have a Federation, but have reverted to the 1885 Federal Council of Australia? Ask yourself how local councils in Victoria can levy a tax per acre of land sold, if the people are sovereign? Ask yourself how the Queensland government can enforce an Environmental Assessment and a A\$5,000 levy if you want to sell your home? Ask yourself why there was not a referendum to sign international Treaties which effectively breach our Constitution? Ask yourself why the High Court, the protectors of the Constitution, did not speak out in this matter? Ask yourself how a government corporation can be in business in contest with the people who voted them in? Ask yourself who this Australian government and Australian parliament are? Our Commonwealth of Australia Constitution Act 1900 (UK) only recognizes the Parliament of the Commonwealth."

There are tens of thousands of case of government abuse against Australians, well concealed and with little interest to the media. Australians *"flicked off, one by one .... with tactics of harassment and attrition rather than head-on battles, by those whose purpose is to advance the principles of socialism via gradualist and reformist, rather than revolutionary means.* By those who have sworn an oath before God to Australians who voted and placed their trust in them, to protect and serve them.

Here are just a few cases from Queensland and NSW for your information:

A Queensland man was prosecuted by an officer of the State for cutting native tea tree to feed his starving livestock in this time of severe drought. The Warrant to Enter executed by the public officials of the State was not for his property but was for a property approximately 17 kilometres away. The District Court Judge stated that the man had purchased the property in the 1980s in fact he had never owned that property. Cost of remediation: A\$350,000.

Another Queensland man was prosecuted by an officer of the State for repairing severe erosion on a watercourse on his property by filling the degraded areas in with dead and dying black wattle and other vegetation and weeds which were of no value to the livestock as a food source. He then covered the vegetation with soil and replanted the areas with pasture grass. Fine: A$27,559.25

A Queensland couple in their 60s were long-term lychee farmers, using regulation low-voltage electricity structures to deter common fruit bats, while obeying all necessary legislation. A university lecturer, with a fondness for bats, complained to the Environmental Defenders Office EDO, who instituted legal proceedings. The farm was raided by police, who went through every cupboard and drawer in the house, including the family's underwear drawers, ostensibly searching for paperwork and dead bats. The bat protection was removed and within one week, the entire orchard and farming enterprise had been destroyed by bats. The couple have had no income for 4 years and are unable to access Government financial support while the case is ongoing.

And another Queenslander, who dug a huge dam on his property with the view of supplying free water to a nearby retirement village in exchange for future accommodation. The Department of Lands Queensland refused him the right to fill the dam, and ordered him to pump the water out of the dam when necessary.

Mrs Burns is a Queensland lady in her late 60s who wanted to develop 23 acres and sell it off in order to build a home for her retirement. Most of the land surrounding her property had been developed with the exception of a parcel that had a restricted animal order over it for the Mahogany Sugar Glider. Mrs Burn's land had been checked previously and was not included. At this time, she was refused the right to develop in case the animals wanted to visit her land. Judge White of the Planning and Environment Court in Cairns stated, *"I just find this astounding. Soviet Russia would be proud of these laws."* Yet he upheld them.

A Warwick couple applied for permission to extend decking and received it. They notified council who did not come to inspect it. A year later, Council contacted them wanting to know who gave them permission to build and demanded it be pulled down. The couple protested, police came with a warrant, the owner was arrested, now faces a A$125,000 fine and/or 5 years in jail. After high level complaints about the police treatment, the couple have had their computers bugged, they have been followed and returned home to find an attempt had been made to destroy the decking, with drill holes, piers knocked askew and etc. They received 3 different copies of the same Court transcript, none of which matched their witnesses versions.

A Queensland lady bought 18 acres and received Council permission to move a house to the land, providing she put a veranda around it. She moved the house and lodged a DA for the veranda. Since Christmas 2006, she has been both refused the DA and yet has received threats from the Council for not having the veranda finished. Her land is adjacent to a large development in which her local Council has an involvement. She finds gates left open, tyre shredding devices in her driveway etc. She believes she is being forced off her land.

In NSW, a farming family cleared land adjacent to the protected Gwydir Wetlands. Their land was not protected and they had all necessary departmental permission. The Wilderness Society flew over the land taking photos and the EDO began legal proceedings. Both that farm and a property they owned in Queensland were raided and all farming operations on both properties were forcibly closed down. This story is still being used by the media and the Wilderness Society to point the finger at farmers re land clearing, even though the government themselves agreed this family had been given permission. Yet that family are now having to fight this issue legally, trying to recover their rights to farm. Note: the aerial photographs were digital, which are illegal to use in court.

A NSW family retired on a small holding in 2 portions. Being environmentally conscious, they were prepared to keep the land natural because of eagle eyries. Minerals were found on the property, right at the access between both properties and the owner was expected to allow ongoing truck access through his main acreage, and to forego his right to enter the second property. Local council passed the miner's DA before any financial negotiations had begun, and the owners were told to agree or the Warden's Court would decide for them. The Warden's Court is specifically for mining issues.

A farming family had a portion of creek through their property, where a rock bar had become exposed and is spearing the water into soft soil on the banks, causing very considerable erosion. After discussion with the local Catchment Management officers, they were told that the "creek had the right to do whatever it wanted." These same officers, from the same government organization, entered into a scheme with the farmer's neighbour to fence off the creek to a distance of 40 metres from the watercourse, on the family's land, without any discussion with them whatsoever. Needless to say, the CM officers were informed of the rules of trespass.

A Queensland man purchased mangrove infested land frontage on Morton Bay many years ago. In recent years, he attempted to build a retirement home on it, however was refused the right. The local Council re-assessed all remaining blocks in this area down to flood zoning, rendering them unusable. The Valuer General re-valued each block down to A$1,000, although most blocks were carrying rates of well over that amount. Many people therefore defaulted on their rates and lost their blocks of land. Yet, all of these blocks had land beside them with houses that had been built before the new environmental laws were created, all with minimal or no flood problems.

Peter Spencer at 61 years of age, spent 52 days on a hunger strike, chained 10 metres on top of a wind tower at his Alpine property "Saarahnlee" near Cooma in NSW. He was protesting about the loss of his land rights after the Federal Government declared his land a carbon sink under the Native Vegetation Act in order to achieve its Kyoto targets. As a result, Peter Spencer was unable to use or develop his land, rendering it useless. Under the Australian Constitution, if the Commonwealth wants to acquire a person's property, it must do so on just terms, ie pay fair compensation. Peter Spencer's property use-rights were confiscated along with his livelihood. Despite 200 Court appearances, Peter Spencer has been denied compensation. Mr Spencer is one of many casualties of the reappropriation of an asset from an individual to the State and by the State, without payment.

In February, Peter Spencer could not meet his financial commitments and was evicted from his property. **Peter Spencer is now the spokesman for thousands of Australian farmers. He is demanding the Australian Government pay fair compensation to him and all Australians whose property rights were taken without compensation. He has demanded a Royal Commission into the way governments acquired their property rights. A well contrived conspiracy, deliberately intended to, and did, subvert the constitutional protection against the unjust acquisition of property.**

Faced with Peter Spencer's hunger strike, the Federal Government blamed State Governments. Although they sponsored the acquisition of his property, Peter Spencer can't sue the Commonwealth because, even though they acquired the benefit for their purposes, and are constitutionally liable to pay just compensation, they didn't actually do the deed themselves. It was deemed that he could not sue the State Government because they aren't legally liable to pay for it, as under the State Constitution there is no provision for just terms. The Commonwealth argues in the High Court that the Constitution was not intended to protect against forced acquisitions of property by the executive arm of Government. **From June 2007 till 1 Sept 2010 Peter Spencer has had to fight for his right to legal recourse** and finally at the unanimous discretion of seven High Court Judges, they granted Mr Spencer special leave to appeal and allowed the appeal with costs for him to take his case to the High Court of Australia. The cost to Peter and his legal team, the time invested in 200 court appearances to achieve the right to go to court, the loses of livelihood to so many Australians who could not afford or endure the arduous trip Peter has had to suffer and ultimately what this case will mean not just to Peter but to every Australia remains to be seen. The dishonesty of the government's argument is breathtaking because if it is accepted, it will make the idea of private property constitutionally limited or rather, meaningless.

According to the Opposition, there are approximately 30,000 farmers affected by this legislation. The Federal Government cannot afford to compensate these farmers as estimates run into billions of dollars. Mr Spencer personifies the frustration held and injustice suffered by so many people in regional Australia who have had to pick up Mr Rudd's tab for the price of Australia meeting its Kyoto obligations. Farmers like Mr Spencer and his family have had their lives ruined. Anecdotal evidence is that many have committed suicide. It's up to all Australians to fight for Peter Spencer's rights and thus the rights of all Australians, to **stop the land grab and *"turn back the tide of corruption"*, as Father Frank Brennan clearly warns us.**

The ruling government parties at the time, Liberal Federal and State Labor, initiated oppression against our most vulnerable but yet our most vital sector of our community, while the Oppositions, Labor Federal and

Liberal State sat on their hands without protest, to the ultimate benefit of the current Labor Federal government and its globalization focus. Were both the State Liberal and Federal Labor Opposition parties negligent, or uninformed, or tricked, or were they in collaboration with their government opponents? In any of these scenarios, this is the clearest example of how the party system is no longer a reliable form of government in Australia. Not only do both major parties fail to stop ramped corruption but they are at the very seat of it, as the most fundamental instigators of corruption in this country. All combining to further the process started by Gough Whitlam, whose role as the Grand-Poobah of the Fabian Society in Australia, included upholding the society's ethic of *"the extinction of private property in land . . ."*

From John Howard's crafty hand, he (perhaps inadvertently) made Kevin Rudd the winner with the Kyoto Protocol. All Australians should understand that the Commonwealth (both sides of the political party system) are implicated up to their necks in what it blames on its accomplices, the States and we should be demanding a Royal Commission into this devious and appalling abuse, see the Petition at our website. This unconstitutional device, this perverse loop-hole was relied on to rob of fair compensation all of those persons affected by this unprecedented case of massive governmental theft, even though the basis of the acquisition, ie greenhouses gases, remains flawed as to accuracy. **If you think you're immune and your property rights are safe because you're not a farmer, think again, everything in Australia starts and finishes with the farmer.**

For the success of a Single World Government there are two requirements:

1. Money – A Carbon Emissions Trading Scheme (if that fails, increased tax) to reduce us to poverty while empowering others, and
2. An International Treaty with severity for non conforming to a Single World Government, to be signed:

1. A Carbon Emissions Trading Scam – It's A Tax On Everything!

There has, and always will be climate change. It's a fact of life. What is in dispute is whether climate change/global warming is caused by humans (AGW – anthropogenic global warming). The science is unproven with over 31,400 scientists signing a petition against the theory of manmade climate change. Many academics, high profile scientists and environmentalists such as David Bellamy, Patrick Moore (the founder of Greenpeace), Professor Bob Carter (former Professor of Earth Scientists and Palaeontologist, Marine Geologist and environmental scientist), Professor Ian Plimer, PhD (Professor of Geology, School of Earth and Environmental Sciences, University of Adelaide and Emeritus Professor of Earth Sciences, University of Melbourne) and William Kinninmouth (head of Australia's National Climate Centre between 1986 and 1998) just to name a few, have spoken publicly against human induced climate change.

As the global warming hysteria grew into religious proportions, those who dared question AGW were branded heretics and 'Flat Earthers'. This did not stop the scepticism and global warming remains unproven, especially in lighted of the leaked emails from East Anglia and the data now discredited from the IPCC. The earth is actually cooling and the fear campaign has transformed or switched from global warming into climate change. Increased carbon dioxide has being blamed for an increase in global temperatures, polar ice caps melting, polar bears drowning, islands sinking and oceans rising in the next 50 years by 20 feet. Never is the finger pointed at "Sun Spots" and perhaps with the deluge of water over Australia of recent times, we may benefit from this "climate change" to enjoy lush pasters which were once desert, if the resources are put into capturing this vital resource.

All this hysteria was generated with Al Gore's film, 'Inconvenient Truth' – the film Mr Justice Burton from the High Court in the UK ruled that schools could show to children, as long as it was accompanied by guidance, giving the other side of the argument. The Judge said that nine statements in the film were not supported by mainstream scientific consensus. Al Gore, the architect of the Emissions Trading Scheme and institutions such as Goldman Sachs, stand to make trillions of dollars through carbon trading fees.

No media outlet has clearly identified where this whole fiasco started. Margaret Thatcher, newly installed as the first woman prime minister of a first world country, needed something to build her government on. Mining strikes were crippling Britain, people dying from the cold. The government wanted to bring in nuclear power, but the people were very wary of this. So a way was found to make coal a more dangerous energy source, hence the global warming, carbon emissions propaganda was resurrected from the work of one 19th century scientist. Government money established a research centre and succeeding governments, both in Britain and worldwide saw the advantage in a new 'industry' that would create a massive money source. Add the Green element, and the stage is set for a massive attack on all private enterprise and ownership.

The new carbon credit market is a virtual repeat of the shoddy commodities-market trading, except it has one new twist: If the plan goes forward as expected, the rise in prices will be government mandated. Brokers won't even have to rig the game as governments will have done it for them. If the US or Australian Labor government bill passes, there will be limits for coal plants (concessions for perhaps favorable trading partners in China), utilities, natural-gas distributors and numerous other industries on the amount of carbon emissions (aka greenhouse gases) they can produce per year. If the companies go over their allotment, they will be able to buy "allocations" or credits from other companies that have managed to produce fewer emissions. President Obama conservatively estimates that about US$646 billion worth of carbon credits will be auctioned in the first seven years. One of his top economic aides speculates that the real number might be twice or even three times that amount.

The feature of this plan that has special appeal to speculators is that the "cap" on carbon will be continually lowered by the government, which means that carbon credits will become more and more scarce, and more and more valuable or expensive as each year passes. Which means that this is **a brand new commodities market where the main commodity to be traded (hot air) is guaranteed to rise in price over time based on nothing tangible**. This is no different to Fractional Reserves ie the creation of 9 times the value of the gold but even more lucrative as it is based on air. The volume of this new market will be upwards of a trillion dollars annually. As a comparison, the annual combined revenues of all electricity suppliers in the US total US$320 billion.

Goldman Sachs (the masters of the sub-prime fiasco and inflated oil and other commodities markets) wants this bill. The plan is (1) to get in on the ground floor of paradigm shifting legislation, (2) make sure that they are the profit making slice of that paradigm and (3) make sure the slice is a big slice. Goldman started pushing hard for cap-and-trade long ago, but things really fired up last year when the firm spent US$3.5 million to lobby climate issues. One of their lobbyists at the time was Patterson, now the US Treasury chief of staff. Back in 2005, when Hank Paulson was chief of Goldman, he personally helped author the bank's environmental policy, a document that contains some surprising elements for a firm that in all other areas has been consistently opposed to any sort of government regulation. Paulson's report argued that "voluntary action alone cannot solve the climate change problem." A few years later, the bank's carbon chief, Ken Newcombe insisted that cap-and-trade alone won't be enough to fix the climate problem and called for further public investments for research and development. Which is convenient, considering that Goldman made early investments in wind power (it bought a subsidiary called Horizon Wind Energy), renewable diesel (it is an investor in a firm called Changing World Technologies) and solar power (it partnered with BP Solar), exactly the kind of deals that will prosper if the government forces energy producers to use cleaner energy. As Paulson said at the time, "We're not making those investments to lose money."

The bank owns a 10 percent stake in the Chicago Climate Exchange, where the carbon credits will be traded. Moreover, Goldman owns a minority stake in Blue Source LLC, a Utah based firm that sells carbon credits of the type that will be in great demand if the bill passes. Nobel Prize winner Al Gore, who is intimately involved with the planning of cap-and-trade, started up a company called Generation Investment Management with three former executives from Goldman Sachs Asset Management, David Blood, Mark Ferguson and Peter Harris. What is their business? Investing in carbon offsets. There's also a US$500 million Green Growth Fund set up by a Goldmanite to invest in green-tech . . . the list goes on and on. This will be a market bigger than the energy futures market. Note: Futures Markets are like betting on something that might happen, e.g. that there will be a bumper wheat crop etc. Cap-and-trade, as envisioned by Goldman, is really just a carbon tax structured so that private interests collect the revenues and brokers get their commissions on every deal.

The push by the Australian Labor government for a carbon tax saw the then Opposition Leader, Malcolm Turnbull side with the Labor government in pursing this tax. It would seem that Mr Turnbull's interest remains with Goldman Sachs, paid with the small price of the leadership of the Liberal government.

Instead of simply imposing a fixed government levy on carbon pollution and forcing unclean energy producers to pay for the mess they make, cap-and-trade will allow a small group of greedy grubbing Wall Street "white collar pigs" to turn yet another commodities market into a private tax collection scheme. This is worse than the "Global Financial Crisis" bailout, as it allows the bank to seize taxpayer money before it's even collected. If it's going to be a tax, shouldn't Washington or Canberra or any other government set the tax and collect it? But no, Wall Street will set the tax for the world and Wall Street will collect the tax and keep the money for their white collar purposes while destroying the blue collar society, irreparably.

It is said that Cap-and-trade is going to happen. Or, if it doesn't, something like it will. The moral is the same as for all the other bubbles that Goldman helped create from 1929 to 2009 In almost every case, the very same bank that behaved recklessly for years, weighing down the system with toxic loans and predatory debt and accomplishing nothing but massive bonuses for a few bosses, has been rewarded with mountains of virtually free money and government guarantees while the actual victims in this mess, ordinary taxpayers and superannuation funds are the ones paying. Was global warming ever an issue?

In 2003 Stephen McIntyre, a Toronto minerals consultant and amateur mathematician, and Ross McKitrick, an economist at Canada's University of Guelph, jointly published a critique of the hockey stick analysis. Their conclusion: Michael Mann's work was riddled with "*collation errors, unjustifiable truncations of extrapolation of source data, obsolete data, geographical location errors, incorrect calculations of principal components, and other quality control defects.*" Once these were corrected, the Medieval warm period showed up again in the data. This should have produced a healthy scientific debate. Instead, as the Journal's Antonio Regalado reported, "*Mr. Mann tried to shut down debate by refusing to disclose the mathematical algorithm by which he arrived at his conclusions. All the same, Mr. Mann was forced to publish a retraction of some of his initial data, and doubts about his statistical methods have since grown*". Statistician Francis Zwiers of Environment Canada (a government agency) notes that Mr. Mann's method "*preferentially produces hockey sticks when there are none in the data.*" Other reputable scientists such as Berkeley's Richard Muller and Hans von Storch of Germany's GKSS Center essentially agree. <eastangliaemails.com/emails. php?page=1 hockeystick>

This did not stop the scepticism and global warming remains unproven, especially in lighted of the leaked emails from East Anglia and the data now discredited from the

IPCC. On 20 November 2009 emails and other documents, apparently originating from with the Climate Research Unit (CRU) at the University of East Anglia were released.

The authenticity of these emails has been confirmed by most of the relevant parties including the CRU at University of East Anglia and many of the authors. These emails contain some quite surprising and even disappointing insights into what has been happening within the climate change scientific establishment. Worryingly, this same group of scientists is very influential in terms of economic and social policy formation around the subject of climate change. A full list of emails appears on this website <eastangliaemails.com/index.php>

When scientific evidence showed that the earth is actually cooling, the fear campaign was transformed or switched from global warming into climate change. Increased carbon dioxide is blamed for an increase in global temperatures, polar ice caps melting, polar bears drowning, islands sinking and oceans rising in the next 50 years by 20 feet. These hypotheses are suspect to say the least as the number of polar bears is increasing and the sea ice is thick enough to recently trap 50 ships off the coast of Sweden.

Two years ago the Intergovernmental Panel on Climate Change (IPCC) issued a benchmark report that was claimed to incorporate the latest and most detailed research into the impact of global warming. A central claim was the world's glaciers were melting so fast that those in the Himalayas could vanish by 2035. Scientists behind the warning have admitted that it was based on a news story in the 'New Scientist', a popular science journal, published eight years before the IPCC's 2007 report. An article published in the Times Online dated 17 January 2010 stated that *"a warning that climate change will melt most of the Himalayan glaciers by 2035 is likely to be retracted after a series of scientific blunders by the United Nations body that issued it"*.

It has also emerged that the 'New Scientist' report was itself based on a short telephone interview with Syed Hasnain, a little-known Indian scientist then based at Jawaharlal Nehru University in Delhi. Hasnain has since admitted that the claim was "speculation" and was not supported by any formal research. If confirmed it would be one of the most serious failures yet seen in climate research. The IPCC was set up precisely to ensure that world leaders had the best possible scientific advice on climate change.

Professor Murari Lal, who oversaw the chapter on glaciers in the IPCC report, said he would recommend that the claim about glaciers be dropped: *"If Hasnain says officially that he never asserted this, or that it is a wrong presumption, than I will recommend that the assertion about Himalayan glaciers be removed from future IPCC assessments."* <www.timesonline.co.uk/tol/news/environment/article6991177.ece>

In comparison to the Y2K bug scam (where billions of dollars were also spent), the threat of anthropogenic global warming/climate change is emerging to be the biggest scam in history. Information is emerging on a daily basis that debunks many of the wild claims that have scared people across the globe. In this state of anxiety, people looked to their Governments to 'do something' – they are willing to accept anything that will stop the catastrophe of the world disintegrating in the next 10 years. The Australian Government has taken the opportunity to capitalise on this fear with a vigorous pursuit for the introduction of an ETS and uses data from the discredited IPCC as a basis for action on climate change, despite Dr Phil Jones' stunning admission that there has been no global warming: "*Dr Phil Jones, the academic at the centre of the 'Climategate' affair, whose raw data is crucial to the theory of climate change, has admitted that he has trouble 'keeping track' of the information . . . The data is crucial to the famous 'hockey stick graph' used by climate change advocates to support the theory. Professor Jones also conceded the possibility that **the world was warmer in medieval times** than now – suggesting global warming may **not be a man-made phenomenon**. And he said that for the past 15 years **there has been no 'statistically significant' warming.**"*

Can you see a conflict of interest in any government supporting such a scam over the interests of their citizens and the development of their country? Carbon trading profits aside, what is disputed is that an Emissions Trading Scheme (ETS) will stop pollution by decreasing levels of Carbon Dioxide (C02). **Carbon dioxide is essential to life on earth with 70% coming off the world's oceans,** dwarfed only by the emissions from volcanoes (can't imagine God paying for carbon credits), however our children are being taught in schools that it's the bogeyman of climate change. That it's a threat to the environment and if we don't act immediately, the planet won't survive. **When a problem of physics becomes an issue of ideology, it has more to do with ideology than physics – scare tactics used to strip assets, starve and enslave citizens based on the ideologies of elite organisations.**

The ETS is set to be a tax on energy and will affect electricity and petrol prices resulting in higher prices for everything produced using electricity and transported by road. For Australia, in its first five years, the ETS will cost Australian coal A\$5 billion and the gold industry A\$850 million respectively. Australian beef producers will be slugged A\$450 million dollars a year on slaughtered cattle, in addition to the costs they will bear through their own farm inputs. Those additional costs will be highest on power, fuel and fertilizer, but will also be included in everything that is manufactured in Australia and used on a farm.

The effects on prices will change and will drive many industries offshore adversely affecting our exports further than suffered today. These increases will lead to a higher cost of living and ultimately increased interest rates, pushing struggling families onto the streets or reliant on the almost nonexistent government housing, if they are lucky to secure these homes, with demand unable to be met today. The obscenity is that an ETS will not change the temperature of the globe or even reduce pollution.

To get a deeper perspective: Major cities constitute 2% of the worlds surface and 41% of emissions comes from this 2% – while Australia represents less than .02% of total world emissions and it is hardly a reason to impose billions of dollars in undue taxes on us. Harsh as it may sound, most third world countries consist of people who burn wood to cook their meals and due to their sheer massive numbers are greater polluters than we could ever be. Therefore, if there were any logic to this imposition, it is wrongly placed on Australians, Americans or most democratic countries.

The Rudd Labor Government stated that the majority of people want an ETS but this is not true (any untruth is a lie), as the vast majority of people don't even understand what it is. This was yet another Rudd mentor designed statement to create the illusion of positive support, directed at people who could be persuaded to swing Labor's way ie they are undecided who to vote for, and towards those who have been bought off with stimulus (free lunch) payments. Australians don't need or understand the ramifications of an ETS. **Senator Barnaby Joyce, Leader of the Nationals in the Senate, on** 13th October 2009 stated *"A survey on the Emissions Trading Scheme (ETS) to establish what percentage of people actually understood what an ETS was. Based on a few simple questions, such as 'What is your understanding of an ETS', 91.5% of respondents did not understand how an ETS works.*

The Labor Government says that the majority of people want an ETS but how can this be the case when the vast majority of people don't even understand what it is? This is part of the dishonesty behind this new revenue raising campaign. The ETS for all intents and purposes will be the Extra Tax System and a new Australian tax will not change the temperature of the globe. There is something definitely fraudulent about delivering a guilt trip that appeal to the greater anxieties of the community and then implying that the remedy to these anxieties is a new tax when you know, categorically, that the new tax will deliver nothing but revenue to the treasury and commissions to the brokers. The majority of people have no idea how it works because it has never been properly explained to Australians. The ETS's affect on prices will change the buying and supplying patterns of our economy. In fact that is the underlying principle of the plan."

Constitutionally, there is no such jurisdiction as Environment. This is a jurisdiction of this new "republic" of Australia government. Being used, as mentioned previously to 'enslave' the people and their assets. In fact, under the Commonwealth of Australia Constitution Act (UK) 1900, not one International Treaty, most particularly in this area, should have been signed without a referendum of the people, because each and every one of them removes a "right" of at least 1 person, on behalf of the many. That is the soft definition of communism. Are these legislative controls therefore legitimate over the rights of the People? Only the High Court can establish that lawfully and they have yet to be asked this question.

Question: If the Rudd Labor government truly has no hidden agenda and only has the best interests of the Australian people at heart, why hasn't a comprehensive paper been produced ie "The Plan", or debated the details of the ETS as Rudd was invited to by Tony Abbott, and then give the **Australian people a chance to vote in a referendum**, as it's the Australian people who stand to be affected the most when he takes up a higher posting on the World Government.

Answer: You don't ask the question if you know the answer will not be in your favour or against yours and your backers' objectives.

Out of the 44 referendums, the people have only given a Yes to 8. Never have the people voted to allow government to assume more power – the Yes's only assenting to 'house-keeping' issues. Most people do not realize that a No is as effectively lawful as a Yes – indicating that things must NOT be changed. Government in Australia very clearly ignore that fact, stating quite erroneously that they are given a Mandate when elected to do . . . . whatever they want.

The ETS is the single most salient example of what could possibly divide our nation and create revolt against government, similar to the current US "Tea Party Movement"

The Labor Government's propaganda is aided by a complicit or perhaps compromised media who are unable or unwilling to scrutinize the effects on Australia if the Rudd/Wong ETS is introduced. The Government's lack of public debate on the ETS issue is bordering on totalitarianism and exposes the dishonesty behind the introduction of the carbon tax. It is unethical to cause anxiety to deliver a guilt trip that appeals to the greater anxieties of the community and imply that the remedy is a new tax. This would be the ultimate "white collar takers" demise of the "blue collar maker" but with no one here left to feed those who still have a few bucks. Australians must understand that if they are employed in any sector affected by the ETS, their jobs are in jeopardy. The Unions have been strangely silent when it's their members whose jobs are at risk – it's time they forgot their leftist ideology and started to think about Australian workers. The only way Rudd & Co would back down on this issue is in facing an election, when all of issues of poor governance, incompetence and corruption are exposed in defeating them.

As stated by The Fabian Society's Grand-Poobah, Gough Whitlam at the sacking of his Labor government by the Governor General Sir John Kerr in November 1975 *"Well may we say, God save the Queen because nothing will save the Governor General"* and may we say, **"God save us if we don't put on a Royal Commission into all of the activities of the Labor government and the cohorts of adverse UN Treaties and those who are running our current inept system of government".**

The Labor Government's pursuit of the ETS is based on false, misleading and deceptive information and these motives amount to treason against Australia, still a punishable crime. Since April 2009 the Labor government stayed silent about the ETS. George Orwell wrote that *"During times of universal deceit, telling the truth becomes a revolutionary act."* The Australian Constitution is not only under threat, it has been undermined or rather sabotaged, yet why has there been no Opposition Government at either State or Federal levels oppose these violations? They have both been party to this when in government, and by abstaining from action today.

Thomas Jefferson once said, **"When injustice becomes law, resistance becomes duty."** It is every Australian's right and duty to be proactive because as Plato said: *"The price good men pay for indifference to public affairs is to be ruled by evil men".*

There was nothing at Copenhagen nor will there be at any subsequent venue to benefit Australia or any other developed country. Measures to reduce pollution must be made locally by each country individually, as global enforcement is as practical as changing the mindset of those who have alternative objectives and mindsets.

There was to be a signing of another International Treaty at Copenhagen, the signing to a Single World Government under the disguise of global warming but because of the slow waking up and of citizens of democratic countries, this has been deferred. As the leader of still the greatest Democratic country on this planet today, the USA, President Obama has no business agreeing to any such treaty, nor does any democratic country that values *"the right to freedom, liberty and the pursuit of happiness"*.

I urge all readers to listen to the pod-cast of Alan Jones' interview with Lord Christopher Monckton on Radio 2GB called *"Is the Copenhagen treaty about creating a world government?"<www.2gb.com/index.php?Itemid=41&id=2&option=com_ podcasting&task=view >*

2. An International Treaty:

"Article VI taken with the Vienna Convention on the interpretation of international treaties. This means that an international treaty prevails over your Constitution." – Lord Monckton's interview with Glenn Beck on USA Radio <unfccc.int/resource/ docs/2009/awglca7/eng/inf02.pdf>

Australia a signatory to Article VI. Had Kevin Rudd implemented the ETS or if his successor does and signs the Copenhagen Treaty, Australia will be a signatory to a Treaty without an **exit strategy for countries to opt out of, if signatories discover the Treaty is detrimental to their country and there will be no voting rights.**

This is the epitome of a Communist dictatorship and that of elite association on the global scale sought for centuries, as the world has never witnessed. In effect, it will be the end of democracy, giving complete control of our Constitution, our rights and our very lives to an alien government. This is madness like never before and at the hand of those with the supremacy egos of the greatest tyrants this world has witnessed and their money to enforce it.

Developed countries such as Australia, NZ, the US and Canada will have to compensate third world countries like Zimbabwe, Somalia and Columbia. Not loans or financial aid to help build their nations, but massive monetary gifts to their corrupt governments. Compensation to countries like India and financially booming China!

Western democratic countries already greatly contribute resources to third world countries and extend loans but the imposition of fines or taxes that would be placed on democracies by such treaties and agreements will see all democracies turned into third world countries – is also equality? Why should *countries in* Africa be "compensated? Hasn't the world thrown enough money at Africa and African governments with no result but to feed corrupt governments? The African nations have seen an opportunity to cash in on this madness and are lining up to take the cream off the top of the developed world's cake. There is no proviso in this Treaty that states these countries must have to have good human rights records so it'll be business as usual for despots like Mugabe.

There are many other treaties and agreements, with one that ties it up neatly – the United Nations' **"Agenda 21".** Private property and single family homes are deemed non-sustainable. Cap and Trade (ETS) is clearly outlined in Agenda 21, as you may be aware. If this passes, it gives a government which is not ours, almost full control over our properties and our country. This Government will determine if your house meets energy standards, which it decides from one moment to the next, what is acceptable to them so you can re-sell your home. This is one insidious slippery slope. Yes, your name will still be on the deed, but the choices on how you live in your house will not be left up to you. You get to pay the bills, you have to pay the taxes and you will have to pay the fines levied against you as the Government starts handing out violation notices. Your house will become your nightmare! Your electricity, air conditioning, heating, water, insulation, roof, windows, doors, etc., will all be subject to new regulations. Look it up: there are hundreds of sites – no secrets and no conspiracies, remember you're judging. As usual, we are not going to have the choice or vote to agree, particularly because our Local governments have already done that. That is, without any consent of the people, Local Governments have signed agreements and committed to the **United Nation's International Council for Local Environmental Initiatives** "ICLEI" – read further, you'll be shocked at what is happening while you're at work so you can pay your local government to go forth and wreck our lives.

For all of the reasons covered, it supports that governments have caused the problems which have led to our economic slowdown (meltdown in the US) or "World Financial Crisis". On its current course this could led to a pending depression and to the planned demise of our society. From shunning responsibility in deregulating banks and big business; from not regulating or providing adequate fair trading; to removing tariffs; to failing to act in the interest of the people for the long term and in being more concerned about the goings on in our neighbours backyards than in our own. One example: We (in Pacifica) have always had a thriving meat industry, we have enough to feed ourselves and sustain a very viable export market, so why would we import meat from any country, let alone countries known to have "Mad Cow" disease"? Inept management or better buying prices won't cut it this time! The reasons are obvious: Meet the bizarre commitment to reduce emissions under the Kyoto Protocol and with the same bullet, financially benefit other countries from our destroyed beef industry?

Australians can no longer profess to have a government by the people for the people. In ever increasing numbers, Australians are appealing to Queen

Elizabeth II for her help in recovering our rights and our country and she is preparing to appeal to the Privy Court, we can only pray that she will act quickly and while there is a way back.

I used to be in favour of a Republic for Australia but now I bet many Americans wish they were not, and many Europeans would prefer that their country never joined the European Union.

Many European and Baltic countries continue to be on the verge of civil revolution, while countries such as Greece continue to defy bankruptcy. The US Patriotic Tea Party Movement are well aware of their governments plans for the North American Union to be modelled on the now fragmenting European Union. We are witnessing people in once buoyant economies going hungry, they're angry with their governments for the lack of jobs, as the jobless rate increases to more than 20% in some countries. Discontentment rises and upheaval replaces harmony with devastation that comes with unemployment, homelessness and hunger. It was hard to hide the distension of demonstrators at the G20 Summit Meeting in London in April 2009 Anger culminates in resentment for government failure to protect them from corporate greed and for the lack of work, while government ministers and corporation giants receive tens of millions of dollars for their negligence and the lack of compassions, kindness and good government towards their citizens.

Daily headlines read "Gang Wars on the rise" and "Crime Wave hits". Is this any different to the regime of Czarism prior 1917 and then the collapse of communism in Russia some 70 years on? Do we need to relive Russia's experiment over the next 70 years, if we still exist? The G-20 approved US$100 billion towards fixing the world financial crisis but only US$23 billion of the required US$30 billion was to be provided to help feed the 963 million who are starving in third world countries, while Western governments must seriously consider the ramifications for their own people who are now moving into the hunger sector. When a desperate unemployed Dutch security officer about to be evicted from his home with nothing left to live for, makes a shocking international statement with his life in wanting to drive into the Dutch Royal family's vehicle killing himself, it is truly time for us all to take stock of the entire situation. This is a statement, a wake-up call we must all listen to. It is the voice of the unrepresented, powerless poor, who are suffering and none of us want to be in that situation but there are thousands like him in Australia, America and other once sustainable nations today, and their numbers are growing.

Civil unrest can lead to uprisings and then chaos, not counterproductive, but destructive. For example: It starts with resentment of a A$1.6 million salary paid to the CEO of a profitable company, say Pacific Brands. Each worker earned less than 2% of what the CEO took home, then the decision to terminate 1,850 jobs to give production jobs to China and thus a greater profit to Pacific Brands and perhaps justifying bonuses for the CEO. This is seen as a total betrayal of those who have worked the business and created the value in it and then through to those of us who supported their products. Were there no Australian options offered by government?

No cost competitive factory premises with more cost effective environmentally friendly fuels, no competitive wage options which would have achieved a compromise for this profit driven enterprise to stay here and for the workers to receive a wage versus welfare?

Rather than government throwing into Pacific Brands an unconditional A$17 million those funds could have provided a relocation of that business (and others) to new more cost effective premises. Say in a semi-rural area, with an injection into re-establishing a frail semi rural town's infrastructure, improved rail transportation and with more competitive cost of housing and cost of living, we would all benefit. Work opportunities could have been taken up at more competitive rates of pay, versus retrenchments and unemployment benefits and for that industry to remain here as an asset to this nation. It's not too late, Pacific Brands may be gone but this gives rise to a new opportunity for the establishment of a like business. There is no reason why the Australian government does not invest funds into this same type of manufacturing, see section on Bank of Australia.

What starts out as a heated but peaceful demonstration (not unlike the Pacific Brands employees) can turn nasty with many other people joining the protest in solidarity. Tempers fly to civil unrest and contempt for authority, then if the big "R" (Recession) bites and hopefully doesn't becomes the big "D" (Depression), crime increases and laws are tightened. When we get revolt by hungry, desperate people wanting to survive, this is a revolution.

As productive work dries up, motivation will also dry up, and we could end up a third world welfare country. On this course, revolution against those empowered is inevitable. Against those who not only created the mess, but failed to act (now the bunkers are making sense?) It's no different to the French or Russian Revolution of yesteryear and the revolts in Thailand against their Prime Minister or the Fiji military takeover of government and thus media censoring. It's no different to the once flourishing Capitalistic Japanese society now contending with more than 1,000 citizens each month turning to and joining up the Communist Party, rather than starve. It's not necessarily those in the hot seats today who caused the demise of industry and adverse legislation but they are the office bearers seen not to be fixing the problems with their broken election promises but unable or won't deliver any fix-its on the horizon to their predecessors offences.

As history is continually being created and the cycle of human social evolution continues, it will be interesting to see of the United States, Russia and China who over the next 20 to 30 years will be classified as the world's Super Power, a title the Capitalist Democratic US and Communist Russia both shared in the mid 20th century, although their mode of government were both to the extremes.

Our success as a nation is based on our ability to adapt to our environment, to work in harmony with the land and each other and in understanding that the climate and environmental change is to the world, as the various levels of emotion, intellect and objectives are to each of us. While there are many adverse conditions and people throughout the world, it is our right and obligation to think and act locally. It is then with this stability that we can extend a stronger hand to other nations of the world. It will only be with this directive and attitude that will have the positive impact to achieve what Copenhagen or any treaty will always fail to do.

Growing Powers Diminish Our Rights –
No Right To Defend Ourselves & Guilty
Until Proven Innocent!

SELF PROCLAIMED GOVERN-MENT powers are increasingly pre-venting demonstrations. Like the unconstitutional intervention by authorities at Pine Gap and new government legislation will be introduced under the disguise of "National Security" to protect the government from the people. We are not so slowly witnessing the erosion and possible demise of our Democracy. While terror attacks are more than possible here and our laws do need to be tightened but we must not lose the perspective that more people die in car crashes each year than in terrorist attacks, but protecting our democratic rights are just as necessary under a Charter of Rights.

With the *"War on Terror"* we are not just witnessing the tightening of laws, which over the past 50 years reduced police powers, but now laws are heightened and seek extraordinary crossing of boundaries in diminishing our basic democratic rights. There are more people killed each year on our roads and from cancer than from terrorist, this has been an excessive exercise in social control. Strengthening powers for a perceived explosion of social tensions as the global economy remains very unstable and governments seek alternative agendas and I remind you of Father Brennan's earlier comments.

Here is just one case which highlights this erosion: Genargi Krasnow was the owner of a company K-Generation Pty Ltd. In 2005 he applied for a Liquor License. With the new laws, the South Australian government permitted the Commissioner of Police to intervene in the court proceedings and put forward "Criminal Intelligence" – evidence that the Liquor and Gambling Commissioner and the courts were required to keep secret.

From these amendments, evidence that neither the applicant nor his legal representative were entitled to see or challenge, evidence brought against him and that which was relied on to refuse him a licence. The presiding judge in the Licensing Court, Judge Rice described the secret procedure under the Act as *"odd"* as the judge and police conferred in private, in the absence of the applicant and he Stated, *"It seems to be draconian legislation . . . but that is what Parliament has said and I am stuck with it".* On the basis of *"Criminal Intelligence"* he ruled that Krasnov was *"not a fit or proper person to hold a licence".* This determination was upheld on the same basis by the High Court of Australia on 2 Feb 2009 with acknowledgement by Justice Gray that the secret process subverted the independence of the judicial branch of government in contravention of Chapter III of the Australian Constitution. The legislation forced the Licensing Court to *"act as an arm of the executive"* and dictated to the judiciary an unfair procedure that *"cuts deep into judicial integrity and independence".* It may have been correct that he be denied a Liquor License but for his inability to know why not or to be able to challenge any allegation against him has never been constitutional.

Non-democratically determined changes are cutting new roads into our civil rights and are expanding police powers throughout Australia, enabling the carrying out of "covert warrants" to secretly enter anyone's home for almost any reason. This is disguised under "anti terror laws" and with no Charter of Rights to protect the rights of the individual – the Human Rights Commission stands as our only advocates and thus each of us individually becomes more vulnerable. Citizens have no due process to change or amend our Constitution or legislation as this is at the hand of the government to initiate; nor are we able to remove inept government but to wait for the next vote; no due process against the State, yet we are still spun the yarn that the Judiciary is independent of the government, but truth is, only when it suits the government! Please bear this point in mind when you get to the section on One National Judicial System.

The notion that a court or any authority can deprive a person of the right to see any or all evidence against him, let-alone afford him the right to be able to challenge it, provides a cloak for the malicious, the misinformed, the meddlesome and the corrupt to destroy innocent lives. They can play the role of an undetected, unreliable, uncorrected informant but one who is relied on for the wrongful determination of litigation or court process based on perhaps false evidence or victimisation and persecution by government, police and any other security or government agency, no different to the KGB. Democracy has always prided itself on participating in fair trials and that an accused person is deemed innocent until proven guilty but this is changed. That is, the accused is deemed guilty and is not even afforded the opportunity to try and prove his innocence.

The Australian Taxation Office "ATO" has now been given the power to come into your home and cease documents and goods, if it is suspected you are withholding documents sought by the ATO – no court order required, just invasion of privacy and seizure of "evidence". It would seem that these powers of invasion would also enable notification to other government agencies of matters irrelevant to the ATO if the intruders had directives or perhaps to frame you on say money changing hands in a game of cards or if the ATO were to be the cloak for any government agency to trespass without a court warrant.

We are witnessing not just the erosion of democracy in Australia but a strike to the very heart of democracy. It is laying of the foundation for an authoritarian rule so transparent that we as individuals have no inalienable right to a fair hearing or trial in Australia today; no right to defend ourselves against any wrongful accusation and to not even know what we are being accused of – so how much more will draconian laws change against us in the future?

Censorship Begins – The Rudd Governments introduced new censorship laws, no doubt to be expanded. A new law came into effect on 1 October 2009 that will deliver a massive advantage to the Government of the day (both sides). Every newsletter must first be cleared by the Department of Finance before it is distributed by any member of parliament. This crackdown follows the Auditor-General's criticism of the A$300 million parliamentary entitlements scheme. The Rudd Government was accused of censoring any voter handouts which are critical of controversial programs run by the Rudd government, such as its A$42 billion economic stimulus package or the Emissions Trading Scam, yet not a peep from the Liberal Opposition! Why? They would benefit if they were to win a next election, so why would they stop it!

These new regulations mean that any ruling government of any political persuasion or those having the governments delegated authority by say, an International Treaty, will have the power to suppress full disclosure or free expression against any opponent – whether the opposition is a political party or anyone else. To expand on this, it would be just another flick of the pen to suppress the media and people individually and thus collectively. This perhaps start with the internet and innocently under say, stopping pornography but it would transgress into anything deemed to be adverse to government. What we now have in effect is that there is one rule for the Government (or no rules) and another for everyone else including our elected MPs. Australians will be denied access to the truth in an attempt to keep Australians in the dark and allow the government to do anything at their will (see the movie *"V for Vendetta" it is as a premonition of what may come, if we allow it*).

Words that have been blocked from MPs communications in the past month include: *"dreadful", disgraceful", "inept", "responsible for "mismanagement", "reckless", "guilty of incompetence" and "irresponsible".* NSW Senator Marise Payne was forced to black out offending words after she had printed 5000 newsletters criticizing the government's 'education revolution' for schools, claiming it was littered with examples of *"inept management"* that speak volumes for the financial *"mismanagement"* of the Rudd Government. Victorian MP Jason Woods has also had his newsletters censored.

Senator Ronaldson, Finance and Public Administration Legislation Committee, in Hansard said on Tuesday 20 October 2009 *"Oppositions are unable to use any language that appropriately attacks government policy, but government members – of whatever political persuasion – are able to extol the virtues of a government policy as long as they do not tag it with the requirement that someone should vote for the government on the back of that policy that is the real issue that we have here. Opposition MPs or Senators cannot use taxpayer money to distribute anything that is critical of the Government, even actual Hansard text has to be censored before being approved. Yet the Government, ALSO using taxpayer dollars, may extol the virtues of their own policies (which can rightly be called 'electioneering') without fearing the red pen of the censor. This is outright hypocritical."*

Free speech in 2010 is now limited to talk back radio, but for how long and if it is of interest to the station in the ratings war. Censorship continues to facilitate government's treatment of taxpayer's money, treating money as if it belongs to them and their party. The Rudd Labor government continued the threat to withhold billions of dollars from the States and seize key planning controls under their agenda for growth cities. In an address to the Business Council of Australia, Rudd said it was time his Government played a greater role in preparing the nation for 35 million people by 2049 This is despite an environmental study in the 1990s stating our population should never exceed 19 million because anything larger would destroy the environment forever. The Rudd Labor government's control over his own Government MPs is well documented as are his 'interests' in the daily activities of the Canberra Press Gallery, where he would send his staff to report on the stories of the day. If the news items were not considered to be in the Government's best interests, new 'announcements' were made to be included in the evening news thus deflecting attention from the real issues and concealing the truth. The media are very reluctant to report on anything detrimental to Rudd's government and this was reflected in the opinion polls where a huge majority of voters still think Rudd was doing a great job.

These censorship constraints and changes hide vital information from the public, to enable adversity to go undisclosed. Google are up in arms over China's censorship but how does Google handle the American Tea Party rallies, with Al Gore on their board of directors? Censorship by government is a first in our 220 years and demonstrates that what is left of an Australian democracy is under threat as it supports agendas of "Chinese Politics" and "Globalization", with the culmination suspected to be subject to the signing of a UN Treaty, disguised as "Climate Change". Kevin Rudd as Prime Minister was appointed as one of three 'negotiators' at the Copenhagen Climate Change conference, now deferred until after the next election or under pressure at the next convention in Mexico. Mr Rudd will continue to tilt his ambitions towards the UN Security Council with anticipated unprecedented concessions to corrupt African governments and others as the newly appointed Minister for Foreign Affairs and may I say God help us all.

Censorship worked to conceal Kevin Rudd's reluctance to join the boycott by other democracies of the United Nations' bizarre conference on racism, a *"festival of hate against Israel"* held in Geneva in April 2009. Rudd desperately wanted to secure a temporary seat on the United Nations Security Council where he would join countries who have betrayed the most basic of human rights. Countries who inflict racism, yet censorship conceals questions as to why Rudd has donated A$10 million, unaccountable taxpayer dollar, to corrupt African nations. Who approved the costs for Governor-General Quentin Bryce, Rudd's preferred representative as our "Head of State" who he deployed for a 19 day tour with her entourage to these same African nations to seek support for Rudd's nomination for a seat on the UN Security Council?

The Governor General, Ms Bryce, Australia's representative of Queen Elizabeth II under our Constitution is not supposed to be holding any position of a political nature, yet Rudd deployed her on "his" mission. It has now been revealed that the cost of Ms Bryce's African escapade to Australians taxpayers was more than A$700,000 This revelation came days after Parliament was told 30 of Ms Bryce's staff of 85 have quit since her appointment (while 8 of her Queensland staff quit when she became the Governor of Queensland). Mr Turnbull was not inspired but perhaps Mr Abbott will be, to investigate as to why such expenditure was possible for Rudd? Does the Labor government hold an open cheque book for such 'purposes' particularly when we have hundreds of thousands of homeless and unemployed and growing in this country?

If an adversarial party system is truly effective governance, then why doesn't the Opposition veto such extravagant and wasteful expenditure, especially in times of a "World Financial Crisis" which resulted in a world downturn to where poor "economic conditions" have seen thousands of Australians join the growing jobless and bankrupt, if not for the appeasement of the United Nations?

The UN held a conference in Geneva in April 2009 where there was a draft declaration that had been produced with its tirade of emphasises on the *"Sins of the West above those of the rest"* suggesting restrictions on free speech to save Islam from criticism. It was also blaming Colonialism for Third World dysfunction, for which it demands compensation. Only one country was singled out for denunciation – democratic Israel, which is accused of torture, collective punishment of Muslims, "apartheid" and "crimes against humanity".

Only one faith is singled out as needing protection from free speech – Islam, which should not be insulted *"through publication of offensive caricatures"* or as an association of terrorism and violence because a most disturbing phenomenon is the intellectual and ideological validation of Islamaphobia. The West is frowned on for allegedly "creating a hatred of Muslims" by taking steps to protect itself from the hatred of Muslim terrorists who have slaughtered so many innocent civilians in London, New York, Madrid, Mumbai, Lahore, Jerusalem, Baghdad, Bali, Nairobi and in their own countries. In fact, in recent decades the worst genocide and atrocities have been in Africa. The most savage terrorism has been launched by Islam, the worst ethnic cleansing has been in Africa and Asia and those most likely to kill for their faith, are Muslim. *"Certainly not all Muslims are homicide bombers but almost all homicide bombers, are in fact Muslims".*

Our then Foreign Minister Stephen Smith advised that our officials tried to improve the draft declaration but as the 2001 Durban meeting was *"an anti-Jewish, anti-Semitic harangue"* this was more of the same. Why would any "democratic" leader try so hard and at such moral and financial expense to win a seat and mollycoddle those scum bags? Where is the justification and what is the motivation and what would be the "initiation requirement to be imposed on Australians" in joining this unholy racist club? Labor Senator David Feeney and Family First's Senator Steve Fielding spoke against Australia's attendance. Senator Fielding said *"It seems the government's fanatical obsession with winning a seat on the* UN *Security Council has caused it to lose its moral compass".* Senator Feeney said *"I believe that Australia should give very serious consideration to what interests we would be serving by dignifying this conference with our presence".* In that pursuit Rudd broke the Howard government's policy and voted for two anti-Israel motions in the UN, a betrayal of our principles and a total insult to all of our democratic allies in a vote for the enemies of our freedoms. It seems apparent that Mr Rudd's ambitions are well beyond Australia to be "Kevin-11 UN Secretary General" or Chairman of the World Government.

I have heard the best, most passionate outspoken Australians speak up against an Australians Charter or Bill of Rights but I feel they have not taken into consideration the new laws which are in direct contravention of the Universal Bill of Rights 1948 Article 10 *"Everyone is entitled . . . . to a fair and public hearing"* and Article 11 *"Everyone is presumed innocent until proved guilty".* Our Constitution was established to protect us, but new laws through legislation are not always in the interest of the majority of Australians. For this reason assurances through a Charter of Rights to defend and protect us, is imperative.

Webster's dictionary defines Capitalism as: A system under which the production and distribution of goods and services are privately managed – ***Free Enterprise – not Free Trade***. A Capitalistic society is supposed to allow for and provide incentives to produce more and to the benefit of those who have invested time, money and effort. This is right and just, but only up until the want for more and more creates greed, resulting in many levels of crime by individuals or collectively under a business or government, based on inequality between people, this is beyond Free Enterprise.

Corruption and Greed comes in many forms and starts at the top, in providing and receiving funding or donations to political parties and this "leadership" works its way down the food chain. In many cases political "donations" are repaid with favourable consideration in allowing the donor to have an unfair advantage, often preventing fair trade practices and creating injustices through inequality to an industry or business over the interests of the majority of people. This is where the pursuit of money under the banner of Capitalism for any individual or an industry or a government party's business causes damages.

This is the one most destructive force against individuals or an entire society. Greed and ego are responsible for division in our society with improper financial budgets and deregulation of industry sectors. It leaves homeless people on the street and fails to address social problems which breeds gang mentalities and makes it unsafe to walk the streets in many western cities. Poor governance is what is responsible for unregulated freedom associated with Capitalism and therefore Capitalism has been blamed for the demise of morals and modesty [in many forms] and for the perversion of equality which is not in the interest of a decent society.

What Is Democratic Government?

TO ASSESS WHAT we need and what we want, we must clearly define and understand what we actually have. Webster's definition –

"Political" – having a fixed or regular system for the administration of government; relating to civil government and its administration; concerned in State affairs or national measures pertaining to a nation or State". This would not include any government's ability to deregulate any industry sector making that industry unaccountable and inequitable in its dealing, be it the banking industry or any industry, and

"Government" – is the exercise of political authority, direction and restraint over the actions of the inhabitants of communities, societies and States; the administration, management or executive of power of supervision; the mode or system according to which the legislative executive and judicial powers are vested and exercised". This does not deem that a party system is the only system available to the people, and

"Democracy" – is Government by the people; a form of government in which the supreme power is vested in the people and exercised by them or their elected agents . . . a State in which the supreme power is vested in the people and exercised directly by them rather than by their elected representatives; a State of society characterised by normal equality of rights and privileges; political or social equality.

This is why Australian government currently stipulates a compulsory requirement for Australians to vote. That is, you can never have any come back in that you didn't get a say as to who was democratically elected, irrespective of the determination or passing over of your (preference) vote to a major political party who you did not vote for.

A DEMOCRATIC GOVERNMENT is, by definition: **The supreme power of the people being vested in the people and exercised by the people in the administrative authority and direction in obtaining equality of rights and privileges for all of the people. What has evolved is the party system with its survival is its first objective but Government by the party for the party is not democracy, it is communism.**

Political parties in democracy are a mere invention – having become accepted over time, as history legitimises their unconstitutional existence while hiding the theories and agendas of faceless elite people in organisations.

Unfortunately this is not what the current system of government provides. What we have is something else, something politicians have transgressed to. So far, I have attempted to highlight some of the shortcoming and abuse of power by individuals and their party, but our constitutional rights, our equality and privileges for all of the people by the people – is no longer reflective of the essence and the intention of democracy. Democracy has been abused by individuals and corporations, facilitated by inept government in manipulating legislations, to enable those weak of character or with little moral fibre, to prioritise "profits before people" and thus profiteering at the expense of the majority of Australians. Excessive governments waste for ineffective and often detrimental function, with little if any accountability. Australia and most western democracies require a system that does not provide for any mechanism to facilitate government party priorities or ego related personal career agendas, in providing effective and efficient government, rather the merit of the individual and thus collective citizens through independence representation.

Debate on all issues is healthy and while Australia has been running an adversarial political party system, the close alignment of the parties and the many bureaucratic impositions, particularly pertaining to the many levels of government has seen politicians and their employees moving away from being our employees, to becoming our rulers. God forbid that we should end up with a dictator under an autocracy and find ourselves without there being any election system or even the requirement for our vote. With such a tight alignment between the two major parties in both Federal and State governments, who do you vote for? The devil you know or the devil you don't, or for perhaps an unknown, possible devil! You can get all excited about say the "Greens" and be hell bent on not voting for "Labor" or "Liberal" and it is this which gave the Greens a massive protest voting success in the 2010 elections. But the discontentment with the two party system only saw a vote for the "Greens" passed on to "Labor" as a preferential vote, same applies in voting for the Nationals, votes going to Liberal. That is, the party you may have particularly not wanted to vote for gets your vote, so you are the loser and your vote has been to the detriment of your wishes! This is not a democratic election. Your vote did not go to whom you wanted to receive it. In this event, the Greens!

◆ All preferential votes should be abandoned, not passed on by a losing person or party. Destroy the vote rather than pass it on to any person or party to whom the voter had not agreed to.

The irony is – that the disdain for party politics and politicians has led to the creation of so many new "parties" but individually we maintain a false fear of voting for an independent or a small party, in that they do not have the experience of the major parties.

As mentioned, from the Socialist, Communist, Republican, Democrats we now have Christian Democrats, Greens, Liberal, Labor, Nationals, Family First, One

Nation, Shooters, Smokers, Climate Change Sceptics, all "parties" and every so often, there is a new kid on the block. A party known as the "Citizens Electoral Council of Australia" (CECA) and all of these parties are singing a new/old song that we so desperately want not just to hear but to see implemented. They all purport that their objectives are based on sound financial planning and good government objectives and they all appoint local members for your choice. Imagine your vote reflects your support for a particular person and he is a member of say the Liberal government. That local member has been out canvassing for votes and you decide to give him your vote and he wins, but all of his promises come to nothing as they are not ultimately the direction of his party. That is, you might get the bloke you wanted but he is not able to deliver what he promised, is he a liar or just a puppet?

The "Greens" – such an unfortunate name, as it implies care, concern and the fight for the environment, but the farmers know better. They have a chant at their rallies: *"Green on the outside and red* (communist) *on the inside"* As the "Greens" are gaining ground their party policies are becoming apparent and they are known to many for their support of adverse UN Treaties and holding global ambitions as covered by Cory Bernardi 25 Aug 2010: *"The nature of the Greens' totalitarian agenda can be seen through a careful examination of their policies and party platform. Their support for global governance, manifested in the United Nations, includes a "stronger UN capable of dealing with threats to international peace and security." Given the Greens oppose every type of conflict except the 'just wars' mounted by radical eco-terrorists like the Sea Shepherd organisation, one must ask what benefit a stronger United Nations would be to their objectives? That is, unless the UN was entrusted to enforce some of their more interventionist treaties and agreements. Actually, that's exactly what the Green lobby wanted through the Copenhagen treaty. An unelected, unaccountable body was to be funded through the wealthy Western nations to act as the global policeman, judge and jury determining who could do what, where and when including one that trumps parental responsibility with government bureaucrats under the guise of 'children's rights'.*

The Convention on the Rights of the Child *treaty is part of an international plan to give children a long list of rights. It was implemented in 1989 and most nations, including Australia, are signatories to it. Some of the clauses in this treaty give rise to some concern. This includes* **the rights that give 'the government the ability to override every decision made by every parent if a government worker disagreed with the parent's decision.'** *Further, children would be able to seek a 'governmental review of every parental decision with which the child disagreed.'*

Teaching children Christianity in schools would be banned, as would raising your children in any particular faith. In fact, parents would be limited to giving 'advice' to children about religion under this treaty. According to the United Nations good parenting guide, children would have a right to abortions without parental consent and would have a legally enforceable right to leisure. Exactly what constitutes leisure is left open to interpretation but I feel confident that campaigning for Green causes would meet with UN approval!

Of course, the UN doesn't stop there. Under their treaty it would be illegal for a nation to spend more on national defence than it does on children's welfare. Who cares that strong nations protect children from tyranny and abuse, or that orderly societies provide a safer environment for children than lawless ones? Such trifling matters should never interfere with the United Nations' ability to dictate how sovereign nations are allowed to spend their taxpayers' money.

At present, although there are reporting obligations by nations that signed the treaty, there are no penalties for failure to comply and nations can opt out of the treaty with little notice. So it is basically another UN motherhood statement that achieves nothing except for providing the UN with the appearance of achievement. However, under the Greens' world view, that could change. They want to empower the UN to have an enforcement role for all existing and future treaties and conventions, which the Greens will unilaterally endorse. Don't take my word for it, read their policy platform.

This includes the Rights of the Child *treaty where an enforced UN treaty could actually direct how parents can raise their children. It's alarming enough that **a party with a Marxist heart covered by an environmental skin can achieve electoral success and balance of power status without effective scrutiny of their policy positions.** However it is downright scary that they are prepared to effectively outsource aspects of Australian sovereignty to an external organisation and further want to empower that organisation to be the global policeman – directing, amongst other things, how we can raise our children"* Still more on UN Treaties later.

Human nature dictates a protective mechanism irrespective of the level at which any one sits in the pecking order. That is, if you are struggling financially you must feed yourself before you can pay your creditors and – in party politics – the maintenance of the party's interests are a priority for its very survival. It's what keeps the party functioning and a politician protecting the party, even if this is to the detriment of the people. This has been proven to be just so and this in itself is the greatest conflict of interest, adverse to our society and our democracy.

Never would a politician commit or personally guarantee his representations or to rectify the grave concerns of constituents or commit to anything within a strict specified time frame. Government are supposed to exist to facilitate one essential thing – that, **we are first and foremost a society not an economy, albeit a society reliant on an economy as the means of supporting society. It was never intended that society exists to support an economy or any political theories or agendas.**

Our democratically elected leaders are entrusted with having our individual and collective equality, justice, peace, privileges, security and benefits as their only objective. This together with managing our assets, but not only have we been exploited, we are vulnerable to further exploitation at every corner as the objectives of party politics out ranks the people's objectives.

Workers Unions are yet another "party" although the union movement was so purposeful early in the industrial revolution. Unions were brought about to overcome the exploitation of workers by ruthless aristocratic employers and to lobby government for the fair rights of their members. Today the Union Movement is a forceful mechanism able to hold the whole country to ransom in meeting their demands, even if the demands are detrimental to long term business and hence long term employment. Members contribute to the administrative costs of their union but membership fees have not been restricted to only covering the costs of maintaining the administration and lobbying government.

Millions of excessive dollars are charged by unions to their members with massive "donations" by the leaders of the unions to political parties without the approval of every member. No union or person would "donate" such funding to a political party if there were no deal done or advantage assured. Disguised any way you like but this is callous corruption by the provider of the donations and the recipient government party. We all know it is happening, it's no secret and there is no attempt to stop it.

The determination of our governments is based on our selection of our local Federal, local State and Local government members and if the number of members of one party succeeds in exceeding the members of the other, their party wins! It gives the appearance that we are voting for a particular individual representative who stands for his party and the deterrent for our choice is provided by the opposition. This is often based on the opponent's ability to rake up as much muck as he can against his opponent and if he can make this muck stick we are supposed to give him favourable consideration with our vote.

Pauline Hanson and her One Nation Party was seen as a threat to the major political parties and she was labelled a racist, with frenzied attacks on her or anyone brave enough to support her. Although she was defeated, topics contained in her maiden speech were gradually adopted by the Howard Government. Ms Hanson was found guilty of electoral fraud and imprisoned only to have the charges against her dropped after her stay in prison. We are all aware of the indignities she experienced and to date Ms Hanson has not received compensation or an apology. More recently, nude photos were published throughout Australia and the international media, claiming to be of a young Pauline Hanson. The feeding frenzy continued with the media hysteria that followed. Unfortunately for her enemies, the photos were of someone else, a girl who looked like Pauline Hanson. The aim of the defamation was to discredit her but her popularity continues despite the media attacks. She may not be perfect but who is. One thing is for sure, she is an Australian, she cared enough to speak up, she made a huge effort, and she made a huge impact, one that many in and outside of the powerhouses have not!

Then of course there are the in-house party contests or infighting for leadership, branch stacking etc. which is kept from the public arena as much as possible and that gets as dirty as it can get. Malcolm Turnbull's succession to the seat of Wentworth was at the demise of Peter King. It was not based on what the constituents wanted but on who Mr Howard thought would get greater support from the constituents in an election. It was not based on any track record of performance by King or Turnbull's ability to perform better, the motivating factor remained with John Howard. Perhaps the Wentworth constituents may have agreed with Mr Howard but they were never consulted.

We hear contenders for the prime ministership and other ministerial jobs defaming each other every day. For example, John Howard vs. Kevin Rudd *"the Prime Minister is past his use by date"* or the Prime Minister will say about Rudd *"he is young and inexperienced"* (and *"he goes to strip joints"*). This rather than highlight their own positive skills and attributes which they are able to bring to the table. Politicians opt or rely on negative personal attacks and school boy antics towards each other in our parliaments at a tremendous financial and moral cost to us all. Party politics focuses on the shortcomings of their opposition. One politician trashing the other in some demented form of trying to elevate him or herself. This reduces productivity and losses sustained in paying for digressing or bludging on the job. We teach children not to name call and to be respectful while our public "examples" deface this intrinsic value. Not only publicly "bullying" in bringing down their opposition but in bringing themselves down firstly. This self character assassination is costing more than money can ever compensate for. Failing to tread carefully with humility and wisdom provides poor long term damaging effects for everyone.

Although on a much larger scale, running the country is no different to the way we run our individual households, rules are rules and responsibilities are responsibilities for everyone. We don't accept schoolyard antics of yelling abuse, name calling, lies, bullying and muck-raking at home nor should we from adults in parliament in demonstrating their bad behave, bad attitudes and poor performances to disguise their ineffectiveness or lack of communicative skills or being unable to present their views in the most professional manner. Government sessions are chaired by the "Speaker" and if government were half serious, the speaker would permanently remove anyone who calls out without invitation to speak or who is out of order, and have that representative replaced. This would fix the problem, no warning – out never to return, no more wasted time and money during government sessions and in working towards providing greater productivity.

For Queen and Country
or for the Party and the Media?

THE GOVERNORS OF each State and the Governor General are the British Monarchy's delegated Officers in Australia. The Australian people pay the Governor General A$400,000 pa tax free for this post (and we pay Queen Elizabeth some A$19 million pa). That, plus the lurks and perks while on the job, then a A$200,000 pa pension on retirement, free holidays and yet we had to find another A$28,000 for her new clothes! Great distaste was demonstrated in the Governor General accepting A$28,000 from the Australian taxpayers before Xmas 2008 for her new clothes when thousands of Australian families could not put food on their tables. This may appear trivial but it certainly demonstrates contemptuous, excessive waste and disregard, rather than concern for the Queen and her subjects.

The position of Governor General is embedded in our Constitution and while the responsibilities of Governor General are less than that of the Prime Minister, the remuneration is greater. In recent times she has tried to elevate her role to the dismay of Labor party members. Perhaps it was this lack of function in her position or perhaps it was for previous assistance to Rudd while he was with the Queensland Goss government but Rudd was inspired to delegate sending Her Majesty's Governor General Quentin Bryce, on a 19 day tour of 10 African nations in hot pursuit of a seat on the UN Security Council. It would seem Mr Rudd has a special interest in Ms Bryce; firstly he blocks an inquiry before she was to be sworn in, against a recommendation by the outgoing Governor-General Michael Jeffery into her part in the Heiner affair and in giving her an unnecessary all expenses paid trip to Africa, as his "Head of State" for an issue detrimental to Australia.

Our constitution does not give a prime minister any standing to speak on behalf of Australia, particularly when it comes to apologies for abuses eg to the stolen generation or those abused as children in church or other institutions, but Mr Rudd assumed this responsibility when responsibility is vested in the Governor General and so his apologies are mere rhetoric.

Greg Melleuish, an Associate Professor in the School of History and Politics at the University of Wollongong, says (sic) ". . . there is *a real problem here. Rudd, like his predecessor, has increasingly sought to bestow upon himself activities in roles that go beyond politics. He constantly comments on matters that are not political* *in nature. The consequence is to bring politics into matters that should not be political in nature. Rudd is a political leader, he is not head of State nor is he in a position to act as if he is head of State. Unfortunately Rudd is behaving like some sort of monarch. Rudd seems to believe he can cure the psychic ills of the nation through a wave of the hand and a bit of waffly rhetoric. Our system of government has traditionally divided ceremonial and symbolic activities from political ones. The ceremonial activities, those that are non-political and unite us are carried out by the governor general and the various State governors. The political activities belong to the politicians. This system has served us well. It has helped to keep the infinite egotism of political leaders in check. However, recent times have seen political leaders attempting to become more than just political leaders. Now we have Rudd seeking to be the Father of the Nation. It is important that politicians like Rudd be confined to politics."* Rudd is not empowered to represent Australia, this remains the liberty of Queen Elizabeth II and the proof of the pudding will come in July 2010 when she will represent us at the UN General Assembly.

While Rupert Murdoch, in his first 2008 Boyer Lecture, urged Australians to declare their independence from Britain, he stated, *"The establishment of a republic will not slight the Queen nor will it deny the British traditions, values and structures that have served us so well"*. He said that *"the 1999 rejection of the republic referendum was more of an expression of mistrust of politicians than an indication of royalist sentimental attachment"*. The Queen has stated, *"I have always made it clear that the future of the monarchy in Australia is an issue for the Australian people and them alone to decide, by democratic and constitutional means"*. Under normal circumstances (prior 1973) I would say that: Perhaps what needs to be determined in a non-contrived referendum is whether to sever our allegiance to the Queen and Britain constitutionally or not, but under the current shadow of UN treaties, this cannot be on our horizon. Australians voted not to become a Republic yet without any authority Prime Ministers starting with the Labor PM Bob Hawke in 1984 ditched "God Save the Queen" as our national anthem and now it is being suggested to ditch it from anything that is not directly connected to functions where Royalty is present eg ANZAC Day ceremonies. **The Queen remains Australians protector and our get out of (United Nations) jail card, free of adverse treaties and agreements!** One thing is certain, no Australian wants to see more taxpayer money wasted on yet another expensive and drawn out inquiry to determine our future, rather put it to the Australian people in a vote. Labor PM Paul Keating sought to ditch our flag, and State Premiers have without any authority disregarded our Constitutional Rights while both levels of government have been pretending and acting as if we are a Republic. That is, pretend it is for long enough and it will be as if it always was! It has been suggested by politicians and others, not the people, that removing the Queen and God from all ceremony will be more attractive to our younger generation but in these times, it is far more appealing, more appropriate and more relevant for unity, peace and purpose than ever to align and respect our heritage, as without roots the tree cannot grow and flourish. If young people do not know the Royal Anthem and their National Constitution it is because we have allowed politicians to dictate it out of the education system making civics education in this country, a complete failure.

There may appear to be little evidence left of purposeful Royal governance but for the protective mechanism in Her Constitution. Perhaps the greatest contribution the Queen has made to mankind albeit to womankind is the Queen's ability to portray a regal and refined inspiration for all people, particularly women. She represents the epitome of womanhood, of modesty, of correctness, of good behaviour and grace demonstrating women's ability to rise to a level well above common, with her staunch sacrifices to the position. Without snobbery, every woman in western society has the ability to rise to greater challenges which can only be yielded from the same commitment to dulcet and decorum in every facet of our lives. Live the part and you'll be the part!

As an alternative, the Republic Party has not provided Australians with sufficient advice or information as to benefits to enable any informed decision to support it or not. Perhaps, as there are no murmurs from the Republicans they are aware that what we have today is a quasi Republic. A change to a Republic could alter the direction of this country and one which both Mr Rudd and Mr Turnbull had both previously advocated for, but they are no longer pursing, why – because international treaties and legislations have achieved the same results. If we adopted a similar system to the USA we would still end up with "party politics" but instead of "Liberal", "Labor" and a heap of others, it might be "Democrats" and "Republicans" and a heap of others, so one would suppose, why bother!

The Democratic Liberal (holding conservative theories) Prime Minister, John Howard posed the question to voters regarding our support for a Republic but the wording on the ballet paper was so ambiguous, very few people knew if they were voting for or against this "tricky question". This was to his political advantage, in purporting to be doing the right thing in asking the nation, "the big question" under a referendum vote. While there has been nothing but talk about establishing Australia as a Republic and with more than 60% of Australians in favour of a Republic, the Republic issue did not even make the top 9 issues from the 975 recommendations posed from last year's "2020 Summit" – no need, it's been put to bed, but no referendum!

That is less than 1% of the proposed 975 issues from 1,000 prominent Australians, is to be "contemplated". What a great public relations scam the 2020 Summit was. This Summit was nothing but a bright new marketing ploy by a political party in winning popularity poles and our confidence!

Over the past few years governments have moved their focus away from good governance to good marketing and great public relations. The prize would have to go to the current Labor party's marketing and public relations team. The 2020 Summit concept achieved little other than to appear as if the government was interested in listening to all Australians but – Eric Abetz the opposition spokesman for industry and science said, *"the summit cost taxpayers A$2 million and 12 months later only 9 out of more than 900 ideas had seen any action* (needless to say that after 2 years there was also no action on his political promises). *I think every participant and Australian would have every right to feel let down and deeply disappointed with the outcome".* This was followed by the indulgence of cash handouts which achieved little if any long term benefit.

The government's public relations people work hard at coming up with these "good guy" schemes facilitated by the media in propping up the perception, while real governance is left begging. Again, when stuff ups are exposed the government's mentors create diversions, for example the very quick switch from the ceiling batts disaster of Garrett and Rudd, and the massive deficit, and the focus on an ETS all were just swung right away to national health, all to be forgotten and forgiven. In just one week, we saw this switch in the hope that the voters will forget the waste of resources, the lack of performance, the demise in living and life standards and the pursuit of adverse objectives, but I don't think so this time. Unfortunately inequality has reached the highest ranks in the country with the **Liberal government's inability to procure as creative a public relations organisation as Labor, now sees Australian politics boiling down to "Propaganda, Lies and Showmanship".**

Public relations more than often is nothing more than smoke screens relied on to cover up government failures and glorifying those needing to demonstrate a glory they don't have. It is a well known fact that Kevin Rudd sent staff to visit the Canberra Press Gallery to see what stories are being reported and the Gallery has been having an inexplicable relationship with the Rudd Labor Government, despite their massive failures. Diversions created to "look after (Labor) politicians" or their political agendas and thus the media are looking after themselves. If the media does not complying with the governments mentors they risk being kept in the dark or out in the cold, which would be disadvantageous to their respective network and so the media must comply with what the government wants reported and how, or they miss out on information and ratings but this is just another form of communist censorship.

More than 60% of all political news is taken up with government gossip, corruption, personal sex lives, etc rather than on real issues. For example: creating headlines in focusing on the lack of performance or negative aspects of the Opposition rather than reporting on why Government has not built the promised new aboriginal houses. Scarcely anything has been said or written about the Labor Government giving hundreds of millions of dollars away to other nations and on consultants before one aboriginal house has been constructed. Aboriginal Labor MP from Central Australia, Ms Anderson, challenged Jenny Macklin to start 'keeping an eye on her money' after it was revealed that as few as 300 houses may be built with the A$672 million Strategic Indigenous Housing and Infrastructure Program, or why 75% of government grants to Aboriginals ends up in administration costs while the balance has not been expended to Aboriginal communities etc. Nothing about why government has an open cheque book for Mr Rudd to have committed us to A$11 million towards the cost of setting Tim Fisher up in a new embassy in the Vatican City, a country that we do not trade with, while our homeless and unemployed numbers grow, tens of thousands of Aussies are on waiting lists for surgery and our kids, many needing glasses get a second grade education in leaking classrooms, many with no air conditioning, but they have new halls whether they needed them or not.

Nothing about governments broken promises regarding the hospital crisis but the media coverage was of Mr Rudd visiting patents on his tour of hospitals asking doctors (for the benefit of the TV audience) "so what do you want" is nothing more than deplorable public relation's spin. Only when all else fails and it looked like government will not be elected again does the swing revert to the hospitals crisis. Nothing about the computers for schools program, originally to cost A$800 million but will come in at about A$2.2 billion and nothing about continued inaccurate projections from our National Treasury, just rub it out and change the numbers.

The mentor propaganda machine with unlimited funds continues: Placing thousands of unnecessary stimulus improvements signs at schools can only be viewed as a Labor indoctrination for our children (then give 16 year olds the vote?) but at A$3.5 million for signs, it is a very expensive back patting exercise in wasting taxpayer's money. Then the government stimulus to schools in building the "Rudd & Gillard Memorial Halls" across the nation whether the school wants or need such a hall is irrelevant to the Labor government. *If the school would have rather spent the money on other vital resources, forget it, this does not conform to Labors public relations and other agendas. In other words, the national infrastructure, as with all stimulus payments and investments, are firstly a Labor government promotional campaign.* Now that the horse has bolted, Labor would spend A$13 million to purport to be determining valid expenditure, when a quick calculation by anyone let alone the Auditor General, would demonstrate that the construction cost per square metres of each building is between A$1,500 and A$2,000 per square metre and anything above this, is just a rip-off. The real inquiry ought to be into who got the jobs and why their quotes were accepted if excessive. We will probably not hear about this or where the ripped off money went? It has been suggested that it has been channelled back into the Labor Party's political campaign and into consultant mate's pockets? Will Liberal be investigating Labor's campaign funds?

In other words, the national infrastructure, as with all stimulus payments and investments, are firstly a Labor government promotional campaign. Inept government cannot justify spending A$800 million on consultants (the cost of 3,000 new semi-rural homes for the homeless with repayable mortgages from newly created jobs) to determine where A$300 million will be expended. This is just continually wasting taxpayer's money for nothing but a debt in propping up the excellent packaging of the Labor government, but there is nothing of substance in the Labor package for Australia, where highly skilled expert consultants advice is ignored when it is not on the governments agenda eg the Minter Ellison report regarding the batts.

As the roof batts scandal was to Garrett and the Environment Ministry – the school buildings rip-off scandal is to Gillard and the Education Ministry – as will be Rudd's decisions as Foreign Affairs Minister, but in what light will the media report this?

The NSW State Labor government appears to have a similar relationship with the media. Nothing mentioned about Mr Rees referring to *"climate change sceptics as Hitler sympathizers"* this ought to be headline news, as is the mismanagement of the NSW government. Taxpayer funded propaganda signs are no different to, as stated by NSW Shadow Treasure Mike Baird, *"Total handouts given to first home buyers as part of the NSW Housing Construction Acceleration Plan was A$2.8 million similar to the amount ie A$2 million the NSW government spent on advertising this State Budget initiative"* and this was conceded by Mr Rees. Mike Baird also stated that, *"In two months the Rees Labor Government spent only A$2.8 million on its Housing Construction Acceleration Plan to 377 recipients, after claiming the package would be worth A$64 million over six months but at this rate the Government will only spend A$8.4 million on its "major economic stimulus package". The NSW Government will receive A$4 billion in stamp duty revenue this year however it can only manage to give A$2.8 million to first home buyers as part of its major stimulus package."* Spending A$2 million on marketing or rather for Labor's public relations is a ploy for voter support, this must be illegal!

The above examples are blatant evidence of governments contrived misappropriation of taxpayer funds for their party's promotional benefit. **Misappropriation of funds, irrespective of the circumstance is fraud on par with legislation which digresses from the intended effect of the Australian Constitution, acts of treason, against the Australian people.** These examples are but a "tip of the ice berg" yet no authority or the media challenges the misappropriation of funds or pursues. As a result of the prospect of isolation, many reporters have become lazy, relying on government press releases to write their stories. Political party's taxpayer funded mentor/public relations and marketing people are experts at political propaganda and dirty tricks. Why not? The costs and ramifications don't come out of their pockets, but feather their nests. These expert spin and public relations mentors continued to provide false perceptions in the excellent job of "selling" Rudd and they will continue grooming ministers such as our new PM Ms Gillard and they will continue the political game playing as a diversion from poor governance, where digression from real issues has become the alternative for good government.

With deep seated egos and party priorities running governments, it can be hard if not impossible for government to provide assistance or funding to an opponent minister of his or her constituents. That is, if your Federal member is not on the current winning party team you will never get any real government to address issues. With both parties and between Federal and State governments playing the blame game with each other, for our perceived benefit and with hundreds of millions wasted year in and year out there are very few who deliver anything constructive. Procrastination is the best tool in preventing a government from doing what must be done in an expeditious manner, to where legislation can be a great skirt to hide behind depending on the ruling party's political motives and priorities for which there should be none.

Honest Government Would Be A Change

FACT IS, IF it were not for the allegiances of individuals to political parties, it would not matter which decent Aussies are sitting on the representative hot seats, as long as they are qualified to do the respective good job and able to get the best positive results attainable. But it is only reasonable that those best equipped to hold portfolio positions are those who have extensive experience within their skilled industry. Resources Ministries provided with Senate approved directives for positive initiatives, with full transparency and accountability to all Australians in achieving a common sense approach, but common sense cannot prevail in the current nonsense political system.

Public Officers of every description must be held accountable for their actions and honesty, that is, particularly their representations. The NSW government installed the ICAC (Independent Commission Against Corruption) to keep themselves and their peers honest. Governments over the past 40 years have deemed it in our best interest not only to deregulate so many industries, but they have distanced themselves further with the establishment of independent agencies to do the job we have entrusted them to do, but who are they answerable to? Agencies such as ASIC (Australian Securities and Investments Commission) and the ACCC and other government departments, but just try and lodge a complaint with ICAC, ASIC or the ACCC and see what results you get, if ever.

Other than a national independent watchdog over all public servants, if a government agency or department is deemed to be independent of the government – it means that the government is either incapable or incompetent, or it believes itself or elements of itself to be potentially corrupt, or it does not want to be accountable or responsible for any conflict of interests, or it merely wants to fob off any responsibility to an unaccountable agency classified as "independent".

Then for an "independent" agency such as ASIC to have no power over an industry sector deemed to be "deregulated" it provides every authority with the tool of "unaccountability" and the inability for any government or government agency to intervene or give directive. In these circumstances we must ask, just who is running the country?

I can say first hand that the Minister for Corporations, The Hon Nick Sherry has no jurisdiction over our only corporate watchdog, ASIC. The Minister for Home Affairs, The Hon Bob Debus advises in a letter that I have, *"the Australian government does not direct the Australian Federal Police to investigate matters"* – so who needs any government which has no jurisdiction over our vital agencies? This is the loudest alarm bell in advising us that "things are not as they ought to be". That our government structure is both inadequate and perverse, opening the door for our urgent need for redressing.

If we reduced and consolidated bureaucracy while disbanding political parties and reassess our governmental administrational needs, then appointed those equipped with the best skills necessary to handle each respective portfolio, we would have made the most positive changes. If we amend to a unified national judiciary and conformed to a unified national constitution as opposed to State constitutions (with legislative amendments to reverse adverse legislations and support new) in conforming to the requirements of the 21st century, we would be advancing in the right direction.

By enshrining a Code of Conduct and a Charter of Rights which incorporates: anti-discrimination laws, human rights, defines the extent of freedom of speech, equal opportunities, consumer protection and trade practises for business and government we would ensure regulations are in tune with our current and future requirements, with our democracy stronger than ever. By doing this we reduce our vulnerability to those who exploit and abuse society, aided by the greedy for their own agendas. A protected Democracy, able to administer and provide increased productivity, reduced disputes at all levels of society and never would there be a need to throw out a government for corruption or mismanagement or for placing their party policies and propaganda above the interests of the people.

We have issues that are ethical-community issues and not government administrative issues. While the government is supposed to administer in our best interests, determination or resolve in regards to ethical and social issues must be with the people by the people. With due respect, when Tony Abbott was the Federal Health Minister, although not having qualification as a medical expert to be the Minister of Health (how do we allow and condone that), we must ask what qualifications he has to cast in concrete his personal opinion in relation to abortion, yet his decision nonetheless was enforced for the entire nation. An unqualified decision determined without community consultation, as most decisions are currently made.

The hospitals and water crisis is merely expensive infighting for "control" between Federal and State governments. Both levels of government are buck-passing as to who is responsible, or rather who will retain "control" for the carriage of these imperative national issues, coupled with bureaucratic funding priorities by those ill equipped to overcome the logistical problems. This attitude or power game will never fix our national problems, only compound them.

The hospital crisis is not a matter of inadequate financial resources but a matter of higher party priorities and thus the inability to accept the advice of experts. Financial resources wasted in the political ball game between Federal and States and the inadequate political focus by unqualified would-be health experts on both sides of the many political fences, left unchallenged by the people and ignored experts. In simple maths, there are 8 State and Territory governments and 1 Federal government not including the umpteen local governments. Now times that by two for the oppositional parties and you have at least 18 parties (not including local government) with their own inconsistent constitutions to try and get a major consensus from in attempting to fix problems and move forward. It is illogical to even conceive, let alone remedy.

Malcolm Turnbull is a very astute businessman with a very extensive legal and merchant banking background, particularly with Goldman Sachs, but he had no expertise in water or the environment to become Minister for Water, certainly no more or less than Penny Wong or Peter Garret a singer from "Midnight Oil" for environmental issues. Mr Turnbull rejected the advice of water and geological expert consultants based on *"it's not on our party's agenda"*. That is, it rained and the heat was off his party.

All expert consultants advice is at great cost to the taxpayer and how much more so, if ignored. To reject valuable advice based on it not being the flavour of the day or of interest to the political party or it is no longer a priority on the party's agenda, is not just adverse to our needs, it is contempt. No different to government wanting to sell air or Carbon Credits, rather than investing into alternative power and long term loans to various industries for relocation to rural areas with the installation of alternative power, say Ethanol, wind, solar and particularly geothermal which we have an in exhaustive abundance of, albeit to the financial detriment of electricity and gas suppliers. Hence, after 100 years there are no positive moves on water resources or the environment, rather government just propping up its propaganda, in continuing the fight with the States all just "appearing" to be doing the right thing. But treating the limited water supply as just another asset or commodity governments can sell off or charge extra for, rather than developed and used to achieve greater national (not just State) sustainability.

Are we are stuck in an unfair Federal system or conforming to world government.

February 16, 2010 – The High Court handed down a decision in the Arnold case, which reveals major problems with Australia's structure of government. This case came about when farmers in the Lower Murray region sought compensation for forced reductions in their use of water. A NSW law replaced their groundwater bore licenses with aquifer access licenses, where they lost 70% of their entitlement to groundwater without "just terms". The Federal Constitution requires compensation when property is acquired, but the NSW Constitution does not provide for this and our rights can be taken without any compensation whatsoever. Arnold lost the case and so Peter Spencer would seem to be at the end of any legal attempt for compensation for the loss of his land-use, without a High Court challenge regarding the Constitution. This is why Australia appropriately needs a review of our National Constitution with supporting legislation (not by politicians but by professionals in all fields under an independent Senate), encompassing or replacing all State Constitutions, that is, one National Constitution which portrays benefits in favour of the people and not to the benefit of any party or person individually in gaining unfair advantages for their agendas or in meeting adverse treaties.

George Williams, Professor of Law at the University of NSW says, *"It may be constitutionally valid for NSW to acquire property without compensation, but it should not be. It is offensive in a modern democracy like Australia that the States can acquire property without redress. This should be fixed."* He also states, *"The problems revealed by Arnold do not stop with property rights. The case also highlights the inadequacies of the constitution when it comes to river water. Water was a deal breaker in the move to federation in the 1890s. As one commentator said, without a settlement on water "there could have been no constitution and no federation. Not only have farmers turned to the constitution seeking compensation, but South Australia has begun an action against Victoria to have its water trading limits struck down. Litigation can be a necessary means of resolving disputes, but offers little to better manage our water. Existing problems can be made worse by the inevitable by-products of litigation – long delays and great expense – as well as having outcomes driven by a constitution drafted in the 19th century. Since 1901 the constitution has had the potential to play a decisive role in the management of Australian rivers. It seems now that this potential will increasingly be realized. In the absence of a new constitutional settlement that recognizes Australia's modern water problems, this holds grave risks. Instead of having water regulation determined by balancing business, environmental and other legitimate concerns, the claims of the parties will be mediated through an out-of-date constitution and the technicalities of Australia's federal system".* A reduction in water equals a reduction in productivity, without disclosing the demands dictated by the World Trade Organisation, which has been contorted and contrived as to conforming to reduced manmade environmental impact.

We are capable of protecting our own environment and sustaining ourselves but governments have committed us to many adverse international treaties: **The World Trade Organisation "WTO" which is the most powerful legislative and judicial body in the world.** Promoting and enforcing "free trade" and supporting the agendas UN directives above the interests of local communities, of working families and our country allows the World Trade Organisation to systematically undermines democracy around the world. According to the WTO, our democratically elected public officials no longer have the rights to protect the environment and public health and unlike other United Nations Treaties, the International Labor Organization conventions or multilateral environmental agreements, the WTO rules can be enforced through sanctions. This gives the WTO more power than any other international body even eclipsing national governments. The WTO is continually opposed by poorer countries which has brought the most powerful countries to their knees, where false assurances that agriculture would be fairly reformed. We suffer the "Effects" and these treaties are the "Causes" we are now bound to.

I reiterate: We are not going to have the choice to agree because our Local governments have already done that. Without any consent of the people, Local Governments have signed agreements and committed to the United Nation's International Council for Local Environmental Initiatives "ICLEI"

In an unskilled quest to find a conservative way to be "green" some politicians are compromising and signing contracts with non-governmental entities and accepting funding which ultimately bind cities, counties, and states to radical environmental policies. Regulations and laws continue to be forced onto us by leaders that may not realize they have unwittingly committed us to anti-Constitutional Globalistic plans.

There are now over 600 cities and counties within the United States which have contracts with ICLEI and at September 2010 there are 123 of Australia's 602 Local Councils who have committed. Over 1,000 Local governments are now committed around the world. Right now, in your town, policies are being implemented that will ultimately eliminate your freedoms and destroy your way of life. You need to know what's going on to stop this process. Many town officials are selling us out to global regional development with help from the *International Council for Local Environmental Initiatives (ICLEI): Local Governments for Sustainability*. ICLEI is used as one of the mechanisms to undo the political recognition of unalienable rights. They hold "Consensus" meetings but they have predetermined outcomes. They *pretend* to garner community input but pursue their mandates.

http://video.google.com/videoplay?docid=-8137185398743302029#

The "ICLEI" was founded in 1990 when 200 local governments from 43 countries convened at the inaugural conference, the World Congress of Local Governments for a Sustainable Future, at the United Nations in New York.

During the Local Government Session at the World Summit in Johannesburg, South Africa in August 2002, local government leaders from around the world, as well as representatives from the United Nations Development Programme (UNDP), United Nations Environment Programme (UNEP), UN-HABITAT and the World Health Organization (WHO), joined ICLEI in launching Local Action 21 as the next phase of Local Agenda 21 (LA21)."

In complying with Agenda 21 President Obama's **Executive Order 13547** issued July 19, further extends federal power, embraces global governance, diminishes the rights and privileges of individuals, and brings the United States into compliance with Agenda 21. Obama's expansion of government is taking the nation in the wrong direction. The federal government should be pushed back to those limited powers as defined in Article 1 Section 8 of the U.S. Constitution. States and individuals should reclaim the power given to them by the Constitution and guaranteed by the 10th Amendment. Thirty states will be encroached upon by Obama's Executive Order establishing the National Ocean Council for control over America's oceans, coastlines and the Great Lakes. Under this new council, States' coastal jurisdictions will be subject to the United Nations' Law Of Sea Treaty (LOST) in this UN Agenda 21 program. There are overlapping schemes that quietly and deliberately drown our property rights and freedom. Take a look at U.S. Congress – H.R. 5101 Wildlife Corridors Conservation Act of 2010. This bill is intended to lead to the formal creation of several continental-scale "wildlife corridor systems" that will negatively impact livelihoods, homes, the environment, ranches, farms, access to resources, outdoor recreation and more. This is why the American Tea Party Movement has been created – the yanks are growingly aware and very active in defending their country from becoming the North American Union, same as the failing European Union.

KICK'EM OUT – A group from Spokane, Washington called the "Spokane Patriots" will issue a demand that the city council withdraw from "Sustainability" policy and terminate the city's contract with the international Non-Governmental Organization called ICLEI. The Spokane group presents a city charter amendment along with an ordinance asserting the unconstitutional alliance between the City and ICLEI and Australians must do the same, before rates go through the roof under the disguise of environmental works or other deceptive initiatives to bankroll themselves. Are you saying *"No way could this be happening here, our Federal government wouldn't be facilitating this"* or would they?

Feb 24, 2010 a massive contingent of more than 800 Farmers converged on the NSW Parliament in Sydney in a show of solidarity for their loss of land rights and for compensation. There was not a murmur in the media of this rally and most of the people of Australia have no idea about this event and many other rallies. Remember: This country started with our farmers and it will finish with our farmers! We cannot sit back and let the destruction of this country happen by our very complacency or digression to other interests will allow it to, just happen.

I reiterate, our Constitution has been derailed, governments have entered into UN Treaties and are forcing towards World Government. Our most imperative and fundamental issues of national health, education, resources and justice, even if there were an overwhelming 100% support by Australians, could not get through as the red tape and legislation enshrined by government parties will prevent amendments or delaying it for a very long time, if ever. Our issues are secondary or of lesser importance to the protocol and procedures, leaving us little or no chance of amendments. As it stands, changes or reverting to our Constitution may never be able to take place without some form of revolution. We have seen a small sample of this with the protest votes against both Liberal and Labor in the 2010 election but alas with Labor's "Greens" support and that of the Independent Members, who were thrown into a conflict of interest with their constituents, Labor won a minority government. It is overdue that we address the manner in which our political system operates and the push for these changes must be now, or our kids and theirs will still be whingeing Aussies, indefinitely!

This is synonymous with how the current system does not work, and why most Australians are fed up with an illogical, antiquated system that is well and truly past its "use by date". The example of: Prime Minister after Prime Minister and each State's Premier, one after another, to end a century of arguing over water sharing. One hundred years with losses and damage to at least 5 generations, not to mention future generations – to get an agreement just "to agree" which has fallen apart with nothing destined to be achieved in the next one hundred years, not one drop of water created by politicians. Thank God we have finally had excellent rain falls that will satisfy the farmer for awhile, but this agreement to address the water problems across the country which prohibits the viability of our farmers and our entire economy, slows the WTO and UN Treaties objectives. As a nation we have had one hundred years of feeding bureaucratic costs that would have alleviated the water problems across the entire country and now that agreement is stopped dead, because of the intervention of the South Australian government, see section on Water.

Again, millions of dollars are spent by taxpayers at the instigation of politicians for research and consultants with many of the reports just shelved or dismissed to pursue other party objectives. That is, these educated recommendations often just don't conform to the party of the day's polices. This is regardless of whether it is done by the various States, Federal or other government agencies, and then new policies and directions change every time there is a new government and it starts all over again with new research commissioned. Often the same expensive research is conducted by each of the 8 States on the same issues and then, shelved or disregarded in appearing to be doing the job!

Enough games in playing with peoples lives from generation to generation. A new form of government is needed so that this pretence can stop and we can create a highly efficient body, ongoing in meeting the country's needs. That is, results achieved within specific timeframes and at the projected costs. Election promises would no longer be necessary and those who do not perform can be dismissed and replaced.

If a politician is voted into power, it's not because of his or her looks, it's because he or she has purported to have the skills and passion needed for the job and has presented an image of goodness, decency and determination for what he or she can provide to his or her constituents, instigated within the stipulated timeframe from his or her successful appointment to the office, without delay or excuses.

To our loss, most politicians do not have specialised skills to handle a specialised portfolio and more than often, they posses no commercial or business background to rely on. Many have completed University courses in law but have chosen political careers, yet these people have been making commercial decisions in relation to the direction of this country and the dissection of the National, State and Local governments' finances. It's the specifically skilled ability to address the issues effectively that ought to gets a politician into the hot-seat and it's the lack of achievement that ought to be relied on to remove him or her without bureaucratic red tape. It's a fair industry payment in accordance with the job, without the inequality of long term pensions or benefits when the job is vacated, that should be sufficient for those who are passionate enough to want to make a difference to our whole country and to each of us individually.

We have always regarded ourselves as fortunate to be living in "The Lucky Country" but there are many long term unemployed Aussies would sadly disagree and they ask why I am not one of the lucky ones?" With forethought and planning by experts in their respective fields and within the next five years every Australian could be well above the poverty line. They could be the asset they want to be and are needed by this country, providing collectively we address all of the pertinent issues and disregard waste, digression, flawed legislations and an antiquated bureaucratic system. Every State in Australia has its stories of worries, corruption, mismanagement and wasted human and financial resources which could probably fill a library and only through a unified and consolidated National Constitution, Code of Conduct, Charter of Rights and in alleviating party politics and international interception of our resources, can we even begin to fix the big picture and the future.

Isn't it time for our country to develop alternatives to political "parties", their philosophies, their members egos and agendas, and their abuses both wilful and through neglect, which is inflicted on all of humanity in varying degrees? As you would have gathered, I do not endorse any political party. In fact I am absolutely and without reservation against any form of political party system and every form of "Party Politics". However, we should be mindful of the options and access the information in determining the most reliable direction in achieving our common objectives. Individually we all want to achieve the best objectives for our country and it is time all minor parties consolidate for our national benefit in rising up above the party system?

Vernon Bogdanor, Professor of Government at the University of Oxford states, *"What is clear is that we must fashion our democracy to meet the needs of an age in which participation has to reach beyond the [political] party"* **and this is overdue.**

It is now Sept 2010 with the first edition of this book published in June and since then, we have seen Rudd booted out by his own government; an election resulting in a hung government, that is a vote of no confidence, with the Green arm of Labor and four independents holding the balance of power, not catered to in our 1901 Federal Constitution. We have witnessed both parties offer all sorts of blackmail incentives to the independents, with Labor offering the juiciest deal so it could form a minority government. The incentives of A$3.29 billion won the support of the independents for Labor, which in itself is the greatest contempt by the independents for their own constituents in that had the constituents wanted to vote Labor they would not have voted for their independent members. This proves that everything in this country can be bought.

We have witnessed Prime Minister Gillard voted in twice – once by her party and once by the Greens and Independents, but she was never voted in by the Australian people. In fact most Australians voted Liberal, so where is democracy in this equation? History, rather than the Constitution, has become the rule of the land – that is, political parties have in someway become acceptable but are not within our Constitution. We now have a government with approx half of the seats, which could change the balance of power at anytime due to say, an adverse by-election and an early election. We have a government on very shaky grounds, appointing, training and implementing policies, at great expense for what could be a temporary government.

Summary: Even though more Australians voted for the Liberal Party, Labor wins? Even though Ms Gillard was not elected by the people on both occasions, she becomes Prime Minister while Peter Garrett, renowned for the pink batts fiasco gets from Ms Gillard, the schools portfolio; Bill Shorten gets to be assistant Treasurer while Penny Wong becomes the Minister for Finance; Mark Arbib gets the Ministry for indigenous employment, sport and social housing; Steven Smith becomes the 3rd Minister for Defence in 3 years and Rudd gets the Ministry of his dreams becoming the Minister for Foreign Affairs, for his inability to work with people. This will no doubt bring Mr Rudd closer to his United Nations objectives and his ability to create a greater power base to enforce UN Treaties and Agreements. Five minutes into his new job "Kevin-747" as he has fondly been referred to, hit the airways again, off to far destinations and leaving his massive carbon footprint to follow.

What Professor Vernon Bogdanor recognises, as have so many Australians who have signed our petition at the website to date, is that a non party affiliated government system will not pursue philosophical agendas or compromise Australia with Treaties and agreements. One that will ensure House of Representatives Ministers only agenda is the objectives of their constituents and that of all Australians in a transparent government.

We can, and no doubt we all want to reduce chemical emissions in our country and this can be achieved without international treaties and without abusing any Australian. We can care for and maximize the potential of our environment with renewable energy, while we improve our productivity. We can also change our form of government to provide a focus on Australia and Australians before the egos of supremacists and party agendas and this must be done before adversity spreads with censorship and further individual abuse. The people and business of Australia are our primary objective and this lends well to providing third world countries with produce on extended terms (loans are assets) and assistance in overcoming their own adverse conditions, but in trading with other sustained nations, we must be competitive and by lifting taxes and tariffs on imported goods, it will ensure Australian products and services are competitive and attractive on our own market firstly.

Cut the Dead Wood – Build a Transparent Government

T HE MAJORITY OF Australians are not and don't want to be political scientists or (generally) legal practitioners. They don't choose a political career and most don't want to be bothered with politics, which is why we pay ministers to do "their best" for us. The majority of Australians have been extended little if any knowledge, through the school system, of the political process or the relevance of our Constitution. Student's knowledge of the Australian system of government is lower than expected – only one in three year 10 students know what the Constitution is. This lack of such fundamental information restricts the capacity of students, come voting adults, to make sense of many other aspects of the Australian Democratic processes. Many people are therefore disadvantaged in their capacity to engage in meaningful levels of civic action or discourse. Many tick the various boxes on Election Day because they have to – not because they want to, or do they understand the ramifications of their vote.

By year 10, students are expected to recognise key functions and features of parliament, analyse the common good as a motivation for becoming a whistleblower, explain the importance of a secret ballot, and recognise how the independence of the judiciary is protected, although unaccountable. A test was given to year 10 students with only 34% (ie 1,870 of the 5,500 year 10 students in 2007) identifying the correct answers, making it clear that students have not been taught or at least have not learned this most basic information. There can be no doubt that both Federal and State governments are aware of this impediment, so we must question why government would be suggesting reducing the voting age to 16 years of age.

The real question is, why governments through the education department (although inconsistent through various States and nationally) have not ensured our kids are taught government process? Could it be that "knowledge is power" and we don't want any more "whistleblowers". I suppose, if kids get too smart, questions may be raised as to why we have no Charter of Rights or a Code of Conduct to rely on. It cannot be assumed that society and its individuals have an inherent or genetic understanding of these matters. A Code of Conduct must be taught based on sound morals, ethics and virtues, which may have been initially religious teachings, but are the very foundation for a cohesive society. Same as a

Charter of Rights which kids cannot be relied on to make their own inquires for fear of being kept in the dark, and therefore how can kids be held accountable for poor behaviour, poor priorities and ignorance. Ms Gillard deems it necessary that kids be taught as part of the national schools curriculum, Chinese medicine and Aboriginal Dreamtime, but shouldn't our kids also be taught about an Australian Culture and what is happening in Australia? What qualifications or what expertise has Ms Gillard relied on to make these decisions? Should she not be teaching kids that legislation is removing their rights, taking their assets and endangering their mental health. How men and women are fighting parts of the problem, such as Peter Spencer, but the question kids must ask is how have government been able to do this without the permission of the People? Sue Maynes says what we should be teaching our kids, is that:

1. Prior to the formation of the Federation, all colonies but SA were independent penal colonies, under the authority of the British Empire.
2. For purposes of trade, these colonies operated under the 1855 Federal Council of Australasia.
3. The planning for a Federation took 10 years of conventions and referendums.
4. The draft Constitution was formed and sent to England.
5. On 9 July 1900, Queen Victoria signed the amended Commonwealth of Australia Constitution Act (UK) 1900 and returned it to Australia.
6. This constitution required a final referendum of the People to approve it. Why?
7. Because it was a contract between the owner of the land, the Queen's most Excellent Majesty, and her loyal subjects under the Seal of the Crown of the United Kingdom of Great Britain and Ireland. And any contract must have the full agreement of both parties.
8. The details of this contract were that she and her heirs would protect us, we would pay into her consolidated revenue our taxes, she would then pay the public servants wages, and the public servants would obey our Constitution in their administration of her lands on our behalf.
9. Who are we in this Act? We are the Commonwealth. The actual Constitution at part 9 is the rules applicable to government.
10. And it states at part 9, section 117 and section 128 of the Commonwealth of Australia Constitution Act (UK) 1900, that government can not remove our rights without our permission.
11. Unfortunately, for reasons of State, the heads of those independent colonies decided not to have another referendum, but instead agreed to this contract "for and on behalf" of the People. Creating the first loophole in Federation.
12. In 1973, Gough Edward Whitlam came into power and immediately created the Queen of Australia and the Great Seal of Australia.
13. From that time on all government legislation has been created under that Queen and sealed to the Seal. What does this mean?

14. The Queen of the People of the Commonwealth is Her Majesty Queen Elizabeth II of Great Britain and Ireland – not the Queen of Australia. The Queen of Australia is an entity completely unknown to our rights. She did not sell us her land, she does not guarantee our protection.

15. The Seal of the People of the Commonwealth is the Royal Seal of Great Britain with the Lion and the Unicorn. The Great Seal of Australia with the Kangaroo and the Emu is a seal completely foreign to our laws under our Constitution and our rights.

16. A Queen and a Seal are not just pretty pictures on a page, they are profound legal elements telling anyone who understands them that they must operate under them, ie what laws, what government, what power they **must** obey.

17. Anyone who has been taken to court under these draconian laws should know that the first thing a judge must do is look at the Seal on the charge. If it is the Royal Seal he must rule under common law. If it is the Great Seal he must rule under the legislation of the Aust government. If it is the State Seal he must rule under State legislation. **And he cannot look at any other legislation in his decision**. He is bound to the Seal and your rights are completely ignored.

18. Our rights are found under the Royal Seal, at common law and equity, as found in the judicial system created in the Commonwealth of Australia Constitution Act (UK) 1900 and protected by Her Majesty Queen Elizabeth II of Great Britain and Ireland.

19. Our rights are not found in the courts of Australia which are bound to these government creations – hence – we lose!

20. In essence, what Gough Whitlam created in 1973, was a Republic in all but name.

21. The progressive removal of our Queen and our Seal from all legislation in Australia now sees the sovereign power vested solely in the Prime Minister, who has never been given that right by the People. Nor does he have the legal ability to represent us as our Head of State.

22. Under that sovereignty we have been made their commercial chattels, we provide them with our money/our taxes, we must obey their laws on political grounds, we are taken into their courts by their employees and tried in their system under statutory law, where, under the Criminal Code 1995 a person is defined as being a 'nothing" and an act of Treason can only be committed against a Prime Minister (rather than his act of Treason against us).

23. This is not our government. This government is completely foreign to our 1900 (UK) Commonwealth Constitution.

24. In this foreign government all dealings are now contractual under the corporate structure.

25. Our government was authorised by Queen Victoria to operate under common law and equity, and their permission stopped at making laws for Peace, Welfare and Good Government only.

26. What have they done with our Constitution? They have placed it inside a consolidated act referred to simply as The Constitution. Inside that act is

the Australia Act 1986 (their constitution), the Westminster Act and our Constitution – all Sealed under the Great Seal of Australia.

27. In simple words, under their control. We have been enslaved.

28. The States have all returned to their independent colonial status, reworking those 1800's constitutions back into modern terms.

29. COAG is now the trade agreement between all government entities including local councils. You do not get to vote who sits in COAG, yet all agreements over your land rights are under the power of COAG.

30. They have removed your civil and political rights – did you agree to that?

31. They have removed your private ownership rights to your wealth, your land, your goods and your chattels. Did you agree to that?

32. They have created a 'republican style' government and removed our Constitutional Monarchy. Did you agree to that?

33. Her Majesty did not give this foreign government permission to steal Her land and she has recently re-affirmed Her role as the protector of the People when she stated she was the Head of State in this country.

34. We are the People of the State of the Commonwealth, so she was telling this government that she is now stepping into the battle to protect us.

35. People of the Commonwealth, this foreign government has taken the assets of Her Majesty, kept in trust for her People, they have sold those assets and pocketed the money. Did you agree to that?

36. This foreign government rules with fear and statute law.

37. They are nothing but thieves – do not allow them to force us to live in fear. We are much, much greater than that.

38. If you do not know who you are and what you own, you will not know what is being stolen from you.

39. Stand united, know who you are, where your protection lies and speak out. Make your voices roar through the offices and halls of their corporate headquarters. Let them know the People of the Commonwealth have had enough!

Learn more at

We profess to be living in a democracy but this has evolved into merely a Clayton's Democracy, purporting that the supreme power of the people is being vested in the people and exercised by the people. What we now have is reduced freedom of speech with censorship on any government opposition; we are not afforded the opportunity or the capacity to action our legal, personal or communal needs or to defend ourselves and we have almost no ability to initiate changes for our collective good; government mismanages with our most valuable assets, sold off from under our noses; we have unaccountable government ministers procrastinating and making illogical decisions, using the best resources of bureaucratic spin doctors; we have inequality not just between small and large business but between those employed in the government sector and the public at large.

Billions of dollars have been spent on research, reports and investigations over the past 50 years for results just "stashed or shelved". Investigations; Royal Commissions; Independent Inquiries into transport; hospitals; water and other resources; government and departmental foul ups, mismanagement and incompetence. Most results achieve little if anything positive or productive, let alone alleviate reoccurring problems. In many cases this is but a mechanism to shut us up and to convince us that we have competent government, but this philosophy does not work anymore. In simple English, change is needed in how and who operates our government.

Time for a Change has always been a great political slogan to gain our confidence in giving an opposing party our vote but the fact is, it's **time to rid ourselves of useless and redundant pieces of bureaucratic baggage.** This is the prime motivation of Americans in their "Tea Party" organisation and rallies as it ought to be here, to explore the options for improvements and amendments to our political system and legislations. For Australians born here and those who have chosen to come here and who truly want to be a part of us, there could not be a more appropriate time than now in these times of shady politics and shaky world markets to review, consolidate, and to install new initiatives.

Many of the following concepts will be vigorously fought by bureaucrats who are against promoting the governance be given back to the people. Heaven forbid! Also, to rid ourselves of counterproductive waste from political "parties" but this resistance can be overcome with our majority support in the "Petition" at <www. aussieswannakiss.com> Our collective submission and participation in determining a strong, long term and focused political direction. Please discuss the points with your friends, neighbours and relatives, particularly those who are preoccupied with other interests because it is our long term future that is at stake and only this course in help- ing ourselves, will we achieve the best results we all need, sooner rather than later.

Acknowledging our problems is half of the solution . . . . It is imperative firstly, as it is in our personal lives, our business sector and for government to:

Consolidate – from the many duplicated Local, State and Federal government departments, agencies, associations, State and Federal Constitutional legislations; from the many inconsistent and diverse State judicial system; from the many groups and organisations.

Speculate – to the real Australian community priorities and needs and then refine systems and national Infrastructures and

Accumulate – opportunities where all Australians will benefit efficiently for the short and the long term. When all Australians are more secure, we will be a greater asset to developing countries, rather than swapping places.

Government at all levels needs to be redefined and the process streamlined with all of the respective transparent checks and balances provided to the people. The following initial working paper is for the further development and refinement by experts in constitutional affairs.

◆ Consolidate to one National Government from the Federal, State and Local Government system. Individual State governments cause division of laws and codes while National creates unity, ease of conformity and an efficient means of maximising the potential of all of our accumulated resources. Develop new assets to replace those which were inadvertently sold off

◆ Consolidate to one National Constitution rather than having a different Constitution for every State and Territory, many conflicting with each other and providing disparity and inconsistencies between the States. Relying on successful points taken from constitutions of States and from other countries in defining a National Constitution would produce a product that has been tested, works and is effective, without years of procrastination.

◆ Consolidate the Legal System to one National Legal system with its mandate of accountability to the people. Offering various legal options for efficient legal recourse, see section on Legal Options.

◆ Redefine the High Court, the Senate and their responsibilities. The job of the Senate and its Senators would be separate from the government and the courts. It would facilitate the needs of the people through the government and the courts. The Senate would be responsible for Legislating the National Constitution; the Local/Federal Constitution; the National Code of Conduct and the National Charter of Rights while the High Court, as the highest level of recourse is available for issues which cannot be resolved at lower levels be it by individuals in civil or other matters, or by any government minister, ministry or opposition.

◆ Is this a form of Republic? Maybe, or maybe it's just a common sense working paper, one that perhaps the Republic Movement could have considered providing. Besides a name is just a "Label" which restricts our scope!

Protect Human Rights

JUDGE MCHUGH, A former High Court Judge spoke at the Australian Human Rights Commission and emphasised the possibilities of protecting rights in this country beyond a charter. That constitutional entrenchment of rights empowering courts to strike down legislation, if found in breach of a protected right, was not an option. *"Courts are required to interpret the law and are not to be the author of statutes"*, Judge McHugh highlighted the need for a Federal charter to be nationally applicable to all States and Territories. The logistics of enshrining a national Bill or Charter of Rights under our current State and Federal political system requiring national support by all States as is currently with every issue is to say the least, optimistic, as the chances of achievement are dubious with every State being protective over its sovereignty and egotistical politicians.

There have been many politicians seeking to instil a Bill of Rights. In October 2007, Clover Moore MP stated, *"Australia is the only democratic nation in the world without a legal instrument to protect human rights. While human rights atrocities are not as common here as they are in some other countries, the widespread feeling is that civil rights are being eroded".* Her call was on the NSW State Labor government, need more be said than to the "masters of mismanagement" and while the country of Victoria has its Charter of Rights, the country of NSW is still out on that decision.

The following extracts are from exchanges of public letters between John Hatzistergos, NSW Attorney General and Catherine Branson, President of the Australian Human Rights Commission. At the time of her appointment, she had been a judge of the Federal Court since 1994 she was Crown Solicitor of South Australia and Chief Executive of the South Australian Attorney-General's Department in the 1980s. These letters are regarding a Bill or Charter of Human Rights for Australia. Note the Victorian model has excellent support and would be a perfect model to develop from, for national implementation, by an unbiased, dedicated Senate.

Catherine Branson: *"I believe Australia needs a national law setting out basic human rights and freedoms to which all people in Australia are entitled. In my view, this should be a human rights act. This would not involve changing our Constitution . . . . A human rights act is about creating a human rights culture.*

I want to live in a country where all people know about their basic human rights and understand their obligation to respect the rights of others . . . a country where consideration of human rights is an important part of government decision-making. This will make Australia a fairer, a more respectful and a more inclusive place . . . .

Our courts are accustomed to making judgments that involve balancing competing rights and interests. The independence of the courts means they can do this without fearing political or other disadvantage and without regard to the views of powerful media or other interests. I believe the public understands this and would welcome the courts' contribution to this important dialogue.

Perhaps more importantly so far as the "system" is concerned, a human rights act would require consideration of rights at every stage of public decision-making – when laws are proposed, when government policies are set and when public servants make decisions. This can only improve the lives of ordinary Australians". Wouldn't this be a good thing for our democracy?

Your argument relies heavily on lawyer and judge bashing . . . . A human rights act is not about "legal theatrics". The truth is that courts have always played an important role in protecting the rights of individuals against excessive uses of government power. But not everyone has ready access to the courts . . . .

We learn from other jurisdictions that a human rights act achieves greater protection of human rights without the need to go to court . . . . The people who most benefit from a human rights act are those who cannot afford lawyers . . . . This is already happening in Victoria . . . .

The Department of Human Services has reported on the positive impact of the Victorian Charter of Rights. It has provided a framework for reviewing mental health legislation and for improving disability services. It is changing lives . . . . I don't think Australia is so different from every other Western democracy that we alone would not benefit from comprehensive human rights protection . . . .

Of course, where democratic institutions break down, human rights protections are of limited value. But this does not mean that a human rights act would not enhance our well-functioning democracy and strengthen our institutions. The overwhelming weight of evidence from other jurisdictions is that a human rights act would make Australia a fairer, stronger, more inclusive, and thus more secure, nation".

John Hatzistergos, Minister for Justice and Minister for Industrial Relations in the NSW Labor Government. He was senior legal officer with the commonwealth Director of Public Prosecutions in the late '80s

*"My view seeks to protect the judiciary by acknowledging its traditional role rather than politicising it as has occurred in the countries you suggest we should emulate . . . . I think it best we agree to disagree **and put the proposal to the rightful owners of these rights, the Australian people, by holding a referendum** . . . .*

Two former justices of the High Court have expressed doubts about the constitutionality of the dialogue model of rights that you advocate. If it is the great white hope you suggest, then surely you wouldn't object . . . . History suggests that Australians wouldn't support it. A referendum in 1944 (65 years ago) to guarantee freedom of speech, expression and religion was defeated.

The Hawke government's 1988 referendum to constitutionally extend the right to trial by jury and freedom of religion was also defeated. Even John Howard's attempt at a non-justifiable preamble failed to arouse popular support".

The NSW Attorney-General appointed Father Frank Brennan to chair a group to examine the nation's human rights framework. At the onset of this examination Father Brennan suggested that *". . . no change to existing arrangements is an option for the committee".* It could also determine if we need a Bill of Rights and if that Bill of Rights should be enshrined in the constitution or whether it should be created in law but be mindful that it does not *"violate parliamentary sovereignty".* In his conclusion, Father Brennan expressed concerns involving *". . . human rights, civil liberties and freedoms having been most challenged when government controlled the Senate, when political parties (purporting) to act in "the best national interest" agreed to overlook the rights of the powerless minority, and when High Court Judges failed to uphold long and treasured common law rights and freedoms".* This only acts to highlight the need for national consistency, transparency and disbanding the "political party system".

Summary: Judge McHugh highlighted *". . . the need for a Federal charter to be nationally applicable to all States and territories . . ."* This is strongly supported by the President of the Australian Human Rights Commission, Catherine Branson, there could be no best authority and without more research dollars. While the NSW Labor Attorney General John Hatzistergos states, *"My view seeks to protect the judiciary by acknowledging its traditional role . . ."* and Frank Brennan who, up front stated *"no change to existing arrangements is an option for the committee."* On 15 May 2009 Mr Hatzistergos assumed there is a *". . . shrinking argument of those campaigning to foist a charter of rights . . ."* But this has never been put to the Australian people or more so, to the people of NSW for him to make such an ill conceived assumption as he continues to *"**guard the sovereignty of government and the judiciary**"* **from the people.** This would deem parliamentary sovereignty to be separate from the people and not representative of the people. This is not a government of the people for the people.

After completing this assignment Father Frank Brennan stated, *"**I rarely comment on political events unless they are of exceptional importance for the correct and free functioning of human society. Enshrining good moral choices and behaviors in government should not be necessary . . . but realistically this** is **a fallen world and therefore it IS necessary.** When the fabric of society and the functioning of government is unable to treat all of citizens of their countries with common dignity, and decency then the sanctity and integrity of human beings must be legislated and protected."* And supports the fact that it is time to, as Father Brennan states, *"**turn back the tide of criminal behaviour in powerful governments**"* and *"This issue of **establishing a culture of human rights** in societies which were corrupted by George Bush, Dick Cheney, John Howard and Tony Blair (plus others) is of absolute importance . . ."* Father Brennan urges everyone to pray and I would suggest that, as God helps those who help themselves, that as well as praying, inform your friends and family of the detrimental consequence to us all, of complacency and in not being pro-active. In protecting the judiciary who carries out government legislation, it is more than apparent that the objective is not to protect the judiciary but also the government. I'll bet Hatzistergos didn't see that result coming when he commissioned Father Brennan! The result has produced no referendum and no Charter or Bill of Rights based on bogus excuses in appearing to protect the sovereignty of government (not the Commonwealth) and the judiciary.

While holding a Bachelor of Economics, Bachelor of Law and Master of Law and is a barrister, Mr Hatzistergos is synonymous with the many academic political Ministers, from the legal fraternity who hold a conflict of interest, that is, interests above the interest of the people and all too easy to dismiss. With no disrespect intended to Mr Hatzistergos, but looking to the crisis in the NSW hospital system which NSW has been enduring over the past years and his having been the Minister for Health for 18 months Aug 2005 till April 2007 it clearly demonstrates not only the ramifications for the lack of expertise in handling specific portfolios, but also the tremendous cost and loses to the community in an ailing system and from the reshuffling and re-educating of those ill equipped to handle those Ministries.

An Australian Charter of Rights is equally as important as an Australian Code of Conduct, in giving and receiving. A Charter of Human Rights ought to be viewed as a protected entitlement of our national constitutional rights, unable to be compromised by any person or government and as such not open to judicial or any other interpretation and subsequent misinterpretation or perversion in what is afforded to every Australian. Although not to be construed as interdependent, every person must also be afforded a Code of Conduct. Each of us must have the equal right to demand that we all conduct ourselves under a Code of Conduct to preserve our own rights and those of everyone else, as anything other than that would be an imbalance or denial of equality.

An Australian National Code of Conduct, a guide for good life and social skills are just as important as Maths or English studies. These are life lessons needed to be taught as a priority to school children from as early an age as possible, together with the ramifications of non-compliance. This is tolerance and respect and is the equal right of everyone, uncompromised and supported with zero tolerance for those who are intolerant or are non-conforming. There are many ethics, morals and virtues which would be included in a National Code of Conduct but perhaps the most pertinent to civility would include basic demands, starting with (to be greatly elaborated from): Honesty; Treating others as you would treat yourself; Respect for all persons and their property, for our flag, our anthem, our laws, parents and authorities, each other's beliefs and opinions; No profanities or offensive behaviour in any public place; Equality for all persons and all ethnic groups (this is political correctness); Friendship and fairness to each other.

These virtues have been lived by for hundreds of generations and have somehow been lost by many, perhaps for them buried in the same grave as "common sense". These are the same standards and way of life our soldiers fought to defend for us. The

Universal God-given laws of honesty, decency and fairness and the correct authority to ensure a National Charter of Rights is adhered to, would most appropriately be the independent Australian Human Rights Commission, under the auspice of the National Senate, not some here today, gone tomorrow, one State minister with his "party's" agenda and the interests of the judiciary as his concern.

◆ An Australian Charter of Rights is our entitlement as citizens, and a Code of Conduct is what Australians must adhere to and taught to new Australians who must agree to adhere this when accepting citizenship, rather than knowledge of our famous cricketers. Citizenship must be conditional, able to be forfeited in the event of serious breaches of these standards of conduct.

Police suffer from verbal abuse and profanities and are hindered from doing their job for the lack of co-operation and respect from scum-bags. This results in many police resignations and our inability to retain police in the force. Our standard of education has dropped in many demographic areas as a direct result of the conflict in authoritarian powers between teachers and students. Students bully teachers as respect for teachers has diminished due to the reduction in authority by those seeking and confusing rights for children over the rights of those who must be empowered to teach and discipline. Bullying by kids has cost the lives of children as young as 12 years of age, while government has no remedy, rather compounding the problem by adapting to the *UN Rights of the Child Treaty*, which includes the rights of *'government to override every decision made by every parent if a government worker disagrees with the parent's decision"* Many parents now may be deemed to have failed in teaching respect and social behaviour or they have had little influence if a child seeks attention or just wants to be disruptive to the objectives of the teacher and long term, to society in antisocial drunken behaviour – the tail now leads the head to destruction.

◆ The Senate to work with experts in specific fields to develop from all prudent constitutions and legislations a National Constitution and to implement it through local governments and monitor it. Formulate with experts a National Charter of Rights and a National Code of Conduct. Amend legislations to protect the majority from criminals or would be criminals by creating basic standards of acceptable behaviour in this Code of Conduct. Support these documents with full disclosure and the minimum sentence ramifications for the courts to impose for non conformity or non compliance to the entire nation and to all migrants.

CUT OUT ALL STATE GOVERNMENTS – State government is as redundant as a one legged bloke in an arse kicking contest, yet this burocracy consumes 40% of all State revenue. Other than for geographical defining, the States have no real purpose. This level of government is not just the greatest liability in purpose or function, but the greatest waste of money. There is nothing the State Governments do that the proposed local come Federal government ie the proposed new National House of Representatives and the Resources Ministries cannot do, but more expeditiously and more cost effectively by skilled persons. Most functions of State Ministers are at best, defunct and in more recent times, not just a liability to growth and development or even sustainability, but destructive. Functions of health and education have had to be aided by Federal government for the inept practises and poor money management of the NSW State government. The State governments are not totally blameless when federal government holds the national purse and therefore the NSW State Debt Recovery Office has become very creative and aggressive in raising revenue since their instigating the adverse legislation in Fines Act 1996 and other such damaging fines and taxes.

The national saving from cutting out State governments would be more than A$50 billion each year and this would provide more than sufficient funds to remedy all national medical resources and provide a first class health system and the extra services as covered in the Health, Aging and Education sections of this book.

State government opposition ministers appear more and more despondent as their true worth is based on how many questions they can raise in parliament or how well they can rouse the public in the media. This, rather than achieve any real objective. Opposition would be in denial if they were not aware of their redundancy, also becoming more and more apparent to the public with some classified as being in semi retirement. After all, why keep beating your head against the wall when there is nothing an opposition minister is capable of doing to get results. From a constituent's perspective, if you complain to your State member of parliament and if he or she is a member of the opposition, the best they will do is write a letter for you to the unqualified Minister of the portfolio you have an issue with (neither of whom give a rats about your specific problem) and then he will relay the response onto you. He or she is too expensive to keep on as a glorified postman.

All "Offices of State Revenue" and income from portfolios such as transport etc would be taken over by the National (ATO) Treasury.

◆ Redefine the role and responsibilities of Local Government. Local government to represent its constituents locally come regional (or State) and into Federal parliament. To be the single point of contact in relation to all facets of government, if there be a need. This now would be a reduction in both the State and Federal representatives. It would reduce the cost of triple shuffling by inept bureaucratic infrastructures, which would have the most dramatic impact on national revenue. It would achieve both expedient productivity while reducing our financial deficit and put money into where it is needed.

The constitutionally imposed cohesion of 602 local members into regional boundaries, come States boundaries into the currently 150 Federal House of

Representatives would create a greater understanding of the requirements of each municipal area. It would provide the ability for all electorate/ municipality members to work and learn from each other's better methods and by assisting each other with all issues and shared resources. Through a standard Senate provided Constitution, it would provide consistency and benefits nationally and provide a protective mechanism for all constituents from both the ego and agendas of adversaries to our way of life and our assets.

SECTION 2

"The Solution"

One National Government with One Common Direction

FEDERAL GOVERNMENT HAS 150 local branches, the 8 State and Territory governments have 313 local branches and there are 602 Local or Municipal Governments giving us 1,065 individual government offices, in *power!* This does not include the opposition's offices, the senators and the many other parties on all three levels.

Number of Politicians by Federal: State: Local Population:

State	Fed	State	Local	No. per State	State Population	Aussies per Fed Politician	Aussies per State Politician	Aussies per Local Politician
NSW	49	135	152	336	7,019,100	143,247	51,993	46,178
VIC	37	58	79	174	5,340,300	144,332	92,074	67,599
QLD	29	18	73	120	4,320,100	148,969	240,006	59,179
SA	11	10	74	95	1,607,700	146,155	160,770	21,726
WA	15	57	142	214	2,188,500	145,900	38,395	15,412
TAS	5	20	29	54	498,900	99,780	24,945	17,203
NT	2	13	51	66	221,100	110,550	17,008	4,335
ACT	2	2	17	21	346,800	173,400	173,400	20,400
	150	313	602	1,065	21,542,500	143,617	68,826	35,785

Subject to government's statistical accuracy

Do you see consistency in the above? No? Note particularly the number of State and Local constituents to State and Local politician. I can see at least 463 redundant politicians and their oppositions in the above.

Local governments are closer to the people but they seek to maintain their own diverse agendas and constitutions, based on their specific demographic requirements and what is needed by their local constituents. In many cases conflicts arise between the ruling party's objectives and their counterpart oppositions objectives, and more than often, this is in conflict with the needs of the constituents. Add to this, conflicts between Local, State and Federal governments, and we all go backwards. Local governments seek extended powers from their State governments to fix the problems State governments have failed to remedy but State governments jealously hold onto their constitutional powers, irrespective of their failure to resolve problems which are vital State functions nor will they provide authority to local governments to enable them to overcome community problems. For example, the mayors of Waverley, Randwick, Warringah, Pittwater, Manly and Sutherland recently met to discuss the growing issue of graffiti.

Millions upon millions of dollars are lost every year in cleaning up this mess and yet, there are no solutions on the horizon, irrespective of all the man-power invested. Cr. Notley-Smith of Randwick Council said, *"We've reached the limit of powers to deal with this issue, we need the State government to give us more* (power) *as the cost of removal is out of control".* The Councils are seeking NSW State legislative changes to give them the ability to fix problems which are State-wide. Problems which the State government has not dealt with and now powers are now being sought to be given to local government. Also for control of trading hours for late-night venues as a means of defeating the problems associated with drunken and drug related violence, again problems that the State governments have been unable to resolve. Melbourne has become that gang war capital of Australia but Premier Brumby is in denial. Imperative issues that are neglected are not in our best interests, but overcoming these problems are common objectives of all Australians nationally, as we continue to foot the bill in more ways than just financial.

As well as this, there are the State and Federal conflicts of interests and objectives on every conceivable issue. There can never be a consensus with 8 States and territories and one Federal government, so forget about resolving the nightmare of any potential 602 local issues becoming Federal ones. That is, Local governments are not recognised in the Federal constitution, which would see any infrastructural stimulus payments bypass State government as a "no, no" without the current State's intervention. We have an adversarial system, but this only works when there is a final consensus reached. A mass of unresolved issues continue to plague us, decade after decade one government after another.

Inconsistencies create duplication between levels of government and from State to State, and locality to locality. Excessive duplication of functions at all three levels with far too few positive achievements for the mass of politicians and their countless staff, for our just 22 million people, in handling the created mass of bureaucratic procedure. Remember my motto: *"Complexity creates confusion and often is the catalyst of contrived fraud".* Approximately 40% of the NSW revenue is expended on government ministers and their employees. This excessive padding is costing too much money and is only creating too many hurdles for the far too few positive results. The only means of creating effective government is in the consolidation of all departments and infrastructures to provide the productivity needed. This complexity in the political system is a smoke screen for inept government and ultimately this is fraud against the people. How many politicians does it take to effectively administer a population on par with the city of Moscow and barely more than half of California?

Savings on deadwood, duplication and excessive, unproductive bureaucracy are all savings to all Australians. Savings where money is then able to be directed to where it is needed most. Redirecting of administrative "white collar takers" into positions as "blue collar makers" including into national police, defence resource, education and health sectors, trades and areas where human and other resources are in short supply. This is what will provide the positive results in our ability to perform jobs properly and meet justified expenditure which will through attrition develop our country. Our aim as a nation must be to address the shortcomings of having allowed this current system of extravagant waste and duplication to have developed. We must now redevelop it into a system able to cater to the 22 million Australians today and to be just as efficient, if not more so, when there are 50 million of us.

Currently with three tiers of government:

1. Few members of the public know at which level of government an issue sits. Many issues are Local, as well as State as well as Federal (for example, education, child & aged care, health) but few know who does what or why.
2. Often the three levels and their countless staff are doing the same job or (worse) conflicting in their handling of the respective portfolio such as planning, which are handled at all three levels with differing and often conflicting mandates, priorities and budgets. Many planning issues end up in the Land and Environment Courts costing everyone unnecessarily. By contract, just as many plans progress when they ought not.
3. Each State and Territory and local government has and maintains their own diverse constitution. There is no mechanism for national conformity which has lead to vast disparities and conflicting effectiveness, nationally.
4. Duplication between State and Federal levels in particular, creates costly and ineffective confusion. The lack of available finance for constructive initiatives (particularly Health) has seen Federal government having to fund State health constitutional matters and often these funds are misappropriated by the State government into covering the costs of bureaucratic overheads with each level arguing about the other's shortcomings.
5. The many and varying Local, State and Federal objectives and constitutions restrict the ability for compliance or reaching any agreement in regards to issues of national concern eg water. This inhibits progress and overcoming adversity eg drug and alcohol violence and prevents resolving shortcomings and thus restricts providing positive initiatives.
6. Currently, all three levels of government ministers are not specifically skilled persons for the specific portfolio held nor are the opposition ministers. In 1901 with a population of about 4 million the designers of our constitution, had

no conception of the skills and resources required to handle vastly advanced technological portfolios for the massive increase in population from that time.

7. There are constant changes in a Minister's portfolio and then when there is a change in government; there are again new ministers and new policies. For example, Minister for roads one day and Minister for education the next, only to be ousted at election time. This provides tremendous waste in retraining, with a change in direction or policy by a new government, it prevents focused attention by the currently unskilled individual who may not be suited for the specific portfolio assigned. I dare say that some portfolios have had 10 changes in ministers in as many years. Its democracy, but only if you spell that w-a-s-t-e.

8. Federal, State and Local Treasuries budgets are not based on the educated financial requirements of all portfolios but firstly to where it will demonstrate a benefit to their government's agenda best. This leads to under financed thus under productive portfolios.

The primary and imperative issues critical to the benefit of each individual and all of us collectively, irrespective of which State you live in, are all National Portfolio issues:

1. **Law & Legislation** (including fair trading);
2. **Treasury & Taxation**;
3. **Health & Aging**;
4. **Education, Science & Training**;
5. **Employment & Industry**, Workplace Relations;
6. **Security & Defence** (all internal police, military & external forces);
7. **Primary Industry** – Agriculture, Fisheries, Forestry, Water, Natural Resources & Environment;
8. **National Planning, Infrastructure, Transport & Regional Services**;
9. **Family & Community Services** (poverty & pensions), Housing, Centrelink,
10. **Immigration, Multicultural & Indigenous Affairs**;
11. **Foreign Affairs & Trade**

Under the system I am proposing, there can be no fear of corruption between government ministers, government agencies and no ability to pass Bills or Legislation without the direct consent of the people. Government agencies would be answerable to the non party affiliated House of Representatives Federal Government, working under their Senate provided directives, that is, not independent or unaccountable. The Reserve Bank, ASIO, ASIC, ITSA, Department of Fair Trading, the ACCC and others are currently financially dependent on government but are purportedly unanswerable and "independent". Hence the massive lack of performance and unaccountability has been created, against the interests of the people. A non party affiliated government with the proposed division of powers will reduce corruption, provide accountability and ensure performance, thus independence will be redundant.

Of the above 11 primary functions of government, there is not one **"Resources Ministry"** of greater priority than any other. These are our primary issues, with all else falling within the scope of these portfolios or are of a secondary or lesser priority. Although many issues may impact on the primary issues, the focus here and in the following chapters are the primary issues only.

With restructuring to a unified national governmental infrastructural plan, while abandoning State government, there would be **greater financial resources to each portfolio ie Resources Ministries able to provide better services (in the hands of experts) for less money which could provide a fairer tax system.** Redeployment of human resources would help fill the skilled and unskilled Labor markets and facilitate expansion of industries, making way for many more opportunities. In consolidating departments and functions and in streamlining the technology they use, it would provide efficiency, allowing all scales of economy to be maximised. A cohesive national reform would prevent losses currently sustained from the multiple bleeding ulcers arising from segregated or localised priorities. This has prevented and hindered any Federal government being able to obtain or come to an agreement with all of the State governments simultaneously over the past 108 year period, regarding the thousands of issues unable to be put into action, let's not even mention the Local governments who constitutionally don't really count.

Change can only come from one Australian body – its people, because it is the people who have the power to change Australia by referendum. To introduce a body or movement of Australians, namely the ones who want to see Australia change, improve and reinvent itself. The individuals who without party priorities or that of their backers, who care about Australia enough to know, that there is too much wrong with what we're doing now. You could identify these individuals as Modern or Progressive or Advanced Democrats or as the Australian Democratic Public, in the sense that it is the public who wish to remake, redo and reinvent, because the aspirations of these concerned Australians require major changes. A referendum is needed to *Advance Australia Fairly*. I'll get working on it when this book is published, so keep an eye on the website for information. The initiative could be ready for the next election with your support and if you want to get involved, please email me.

The current "Political Party System" only lends to continuing its own objectives and has proven to be far too open to being abusive. Therefore it is proposed to have two categories of Government Ministers. The following is a very simplistic overview but gives an open generalisation for refinement:

1. "National House of Representatives"

By voting for 'independents' with the same objectives unilaterally, we are voting for people who will represent the best interests of their constituents, rather than those from the "parties" who must conform to their parties' agendas, whether they agree with the theories and agendas or not – agendas that take precedence over the interests of the people. The best example of how this is already works is with Senator Nick Xenophon, Tony Windsor, Bob Katter and Rob Oakeshott – not answerable to any party but to their constituents, unless they are forced to sway to support a party. The 2010 election will go down in history as the election where the people, fed up with Liberal and Labor sought an alternative but they didn't get it. What they got was a PM and the Labor party, that the majority did not vote for.

It is proposed that elections be at 4 year intervals, in accordance with a standardised, local come national government constitution. Each Local government would provide information on their website and through local publications and literature produced by every local council (for the 3 months prior to the closing date for the national election). The local website would provide constituents with information regarding each of the candidates, his or her resume, proof of impeccable character, having been involved in various community, civil or charitable activities and demonstrating a solid business or professional background and providing reasons why he or she is worthy of constituent votes. This means, one vote every 4 years replacing 3 trips to the voting booth and saving hundreds of millions of dollars wasted on misleading or bogus promises or "shot from the hip policies" in advertising and most of the costs associated with this expensive process.

During the 3 month election period, all candidates would attend local debates at local venues to be promoted to the local community to attend. The candidates would answer questions and provide the electorate with his or her agenda for the area and views on national issues so that constituents can evaluate the various nominees. Currently party members make all the promises under the sun but once successfully elected, they are delegated to by the party and this is generally contrary to what was promised to voters.

There may be 15 or 50 such local candidates in each electorate (who are all on equal financial footings when it comes to their ability to promote themselves). These candidates may very well include the likes of Malcolm Turnbull, Peter Debnam, Nathan Rees, Kevin Rudd and Ablen Willing. It would be a challenge based on merit, not bully-boy tactics. Prior to the three month closing date of the national local election campaign, a voter need only log onto the national voting security website to cast a vote using his or her residential postcode and his or her exclusive Medicare/Australia card number, see section on National Australia Card, being the voting entitlement if the voter is over 18 years of age. The voter determines his or her local candidate preferences in order from 1 to 10 with the first

5 successful candidates selected for immediate positions and 4 lay persons who may be advanced, subject to later requirement. This will also ensure that every Australian has voted with notices sent 4 weeks prior to the closing date as a reminder of the responsibility to vote.

◆ Voting would be handled by an independent National Election Department, perhaps as part of the National Bureau of Statistics function and overseen by the Senate. Assurances and hefty penalties for tampering or disclosing any individual's details or preferences (if passed onto any party whatsoever irrespective of any circumstances). A secure department with high level computing power would be applied exclusively for this specific function. The overall local come Federal results would be published on completion of every required election. That is, your vote is to remain absolutely confidential to the national voting authority, however more secure. Currently anyone can get hold of your details through the electoral office and this constitutes an invasion of privacy whilst the security of knowing who you voted for must remain sacrosanct.

Every Local Council chamber and Centrelink office would have a dedicated computer, or computers, accessible by the public to access government issues, departments and voting as well as a trained official for the assistance of those who have no computer skills or are impaired in anyway.

On completion of the vote the following would be determined and disclosed:

1. The person who has attracted the highest primary number of votes becomes the **Local, Regional, Federal Member of Parliament**. He or she represents the interests of his or her local constituents as this is their primary and only concern. Through the local council website and media he or she is able to communicate matters of interest and concern for local, regional and Federal matters. He or she would be able to conduct local votes in support of various issues to be pursued for his or her constituents as directed by them regarding local, regional and national matters of concern. That is, we vote on issues if we so choose and our member represents our majority's vote not his own sentiments, nor as a Party directive.

2. The person who attracts the second highest votes becomes the opposition leader. He has the power to oppose the Minister if the Minister does not perform in the interests of the majority of constituents. This Opposition Member also has the power to bring to the Federal Government (firstly) and the Senate (secondly) any matters of impropriety and ultimately to the High Court any evidence of improper conduct by the Minister.

Maintaining the adversarial element of government in bringing to the public's attention any matters of concern.

3. The person who attains the third highest votes becomes the assistant or deputy to the first elected Member of Parliament and is the relief Minister, able to assume the role in the event the Minister can no longer fulfil his obligations temporarily or permanently, for whatever reason, for the duration of the term.
4. The person who attains the fourth highest votes becomes the assistant to the opposition leader, same as 3 above.
5. The fifth person takes the role of the Secretary and Chairperson and if there is a need, he or she becomes the assistant to the side (either side) if either of those positions becomes vacant due to an assistant being advanced to Minister or Opposition Minister. In this circumstance, the person who achieved the 6th highest vote tally becomes the Chairperson who chairs all public meetings, is empowered to monitor both sides of the table for performance or lack thereof and is able to appeal to the collective government of National Ministers or rather, the House of Representatives to resolve an issue that currently cannot be resolved. That is, never a stale mate and never an issue remaining unresolved indefinitely.

This method would ensure no collusion, no corruption, no alternative personal or party agendas, no adverse revenue raising or donations for political agendas and no mismanagement of imperative issues, but a total focus on the best interests of all national constituents who voted for their nominees by majority vote. All costs in connection with these elections would form part of the costs to local rate payers for the services provided locally thus nationally.

The Local Government would be made up of the 5 people as outlined above plus a further 4 individuals. This is to ensure issues can be resolved and do not come to a stalemate due to equal numbers when voting. This also avoids excessive number of local members, currently encumbered on some local government having 13 plus. All local accounting would be audited annually by a National ATO-appointed auditor. The 5 elected position holders would be paid on a full time basis and have daily functions, while the 4 runners-up would be paid on an hourly basis as required, or employed in local government. Of course there are other considerations, including the size of the electorate etc but this is a general overview only.

All 9 elected representatives would attend all Council meetings together with any interested members of the public. By majority vote of their local constituents' wants and needs, they would initiate local issues and represent these at regional meetings for networking of best methods. That is, have matters determined locally which also need addressing regionally and then taking these issues nationally, if and when needed.

Local Governments would individually and collectively work with each Portfolio Ministry under the new national, standardised constitution for Local Government to determine local planning and infrastructure requirements for each area. Planning and infrastructural requirements would be defined by the National Planning and

Infrastructure Ministry based on the demographic and geographic requirements specific to every area and zone across the country.

The Local Council's Chamber would then become not just a place to purchase local parking permits and pay Council rates but it would become the Local, Regional and Federal Government Office. Assisting all constituents with their enquiries, complaints and providing comprehensive government service in relation to all facets of government. This means all Australians are kept fully informed of all situations and issues and are able to be helped with say, a problem with an issue pertaining to the health department or any other portfolio. Helped with issues of say, unfair dealings or irregular activities or if the constituent is unable to get government intervention directly from any specific portfolio when and if the need arises. The fact that there is always someone readily available at the Local/Federal government level waiting to be proactive in taking our matter as personally to them, as it is to us and in providing the help we all so rightly deserve. This is as opposed to being a glorified postman, exchanging letters between the constituent and any government minister in "appearing to do the job".

◆ Local Government would only charge rate payers the cost of maintaining local government services, the administration of the Local/Federal office costs and sufficient projected funds based on the cost of maintaining and providing improvements to community owned properties as determined by majority votes.

◆ Local Council, by vote, can build its asset base but is **not** entitled to develop a surplus of funds for in determinant investments, as this is exploitation of the rate payer. Rate payer money is for the maintenance and improvement of community assets and the meeting of all administration costs of the Local government and its functions. All surplus funds, if not required within a short period of time, would be invested within Australia. For example, with The Bank of Australia. This would ensure that **"Charities and Local Governments do not lose another A$625.6m"** as they did in the past year with sub-prime lenders costing Woollahra Council A$4.274 million alone.

Once again, using funds for anything other than as intended by the giver or payee is misappropriation of funds, that is, fraud. There is a duty of care owed by the recipient or trustee of these funds, that all funds given or paid be it A$1 or A$1 million specifically and directly goes to where the provider intends, without digression or interception. Charities added further to the A$625.6 million by losing more than A$24 million of donors money given to St Vincent's Hospital and it is been reported that the Fred Hollows Foundation lost A$2 million in donations as these funds were invested, rather than immediately used for the benefit of those needing eye surgery. It seems generous donors were conned out of their money which they selflessly donated, but the operators of these charities had other ideas – investment and profits under tax free charity corporation schemes?

Urgent consideration towards a Royal Commission and prosecution of those who have carried out these greedy activities is as imperative as new legislation, advocating that **charities be strictly regulated to ensure donations are immediately handed over to the designated recipient and are not used for investment purposes.** Those who have invested "donations" rather than immediately giving those funds to where it was purported it would go, need to be subject to investigation and prosecutions immediately.

◆ We have many charities operating in Australia, with the legitimate ones struggling to meet the costs of their own specific overheads. These operational costs can be reduced and thus increase the available funds to the beneficiaries of these charities with a government initiative of providing facilities for registered charities to align with and operate within the overheads of their respective Portfolio Ministry and local governments. With fewer overheads, funds for charity or cancer research will go further. This would also cull duplication of charities and potential exploitation by crooks in the name of charity. Those who actually seek to line their own pockets or turn the charity into a corporation, for the benefit of the board of directors while appreciating the tax free benefits.

All these changes would mean that there is very little cost to be met by the National (ATO) Treasury for the National Government Ministers as each Municipality supports their Local/Federal Members and their own costs. In the above, we have now just saved the entire cost of the current Federal and State government system. Further suggested measures include:

◆ **State held (owned) property assets to revert to the ownership of the Local Council in which the asset lies**, and Local Council must adhere to the National Planning for construction requirements in each demographic area. The same applies to rezoning to ensure all municipalities have the required infrastructure for their demographic requirements.

◆ **Local Council cannot sell or develop any property without the majority of voters having agreed.**

◆ Local Government (in its role as the Local/Federal Government office) would receive plans for property construction and improvements only to be passed onto the National Planning authority which may have an officer housed in its locality for final approval, see section on National Planning and Infrastructure. Local planning issues must also be referred for final determination by the National Planning Authority.

After disbanding the current State and Federal governments, many ministers and employees (subject to their aptitude) would be transferred to Local Government and many may be retrained into the health, education, police administration and other portfolios which are critically understaffed or to the private/business sector. They would not be made redundant nor entitled to any benefit other than being provided with retraining and receive wages commensurate with their new role during and after the retraining period.

◆ The person who becomes Prime Minister and Deputy Prime Minister would be determined by the vote from the 602 Local/Federal Ministers of the House of Representatives in consideration of each candidate contender's successful business acumen and most suitability for these positions. There would be no need for Opposition Leaders of parties as the Prime Minister and Deputy office-holders would represent a cohesive government without party affiliations and thus there would be no *"petty party political point scoring"* or losses due to adverse behaviour. The Prime Minister and Deputy would not hold a Local Government position as their function would be to head the cohesive House of Representatives Government and the National Portfolio Ministries Body. Their mandate would reflect the majority of their collective government's Ministry's vote. That is, the **Prime Minister and the Deputy are roles of representatives or subordinates to the House of Representatives, not having the power to delegate or pursue any interest or agenda other than as delegated by the House of Representatives.** It would be the House of Representative who would have the power to hire and fire based on performance.

◆ The position of Treasurer would be the Minister of the National (ATO) Treasury, possibly Mr Turnbull having the right credentials and same would apply to every Ministry from Health, say Kerryn Phelps, to Education and all Portfolio Ministries, and see section on National Portfolio Ministry.

◆ All Ministerial roles would be subject to the majority consensus, be it local constituents or those engaged in any portfolio in determining issues. That is, no issue would be at the determination of any one person or based on party agendas or adverse attitudes towards opposition's constituents. These positions would represent the cohesive determination of a collective government under the revised House of Representatives; (portfolio) Resources Ministries and Industry Constitutions. Legislations would be amended, presented, monitored and maintained by the Senate with the respective regulatory government agencies to ensure all levels of government, the judiciary and all sectors of industry conform.

◆ Australian International Ambassadors would have to be selected from persons well versed in the designated countries where they are to represent us. This would include extensive language, political and social skills of that country. The collective Local/Federal members would vote every 4 years to determine if the Ambassador to a country has performed well in all areas, with his or her continued appointment, or dismissal.

An Ambassador would not be selected based on getting rid of an embarrassing politician or as a payoff in sending them to another country with no accountability for what they achieve there. This has happened in several instances. Similarly, our Minister for Foreign Affairs must be a person well educated in the historical makeup of many nations, the culture of various peoples, and possess strong language and social skills gained from his or her years of expertise, not just someone who loves to travel or needs a bandaid on his broken ego. Their educational standing and ability to take responsibility for all Australian Ambassadors in seeking out and maximising opportunities internationally for trade and public relations in each country would see us leap ahead. An added bonus would be attending to all foreign matters with our Portfolio Ministers from trade, medicine, education to defence. Only such a person can adequately represent us on the international stage rather than someone who was perhaps, just prior, say the Minister for Welfare.

Would a system of independent members rather the party system work? Independent Ministers are able to be more pro-active in government than most party governed ministers in stopping adversity and seeking accountability. Imagine how more productive as a nation we would be if the party system was disbanded and this system installed! I dare say Barnaby Joyce will tire of the Liberals or party system and go it alone and I dare say, he will be very successful as others would be.

2. "National Resources Ministries"

What credentials do politicians hold to determine and delegate specialised portfolios?

Politicians do not solve problems, often they just create them. **You don't get a plumber to perform brain surgery**, or a bureaucrat to carry out environmental planning when farmers and scientists know the land better, and you don't get an unqualified white collar worker to be, the Minister of Health. Then, after acquiring some rudimentary knowledge in that very specialised field, and possibly after having made very expensive, uneducated and wrong decisions or no positive decisions, transfer him to another Ministry for another relatively short interval of mismanagement. Business, industry and every function of government needs specialised industry portfolio leaders, experts in every specific field with a fresh unhindered departmentalised approach based on accurate determination of their industries requirements and objectives.

The aim of good government is to create uniformity and implement consistently high standards across the country; to reduce duplication; alleviate confusion and procrastination and to provide longevity way past the less than 4 year cycle to every facet of government, and thus maximise every tax dollar ensuring it goes where it is specifically needed. Consolidation and standardisation of each Ministry to a general National Constitution with specifics for each portfolio to be in tune with 21st century's standards and requirements must be implemented by each Ministry. We will not eliminate the current A$4 billion a year the Federal Government currently costs but it will be reduced in servicing this specialised level of government.

To digress a little, yet still demonstrating the pertinence of this concept; Contempt for police authority has been the result of the cultivating of superfluous governance and thus under-achieving productivity. Rather than politicians directing police, police would be nationally accountable through their ministry and answerable to the government for their institutional independence, as all proposed Resources Ministries would. To quote Professor **David Brown from the University of NSW Law Faculty:** *"Politicians must respect institutional independence"* and *"Policing in NSW has become overly politicised with politicians of all persuasions seeking to micro-manage the police."* Too many bored politicians, so bored they seek ways to justify their existence, thus hinder constructive "real work" by experts.

This excess of politicians, on all levels, contradicts there being any excuse for any politician to hold more than one specialised position, unskilled as they may be. With respect to the Hon Julia Gillard MP who is the Deputy Prime Minister, but she still finds time to be the Minister for Education, and the Minister for Social Inclusion, as well as the Minister for Employment and Workplace. I'm sure Ms Gillard is very good at multi-tasking and I'm sure she would be more financially astute than her boss, but these four vital portfolios need four skilled and totally dedicated experts in each of those very specialised portfolios. Liberal got the boot because of Workchoices but Ms Gillard's industrial relations theories appear to be more detrimental to workers, particularly part-timers and those who are under-employed as they cannot get full-time work, which many Australians have become.

These trends are not limited to policing, work place relations and the inability to achieve social inclusion for migrants, gangs and kids who come from dysfunctional families. It has become synonymous with all issues of primary concern to the populace regarding every pertinent portfolio. It clearly demonstrates issues of ego or perhaps more appropriately, the lack of usefulness in their current government positions in needing to cease whatever opportunities can be created to justify intervention, and prohibit focused expeditious results. This micromanagement is both costly and counterproductive, particularly with the NSW Police's resources being so restricted that they are now forced to evaluate crimes and complaints and rather than pursue, they are forced to abandon those not easily resolved, for lack of human and financial resources. To be micromanaged by people ill equipped to direct them, is just downright stupid. Over governance or micromanagement and then fobbing off responsibility for financial reasons, to create the illusion of a legitimate political job, determined military bases be guarded by unqualified security guards, rather than allow our highly trained professional soldiers to secure themselves and us.

The essence of proposed Portfolio Ministries run by specialists in each field, is that all national portfolio ministries be individually institutionalised but harnessed under one "National Resources Ministry" fully accountable and answerable to the "National Federal Government body". Each individual Portfolio Ministry would be represented at the Local/Federal government level to address concerns of local constituents, subject to demographic and geographic requirements in determination with the National Planning Ministry.

Delegate and account nationally for consistent administration locally.

Each Ministry would comprise of the Minister and a member of each of the respective sub-portfolios. An example could be: The Health portfolio under the Australian Medial Association (it's there just not listened to) – head of the national ambulance service; hospitals; medical practitioners association, pharmaceutical association, Dentists and Optometrists representation etc.; an industry workers union delegate and 3 members of the public. No different to a board of directors of a public company who provide their individual and collective short, medium and long term objectives, supported by projected expenditure and benefits. This consolidation of all areas of the health industry and all current State's ministries would enable networking and interaction to maximise resources and opportunities for development with reduced operational costs.

Each Ministry and sub-ministry member would have at least 20 years of successful experience in his or her respective field of expertise. Similarly, the Defence Force Ministry would comprise of members with at least 20 years experience from each service; Army, Air force, Navy, Coast Guard, the Federal Police and Internal Police to determine national and localised requirements. This is in contrast to say, one State setting up a specific task force while others are left begging for consideration or resources. This would also reduce duplication and assist with maximising resources.

In selecting a member of parliament to represent each of the portfolios such as the Judiciary, Treasury, Health, Education, Employment, Defence, Primary Industry, National Planning, Family & Community, Immigration and Foreign Affairs etc. persons employed in their respective industry would be elected by the public at the same time their Local/Federal House of Representatives Member is voted, every 4 years. Candidate Ministers would be re-elected based on results during the term. There would also be a respective Union delegate to each portfolio ministry to ensure work place conditions and terms are met and to alleviate disruption and conflict within any industry sector.

Each Ministry would receive from their sub-portfolio ministers their short and long term objectives and costs. The Ministry would produce an overall Ministry plan catering to each sub-portfolio's requirements which provides for immediate short term requirements and long term objectives. These projections would be supported by solid budgets verified by the National (ATO) Ministry for each Portfolio, responsible for inaccuracies if the plan stays on course. There would be many savings through this networking of resources and it would provide better economies of scale at all levels.

◆ Each Ministry would prepare its long, medium and short term objectives with the projected costs submitted to The Treasury for budgetary consideration. Once the accurate costs have been determined, the proposal is to be promoted to the general public to evaluate on the government website and, possibly the government television channel for any constructive feedback. Once this process is complete with any amendments and Treasury support, it is recommended for approval to the "Federal Members of Parliament"

◆ Maintenance of all Resources Ministries, the Senate, the High Court and all government regulatory bodies are direct costs to be met by the National (ATO) Treasury derived from national consolidated taxation and income revenue. This would also include all specific user pays revenue from the public for say, road tolls, transport fares, vehicle registrations etc. However the cost of all government functions are to be "not for profit" generators with these costs absorbed in the budgets approved, rather than as covert or concealed taxes.

◆ Surplus funds, that are above the cost of maintenance, are the specific and limited funds required to provide the long term objectives of each portfolio ministry with historical income streams relied on in determining future requirements.

We are now getting too specific for the intention of this book but clearly demonstrating the relevance for selecting skilled persons to head all aspects of any department reformed government. Giving Australia the ability to take these proposed amendments to the next level of refinement and ultimate submission for reform rather than continue to suffer the current fumbling and stumbling of politically aligned non professionals.

On-line voting for Resources Ministers would save us, the taxpayers, hundreds of millions of dollars in time, money and resources to achieve an educated vote for an *"academic who has gained the expertise from years of practise in a specialised field."* Professionals, rather than collective party members with their vote winning adlib policies, especially as the current system elects the government who then allocates the jobs, usually based on cronyism rather than ability.

◆ The "Resources Ministries" would work together for common objectives and present unified proposals if cross collateralisation of resources is required. For example, Medical or Education infrastructure requirements with National Planning and communicated through the National Communications Ministry. Same would apply to housing and welfare or Aged and disabled care with the Medical Ministry etc.

◆ **The accountability of the "Resources Ministries" would be to the "House of Representatives" whose accountability is firstly to their constituents as anchored in the national constitution, monitored by the Senate.** If issues cannot be resolved, then the issue would go to the High Court if there was a need, or if concerns have not been fairly dealt with by the National Local/ Federal Members.

In adapting the above forms of government, with skilled modifications and refinement, at least we would have removed all and any need for hefty funding of party politics; the maintaining of party agendas, two of the levels of government together with the removal of costly voting, advertising to gain support and would provide a cost effective means of providing the majority of Australians with an effective government at a fraction of the current cost. We would be able to fill the positions of skilled and unskilled labour to the respective sectors of the community, and enable expansion of personal and commercial opportunities. This method will remove any prospects of improper favourable consideration being given by a political contributor whether he or she is say, a developer or a bank or any person who one day may "need a favour from the government" be it to jump the hospitals que, close eyes to unfair trading or get rezoning or poor planning through. **Reducing bureaucracy and eliminating party politics in *"Keeping It Simple"* and will also reduce our vulnerability to corruption at every level and *Advance Australia Fairly*!**

The Senate Legislator

THE TERM "SENATE" is used very loosely here – this arm of government could be called "Congress" or "Upper House" but the basic job description is – **A regulatory body to delegate on behalf of the people, to government bodies, the courts and industries in producing through the Senate's skilled professionals, academic and non academic members of society: Constitutions, Legislations, Charter of Rights, Codes of Conduct etc to be upheld by all levels of society with no room for misinterpretation. It would work closely with the Department of Human Rights, anti Discrimination Commission, Equal Opportunity and Industrial Commissions, Fair Trading, ASIO, ICAC, ACCC, ASIC and all other such regulatory functions. It would determine law and constitutional reform, eliminating redundant references and ensuring the pendulum swings towards the majority of people.** The strict mandate would be to provide equality at all levels of society, with all levels of society.

This would appease Mark Dreyfus QC who recommends, "... *the establishment of regularly scheduled Constitutional conventions. I also propose that a permanent Constitutional Review Commission be established, along the lines of the Productivity Commission and the Australian Law Reform Commission ... to conduct public consultations .... conducted in Victoria which led to the <u>Charter of Rights</u> enacted by the Victorian parliament in 2006".*

The Senate would be a specialised body comprising of the best, say 100 or even 200 heads in the country from all fields; from constitutional, to legal and financial experts, from economists, industry and social experts working with professionals in each field. They would have the sole objective of establishing National Constitutions for every respective portfolio and ensuring these documents are based on successful existing and international constitutions and best practise. The Senate would determine, implement and monitor performance of the above, able to be amended by the people by voting, as society changes over the next 108 years plus. It would be headed by a representative who is voted in by all Senators. No government minister would be able to hold a position on the Senate as it exists currently e.g. Senator Nick Sherry is also the Minister for Corporations etc. The Senate could only be challenged for amendment by reference to the High Court by any Resources Ministry or House of Representatives Minister or by petition of civilians supported by at least 5% of the voting population.

The Senate would be designed to be the voice of the people in securing the fairest equal opportunities to be adhered to by both the House of Representatives and the Resources Ministries (this would include the national judiciary), all industries, government regulators and civilians with all breaches of constitutions addressed to the Senate for remedy. The Senate, by delegating to ASIC would ensure corporations conform to minimum standards and provide protective mechanisms for individuals, and the ACCC would provide protection against monopolising any industry, protection from the use of harmful chemicals and ingredients, unfair dealings or particularly exploitation with legislation to conform with the essence of the National Constitution.

For example, a major shopping chain buying out Mobil so that together with Coles, Shell secures a 75% interest in that industry. Setting industry limitation on market share, which could mean that sectors of existing operations must be separated, and sold off to alternative owners, however, this must not be based on the poorest performing outlets going. Rather, what would make up a limit for the existing operations of those companies and provide for a fair business for alternative Australian owned operators. Ensuring fair market prices are paid to farmers and that retail prices provide a fair margin without exploitation of the public and that together with Industrial Relations, determine wages to be reflective of skills and demographic living costs. Limiting international ownership of industry and property, with no favourable taxation or other concessions and ensuring international workers are paid in accordance with Australia's award wages, also reflective of specific skills and demography, see further.

The Senate, in revisiting and initiating fairer legislation under respective constitutions for government and industry, would be independent of both functions of government and of the new National Judiciary, although no group or individual would be precluded from making submissions. The Senate would work with the High Court and all levels of society through submissions and in particular from academic professionals and business experts pertaining to each facet of the Code of Conduct, the Charter of Human Rights, Trade Practises and National Constitutions. This would ensure there are no conflicts of interest, no inequality of bargaining power and based on the benefit of successful historical precedents and international tried and true successful trade practises. To ensure the pendulum swings fairly between employer and employee which has swung both too far to the left and the right since white man stepped onto this fair land.

There would be one Constitution for the House of Representatives and one general unified Constitution for the national local ministries, with specific attention to any geographic requirements. One general unified Constitution for each of the National Portfolio Ministries, also with specific legislation pertinent to each Ministries specific requirement, in total, upheld by all Ministers.

All Constitutions would contain specific Codes of Conduct pertinent to that industry, and we would have a National Code of Conduct and Charter of Human Rights. The Senate would ensure every citizen and migrant, regardless of their age or communal standing, is aware of these documents and the most pertinent issues would be taught through the National Education system's syllabus. Expected conduct can no longer be assumed is known by everyone at all levels of society and government must ensure it is taught for it to be able to be upheld, with the benefits outweighing any concerns for compromise. This would have particular pertinence for the Charter of Rights although not dependent on the Code of Conduct, with both taught to all Australians and new Australians from an early age, including the legal ramifications for breaches to these social and legal obligations in law. This would perhaps be one of the greatest deterrents against breaking the law and would help provide peace through fair justice and equality for all. In addition, the Senate would:

◆ Create a National Freedom of Information Department – this will ensure government ministers and public companies can no longer hide clandestine or adverse dealings, thus reducing corruption at all levels by providing transparency to the public. Unless it is a matter of national defence security, all documents and full disclosure is expected from all public servants with the threat of penal servitude for failure to comply. This is real transparency and what the Australian public is entitled to.

◆ Ensure all government regulatory bodies conform and are accountable to the Senate and that there is no "independence from government" – see section on Government Regulators, as the proposed system of government does not provide the opportunity for corruption or the pursuit of alternative agendas.

You can be very sure that every effort for these proposed amendments to the political system, the judiciary, the Federal, States and Local powers will be resisted vigorously. Resisted vigorously by politicians and the judiciary who will kick'en scream to maintain their stronghold with debate, delays, more research and more complex arguments. But they should be mindful that their tenure is tentative, as are any of our lives in the scheme of this world. Rather than oppose change they ought to be working with this proposal to seek ways of refining and expediting the initiatives for the good of all Australians. There could be an argument for no change based on *"if it ain't broke don't fix it"* but it (government, at all levels, the agencies and departments) is broke in more ways than one and breaking down further with every passing day of mismanagement and from one government party's reign to the next!

One National Judicial System

"Only Justice Provides Peace"

FOR ALL AUSTRALIANS irrespective of faith, ethnicity, social standing, age or demographic locality, the most pertinent issue to achieving peace and freedom is to achieve justice within the legal system. But for those looking for the ability to overcome the adversities associated with the current legal process, there are also its costs which are detrimental to the interests of the majority of people, business' and employment.

In the most successful book ever published, an "old legal text", the Bible, it says – "*You shall appoint judges and officers of law and they shall judge the people fairly*". This is the traditional role of the judiciary. But fair judgement cannot prevail when procedures and adverse legislation outweigh the opportunity for fair judgement, when the cost of fair judgment removes the ability to pursue or attain a fair judgement, when laws within the borders of one land are so divergent, when officers of the court run their own agenda and when illegal migrants have greater recourse to legal-aid than Australians. *Charity and Justice have equal dominion and there can never be an excess of either, as society cannot exist, let alone excel in the long term without charity and justice.* This is the only means of elevating our very existence, both individually and collectively, in a way that no collaborative form of government, under Communism or Capitalism, or any other, has been able to provide.

John Hatzistergos, Attorney General of NSW (to reiterate) *"My view seeks to protect the judiciary by acknowledging its traditional role . . ."* but the traditional role of the judiciary was to provide fair access to all citizens, it was not intended to be hijacked by government legislation and it does not include amending or reducing police charges to lesser charges. If a person is charged with say murder by the police, with sufficient evidence, how is the judiciary able to reduce the charges before hearing the evidence, to a lesser charge of say manslaughter, warranting a much lesser sentence, just because the criminal has entered into a "Plea Bargain"? This goes entirely against the grain of *"you shall judge the people fairly"* – for the crime charged with, and not for a quick and easy way out for the judiciary and the criminal, where he or she will be let out on the street to re-offend in a shorter period of time. This is cruelty to the kind (victim and the family) and kindness to the cruel and the greatest unconstitutional injustice. This is a short-sighted saving to the community in a quick guaranteed sentence for the criminal and possibly the would-be re-offender. This is not justice for the victim, the family or the police and court resources. More than often the re-offender is back in court again and again.

Any perversion to justice by means of costly and lengthy procedures; unfair or adverse legislation, or due to inept representations are betrayals, not just of the individual's rights but of the rights of every person. **We can only achieve peace through justice** – no decent society can exist without laws and society conforming to a just and equitable legal system, accessible by every member of society, anything else is destructive and abusive.

The Judicial system in western society was, in effect, adopted from God-given-laws with further designs by aristocratic architects of by-gone days, to be independent of and uninfluenced by government as a means of a purported higher authority. It could even be said that all Abrahamic cultures trace the origin of their laws from their religion. A place where the governed could turn to and rely on for fair, impartial determination of matters of legal concern or in the event that the government has failed to act in the interest of the governed, in accordance with the true intent of Constitutions.

Judicial independence from government (supposedly the people) does not provide accountability to the people, and is a contradiction in terms. Unwittingly, or not, the Judiciary has facilitated government "parties" and their own agendas and has placed legal recourse for government failure, out of the reach of the average person or even a group or class of persons seeking recourse. While *"Man is ruled by laws not by other men"*, men and women determine the outcome within the confines of legal procedures and precedents, but these do not always provide for a fair or consistent determination. We acknowledge that the legal system is cumbersome and inadequate and change is needed which is why millions of dollars has been expended on law reform but producing very little. However, it is generally academic legal practitioners who seek and hold these positions of power and determination with many moving to government positions. Unfortunately many of these persons lack the capacity to see the practical ramifications and benefits to the populace, thus denying fairness and equality.

Legislations or the passing of laws are supposed to be designed for society to exist in peace and harmony. If there is no peace in any specific area of society, legislation must be changed to meet the demands of the majority, irrespective of any purported political correctness. Left untended calamity can spread to a point of no return, but unfortunately political correctness has been misconstrued, with far too much faith and hope placed in the ability to reform people who have lost their direction or who never had a direction. In recent times we have had a 'small dose' of racial vilification at Cronulla and other areas. There are serious concerns that groups or gangs are growing, and they are. Groups who have either not been educated in our social codes (born here or not), or those have not integrated into our Australian society. There are those who have no idea as to what is acceptable, but there are those who maintain contempt and derision for our laws and our society – yet if we speak ill of them, this is considered politically incorrect?

What is not acceptable in our society, are those who blatantly defy our weak laws in acts of destruction of life and property. The Australian philosophy, not unlike the American, claims to embrace beautiful ideals. But without the strict legal means to uphold these ideals, society dips to the departments of moral depravity with problems associated with racial, drug and drunken violent riots. If not addressed through legislative reform and minimum sentences widely publicised, we can expect the same scale of internal violence as America and other multinational societies. Our internal police, emergency forces and legal system are under-resourced to endure the current level of violence let alone able to suppress it or cater to increasing problems. Inappropriate sentencing is not the deterrent needed to remedy for social unrest.

We teach and preach tolerance and have developed what we call "Political Correctness" which only works in favour of minority groups but we have failed to consider what is politically correct for the majority, and this must be turned around as currently:

The Greatest Perversion of Justice is the Justice System itself!

In most cases, the average person cannot afford the current forms of legal recourse with "Big Business" or those financially better off able to win by default against small adversaries. Even if your case is "right and provable" well heeled opponents can starve you out of justice, because their pockets are deeper. Government is not blameless, for example; consider the compensation cases surrounding the Maralinga victims. In other words, you don't have to be in the wrong to lose, you can either not get fair compensation or you can just run out of money and not have your day in court. What is required for equality is for legal recourse to be cost effective, prompt and efficient in ensuring an accurate and fair outcome.

The objective must be to bring about **equality between large and small business and between all adversaries**. Inequality of bargaining power or conditions or the inability to obtain legal recourse by one party over another, can only be considered as the harshest and most unconscionable shortcoming in our society. It is one of the contributing factors to the demise of many small businesses. Small Business as we know employs more than 75% of all Australians and the ability to get business and people moving on quickly after adversity is paramount as against being bogged down in the negative world of litigation. What is worse is to suffer the unjust demise due to denial of legal remedy which is certainly contributing to the growing unemployment problems we are all facing.

The Judicial system has become just as intricate a jungle of unaccountable bureaucratic institutions and diverse procedures. As each of the 8 State and Territory governments have a multitude of diverse local governments and the overall Federal Government, our legal system also has 9 different State and Territory Judiciary systems governing each of their Local, District, Supreme Courts, Family Law Courts, Criminal Law Courts, Land and Environment Courts and other such instruments for seeking legal redress. Forms and procedures have been amended and amended from court to court and from State to State to the point that no average person can defend himself without a lawyer and a barrister and often a Queens Counsel, restricted to a State.

We cannot easily use a solicitor in say NSW for a matter in Victoria as the laws and procedures vary between States. Also, it is so easy for the simple facts of a matter to be confused, misunderstood and lost in the process that at the end of the financially exhaustive day, you can lose a case only for technical reasons, not based on facts or evidence pertaining to the matter. In many States you have no ability to submit new evidence which comes to light before an Appeal hearing, even if the new (crucial) evidence was not available at the time of the initial hearing and irrespective of the prima facie evidence proving fraud. In this case you must be able to afford another day in the High Court and what's the chance of that!

Diverse laws between the States and ineffective procedures from one State to another, create not just injustice but the perversion of justice. There was a recent case where a women was granted (by a NSW Court) an Order that her whereabouts be withheld from her abusive husband but when she moved to Victoria, these orders were redundant in that State and this exposed her to discovery by her estranged husband, as if the NSW Orders just did not exist. This is not an isolated case as thousands upon thousands of court orders pertaining to critical matters result in abuse of Australians by our own judiciary in one State's courts contempt over another State's court rulings. This has been tolerated throughout the country for over a hundred years with not one bright spark legal eagle or government minister ever having thrown it open for urgent reform. A Law Reform Commission has been established and countless debates and submissions reviewed, costing hundreds of millions of dollars, but to no benefit or initiation of a common sense reform. It will not happen, unless the people collectively take this initiative from those who jealously guard their stature and their golden goose.

Unfortunately, as with the government, the Judiciary is not beyond corruption or abuse of power in shielding the misconduct of some of its officers. There are cases of corruption to protect their own which go unreported and due to lack of ability of individuals and the unaccountable failure to investigate by agencies such as ICAC, these protected species go unapprehended. A clear example is the case of John Walsh:

In March 2000 John Walsh was found guilty on charges of conspiracy and perverting the course of justice. He was sentenced to 10 years imprisonment. Two months later the Crown confessed to placing fake evidence before the trial jury. In February 2002 Walsh was to go to an Appeal and on the second night before the hearing – whilst on his own behind a locked door he was bashed senseless and hospitalised. Because of his absence from the Court of Appeal the matter of the Crown tampering with the evidence did not see the light of day and instead of walking free, he lost his Appeal. Upon release, as a self represented litigant and with the written confession in hand, he placed the matter into the Victorian Supreme Court only to be told by the presiding judge that the offending prosecutor is immune for prosecution.

There is no legal body in Victoria prepared to assist in exposing the criminality of a senior legal peer. On 31 December 2009 John Walsh lodged an affidavit with the Victorian Court of Appeal as part of a Grand Jury application. See Melbourne *Sun Herald* 21 Feb 2010 **"Trial Flawed, Claim"** This Grand Jury application may well be the last in Victoria as Attorney General Rob Hulls amended the Criminal Proceedings Act to abolish Grand Juries as from 1 January 2010 Under legal precedent the Court of Appeal has no discretion to refuse to empower a Grand jury. Copies of the Grand Jury documents can be sourced from – <johnrwalsh@bigpond.com> Laurie Nowell of the *Sun Herald* states, *". . . under legal precedent, the Court of Appeal has no discretion to refuse to empower a Grand Jury. Barrister and constitutional law expert Dr John Walsh said it was outrageous that the State Government has purported to abolish the common law right of Grand Juries. "This is a sovereign right enshrined in common law. The Government should not remove it without a referendum"* Dr Walsh (NB same name) said. So how did Victoria's Attorney General Rob Hulls pull that off without any referendum? There are thousands of John Walsh stories, none reported and together with the unapprehended perpetrator criminals, they continue to live in our midst.

On the flip side: There are many decent upright legal practitioners who have witnessed major disparities in this dishonest system. They have given up the fight to stay in the legal profession for what they have witnessed and encountered, both in their inability to gain justice for their clients and in contempt for the system. In addition, they know clients who blatantly break the law knowing the system cannot, or will not apprehend them for lack of will or utility.

It is primarily the judiciary who are opposed to a Charter of Rights for Australia. Then keep in mind that so many of our politicians practised law before becoming politicians and now together with their academic judicial allies, want to continue *"interpreting"* and amending the laws often to the detriment of human rights. They remain immune, protected and impartial to the rights of the people, prioritising and collaborating the interests and objectives of those at the high end of our country in what they themselves believe is best for them.

Under these circumstance, it is illogical and an insult to all Australians in the 21st century, for the Judiciary to remain independent, unaccountable and for the majority of us, inaccessible when needed. Judicial independence of government may well have been necessary in centuries gone by, when the church was a fundamental part of government, but under the proposals contained in this book, judicial independence is no longer warranted or reasonable. It is proposed that:

◆ The National Judiciary to be nationally consolidated and retain independence but answerable and accountable within the portfolio or Resources Ministries system.

It is proposed that there be one "National Judicial Ministry" with a national constitution to service each of the national, local, district, county, supreme, family law, land and environment court and other such facilities functions. This overall national body would include all levels of Australian legal practitioners and would fall under this one national portfolio ministry. It would be headed by the National Attorney General who would be voted from within the legal fraternity and answerable, as with all "Resources Ministries", to the "National Federal Members" of parliament, the Senate and the High Court. This ministry would include member of the legal fraternity and interested members from the wider community for transparency.

It is proposed that this national ministry continue to be funded by the National (ATO) Treasury for the cost of operations only and then charged out on a user pays basis, although, as a not-for-profit government service. In the event that a private person or business litigant does not have the funds to pursue litigation, this must be assessed by the judiciary for alternative dispute resolution, be it an arbitrary body or by mediation. Currently there are no minimum productivity requirements from any of the courts in the land and this in itself needs to be addressed in providing accountability for performance and audited disclosure to the public.

Assessment of amendments to a National Judicial Ministry's Constitution would be undertaken by the National Senate, who would ensure that legislations and procedures are formulated from sensible streamline practices, adapted from various successful States and international constitutions for the adherence of all unified courts. Included in that constitution would be how alternative dispute systems of Arbitration and Mediation are to be applied and upheld by all officers of all courts.

◆ All individual State and Territory laws and legislations need to be consolidated into one national constitution and refined into the most effective and pertinent documents for fairness and practicality in providing the ability for application based on the most appropriate common sense practices and procedures nationally.

It is proposed that **The High Court of Australia** would retain independence of the National Judicial Ministry. It would provide the ability for House of Representative members and their local opponents; the Resources Ministers and the public to have access to it in the event that disputes or challenges cannot be resolved at lower levels. The High Court would work with the Senate on developing, implementing and amending legislation based on the wishes and determination of the majority of Australians through an online voting system, particularly pertaining to social issues. There needs to be a mechanism for a percentage of the population who share a common concern to be able to put that issue to the Australian people directly. This could apply to many issues such as marriage contracts, euthanasia, abortion etc.

The de-regulation of the Financial System has enabled banks to evolve into self regulatory bodies which are unaccountable to the government (us) or their customers (us) whose funds they administer (ours). There is the urgent need to have a mechanism in place to create equality of bargaining power with prompt, constructive recourse for both parties which will also reduce the costs of litigation to the litigants and the taxpayer. It is suggested that from the bank's margin a fund be established to provide litigation funding or "insurance" ensuring the bank and the customer achieve equal representation. If alternative dispute mechanisms are relied on, the cost for prompt decision by say an arbitrator would be minimal. This would ensure that if a client has a matter not worthy of litigation (ie a sore loser of a case), that the solicitor be absolutely up front with his client in not wasting the clients money in pursuing a matter that will not win, but will line the lawyer's pocket.

◆ Arbitration between large business and their customers ought to be written into all Industry Constitutional Legislations, bringing about equality of bargaining power and releasing the strangle-hold on the courts, the purses of the opposing parties and the taxpayer.

Nationally there are thousands of court cases each year involving banks and currently the Banking Ombudsman's Office, which is maintained by the banks, attempts to resolve disputes or issues but acceptance of this determination is not an obligatory determination on either party. In general, the complaints received regarding banks encompass – overcharging of interest and unfair penalty rates and fees; wrongful foreclosure on a specific industry sector. For example; foreclosure on a builder in the event that industry is currently experiencing a slowdown in trading and the bank gets jittery or feels under-secured so without a default it calls in the loan. In certain circumstances banks tamper with documentation to:

a) Protect a bank officer, if there is a need to rectify that officer's errors/mistakes or non-authorised dealing.
b) Get out of an agreement.
c) Call in loans or security due to policy change or an apparent problem with a loan, or a change of heart towards lending into a specific industry which may be perceived to be heading for a downturn. In short, changing the rules to suit the bank following a reassessment, while the business has made commitments based on the bank's assurances.

The banks wanting to *"appear to be doing the right thing by their shareholders"* currently rely on the legal system without consideration as to costs or their ability to recoup the costs, as they have very, very deep pockets. They engage the highest calibre of creative legal representation that money can buy. More than often the end result for the bank from a successful litigation is that the legal costs and bad debt may be unrecoverable. A win but with no financial reward, or if the bank loses, the bank in both of these situations will treat it as a tax loss deduction – an expense, ie no loss by the bank in either situation, something the private opponent is not afforded and cannot achieve, it's a case of just wear more losses!

Many legal actions against banks and insurance companies are settled before judgment. Out of court settlements are pursued as the banks best option, rather than see a legal precedent set that could adversely affect their industry's long term dealings. So push the little opponent off the playing field for a fraction of which it could cost in the long term. This in itself is an injustice to the entire business world but, for the bank, it is a small price to pay in protecting its industry. If, prior to expending vast sums on litigation by both parties, an alternative existed which both were obliged to pursue, the cost to Australia might be much reduced. A much lesser cost would be required in engaging in Arbitration. Giving the Arbitrator the ability to rewrite loans and assist in facilitating a positive result for both the bank and the customer, rather than contending with adverse results suffered by both parties:

a) Breakdown of relationship between the bank and its customer.
b) Enormous legal costs for both parties and further financial losses
c) Human resources are lost by both parties in the time required for litigation
d) Devastation of customer's personal and financial affairs

Reducing the time and cost of litigation eliminates aggression and animosities and allows everyone to get on with constructive business. It breeds a culture of care and concern, while creating an equality of negotiating power with resolution as the aim. It is only an unjust justice system (unbalanced) in allowing one party with deeper pockets than the other to engage in continued litigation that prevents a fair and equitable result and in breaking their opponent. It is a legal system which protects its own members which is at the heart of this inequality.

September 18, 1998, the following (part) submission was made to Laurie Glanfield, Director General, and NSW Attorney Generals Department for the National Competition Policy Review of the Legal Profession Act 1987. The results of the Attorney General's Department inquiry no doubt ought to have yielded an equality of bargaining power between large and small business, ensuring every Australian is able to obtain legal redress and not be hindered by procedure or cost, but this has not happened.

With one Attorney General in each State and Territory overseeing their diverse constitutions, courts, legal practitioners and legal complaints services and one Federal Attorney General overseeing the Federal courts – where do you go if you have a complaint? Logically most would see the reliance on the legal system and then recourse to that very same system, as a conflict of interest and it is, but nobody stops it. The Judiciary and the Government know there is a conflict of interest and this conflict is not in the interest of the public but it continues to every person's detriment unless you are a legal practitioner. The legal system and redress to the legal system falls short for those seeking justice and this in itself would be adverse to the proposed National Charter of Rights.

Overview: Currently most commercial litigation involves business people who are expanding their human and financial resources in a lengthy and time consuming legal battle. The end result may be in the claimants favour **if he can stand the test of time and cost.** One must consider what the real cost has been in obtaining justice, that is, how many hours did the complainant dedicate to the litigation instead of future positive and constructive business. This can never be recovered, especially if litigation takes more than three years. On top of that and in the case of many major corporations, they will seek an appeal if they lose an action. Further costs and losses to the small adversarial litigant who suffers physically, emotionally and financially exhausting him, and this is relied on by the big fish which has been allowed to flourish, so if that claimant wins on the round-about, he may well fall off the swings.

Alternatively, if the outcome at the end of this long road goes against the small litigant he has lost on two counts. One, his inability to move ahead much earlier in a positive direction of rebuilding and developing his life and business and secondly, he ought to have had the opportunity to reduce by cutting his losses early rather than lose everything including his own employment and that of his staff. If a business fails it is not just the owner who fails, it is also the employers, suppliers, outlets and everyone connected to that business.

Then there may be the opportunity to settle out of court. Pressure by the small litigant's legal practitioner after hundreds of thousands of dollars have been expended to now, *"settle!"* ie *". . . take the offer* (because I'm happy I've got my dough covered) *sorry you didn't get what I told you you'd get!"* What was initially a very optimistic appraisal of the financial outcome of the litigation is now a *"let's get out of this"* approach and in far too many cases, if the claimant is lucky he may get his outlay for legal fees back and often, that's all.

There would be no denying that many legal practitioners come up against each other on a regular basis and have developed both a professional respect and perhaps a friendship with their counterparts. A relationship which could influence the wrongful forfeiture or backing away from a litigation, that is in favour of the practitioner with the ongoing business of say his major client to consider. After all it's no skin off the nose of the practitioner with the small litigant client to forfeit or compromise his action, as morals do not pay the legal practitioners bills. This is not to suggest a "crooked arrangement" between professional colleagues, but rather a situation where the "small lawyer" decides to advise his client to cut his losses. In reality he is actually safeguarding his fees regardless of the justice received or expected by his client.

If the costs of litigation are not enough, there are many cases of the excessive legal accounts by unscrupulous legal practitioners. There are thousands of reports and investigations into the way lawyers bill their costs and conduct litigation, yet the system grinds along in the same slow, costly old fashion, uninspired by any improvements to this unconstitutional constitutional monopoly. The Australian Law Reform Commission produced a massive review of the Federal civil justice system but the then Chief Justice of the High Court Murray Gleeson and the Chief Justice of NSW James Spigelman were against any ingenuity or creativity of a system that currently rewards for delays and inefficiency with higher remuneration, nothing has changed. Many law firms have been known to *"bill more than six times the amount received by the injured client in a settlement or bill A$100 for sending an email to thank a client for sending an email".* Even the likes of Steve Marks, the head of the NSW legal regulator says *"there needed to be a thorough review of cost assessments, cost disclosures and overcharging by lawyers".*

The court of appeal threw out a matter where Marks disclosed *"gross overcharging"* by a solicitor, saying *"it wasn't deliberate!"* as if that was excusable. Steve Marks receives over 12,000 complaints a year relating to overcharging of legal fees and disbursement costs, yet no government intervenes or rectify. The best form of cure is prevention, and the best prevention is where it hurts most:

◆ Immediate disbarring of legal practitioners if found to be overcharging. There is very little room for error as most accounting systems are computerised and overcharging is theft, white collar crime and must be subject to greater sentences than any novice. Maintaining accurate accounts is imperative in any industry and by every business, particularly this industry which is not subject to providing results and clients have little access to determine correct charges.

◆ Regular Trust account inspectors to check not just money held in trust but all charge out accounts to ensure duplicate times are not charged to various clients for the same or excessive time. The fine, as with the banks – 100% more than the overcharge.

Professional Standards – Review of the Legal Profession Act 1987

"**SECTION 45A DEEMS horizontal price fixing to be anti-competitive, subject to some exemptions".** Firm indication and commitment is required to protect the consumer.** In most industries and businesses with the exception of few, there are fixed quotes for work accepted prior to starting a service or providing a product. This allows the consumer to know what he is up for, and then allows the client to budget to ensure the job can be completed.

But with the legal system there are no set fees. No menu of charges. Often the client runs out of funds before the job is complete. That is, the legal practitioner gets paid for what he has done to date but the client has nothing tangible for his investment into the matter. Standardisation of fees must be applicable, enforced and monitored by an independent body. Currently, legal practitioners are able to charge for every minute and unless the client sits in the practitioner's office all day to monitor the time spent on his matter, he ends up with a bill that is a matter of your word against his. This would be one of the only industries able to get away with a "do and charge" approach to accounts. Then there are lawyers who are more proficient and take half the time to do the same job as the one who charges double, just because he is a slow coach, or not as apt to the job. Of course, not all the time is spent by the lawyer, often it is by a junior or receptionist, but it is billed as if the lawyer did it.

If you are not satisfied with the way your matter has been run or the costs are excessive, just try and lodge a complaint with the Law Society. Example: Your solicitor negated your matter, or was incompetent or negligent in some way, or overcharged you. You lodge a complaint with the Law Society of NSW who appoints a solicitor engaged part time by them to attend to your matter. You write to each other and provide more and more information as if you were re-running the matter in court. Back and forward for about a year and a half and eventually you will get a letter to say *"Sorry but we can see no justification to your claim"* and that's that! Or you could start another action in court against your solicitor if you want to spend another small fortune and the years involved, to perhaps get nowhere! You also will find it difficult to get another solicitor to represent you against your previous solicitor, reason being that Law Cover, the collective insurer of solicitors, is very reluctant to pay out in the first instance and may make life a little difficult for your new solicitor, so you can't win!

The Costs Agreement currently relied on, is not a firm quote. It is a generality of the time and costs required to prepare and present a matter. The Costs Agreement is no doubt intended as an indicative figure but in many cases the solicitor goes well over the cost quoted in the Costs Agreement. This would not be tolerated in any other industry. An electrician may quote A$50.00 an hour where a solicitor A$300.00 an hour, but you would not pay the electrician if he did not give you a completed job within the quotation, yet an open amount for no guaranteed result ought not be constitutional. The client is expected to rely on the honesty of his solicitor for maintaining time information and without cross-checking his other clients records, you may not be satisfied that the hours claimed are correct. For example, if an electrician is working at your premises you know how many hours he has spent on the job. A legal practitioner is open to suspicion which maybe unfair on him, especially if he is a slow worker.

There are industry awards to ensure fair and comparable payments to tradesmen have been established and this needs to encompass this profession to ensure fair market rates are charged as currently this industry, the legal fraternity continues to run a "closed shop" where outcomes (not 'justice') go to the highest bidder.

"The market for legal services is diverse" but most clients are not 'sophisticated' enough to even enquire as to the practitioner's skills, ability or success rate": When a potential (claimant) plaintiff or defendant visits a legal practitioner, which in the average person's life is very seldom, it may have been on recommendation of a friend, relative or through some form of marketing. The person relies on the practitioner who, unknown to the potential client, may have a lack of knowledge in various facets of law pertaining to the area required by the client. The client, in his most desperate need, may, in offering the lawyer to take on the matter, be jeopardising his own legal prospects for success. Hundreds of thousands of dollars may well have been expended with a practitioner who has little experience in commercial disputes, before the client is rightly or wrongly advised that his case has no merit; or to settle what may have been otherwise a winning case; or lose due to poor representation of a case that had it been handled by someone more proficient in that specific area, ought to have had a judgment in the clients favour.

What obligation or liability exists for the practitioner, who may have spent 20 years in criminal law, yet does not advise the client that he has had little experience with commercial law or – worse – has had very little success against his opponents, the major experienced legal firms.

"A proficient legal practitioner in specific areas ought to know the complexities of legal rules and the expectations of clients" and base his Costs Agreement on his knowledge, preventing Costs Agreements blowing out of all proportion and being exceeded many times over. But **". . . guaranteeing consumers a minimum standard of service and protecting consumers from**

incompetence" can only be achieved by legal practitioners disclosing their history and providing the client with testimonials for the client's verification and satisfaction in proceeding with the practitioner.

"All clients, when provided with a Costs Agreement should also be provided with a standard "Information and Costs Document" from the National Attorney General's Department, Senate approved advising the client:

1. To be satisfied and aware of the practitioners' specialised field (if they have one). This will alert the client to the fact that a practitioner may not specialise in the specific area of law which pertains to the client's specific needs.
2. Where and how to verify the information and costs.
3. What to do if not satisfied with the service.
4. Alternative remedies for various legal matter(s).
5. Fair and reasonable costs for all services provided.
6. Redress in the event of a complaint.

"The client should also sign within the Costs Agreement, that he has received the above information and that he understands it and is satisfied to continue with the practitioner. The practitioner must sign that he or she has discussed the court procedure and other options of arbitration or mediation. Each legal practitioner must provide this standard Senate approved document, endorsed by the National Judiciary for all potential clients."

"... corporate clients, whose market power confers advantages in obtaining high quality services and minimising the risk of negligence by practitioners" This works to the detriment of the small business person who have minimal legal requirement ongoing in comparison to their corporate counterparts. Often the interpretation of statements and pleadings prepared by less competent practitioners, as contained in court documents is viewed differently by a judge. That is, either a misunderstanding of the facts by the practitioner or poor presentation by the practitioner, either way, it will yield a negative outcome to a complainant in that "the pleadings were wrong or poorly constructed". The client is in the hands of his legal practitioner, competent and often not. Nevertheless the client has paid dearly for negligence and if he has not paid his legal representative based on a contingency agreement (paid on success only) the client may be denied access to his file of documents and any future redress is compromised.

"Legal Profession Act 1987... properly regulated and publicly accountable" The Government has a responsibility to ensure that the legal profession is properly regulated (through the proposed Senate) and that clients of the profession are properly protected but this cannot be achieved if **". . . the Commission's objective is to ensure the preservation of an independent legal profession . . . ." This is a conflict of Constitutional interest.**

"There does not appear to be any external scrutiny of the profession" and the Legal Profession's Advisory Council has more complaints than they can handle. If a client wishes to have the Law Society of NSW investigate a complaint it is an impossible situation. All members of the society are indemnified by Law Cover, their insurer, who will use all means to dismiss any claim rather than pay. This is not your average insurance company who payout for real claims, you will need to commence an action in court and when you're out of money, they also win by default. It is important to note, your claim may still be correct and provable, but because you are cash strapped you are likely to be axed regardless.

"Further, it should be noted that the proportion of complainants seeking a review of decisions of the Councils by the Commissioner is <u>low</u>" This is because there is a lack of confidence by the public in the Commission, as it appears to be another waste of time and energy for a no result oligopoly.

"Legal Profession Reform Act 1993 . . . Legal practice was understood to be both a professional service and a business . . . ." This could be construed to be a conflict of interest between the practitioner's ability to carry out a matter and his business' financial needs. There have been allegations of solicitor's double dipping their clients. That is, charging more than one client for the same period of time. There is little if any way, a client can determine if the solicitor is correct in the times quoted for work carried out, unless it is overseen by an independent body, for example an inspector similar to the trust account inspectors able to audit and cross check time records of solicitors. Again, more transparency is required.

"Other more radical proposals by the Commission . . . to open up legal work to other service providers . . . ." The Procedure and protocol attached to the legal system does not allow for any competition outside of its own industry interest. That is, due to the technical nature of procedures an individual does not have the ability to represent himself adequately if he so wishes. That is if he cannot afford litigation nor has no confidence in the legal system or his ability against a very experienced adversary. The procedure and documentation is cumbersome and time consuming and the ramifications for failure to comply proficiently often determine the outcome, over the facts of the matter. This is why a client does not represent himself, as the saying came into being that *"a man who has himself as a solicitor, has a fool for a client"* for he is at a great disadvantage, from intimidation of the procedure; lack of time required in preparation versus pursuing daily income requirements; lack of confidence in opposing a highly qualified practitioner; thus the system is not user friendly.

"1994 Access to Justice Advisory Committee" advocated a national reform of the legal profession. It proposed that the Trade Practices Act should be applied to the legal profession. Further it is proposed that amongst the options available for legal recourse today, that commercial litigation be under similar rules and regulation adapted by the Land and Environment Court as many litigants may want to present their own case but there is no compulsion to participate or comply placed on their major corporate opponents – self defeating unless major corporations are regulated and must comply under their Code of Conduct and Senate provided and monitored constitution.

"... **licensing for some categories of work, rather than solely in their professional capacity ...**" would offer some protection to the public. That is, restricted to specific areas of law, say property conveying, commercial litigation etc.

A judge who sits on the bench at 70 years old maybe suffering with Alzheimer's disease or dementia or its precursor stages, but this isn't written on his or her face, thus it is not always obvious. Nonetheless judgments are handed down, costing the plaintiff and or the defendant hundreds of thousands of dollars with the outcome not only of grave concern, but often not in keeping with a correct judgement or the gravity of a crime. As in all industries, ability is as important as attitude, and it is nothing short of culpable to empower a person to this position if they are not competent or lose competence in office. Perhaps in this situation two heads are better than one as almost every day we hear of wrong or poor judgments and inappropriate sentences. In the case of criminal proceedings it is imperative that this be a trial by jury.

In this same vein, it is imperative that legislation be amended to afford the opportunity to tender new evidence into the Appeal process, evidence which may not have been available at the initial hearing, to enable a true and fair outcome e.g. *"The Court of Appeal does not allow new evidence to be brought into a matter".* This may be evidence not previously available or that which has been suppressed for a legal advantage by either party. The legal system must be able to contend with moral and practical issues of facts rather than only rely on rigid legal procedures and precedents from cases long ago, tried in times of inferior technologies and inappropriateness to the world in which we live.

The current judiciaries will fight to defend their right to exist independently although amongst far more competitive alternative dispute resolutions options. The legal fraternity will fight to maintain unaccountability for productivity to the taxpaying public.

Justice French states *"... providing public monies to the courts is founded upon value judgments about their functions in the maintenance of constitutional arrangements, as well as the rule of law and the provision of access to justice"* and *"the community through its elected representatives has the right to demand that measures are in place to ensure public resources are properly allocated. The community should be assured that those resources are used efficiently and that their use is capable of intelligible explanation and justification".* That is accountability is our right, as well as efficiency, productivity and performance for taxpayer funding but every successive government has failed to ensure or provide.

Questions about ASIC's accountability were raised when it came to decisions as to whether ASIC ought to launch prosecutions, as ASIC has failed in several high profit prosecutions, including the case against One-Tel, a case which took 232 hearing days to come up with a 3,105 page judgment. Justice Neville Owen acknowledges the problems regarding "Mega-litigation" where he handed down his judgment in the Bell Group matter, a hearing taking 404 days and the need to digest 85,000 documents. Professor Michael Adams, head of the Law School at the University of Western Sydney along with other academics are seeking methods of curbing complex litigation. Even the wisdom of King Solomon could never have coped with such procedures or complexities, to where confusion digresses from the basic facts. Where cases are lost due to "legal technicalities" and this in itself is a form of corruption.

Academics now propose that there be a revamped arbitration system in doing away with unnecessary formalities and to get on with identifying and solving problems that exists between the parties. Professor Adams has stated, *"that while ASIC has talented staff, recent court decisions suggest its (bloated) bureaucracy was unable to match the skills of large law firms"* and yet he would call on the judiciary, the big law firms and the Federal Attorney-General Robert McClelland to "reform the very essence of their profitable closed door empire". In a fair society, everything needs to be balanced. If our laws are fair and equitable there is little required to determine, right from wrong; legal from illegal; justice from injustice in prompt determination of judgments. In the ASIC cases, we must be mindful that it is the responsibility of ASIC to mount prosecutions against all perpetrators of our corporate laws and those who have acted fraudulently. Failure to ensure corporate laws are understood by directors is as negligent as failure to prosecute, and this is on par with plea bargaining or perversion of justice.

Cost effective alternative dispute resolution avenues are available and these ought to be an imperative first step in the legal process, constituted within trade practise laws and corporate constitutions. This would reduce the necessity for an expensive judicial system, with some courts able to be almost redundant or at best, certainly able to increase their productivity, in getting back to basic justice

In many circumstance the individual litigant is wiser to the facts of his dispute but at a disadvantage in conforming to procedures and complexities of the legal system, many a litigant would be able to opt to represent them in a friendlier environment. Only this would provide a balance of fair dealing and bring about a level playing field with better options for resolution for everyone. While agencies such as the Department of Fair Trading and various professional bodies e.g. Real Estate Institute and the Banking and Telecommunications Ombudsman's offices etc offer dispute resolution services, there are no mandatory stipulation on industry to comply in accepting the outcome. What's the point of winning if the resolution isn't legally binding?

◆ All dispute resolutions functions ought to be under the National Judiciary Ministry to determine the most suitable venue for each specific matter in the most cost effective way and leaving the various industry associations and the Department of Fair Trading etc to be responsible and more pro-active in preventative measures associated with education in work ethics, licensing, tenancy, corporate obligations and other such matters.

A point to note: In dealing with all professionals in every industry, from accountants, architects, tradespeople and any professional consultant, make sure you always get a fixed quotation before you give the job. Make sure there is no fine print and that you understand every facet of the quotation, ensuring all communications are in writing. Never accept an hourly rate from any person or company or be prepared for the consequences. There are many professionals vying for your business and competitiveness is only competitive when everything is on the table for you to access upfront.

The Australian Social Security Card

THE AUSTRALIA CARD used to be a very touchy subject, one which governments toyed with but stayed away from. But now more than ever it is so prudent for the many benefits it can provide, providing it is handled by transparent government. It has been considered an invasion of our privacy by some, yet 9 out of 10 of us freely bare our all and everything to get a bankcard; a shop charge card; a mortgage; a personal or car loan, we either provide the information or we just don't get the loan or what we want! We join up to "Facebook" and other *purportedly secured internet sites* where many give up the most sensitive "invasive" information; our whole family tree, where we are, what we do etc. From our shopping dockets, paid for with credit or debit-cards, major supermarket chains and card providers can tell us more about our shopping habits than we know or realise about ourselves, from what toilet paper we use to how many rolls a year we bought, no secrets! This information about almost every facet of our selves goes into databases. Do you think it is safe? No! So an Australian Security Card can be of no more risk than what we are currently contending with.

If we apply for a passport we must provide a birth certificate and a guarantee that someone knows us even though some liar might help someone to get a passport, so this guarantee is worthless. Then, every few years we re-apply and provide all of that information again and again. If we need to rely on, say, Centrelink for a pension or welfare entitlements the amount of identity and information needed can be crippling. The time wasted by every one of us and by every one of our government officers in obtaining replicated information time and time again is nothing short of ridiculous. All it takes is to adapt our Medicare card as our Australian Security Card. With a few amendments, there is no better form of security for ourselves and anyone wanting to deal with us. It could slash bureaucratic paper shuffling by at least 70% and reduce Medicare and bankcard frauds by billions each year. Currently millions of dollars are lost every year through Medicare fraud in circumstances where international visitors use their Australian relatives Medicare cards for health care and pharmaceuticals and in government paying false welfare payments to those who have multiple names. This card presented properly, would reduce losses in the costs of fraud while improving our national security and productivity.

The real privacy issue is not who we are or what we've got, but where we and our assets are, that is our address. But pick up a telephone directory or a driver's licence or Google, or check the Electoral records and everyone knows where we are and, after a few simple searches, they can steal our identity and our assets. We can pay to have our phone number not listed as a silent number and we should be able to use a postal box to be contacted by any government agency, but our home and our assets are what is sacred to us and requires privacy in agreements with financial lenders rewritten to exclude sharing of our information with any party.

America like many countries, issues a Social Security identification card to every person born in that country and that unique number stays with that person for their entire life. No card usually means the persons is probably an illegal alien, not legally entitled to be in the country or to receive citizen entitlements.

Computer security systems have proven not to be infallible but government has the ability to provide greater security and provide a guarantee of non-disclosure to any party. What I am suggesting is also a system that will obliterate at least five government offices. The issue of a non-replicable Australia card on the birth of every Australian and on the granting of citizenship, with a unique number, cancelled and not reused after issuing a death certificate (this would certainly ensure no dead people receive pensions and stimulus payment) or if a person migrates to another country and it will provide better security in these very security conscious times.

Shops could install a thumb print reader versus requiring a pin number or signature, eliminating fraudulent purchases and losses. Losses, which are generally passed onto all credit card holders by the card issuers in the fees charged. This could be reduced with these savings passed onto customers. The process and information:

1. At birth or granting of a citizenship certificate comes the issue of the unique Medicare come Australian Social Security Card Number.
2. With photo identification, redone every five years as is a passport or drivers license.
3. The person's names and expiry date of the card.
4. The right thumb print versus a signature for every retail, medical and other use – reducing credit card fraud, loses and costs passed on.
5. Date of birth – stops kids getting into pubs under 18
6. Bar Code on the rear of the card for scanning, with limited information provided and only fully accessible by government for core personal data.
7. The card would be used to register voters and be relied on when voting to stop multiple illegal voting during elections.

◆ Under the proposed Charter of Rights this card would be protected in the interest of each Australian, not to be used as a tracking device or for any purpose other than for identification.

Signatures can change, photos change with age but it is impossible to forge say the right thumb print. Our thumb print is all we would need for verification with the use of the card. It will be impossible for criminals to fraudulently use the card and it will assist police after criminal activities to locate a person of suspicion for questioning. Would-be thieves may then be wary of becoming first offenders, while non law breakers will have nothing to worry about in providing this identification.

No address would to be noted on the card, as the address would be the password relied on by respective government departments, police and other authorities to determine the validity of the person holding the card, ie if you don't know the address on the data base, you'll have a hard time explaining where you got that card! An address on a driver's license or other ID only lends to informing a thief where to go to rob your home or worse. Currently your location is available to anyone who looks for you on the electoral roll or conducts a credit reference check and these may be devious persons with ulterior motives.

This same card and number would be relied upon as not just a Social Security and Medicare Number but also:

1. A voting registration number – enabling unique votes via the internet and changed as a person moves home from one electorate post code to another with notification to the local council.
2. Tax file number – ensuring everyone lodges a tax return although this would be automatic with a new proposed tax system.
3. Passport number – if travelling a visa form may need to be issued for the country to be visited etc.
4. Pension or welfare recipient number.

This one card would be relied on to provide the 100 points for finance and other identification purposes, unique in identification number and finger print. As a government secured site, issue and renewal could **not be an online service** in order to prevent any unauthorised access or forgery of the card.

National census and the costs associated with this massive exercise would be redundant, as all of the information is already on file e.g. name, address, age, wages, employment, information from immigration if the person is a new citizen etc. Information would be updated to the data base when re-application is made for a new card, every five years or on notification of change of address as updated at local councils.

The introduction of a National Drivers Licence system would ensure that if a driver loses his license for an offence in one State the suspension is applicable nationally. The national driver's licence, vehicle registration and Social Security card could be issued by one network of offices, saving the excessive overheads of rent, wages and all other costs of maintaining many redundant government offices. Again, the diversion of this massive administration could inject human resources to the much needed resources of health, education and security. Staff from redundant offices could be re-deployed to the hospital, education, police and other government frontline infrastructural improved facilities. That is, in providing more nurse's aides so we enable nurses to be more efficient and that would coax some of the 67,000 odd needed of the 96,000 registered nurses back to work with better working conditions.

This in itself is a better option than relying on seeking more nurses from school leavers who, under the current over demands on nurses, would provide the same sad results as those who have left the nursing practice. Also, in providing more teachers' aides this would enable teachers to spend more quality teaching time with children, rather than with preparation work. Re-deployments could also provide our police force with more administrative staff to attend to reporting and accountability and therefore enable police to do their job efficiently without being bogged down in accountability issues. These changes could provide police the job satisfaction they so rightfully deserve, rather than suffer demoralisation resulting in thousands upon thousands of lost working hours and sick pay each year due to the stress currently encountered. It will also ensure police don't leave the force in droves or need to claim long term sickness benefits for stress leave. These initiatives are not cost savings but the transferral of human resources to where they are needed, perhaps the same costs but with many social problems resolved.

There would be many other finer benefits and savings achieved through the Social Security card which could include the use of the card by pensioners as transport discount card with the barcode scanner etc. No more lining up to vote on polling day and the millions of dollars wasted at polling booths – just go on line at home or at work or at the local Council to register your social security number and your vote, saving more time and money while improving standards!

National Legislation Reforms –
Voting On Social Issues

OUR FUNCTION AS a society must be a reflection of our collective, majority determination and demands transformed into our standards in our Code of Conduct and formalised in our laws by the National Senate, not predetermined by any person, their party or the party's backers. Governments are instilled to carry out the wants of the people, not to determine and pursue their own agendas, often contrary to the wants of the people.

As a society we have spent the past 50 years lowering the bar of acceptable behaviour and now it's time to re-address this in the best interests all individuals collectively – whether any few individuals like it or not and thus ultimately, to the benefit of the individual and community as a whole. While we are all born with inherited characteristics, our characteristics and attitudes are subjective and greatly influenced by everything we encounter, to where we all create and effect our environment, thus our lives and everyone we come into contact with.

What we see and what we hear is what many perceive as acceptable but in many cases "rubbish in (our eyes and ears) results in rubbish out (from our moulded minds)" which is why authority determines appropriate "Censorship Laws". These protect the young and naïve from damage, both to their naturally unpolluted, healthy mind as it matures into clear thinking adults and physically, from becoming destructive or abused. It is our responsibility to protect not just the young and the innocent but ourselves. Many would consider this as an infringement of their rights in not having access to pornography and violence – both of which cause the demise of standards and often culminates in drunken violent behaviour. Opposing censorship is nothing more than, nearsighted selfishness or egocentrism, with no consideration as to the effect on others and the community overall. Like it or not, each individual is responsible not just to himself for his own actions but to the community if an individual's actions encroach on the liberties of others and therefore we must all be accountable and responsible.

The following are a few of the most pertinent issues to society in reducing crime and in saving our human and financial resources while improving our lives in a safe and sound environment. No doubt you have other issues which ought to be included but initially, legislation needs to be amended to provide that

◆ **Social issues are not to be decided by politicians**, with short term tenure of office, but decided by all of the people for the long term encapsulation in legislation (and the Code of Conduct if need be) by the new National Senate.

Currently most, if not all, of our social issues are determined by various politicians or their appointees whether qualified or not, whether possessing the right moral disposition or not, and rarely if ever, put to the public for determination by a majority in a voting process. Why? We can only assume that irrespective of political affiliations, all politicians treat control of all issues as sacred unto themselves, never trusting or compromising their "power over the people" – adverse to democratic intentions. We have many social issues which are not of an administrative government function for resolve and those which can currently take years of research to progress and determine, if ever.

With the proposed restructure of the government, there is no reason why every Australian over 18 years old cannot get online at home or at their local Council Chambers, log in their modified Medicare card and cast their vote on any or every issue. All the while in full knowledge that the voting is maintained under the privacy laws by the independent National Electoral Office. The results of the votes enabling the most cost effective means of the public receiving what they want, in the most efficient method, by the National Senate with amendments to National Constitutional legislations. This is not to say that we would be running off to cast a vote every other day but perhaps after seeking submissions from the public over a period of say 6 months and then in one nominated month each year all issues are tabled for voting and this may well coincide with the 4 year election of National House of Representatives.

The sort of questions that might be asked would be, for example, should a national asset, say The Snowy Mountain Scheme or Telstra or the Commonwealth Bank be sold off? Should we have minimum sentences for crimes and determine what the minimum sentences should be? I would suggest that no Commonwealth real property asset should be sold but clearly this comes down to a majority vote. Again, in the period 2007-2009 the Rudd government spent A$1 billion on consultants rather than asking the people what they (his employers) want. This would cost almost nothing but a few minutes of our time in providing government with firm directives.

Who decides Abortion, Surrogacy, IVF and Adoption? For decades we have been hearing both sides of the argument – *"It's the woman's body and she should be free to choose what she wants to do with it"* and *". . . it might be her body but she does not have the right to murder a baby and this should not be allowed"*. Both arguments have their merits – a woman should not be forced to have an unwanted baby who will grow into an unwanted person with resentment, anger and pain. Is it right for tax revenue to be paid to support a woman to stay at home just to keep a child she did not want, or if she wants to stay at home just to obtain government support? There are those for and against each argument. It makes for good conversation and for government debate but while the problem continues, and escalates, the community has no resolve or determination.

Childless couples who for no fault of their own, are deprived of the ability to nurture a baby into a happy well adjusted person and in fulfilling their lives, as they look for any option to become parents. Should they receive financial assistance with the ability to expeditiously adopt (due to favourable consideration for girls to keep their babies, there are few given up) from the 143 million orphaned children around the world? Likewise, having a surrogate isn't an option in some Australian States as it is illegal, and often bureaucracy judges and denies them because they are over 40 years old or that they don't own their own home. The injustice is that they so desperately want a child and would be great parents but cannot conceive, while another woman who may be an unfit person can just fall pregnant and expect society to support her and her children. So why not conduct a vote to determine if decent people up to say 50 years of age can adopt efficiently from overseas and produce children our country can be proud of. There are millions of children from 2 to 10 years old who need a good home and a new life. Our life expectancy is longer and chances are we'll be around in our 70s to see these kids married or at the least, able to support themselves.

With these 143 million (and increasing) orphaned, starving, loved deprived and unwanted children throughout the world who need to be fed, educated and loved, there are also thousands of Australian homes who would gladly take in as their own, one or several children. Couples transformed into families would spend their money to provide everything they can afford for this much wanted and loved child. What better way to bring in migrants to this country with so much to offer while combating many social concerns, from the concerns regarding a purported aging population, to national productivity, to having no prior adverse national allegiances.

The ill conceived emphasis has been on not taking a child from its natural heritage but given the choice of starvation and depravation versus maintaining a "natural heritage", well I think most children would choose to live and prosper in a country where they are loved, cared and provided for. What is the difference if a young child migrates at an early age or if he or she migrates at 40 years old, when he or she has to then learn to fit into Australian society and learn a new language? If the child wants to know about their roots, let them learn, and if they want to just get on with being an Aussie, that's great. Common sense dictates that the earlier you adjust to "home", the more that good adjustment (as against maladjustment) shines in every facet of our lives.

This would also assist in combating many problems of food and medical distribution to third world countries. That is, bring orphaned children to these resources as here we have the greatest opportunity for any baby, especially one who is orphaned and suffering.

In-vitro fertilisation is a different question. IVF is a very emotionally and physically traumatic experience and costs a fortune for the participating couple (and the government) with a success rate of less than 25%. It also has less than 1% success rate in women over 43 years of age. With the millions of homeless children around the world, adoption is by far a better option.

Single women have choices to keep their child or to place it for adoption. But in being a responsible parent, should the mother be held accountable for her child financially and for all facets of the child's care, including for a child's actions until at least 18 years of age or an age deemed to be more appropriate?

Failure to prevent an unwanted pregnancy is dumb but is it a crime warranting payment for at least 16 years if the father wanted the child adopted out but the mother wants to keep it? Should the father in this situation be required to pay? He may have been misled into believing the pill or other contraception had been relied on!

We have allowed situations in society to develop where no-one is accountable for maladjusted children or who is willing to accept responsibility. It is like a microcosm of the blame-shifting between Federal, State and local government. The blame is shifted with such blinding speed between parents, government agencies, the police and the judiciary that everyone involved thinks that they're not to blame. If bored, restless and maladjusted young people are wandering the streets at midnight, who is to blame? Their parent(s) who don't know where they are and apparently have no control over them?

Hundreds of millions of dollars are paid in costs and legal services to hear very traumatic cases in the Family Law Courts, the solicitors and the judiciary get richer at the expense of those whose lives are in tatters, especially the children. Marriages break down and the trauma of divorce is always devastating for everyone in the immediate and extended family. It is near impossible to get couples to compromise when they are hurt, or betrayed, and want revenge and to minimise whatever they have to pay out to their spouse at a time when each hates the other with a passion. Rather each would destroy the other with any tool available, especially the kids, money etc. Certainly this is the wrong time to negotiate fair consideration and therefore, we need to consider a vote to determine if:

◆ Should couples wishing to marry or cohabitate be made to enter into a prenuptial agreement where they both agree who gets what in the event of a break-up? A genuinely loving couple on the threshold of marriage or a relationship, with a view and the commitment to a life long relationship together are far more likely to be giving and caring in an agreement prior, rather than under the emotional torture of divorce or separation, when all logical decision making is often taken over by anger, hatred and revenge and where everyone loses! This agreement would also include new Divorce Laws which advise of the responsibilities of each party to the other and for the continuing care of any children. In effect, the savings emotionally and financially to the family are incalculable and also saving millions of dollars to the country each year in ways to numerous to mention.

◆ Should compulsory pre-marriage relationship education programs be required? This could be handled by designated community leaders for example church ministers, magistrates or other responsible community persons able to give guidance in the various positive and negative aspects of marriage and of the serious commitment a marriage contract is. Programs conducted giving advice and getting the prenuptial agreement signed to be registered with the Marriage Certificate.

◆ Should divorce be so easy to achieve? A marriage requires the signing of a legally binding contract, the giving of a "word of honour" as well as in a religious ceremony if both parties abide by a religious belief system.

Australians have been seeking the right to trial by jury as a preference over entrusting their judgement to a single judge for a number of reasons. Similarly, outraged citizens hold contempt as criminals are not given a minimum sentence befitting their crime, and that which is not a deterrent to would-be criminals. This also sees repeat offenders back on the streets in keeping the police and the court system wastefully busy. Civil Libertarians have unwittingly prevented true justice being carried out, which is the greatest injustice to decent people, often providing criminals with better treatment than their victims and their families.

◆ Harsher Minimum Sentences?

In the course of their duty, police are often abused both physically and verbally and this has devastating effects, particularly for Matt Butcher, a police officer, who was doing his job when he was clearly attacked and his life ruined, while the criminals just got off scot-free. Western Australia now seeks to give jail sentences to those who assault police officers. This move is being fought by the judiciary, while a contemptuous judge sentences a man to 6 months in jail for yawning in his court. Every Australian is entitled to a fair trial but the majority of Australians want penalties matching the crime and harsher sentences imposed for violent crimes as *"being kind to the cruel is being cruel to the kind"*. Clearly government and the judiciary have failed at instigating and maintaining peace or effective justice and it must be time for Australians to vote on how we handle these situations, perhaps:

◆ Physical assault should be treated as attempted grievous bodily harm, with income from hard Labor to the victims and, in the event that the victim is a police officer, the penalty ought to be doubled.

◆ Zero tolerance of obscenities, particularly towards police and other authorities with a mandatory minimum jail sentence or alternatively an extensive community service sentence.

Sexual Assaults and Paedophilia – There are six reported rape cases in Australia every day. Based on the severity of the crime, should we impose minimum sentences from 20 years with no parole within that time and with hard Labor to pay recompense to the victim or the victim's family?

◆ What do you do to a person who breaks into a home, kidnaps an 8 year old girl, rapes and murders her? Capital Punishment or try and justify his actions in trying to rehabilitate him? You decide, this is your country.

◆ Is chemical castration too good for paedophiles? Taking away the urge and deflating the equipment will take away the ability to offend again. This will reduce this crime rate, empty the jails and give peace to parents with children to protect.

However barbaric this would seem to any Civil Libertarian, but how much more barbaric and cruel is this crime against the victims and their families, a life sentence for no crime of their own. A sex offender, particularly a paedophile is the worst sort of thief and assailant as he steals the innocence and the self-esteem of a child, a suffering for the child and family forever, long after the sex offender is released from jail.

Most sex offenders are cowards with psycho-social disorders, having inclinations which may never be resolved, but they do know what is wrong from right. Many believe he should never have been released from jail. Is it fair for persons such as Dennis Ferguson and Jack Wade, pathological paedophiles, to be let out into society to re-offend or to be able to live in child friendly neighbourhoods? Instilling fear into parents is taking away their right to happiness, peace and security.

In Dec 2009 the NSW Police sought an Interim Restraining Order to keep Ferguson away from places where children go, but this was refused by the presiding judge. Based on his track record and if Ferguson re-offends, shouldn't the presiding judge who denied the order personally accept responsibility, for not taking all measure to protect the community from a proven predator? Ferguson is one of several who have cost taxpayers a small fortune in court, jail and other costs and now with the constant requirement to monitor his movements and provide him with security. This does not give a fair balance of justice to anyone else, particularly potential victims. This is the height of being kind to the cruel.

The ramifications of chemical castration will certainly have an impact on cowardly scumbag. It will make them think very hard before committing any sex crime and this in itself is the greatest deterrent. It will produce less crime, which is less cost and less demand on the police, courts and taxpayer resources and most importantly, less destruction of innocent lives and provides security for everyone.

Many sex offenders and other criminals go unapprehended for many years leaving unresolved crimes and often these criminals end up in jail for some other offence. British police introduced compulsory DNA testing of all prisoners with many unresolved crimes are now resolved and these criminals prosecuted. There have also seen many cases of wrongful convictions now overturned and wrongful conviction prevented with this testing. In the US alone, 248 wrong convictions have been overturned in ten years, 17 of these were on death row. We will never know how many criminals have escaped conviction and how many innocent people have actually been put to death or served lengthy jail sentence destroying innocent lives. If technology is worth anything, it is worth determining justice. As a nation should we vote on maintaining DNA records? Should DNA be obtained at birth or migration or perhaps of criminals only? Any law-a-biding person need not be concerned about their DNA being on file as long as this information is secured through the appropriate authorities, under the proposed Charter of Rights. It would certainly help keep everyone on the straight and narrow and certainly this is worthy of debate for a secure and peaceful society?

Murder, Manslaughter and (Potential) Death by Negligence – I don't think there were too many Aussies who shed a tear for the Bali Bombers when they were jailed and executed. Although we have abandoned Capital punishment for murder, should we be voting to determine if:

◆ Drug dealers and arsonists who conduct activities which could cause death, ought to be considered and charged as attempted murderers. The reduction, if not eventual, elimination of drug trafficking could be achieved by instigating severe minimum sentencing, for manslaughter, for such cases. For example, be aided by matching the bio-signature of a fatal drug with that found in the possession of a dealer or supplier.

A Royal Commission into Bush Fires cost more than A$40 million and, at best, the only likely determination will be for harsher sentences for those who have wilfully caused the loss of life and property, what a waste of money on a no brainer! These commissions are nothing but money up in smoke, when common sense ought to have prevailed in awarding more appropriate and severe sentences. Arsonists achieve gratification from lighting fires. Yet we treat these perpetrators with kid gloves and consideration as to the cause of their actions, be it an abused childhood or the desperate need for recognition. These are all ill-founded excuses, a "crime is a crime" and unless there is a real mental illness warranting a life time incarcerated. Arsonists and drug dealers and those who harbour them, know that what they are doing is wrong and only a heavy labour sentence will be the deterrent for these cowards.

Not all arsonists are known to police and authorities. However, why shouldn't known arsonists be required to carry locator beacons during declared bushfire periods? This would reduce temptation but at the same time it should help provide verifiable evidence that supports an arsonist's claim to his whereabouts. If not, why not invite them to annually spend a "vacation period" working as an emergency operator fielding calls for fire emergencies so they get to speak to real people traumatised by fire.

We have a national police force of some 45,000 police officers who, subject to resources, are outstanding in their abilities to pursue criminals, make arrests and pursue the charges through the legal system. They are confronted with an enormous amount of bureaucracy in a very lengthy legal process and often the criminal escapes the full wrath of the law on either a technicality or the extreme leniency of a judge. The demoralisation of dedicated police officers, when the judicial system imposes light sentences that sees criminals back on the streets in a relatively short period of time, that is, if they are removed in the first place, contributes to police dissatisfaction and frustration in carrying out their job, with so many seeking alternative careers after extensive training and commitment.

State Governments and their opponents make election promises to increase the number of police in society but this is not the answer. The only way we can retain our police officers and encourage new recruits is to ensure they are suitably remunerated and well respected, by every member of the community. All too often, the police and the judiciary are pulling in different directions: police are trying to enforce existing laws for the community, while the judicial system, however, all too often gives the impression that it is trying to bend the laws to accommodate the circumstances of individual criminals and excuse their behaviour. Criminals are not "recovering alcoholics" who deserve to sit in a knitting circle for weekend detention! For police, the position of authority they hold is constantly undermined. The police force and the public must be able to depend on a justice system operating in the most efficient manner. That is, a common sense approach would be to ensure:

◆ All crimes are dealt with within 3 months of charges being laid. This will ensure police appreciate that they have been instrumental in ensuring that a criminal does not escape through the cracks of the legal system.

◆ Every person must have the right to a trial by a jury (if the crime warrants it) and the sentences determined by the jury, but in adhering to the minimum sentence for each crime.

Drunken Violence – Government Authorities have allowed pubs and clubs to extend their trading hours (without community consultation or agreement) and the result to society is now that we have to crack down on alcohol-fuelled violence which costs more than A$6 billion a year to Australia. We witness young men and women losing control of their bodies, morals and dignity and often their lives in the name of having "*fun*" at a massive loss to themselves and the community overall. Clover Moore stated that "*one in eight acts of alcohol related violence occurs in the City of Sydney and that A$8 million has already been spent in trying to clean up the problems*", just more band-aid measures. Alcohol-related violence happens in the home and breaks up marriages, absolutely destroying kids and creating a tremendous cost to every Australian in unwarranted hospital and police costs. But truth-be-known, we've come the full circle from 6pm closing times to closing way into the early hours of the morning and now at no cost required to slash this problem, if the majority agree –

◆ Close clubs and pubs at midnight and get everyone home to continue to party if that's what they want. Violence is not usually between friends but against other patrons. Regardless, all of the costs of violence, this should fall on the individuals who are responsible for their disregard for others, not the public. Should all community costs of police, ambulances, hospitals, damaged property and courts be paid by offenders?

◆ Dependant children are the responsibility of their parents, should they be made to pay the hospital, the police and the court costs for their child's involvement and for any damage they cause. Should we consider raising the age of minors to 21 in a national vote?

◆ Should parents be held responsible for the actions of their minor children – financially and legally? Irresponsible parents will have to take their responsibilities seriously and they will then earn the respect of their kids through discipline, a skill which seems to have been lost or suppressed over the years.

Many parents just don't know what to do or how to make their kids be responsible and feel they will be judged poorly if they ask for help. So rather than encounter these problems on their own, parents must be made to feel easy about asking for help from friends, family and government support systems. Parents must be able to rely on community and government assistance to help in educating and changing antisocial children. If anyone of any age breaks the law, they must be prepared to be accountable especially for the cost of damage as well as performing community service to pay society for their crime – *"Old enough to do the crime, old enough to do the time!"*. Police and or community agents must work with parents and make them feel that this is a service to them and not a criticism of them or a reflection on them as parents.

◆ Make the sentences fit the crime and people will have to think very seriously about what their intentions and their actions, even in a drunken state. Understandably, manslaughter, acts of terrorism (in its many forms) and other crimes must pose penalties and sentences consistent with the crime they commit. Human facilities to provide rehabilitation must be community facilities, but these need not be at any cost to the community at large. It should be determined what skills and abilities the offender has and how best they can repay society for the crime committed in skilled or unskilled labour.

White Collar criminals are rarely a physical threat to society and in most cases they don't need to be locked up to be punished, but they do need to pay greater recompense to society as their academic or professional skills give them an advantage over most people, in knowing better. Many fail to act as a "whistleblower" in circumstances detrimental to the Australian people and perhaps this should be considered participation by the wilful withholding of information or failure to take the appropriate course of action, in the protection of Australians?

◆ Successful prosecutions of "*White Collar Criminals*" could result in sentences requiring a reduction of civil rights, day release or home detention and working for a government department as retribution for the crime. That is, instead of a 5 year jail sentence at a great cost to the public, the term would be say 10 years Labour in the appropriate job with 50% of the income paid back to society or those he or she may have defrauded, and 50% to sustain him or herself during that period. The term of the sentence would be based on the amount required to pay back the amount lost by the victim of his crime, or an amount as determined by the respective court, no escape to bankruptcy, see that section.

Perhaps the hardest suitable sentence for a judge to determine would have to have been for the perjury by Marcus Einfeld. It wasn't the A$77 fine and maybe initially it was the accumulation of points jeopardising his driver's licence that caused him to tender a false declaration, but that first lie led him to the next, as self preservation. This very peculiar case of a decorated High Court Judge, a person who has so generously aided Human Rights internationally and here, a person of the highest repute, the tallest of poppies that could be cut down. Einfeld, a human with flaws as we all have, but because of his stature his flaws are a greater encumbrance to him than most of us, making him one of the most vulnerable people in this country. He had a much greater need than most of us in having to protect not just himself, but his high profile and the highest office that he represented.

This crime was not one of a government or corporate person committing acts of deception, fraud or corruption against the Australian people, but it was in relation to his bad choices in his personal dealings. To be stuck in jail for two years at a greater cost to the taxpayer for the additional security away from hardened criminals and the ultimate loss, his worth to the community. Would it not have been better to give him day release, or home detention and for him to work in the Supreme Court or perhaps in seeking amendments to reinstate the National Constitution, or provide legal services on a pro bono basis for those who cannot afford legal representation, not dissimilar to the grateful many he has provided this service to in the past? Two years for perjury where Einfeld had not inflicted any loss or damage on one single person, while David Vincent got the same sentence for stealing over A$1 million from the Wesley Mission, money which was destined for destitute families – where is the comparison and where is the appropriate sentence?

People at all levels of the pecking order lie every day of the week; in business, in and out of court, in and out of parliament, although constitutionally protected (wrongly) under "Parliamentary Privilege". Some are caught and most are passed over, but Mr Einfeld's lie was caught and made an example of, as it had to be. The saddest part of this debacle was that many people in our society took pleasure in the misfortune of another person. Many people take pleasure in the parliamentary cock fights, particularly the media, for example the "Ute-gate Affair" with its verbal punch-ups between the parties and the juicy gossipy scandals which gives no consideration for the job at hand, while issues such as the Heiner Affair, and the implementation and devastating effects of international treaties, are passed over.

There are further proposed social and legislative amendments in the respective sections and they are all needed to be put to the over 18s of our 22 million, to determine, that is not just at the whim or in support of an alternative agenda of a select few, short term politicians. **Perhaps the most daunting vote needed is in determining our future. There are two sides of our political ledger, neither requiring us to become a Republic or divest ourselves from England or restrict ourselves with any other "Label". Both able to provide a transparent Democracy – on one side we maintain the past or the other, a revision with lessons from the past, but both workable for the future:**

On one side we have:		And on the other:
1. The Flag – With Britain's Union Jack	V	Symbols of Australia eg The Southern Cross & say the Aboriginal flag?
2. The British provided Constitution	V	Maintaining the solid principals and perhaps including a Code of Conduct & Charter of Human Rights.
3. British Sovereignty	V	Government by and for the people, not a Republic, but a true Democracy
4. The Westminster Political System	V	No division into parties with their theories; be they Communism or Capitalism or any shade in between, but united as Free Aussies.

To make changes to any or all of these issues is *Our Democratic Right* and as a Democracy, the minority will accept the determination of the majority in a non-politically contrived vote by the people not the politicians, FREEDOM WORKS!

Bankruptcy and Insolvency – ITSA Reform

Who compensates for poor "Economic conditions"?

F ROM REPORTS ISSUED by ITSA – nationally we had an increase in insolvency activity of 16.96% for the period June 2007 over 2006 to 31,964 – and 3% increase from 2007 to June 2008 to 32,865 sorry no stats for 2009 but with a withdrawing of bank lending, causing "Recession" this is guaranteed to have escalated. The main three causes, (approximate percentages) nationally are:

1. "Economic Conditions" 29.6%
2. "Excessive Interest" 22.2% – 51.8%

Year after year there are thousands of bankruptcies and businesses placed into liquidation. We have a general pre-conception that a bankrupt is a bad, wasteful, irresponsible person who has reached a lower level of criminality or that he or she has mismanaged their business or personal affairs and deserves punishment. Bankrupts are frowned upon, irrespective of the circumstances of their bankruptcy and they are looked upon as if they have some serious contagious anti-social disease.

3. "Lack of business ability & lack of capital" 19.25%

Some of the factors which contribute to bankruptcies and company liquidations are:

♦ The lack of adequate expert advice or the wrong advice from would-be experts;
♦ The inability of the business person to accept or understand the advice and thus the inability of the business person to act upon the advice obtained;
♦ The inability of the business person to plan;
♦ The lack of acceptance that one's projections may be too optimistic;
♦ The lack of financial injection to cover the expenses of a business for at least the initial 2 years of teething and growing problems (50% of new business fails in the first 5 years);

- ◆ The inability of the business person to monitor the plan or lack of ability to delegate;
- ◆ The inability of the business person to change or modify the plan to suit market or seasonal conditions or a downturn in demand or sales or an upturn in business costs.

More than 40% of bankruptcies and liquidations are a direct result of *"Economic Conditions"* including excessive interest. In this case the "fault" wrongly lies with the individual but it is not due to his or her negligence or mismanagement. These bankrupts are truly victims of circumstances out of their control, yet they are treated or perceived as criminals, denied the ability to get going again with a black mark "bankrupt" on their good name. This prevents their future potential ability of becoming an asset to themselves and to all of us. **Most jailed criminals are deemed to have "paid their debt" to society in a much shorter time than it takes for the average bankrupt to get on their feet again.** Just look at David Vincent, 2 years for nicking A$1 million from Wesley Mission. On release from jail it will be considered that he has paid his debt to society! A common thief free in 2 years, but not someone who took risks, employed people, worked hard to do his bit in building our country and who became a victim of either his own poor management or the poor economic handling by governments.

The paradox is that "Economic Conditions" are generally a consequence of government decisions, yet if you have suffered business failure because of poor or adverse government economic decisions and conditions, you are then subject to and scrutinised by the government's insolvency commission, ITSA! No different to being tried for say theft or murder by those who have actually committed that crime! Clearly appearing a conflict of interest?

Fraudulent business dealings are generally as a result of people becoming obsessed with their own ego and their insatiable wants. They develop a lack of conscience and disregard for those they rip off or mislead, be it by their fraudulent representations or for the lack of empathy as they fail to ensure fair trading, all in the name of achieving a financial advantage. Legal mechanisms and other divisive measures are relied on by crooks in covering their tracks to provide limited evidence for prosecution, while government systems deny victims recourse, as they become just another statistic. Recent years have seen absolutely staggering corporate deceptions. Many people are placed into bankruptcy as a result of adverse economic conditions or the fraudulent actions of others, which ought to be detected and pursued by ITSA in a proposed assessment process.

For Example: If it is a personal matter, the circumstance of the bankrupt should be pursued for the potential bankrupt by ITSA as a government service. If it is found that the intended bankrupt is innocent in the dealings, he or she should be treated that way. If it relates to the liquidation of a corporation and the liquidator is satisfied that fraud has caused the situation, the matter ought to be referred by the liquidator to ASIC for their compulsory accountable investigations or assistance provided to the liquidator to pursue prosecution and recovery and not as is currently, fobbed off by the ASIC as a non-actioned complaint.

Currently bankruptcy is treated as a one size fits all. That is, innocent people are confused with the wilful or fraudulent activities of individuals who break the law. The first thing a person in financial difficulty does is borrow more money, being ever so positive that things will turn around, telling the bank what they want to hear, giving whatever security is required just to get that extra money. That extra injection is an extra opportunity for the business for mere survival and more than often, they don't survive – especially if they continue to do the same old things in the same old way or believe that they can contend with harsh economic conditions until things get better but more than often, the hole gets deeper till it all caves in!

Going into business and taking risks is primarily to make money, but this can become a small part of why we are in business. In most cases it is either a progression from a trade someone has worked in for many years or an opportunity to buy out an existing business or to start a new business. An example, Perhaps it's a farm, the farmer had grown up on, handed down from generation to generation, where he had learnt from his father who learnt from his. But living in "*modern times*" he has better ideas and his bank (touting for new business) encourages him to improve his position in taking on leases or loans for new equipment. While the trade or farming skills may be there, in many cases the farmer now entrepreneur, may have many shortcomings as far as experience in business is concerned. Draught hits and interest rates rise, income is down and costs are up. He borrows more to keep floating and before you know it, he is excessively mortgaged as the mortgage has grown with unpaid interest seemingly to the point that the bank consider themselves now under secured, so the bank move in quickly to sell him up.

Then there is the case of the builder/developer (one of far too many): He proposes a project to the bank for properties he holds options to purchase over and for the development of 12 luxury waterfront apartments. That is, he will not take up the options to purchase or build unless the bank is satisfied to proceed. The bank conducts their own valuation and scrutinises the feasibility and are then happy to lend for the purchase and construction with the project as their security. The land cost A\$3.5 million and the construction is A\$5 million with an end bank valuation of some A\$14 million – but low and behold before completion the bottom has fallen out of the market due to international bankers stuff ups. The bank carries out another valuation but this time the valuation comes in at A\$6 million ie A\$2.5 million below the cost of the project and less than 50% of their original end valuation. Whose door do you think the bank will be knocking on for their principle and interest shortfall? All care but no risk by the lender while the builder/developer after working hard, employing hundreds of people, taking risks and contending with massive bureaucratic hurdles during construction, now stands to face liquidation and bankruptcy, the loss of his home and other assets or as a first, he decides to take the matter to court to determine who ought to bear the responsibility of "Economic Conditions".

Unfortunately, in many cases, the lack of funds (or arrogance) restricts the ability to seek or accept professional advice from accountants and other experts in their field and often when a business collapses we look to blame others as we cannot allow our ego to be damaged and do not want to accept all of the responsibility ourselves. But if every effort has been made and solid independent help has been taken into the equation there is no shame in having tried. The greatest shame is in not getting up and trying again and we have a moral responsibility as a community to help those who would help themselves. Ulysses S Grant, for example, failed in every business venture he tried and took to drinking. Destiny, however, was more forgiving then than society is today – he went on to command all the Union armies and win the American Civil War and was later elected President. As a society we must offer better means and assistance before the inevitable happens.

Generally, trustees in bankruptcy are not retained by ITSA. Like a predatory shark they wait to be appointed by the court in throwing them (hopefully) a juicy morsel. If there is anything on the bone, they will devour it before anyone gets anything. This is a speculative arrangement and the trustee's financial success is based on being ruthless with their bankrupt, when in fact it is often the bankrupt who is the victim of "economic conditions" and now suffers further victimisation under the guise of a government regulator. The trustee pursues debtors in an attempt to satisfy creditors but firstly to satisfy his excessive costs, often charging more than A$500 per hour and this is clearly a conflict of interest to all other creditors.

◆ Grading bankruptcies and providing assistance through ITSA for assessment, rather than putting people directly into bankruptcy with a nominated trustee (whose primary interest is his fees before any consideration for the bankrupt or his creditors) would achieve a more positive result.

For example the grading of bankrupts could be:

A Class – A person who has been the subject of economic downturn, excessive interest or poor health and needs supervised re-establishment. Based on ITSA projections for a long term positive result (to all creditors) perhaps a government fund could provide a loan rather than endless Centrelink payments. This would be **a hand up rather than a hand out**. Grade A must have no mention of this with any credit reporting or rating agency as this is damaging and prohibits the person getting their life back in order. It also reduces future business development for lenders as they base loans on an inaccurate determination of the person's credit worthiness. The ITSA assessor would determine a plan to get the person on track again with his powers to include the re-negotiation of loans and creditors with banks to prevent foreclosure and the destruction of the home and family.

B Class – Due to the lack of capital; failure to keep proper books and records; lack of business ability or adverse litigation and where the person is unable to seek recourse if they have been wronged. Once accessed, if there is a way of providing help be it perhaps with litigation funding or business education, this should be considered firstly. If not, the person must demonstrate having participated in suitable business courses before being able to establish a new business or company. This information would only be noted by ASIC who would prevent acceptance as a company director and with the Department of Fair Trading to prevent the registration of a business name until remedied with advice from ITSA that the person has conformed with their educational and other requirements. Credit agencies would note that the person has had business difficulties, which indicates cautious consideration with dealings until certification from ITSA is provided that the person now meets the requirements to be able to operate a business, reconsidered worthy of credit again.

C Class – Excess drawings, gambling and rash speculation demonstrating that the person is not fit to operate a business or borrow funds and that he or she needs trustee supervision in conforming to a budget from income. This would warrant a notation by credit rating agencies and ITSA which may include sending the person for therapy for obsessive behaviour and gambling are mental disorders, needing rectifying for himself and no doubt for the benefit of his family and future creditors.

D Class – Fraudulent trading; false, misleading and deceptive conduct, criminal and corporate crimes warranting the lifetime banning of a person holding a position as a company director or a business name and a lifetime notation on all credit rating agencies to protect us all who may have otherwise intended to deal with this person as *"a leopard doesn't change its spots"* and many "White Collar" criminals go un-apprehended for lack of authoritarian intervention. *Throw the book at him*, see section on ASIC.

Small business is the first casualty when there is a downturn in economy. In the past 40 years we have seen growing monopolies and duopolies taking out small business with predatory pricing (reducing competitiveness in pricing, with their superior buying power and bargaining power) and thus not only do small business people suffer but there is reduced competitiveness offered to the consumer. It is suggested that government bodies need to focus on providing assistance to borderline and struggling business people and individuals not with "hand-outs but with hand-ups". Providing help to ensure every chance of success is given and also to prevent dragging out the inevitable demise of a business and the devastation this causes personally and financially, if that be the educated projection.

In determining the viability of an existing business or new business the National Planning & Infrastructure Department based on demographic requirements, would be best placed to determine what shops, industry etc should be where. This would assist the small business in determining the demand and justify financial assistance or in relocation to where the business would flourish rather than stay and collapse.

Confidentiality and Reporting Agencies

WHILE GOVERNMENT AND business have expanded **confidentiality laws to the point of the ridiculous, Credit Rating Agencies defame individuals and cause unnecessary damages every day.** All it takes is a dispute for as little as a few hundred dollars that may well have been wrongly charged for, say a power or telephone bill, for us to have a blemish on our credit rating records. Even if the dispute is then resolved in our favour, we are at the mercy of that provider to remove the poor notation, if they want to. If for any reason they don't, we can spend time and money trying to overturn that false, misleading and damaging information against us which often we may not be aware of until we have been knocked back two or three times in our application for a home loan. By then those applications are noted on our file appearing as if there have been rejections and we can kiss that loan goodbye.

Every time we apply for a loan, even if we are just shopping around, if we sign the privacy agreement we give consent for a credit check and this inquiry will be recorded on our record with credit reporting agencies. If there are several listings it will appear as if we have been knocked back, rather than our choosing not to take up the (various) lenders offers. To get the loan we must sign a privacy agreement and thus a loop-hole for non disclosure of our information has been closed. What this agreement has actually created is the lenders ability to nullify the privacy laws in working to our detriment. That is, prior to the change in laws requiring signing a consent or privacy agreement, the credit provided could not share our info, that is, there was no authority to share it but now when we sign this authority we freely give permission for the lender to share information with whomever the lender wants to. No checking with us first. The information about our finances, our assets and liabilities can be shared and often those who our information is shared with can sell it to others, here and overseas. Assurances may be given that the information will remain confidential to those to whom we have provided it. Then all of a sudden, we start receiving junk mail, junk emails and unsolicited calls from marketing companies in for example, India – who suddenly seems to know more about us than we recall having told anyone. Try and stop it or take action against those who have breached the confidentiality! First we have to prove it and without proof we have no recourse and no means of stopping the spreading and selling of our information.

Never give consent or sign the privacy agreement until you are approved the loan and you are ready to take on the loan of your choice – delete the clause about sharing the information. That is, get the approval for the loan subject to a credit report just prior to settlement of the loan.

To protect individuals from misconceptions or misrepresentations it is recommended laws be changed to ensure:

◆ No listing of one default debt for less than A$5,000 or alternatively if there are less than three complaints from credit providers. If the three small individual debts are repaid within 12 months there should be no listing. This would alleviate destroying credibility of individuals for often what is an overcharge by say Telstra or others.

◆ The industry ombudsman should have the right and ability to remove any adverse notation, if he deems the charge or debt is either unreasonable, not owed, has been paid or is due to the default of others ie beyond the control of the individual. Often companies fail to remove notations or are slow to remove and again, causing damage.

◆ No listing on a director of a company placed into external administration or liquidation where it can be proven that defaults were created by others not paying. For example: the building company is placed into receivership, external administration or liquidation due to debtor's failure to pay and creating the inability for the company or its directors to pay creditors. Tradesmen go broke all the time because the builder has gone down and cannot pay him and therefore the tradesman is collateral damage and should not be held accountable or suffer bankruptcy.

On the flip-side – *your right* to withhold private information is (purportedly) denied. You may be breaching privacy laws if and when you reveal information about other persons. For example: When you receive say, a speeding or other fine requiring you to supply information about the driver of a vehicle at the time of an offence. In providing this information, without the express approval of the person you intend to nominate, you may be breaching or betraying the privacy of your nominee. Information provided by you, which may be shared with other authorities without your consent and particularly without the consent of your nominee. It may be that you are intimidated by government or that government has given itself the right to demand through legislation, for you to surrender this information and this in itself maybe both draconian and unconstitutional. The intrusion into privacy by the State Debt Recovery Office is extraordinary and outweighs *the Privacy and Personal Information Protection Act 1998* The Australian Privacy Foundation in its submission to the NSW Office of State Revenue, states: *". . . it needs to be recognised that it is the Fines Act that is anomalous and inconsistent and its provisions need to be wound back more in line with standard practices under other laws"* When it comes to the *revenue grab*, all other laws are off the table.

Government Regulators

THE DE-REGULATION OF any industry sector and the farming **out of our government administrative responsibilities, together with selling off of government installations and functions is both irresponsible and not in the interest of the public. It marks government as inept for considering itself not worthy of the job entrusted in managing the interest of the populace.** Investigations and Royal Commissions are a means of appearing to be doing the job, but are not the job and to what result? Under the current system of government perhaps there is good reason for ministers to suspect each other of impropriety but under the proposed House of Representatives and Resources Ministry, this is no room for improper administration.

Attorney-General Robert McClelland is to review the 107 year old Royal Commissions Act, which has had little change since inception. The Australian Law Reform Commission has issued 49 questions for a national inquiry and they will report to Government in October 2009 The 2003 Royal Commission into the Building and Construction Industry cost taxpayers near A$70 million; the HIH Royal Commission A$47 million (would have been better spent on compensating those who lost) and the Royal Commission into Aboriginal Deaths in Custody more than A$50 million and this list goes on and on.

Inquiry Commissioner Professor Les McCrimmon said: *"A focus will be the high cost of a royal commission, and whether taxpayers are getting value for money"* and *"I suspect what we'll hear about is concern about the lack of implementation of some recommendations"* and *"You spend a lot of money on the process and you're not quite sure what happens as a result of it. The Deaths in Custody inquiry is an example of that."* More files on the shelves of "Investigations; Reports and Inquiries" which taxpayers have paid dearly for and most amount to nothing, just more waste. The Senate needs to have the ability to implement action from the findings.

Independent Commission against Corruption "ICAC" to become the:

National Independent Commission Against Corruption & Crime "NICACC"

Federal and State governments initiate different regulators but overall there is no consistency. Currently the ICAC is a NSW agency but it is proposed that this be nationalised and that this be the only government agency recommended to be independent of any government and able to investigate and prosecute anyone on any level of government (a National Crime Commission), any public officer or public employee in any capacity. This national ICAC would be answerable to the Senate and able to be challenged in the High Court, if there be a need.

It is suggested that the scope of the national ICAC be broadened to incorporate the function of Federal Prosecutor and beyond the limitation of investigating *"Public Officers"* to encompass the investigations currently undertaken by the Police, government departments and agencies including ASIC, ITSA into matters of fraud and breaches of the corporations act and facilitating any government inquiry or Royal Commission.

A National ICAC able to conduct investigations and have the broad power to dig down deep into all issues and across the obstacle courses of borders which would alleviate the need for yet another arm of bureaucracy. The ICAC would, with flexibility and less formality, be able to be more cost effective. The Senate would determine in its directive constitution issues such as, the level of intrusiveness and the ability to obtain court orders for production of documents and for witness co-operation etc.

The Federal Police would assist ICAC as it would any government department or agency to obtain information and documentation to conduct investigations and to prosecute through the ICAC. Although the Federal Police would be within the "Police Resources Ministry", like ICAC, the Federal Police would be answerable and accountable firstly to the Senate and then to the High Court. After determination of any matter, all findings of the ICAC would be provided to the public without contention, under the Freedom of Information Act as would High Court rulings, providing these rulings are not contentious to defence security.

Australian Competition & Consumer Commission & Trade Practices to become the:

National Competition & Consumer Protection Commission "NCCPC"

Price Fixing is purported not to be tolerated but exploitation and predatory pricing by government, a monopoly, duopoly or an oligopoly is okay?

These terms reflect economic conditions in which there are so few suppliers of products that one supplier's actions can have a significant impact on prices and on its competitors, for example: Currently Shell/Coles and Caltex/Woolworths hold more than 80% of the market and one's pricing is reflective of the other.

The ACCC has closed its eyes to exploitation by these economic power houses in their large supermarket and petrol operations. The public have become not only contemptuous of government for allowing this but feel they are powerless under our current government structure. There have been so many investigations which have whitewashed obviously unholy dealings that we can despair of ever seeing a fair outcome, let alone a just one. We need a really independent and "toothy" agency to investigate and prosecute such unfairness – but what is happening is government limits disclosure and (in the case of petrol) goes back to sucking at the teat of the petrol pump, where every pump is a taxman with his hand in your pocket and "independent government agencies are not held accountable".

◆ The ACCC must become the **ACCPC Australian Competition & Consumer Protection Commission**, to have as its only mandate accountability for performance to The House of Representatives of its Senate directive constitution. The objective of the ACCPC must be to provide equality of bargaining power and a level playing-field to ensure true competitiveness between businesses at all levels of our community and to protect the consumer from exploitation, harm and abuse.

In accepting the redundancy of donations to political parties there will be no ability or need for favourable consideration to any industry sector.

The petroleum industry has driven our economy and thus our way of life for the past 90 odd years being the one commodity we have allowed ourselves to become so reliant on in every industry. The ACCC alleges there is no price fixing or collaboration between the oil companies but it has been proven when the Independent stations banded together with Today/Tonight and dropped their prices by 10 cents a litre, the major oil companies followed suit immediately and without reservation.

Having been personally involved in a Shell service station back in the 1980s we would see the Caltex up the road lift its price, we would report it to Shell who would instruct us to move our price up or down to remain competitive. Now that sounds very competitive on the face of it but in having the ability to lift the price overnight, it clearly demonstrates exploitation on a grand scale.

Petrol has provided government with a massive tax component per litre of fuel, so there is plenty of room for tax reduction in a fairer tax system, see section of Taxation Reform, but government would have us see the petroleum industry as the exploiters, rather than themselves, be it either side of the current political system.

For undisclosed, no doubt political motifs, the ACCC has allowed adverse takeovers by the big 4 banks; the 2 petrol companies and the 2 major retailer chains. This has reduced competition in every spectre of business. With predatory pricing; increased prices and interest rates and screwing suppliers, small business and individuals have been destroyed, giving these major players "control" over every major fundamental of our economy. That is, both Liberal and Labor have allowed this to transpire.

◆ The ACCPC would regulate all business/industry from the Retail Traders Association (ensuring both the landlord provides equal consideration to all tenants); the Real Estate Institute; The Farmers Federation: The Petroleum Industry and other business collectively working together to ensure there is fair competition and no inequality of bargaining power and that there is no exploitation of one party over any other at any level of society. To ensure the pendulum is balanced equally, for the benefit of all.

◆ Those commissioned to undertake functions within the ACCC must have a strong commercial business background rather than bureaucratic or just academic and thus less likely to grasp commercial reality and subsequently cannot come up with a prompt, efficient and inexpensive means of effecting solid commercial decisions and amendments to legislation.

◆ Mandatory regular checking of scales and measures relied on from service stations to supermarkets, as say underweight tins of tuna, filled with water, are perhaps one of the most serious forms of theft from the consumer, no different to being ripped off for cash by any company.

◆ Regulating Insurance companies to ensure minimum coverage and transparent documentation is provided to the insured to enable determine of the level of cover required for the varying costs ie without the insurance company relying on fine print to get them out of paying. To ensure all claims are paid within say

30 days, as many insurers withhold payments to their financial advantage and to the detriment of the insured.

◆ Minimum price standards to be provided to all sectors of the farming industry and maximum price margins for electricity, gas, public utilities and produce to be set by ACCPC to ensure consumers are not exploited for undue profit while farmers are left begging.

◆ Standardisation of demographic shop rentals to ensure there is equality between all retailers. This may include say a 10% discount for shops over 500 sq metres which would only be reasonable but an 80% discount is not, and this is one of the main causes for the demise of small family owned retailer business in failing to be able to compete with mass merchants who appreciate this major disparity but as an imposition on small business.

◆ Set maximum market share for all business to be able to hold, including banks. This will require many to be broken up and sold off. This would ensure there is *"never any company too big to fail"*.

There are many forms of theft – be it from over-charging; to under-providing; from providing inferior products and purporting that a product is superior; from under-regulating and over-taxing. Many of these issues are taken up and reported by Choice Magazine and others. It is suggested that the ACCPC work in close alignment with Choice and others to ensure every sector of every industry provides what they are supposed to, good quality products at fair and equitable prices. This is not to be construed as providing a barrier to competition but to ensure the consumer, all of us, are not exploited by say a bank working on 200% mark-up on cost relied on as "fees" or any other government agency charging interest on parking or speeding fines ie interest on something that has not cost the provider be it the Road Transit Authority, local government or any other.

Predatory Pricing is not restricted to corporations but also enjoyed by government. In acting as a collection agent for private road operators, *our* NSW State Debt Recovery Office allows, for example: A $10 administration (for a computer generated letter: envelope and stamp ie 57 cents) on say a $3 road toll which the SDRO collects under the *Fines Act 1996* If you don't pay that in their nominated timeframe, you might just get a $350 penalty (for no cost incurred) but don't expect the ACCC to fight for your rights, you don't have any and you don't have a toll booth to pay the toll, rather you have to pay upfront for a service you may never use, which is why there is more than A$5 million sitting in accounts of private road operators and not in your account or the account of our government for our roads.

Inequality of Bargaining Power

FROM THE FARM to the shop shelves, small business suffers from predatory pricing and unconscionable trade practices up against super power retailers, landlords and banks. This needs to be addressed by the ACCPC in consultation with economists, retail and all industry experts. Unfortunately the demise of small business has not been prevented with adequate or fair trade practices and thus the demise has been allowed to occur for so long. There will be very strong resistance to rectifying from the monopolies and oligopolies who have gained and accumulated assets for so long and nothing will be rectified while we live under the current political party contribution system. It is up to every one of us to seek reform and I stress, go to the petition at <www.aussieswannakiss.com>

Retail is governed by the economy and is the yardstick government relies on in determining how the economy is going and factors associated with consumer spending are subject to the consumer's available or disposable income or how high a debt they are prepared to wear on credit. Imagine: the economy is bubbling along *so very nicely* that the government decides that it is in "our interest" to slow things down and:

1. Interest rates rise and you are now paying more on your business loan or increasing your level of debt by, say another 1 or 2 % that you didn't budget on, then

2. Your customers are forced to spend less or look for bargains, reducing your turnover and income with the increased interest expenditure.

3. Meanwhile the major chain stores who can be more price competitive and do not provide the same level of customer service (with fewer staff per dollar turnover) and are paying approximately 12% of your annual rental per square metre, and then

4. They sell stock often below cost, as a loss leader to get customers into the stores, while you go broke. Due to the sheer volume of product purchased by the major chains they are able to demand advertising contributions and sell premium shelf space to their suppliers and if you are a supplier and you choose not to participate with the majors demands, you're out or your product does not get the premium shelf space!

Major retail chains require about 10,000 sq metres in hundreds of centres nationally and they pay landlords a rental at approximately 12% of what specialty stores pay per square meter for their floor space. The majors have buyers overseas who manufacture exclusively for them the thousands of items they import and sell at higher margins than a specialty store could ever dream about, getting consumers into their stores and away from others. Australia has no increased tariff on imported goods, thus local manufacturing has also dried up along with those jobs.

There is a retail philosophy that says 80% of your sales come from 20% of your stock, but which 20%? Do you ditch the other 80%? No, you can reduce a range or sell off slow moving stock at reduced prices, but if you did this across the board, your shop would lose its appeal, losing you more sales and before long, you go broke, close the doors and suffer legal action for breaking your lease! This is why even the likes of Disney and Warner Bros stores closed down nationally – they could not even compete with the major chains! You rely on verbal representations to go into a shopping centre, because of "Confidentiality" you can not be told how other stores are trading, then low and behold, you are congratulated by your centre management for being *"Number One in your Specialty Store Category"*, what an honour, only one problem – this is when you realise that your highest sales achievement is A$5,000 per sq metre and not the A$8,000 per annum (that you were told is the average, not the highest when you signed your lease). So who was telling you "porky pies" and what do you think you can do about it now that you are trading in the negative? You start paying suppliers slower and less than their monthly statement amount to keep the stock flowing in, but eventually they stop supplying you and you go bust!

In selling product say, videos or DVDs the mass merchants use this as a "Loss Leader" to get the customer in they sell the product at cost price in the hope that the customer will buy other products with real margins. You can't compete, you send back unsold stock trying to clear the debts on your accounts; sell off your depreciated shop fitting for next to nothing and are left with a massive shortfall to suppliers and the bank. You have now lost your initial investment but the bank gets your house if you cannot re-finance to include your losses, and you are left with your poor credit rating or bankruptcy under *"economic conditions"* which *you are guilty of!* You have lost motivation and rely on welfare to support your anxiety and depression. Your family suffers from your inability to make ends meet, you and your wife start fighting until you separate, destroying your family and while the shopping centre finds another mug tenant like you were, who is positive and eager to make a fortune while only the mass merchants do! This is Predatory Pricing, responsible for the demise of many businesses, shops and chains of franchised stores. Sounds familiar, your story? This is the story of thousands of Australian mum and dad business owners!

◆ Confidential but full disclosure of sales incomes and rentals should be made by shopping centres to potential tenants to ensure educated determination as to the chances of success in a centre.

◆ Equality of rental must be provided to all retailers and suppressive dealings with suppliers must be fought.

The impact of our failing to support the mum and dad corner shop which gave great service and a good range of product at fair prices is being felt as they're now all but closed down. We blindly turned to mass merchants who have greatly impacted on local suppliers, opting for imports and reduced prices paid to our farmers. Now major supermarkets are infiltrating the shelves with their own "Brand Products" products, reducing the shelf space of local wholesalers but providing massive returns to themselves with prices 40% higher than just 10 years ago. Who loses out? The producers, our farmers (with more than 30% on the dole) having to sell at greatly inequitable prices and the consumer. It has been proven that Australian consumers pay higher prices than in New Zealand or in Europe for the same products.

Then every so often we get an entrepreneur like Dick Smith who has been busting his butt for years trying to get us behind his Australian brand and God bless him, he's still in there up against the majors, so surely we owe him and small operators especially Independent Grocers, our business.

Until we establish regulatory bodies with teeth which protect consumers the only way to ensure competition is to "look after the little guys" because it is the little guys that bigger chains and corporations are trying to squeeze out of business. Sure, their loss leader products may offer some bargains now and then, but if the little guys disappear altogether, it means the big corporations will have greater control over prices which, overnight, will cease being low because they were only low to kill off the little guys, not because the corporations feel their customers should pay less.

Until now the major supermarket chains have negotiated with major shopping centre chains to keep supermarket competition out or limited in the centres they are in. IGA and others are contenders to take up occupancy in shopping centres and we can only trust that these independent franchisees, through their head office will ensure rents are competitive to that charged to major supermarkets in preventing a catastrophe.

Craig Kelly, South Sydney Retailers Association who recently became the successful Liberal MP for Hughes, has presented evidence in various submissions proving that, under the current policy settings, the farmer is getting less and less and the consumer is paying more and more, while the government and the ACCC sticks their heads in the sand, remaining in denial and inept to remedy. The following is a submission from Mr Kelly:

The Australian Dairy industry was de-regulated on 1st July 2000 at the cost of A\$1.94 billion to the consumer. In the light of the overwhelming and irrefutable evidence in this submission, anyone who continues to claim that *"Australian consumers are benefiting from a competitive market",* is nothing other than a shameless hypocrite or a stooge with vested interests, read: <www.insideretailing.com.au/articlespage.as px?articleType=ArticleView&articleId=2465>

The self-proclaimed competition law *"experts"* theorized at the time *". . . . it was the consumer that was most likely to benefit significantly, from lower costs for fresh milk . . . ."* While the economic theories of *"free marketers"* speculated that all de-regulation is good, leading to their naïve and mistaken belief that de-regulation of the dairy industry would result in significantly lower prices for consumers, this group's total ignorance of the workings of the real world resulted in their failure to understand the hyper-concentration that had evolved in the Australian retail sector, and how with Australia being one of the few countries in the world without any Price Discrimination laws, that de-regulation would simply result in Woolworths/Coles exploiting their brute market power to the detriment of their smaller competitors, farmers and ultimately consumers.

These misguided theories of self-proclaimed competition law "experts" have simply exposed dairy farmers to giant predators, whereby the farm-gate price (price paid to producers) for drinking milk they receive today is lower than it was 20 years ago – meanwhile, Australian families have been punished, suffering with the fastest rising retail prices of milk in the developed world – which have increased an incredible 113.5% since 1990 – making inflation look like a gift.

"And all this has been happening while Woolworths/Coles, in defense of their monopolistic interests, have been claiming to have reduced prices to consumers in a "vigorously competitive market". Then, Governments of both political persuasions, having swallowed Woolworths/Coles' propaganda, hook, line and sinker have structured the legislative settings of the Trade Practices Act to favor and protect Woolworths and Coles. The failures are now obvious for all to see. Protesters signs sum it up, *"Dairy Farmers paid less, and consumers pay more".*

In the UK, the leading Supermarket chains; Sainsbury's, Asda and Safeway have all admitted that they were part of an illegal price fixing conspiracy that increased the price of milk during 2002 and 2003 and stole £270m (A$569 million) from the wallets of UK families. The supermarkets have agreed to pay fines totaling some £116 million (A$250 million) after an Office of Fair Trading (the UK equivalent of the ACCC) probe. Sean Williams, Office of Fair Trading Executive Director, said; *This is a very serious case. [The] supermarkets have been colluding to put up the price of dairy products. Consumers have lost out to the tune of hundreds of millions of pounds. This kind of collusion on price is a very serious breach of the law. Businesses should understand that where we find evidence of this kind of anti-competitive activity we will use the powers at our disposal to punish the companies involved and to deter other businesses from taking such actions."*

But the government solution is to levy fines which go into government coffers, not consumer's pockets. Worse, corporations deem fines as they would an Emissions Trading Tax part of the "cost of doing business" and it is no real deterrent to future collusion. If it was a cost overrun on a government project, someone might be jailed, ha! If it was a private individual they would certainly be jailed. But governments need big business and loathe handing them jail terms. So very soon after it's "business as usual" and the planned 5c per unit rise may go up to 7c per unit so consumers effectively pay the corporation's fine back to them.

If this criminal price fixing conspiracy can help explain why the retail price of milk increased approximately 5% higher in the UK than it has in Canada and USA – what is going on in Australia where retail prices have increased 40% higher than in USA and Canada? While this has been happening, Woolworths/Coles and their apologists have been telling the Australian public, "relax", the market is highly competitive! It isn't! Clearly, it's time for the charade that the Australian retail sector is highly competitive and is delivering low prices for consumers, comes to an end".

It's not just our dairy farmers but also our beef farmers and all fresh food farmers who are subjected to poverty line pricing dictated by Coles and Woolworths and competition from cheaply imported products, but every family suffers with much higher prices for food, while our farming community diminishes our ability to feed ourselves. On its current course we will eventually be 100% reliant on Coles and Woolworths becoming the growers and retailers with powerless government and their useless "independent agencies" continuing to do nothing unless we collectively put a stop to this, see the Petition at <aussieswannakiss.com>.

Fifty years of diminished political responsibility and Australia can no longer wait for any political party to openly admit that the Trade Practices Act has failed Australian producers and consumers. If allowed to continue, the market will evolve into one where just two corporations act as the only gatekeepers to all of the nation's supermarket shelves. This has been foolish and has undermined our national economic prosperity.

Mr. Kelly advises, *"the most pertinent issues for addressing our political and social inequalities lie in the banning of political donations and if needed, have public funded elections; that no politician after leaving office is able to be employed in an area where he or she had made decisions while in office; that we implement a Small Business Act similar to that relied on in the USA; we repair the Trade Practices Act to effectively ensure there is no price discrimination; toughen merger regulations, where the merger is banned if there is likely to be any reduction in competition; divest powers to break up duopolies and oligopolies; introduce legislation against "unfair contract terms"; triple damage penalties for contravention of the Trade Practices Act* (against the directors personally) *where a large firm 10 times greater in size or more than a small firm; introduce the UK Landlords and Tenants Act to protect goodwill; Instigate high standards of disclosure in shopping centre leases – as to what rents are paid by all stores, what is the average turnover for wide range of retail categories; free up the issuing of poker machine licenses. This seems crazy, and many will disagree, but history shows where there is more on a "vice" freely available, the less damage it has on society".*

NCCPC Incorporating Health Standard Regulators

WE ARE ALL consumers and we would no sooner put nicotine (which is more addictive than heroine) into vegemite or sprinkle it on Weet-Bix, so why is nicotine and other harmful drugs and chemicals; additives, preservatives, excessive salt and sugar and artificial flavouring allowed to be included in processed foods, consumables and tobacco products?

A major contributor to the hospital and health crisis and the inability to meet the medical financial demands on our health system is largely caused by our own negligence in accepting and consuming unacceptable food standards. Standards violated and lives forsaken, for profit. Cancers and many other fatal diseases are on the rise, and quality of life has been compromised for food which is slowly poisoning us. Our food regulators failure to intervene in preventing chemical, additives and preservatives being used from the ground to the shop shelf have enabled the problem to fester over the past 50 years, by allowing profit to have priority over the health and well-being of the people. Poisonous pesticides to eradicate insects to increase crops are used when organic pesticides can replace them. We can wash fresh produce but as skin absorbs toxins, so does the produce and we eat these pesticides unless we pay steep prices for organic produce. Health regulators allow chemicals as preservatives to be included in the preparation of processed foods without intervention. Excessive fats, salt, sugar and cholesterol are used as fillers in meat pies, sausages and most other processed foods. Drugs in power drinks and poisons are used by tobacco companies in manufacturing cigarettes with millions of dollars then spent on "Quit" programs when all it would take is for our health authorities to step in and stop any company including these poisons in the preparation of our foods, tobacco and all consumables.

Margarine was a product that was rarely used before the 1950s and today it is being touted as *"a healthier option than butter"* but this cannot be further from the truth, and is used in most processed foods. Margarine makers start with cheap, poor quality vegetable oils which have already turned rancid from being extracted from oil seeds by using high temperature and high pressure. Rancid oils are loaded with free radicals that react easily with other molecules, causing cell damage, premature aging and a host of other problems. The last bit of oil is removed with hexane, a solvent

known to cause cancer. Cottonseed oil is one of the most popular margarine ingredients and it has natural toxins – unrefined cottonseed oil is used as a pesticide. Cottonseed oil also contains far too much Omega-6 fatty acids in relation to Omega-3. While both Omega-6 and Omega-3 are essential fatty acids, an imbalance between the two is widely believed to cause various health problems, including heart disease by clogging the arteries and perhaps is a major contributor to our Obesity epidemic [something also never heard of in the 1950s]. Cottonseed is one of the most heavily sprayed crops with resulting concern that cottonseed oil may be highly contaminated with pesticide residues. Canola oil has been linked to Vitamin E deficiency as well as growth retardation and blindness. For this reason, Canola oil is not allowed to be used in the manufacture of infant formula. There are other processes introduced to rearrange the molecules till it turns into a hard solid that comes out, as smelly, lumpy, grey grease. To remove the lumps, emulsifiers – like soaps – are mixed in. The oil is steam cleaned again to remove the odour of chemicals, this step is called deodorisation and it again involves high temperature and high pressure. The oil is then bleached to get rid of the grey colour and then synthetic vitamins and artificial flavours are mixed in. A yellow colouring is added to margarine as synthetic colouring is not allowed. Early in the 20th century all colouring was not allowed and margarine was white, not to confuse margarine with butter and its healthy natural yellow colour from the simple process of churning milk. Margarine doesn't decay and bugs won't even go near it! The following initiatives are urgent:

◆ No drugs or chemicals, referred to as additives, flavourings or preservatives are to be fed to or administered to animals used for food products.

◆ Sparging, a process which adds water and dilutes the milk must cease, together with the restrictions placed on retailer by regulators in protecting those who have had a free hand with additives and preservatives to lift their profits while preventing the consumer access to just pasteurised and homogenised milk in its most natural form. That is, milk to revert back to being the natural product fed to thousands of humans for generations before cancer was so rampant, removing all additives particularly those which extend the life of the product for financial benefit.

◆ Natural pesticides to be used for spraying crops and no chemicals or unnatural products to be allowed in the preparation of processed foods.

◆ Date of harvesting and preparation ought to be displayed on the product, deterring extending the life of the product to the point that it has no nutritional value and thus avoided.

◆ Maximum salt and sugar limits to be determined by the medial association.

The above are just a few very explicit examples of what our raw and processed food-stuffs contain and we consume. Needless to say it is imperative to ensure what goes into all foods and consumables has to be of the highest standards and one of the most important roles of any government is to ensure the health and safety of Australians and those we export our produce to. Is it any wonder we as a nation suffer not only from obesity but also many forms of physical and physiological illness which reduces our quality of life and contributes to the crisis in the health care system?

The vitamin industry has flourished due to the lack of vitamins in our foodstuffs. This is in part due to contributing factors from lengthy refrigeration to modifying and processing foods. Retailers and government have allowed foods from thousands of kilometres away for profit and other reasons, rather than insisting foods should are sourced over shorter distances and delivered "fresh and local". In decades gone by, vitamins were always sufficient in our fresh foodstuffs, but now supplements are relied on as the processing of foods and the additives and preservatives have stripped away most of the nutrients. Also because of the financial return to the farmer is inadequate, he does not have the resources required to replace trace minerals into the soil or allow it to rest every few years. There is no reason why a few cents per kilo cannot be passed on to cover the cost of trace mineral replacement into the soil after harvesting.

It has been suspected that aluminium in cooking is a contributor to Alzheimer's disease. Heating food in cheap aluminium pots softens the metal which can permeate the food content and until it can be proven to be 100% non toxic, it should not be allowed to be used, rather cast iron, stainless steel or better still, Pyrex. Pyrex, that is hardened glass, great in any oven or dishwasher, for mixing, for storage, for serving, it's re-usable, doesn't absorb, is environmentally friendly and it's cheap to buy. Tests have proven that soft plastics break down when used in a microwave oven, leaking cancer-causing toxins into the food, we then consume. You wouldn't eat it or especially give it to your baby! Given that society relies so heavily on microwaves regarding food, no container in which food might be micro-waved should be sold unless guaranteed against carcinogenic leakage. In reducing pollutants, think about using white vinegar for cleaning, no more chemicals down the drain and Bi-Carb Soda will make your teeth pearly white as well as get stains off the bathtub, while saving a small fortune.

Not only have we almost totally negated our manufacturing industry for cheap imports and the many "things" we really don't need, we have jeopardised our health in the pursuit of these cheap "things". Compared to many countries, our produce has been grown under strict conditions and quality laws, with the financial benefits due to our farmers and to all who handle the product to the end-consumers. There are very few Australians who do not share these wishes and sentiments and many persons have become proactive in promoting the Australian symbols. Ausbuy has established a catalogue of Australian products which can be obtained from supermarkets and their website <www.ausbuy.com> which also familiarises Australians with issues pertinent to our many concerns of government shortcomings.

◆ Only products which are **100% made or grown and packaged in Australia ought to be able to flying our logo and all Aussie products should clearly denote that it is Australian, including meat.** This would increase patronage, increase demand and sales for our products over alternative imports and it would ensure we can support our industries. The clearly marked Australia Logo must be depicted on every qualifying product to provide immediate identification on our shop shelves and for the greater recognition of Aussie products on the world market.

It is impossible for Australian health authorities to inspect the conditions, fertilizers, pesticides or chemicals which are used in all of the stages of primary agricultural production and the treatment of all manufactured products we eat, wear and use which are imported into Australia. Australian health authorities have failed to protect us, so what capabilities do they have to ensure safety and high standards from imported food stuffs? It has been revealed that vegetables have been grown in human faeces, lead has been used in paint in many products particularly kid's toys (which kids chew on) and formaldehyde (cancer causing) has been used in the manufacture of clothing. Food stuffs have been injected with steroids and antibiotics. Ever wondered why girls as young as 7 are menstruating, why cancers are at epidemic levels and why imported new clothes and some furnishings itch? It's because it's chemically reacting with your skin! Cheap isn't cheap if it costs your health or worse, your life!

◆ The government Resources Ministry for Health Standards through the ACCPC must focus on and implement strict guidelines preventing and eliminating all contaminants and non-natural preservatives and colourings from all of our food products, clothing and the environment, ensuring all producers are overseen. Every entity breaching the new codes must be banned from importing to Australia and closed down. **This is not the denial of freedom of choice – the denial of freedom of choice is the inability to buy produce without harmful additives and preservatives.**

◆ A vote to determine if the majority of Australians approve and will accept genetically modified products or if this practice should be abandoned.

◆ If the farmer or food processor does not have natural alternatives available to replace the chemical, the product ought to be withdrawn from use and this may mean the removal of some products we have become dependent on. That is just the price we must be prepared to pay for improving, lengthening and strengthening our healthy lives and in reducing our national medical costs. Prevention is always better than cure and many of the cancers we are effected by can be greatly reduced if this stance is taken.

If someone wants to smoke or cannot stop, the lack of nicotine and harmful chemicals will assist in stopping the effects of this terrible habit. It won't be from hiding tobacco products under the counter or plain packing, it's the removal of the addictive additives. If we as a nation are serious about helping people to stop and save a small fortune in wasted TV and media advertising to "Quit" – then stop allowing the use of these harmful drugs:

◆ Ban nicotine, addictive drugs and chemicals from being used in tobacco products sold or brought into Australia as a moral, ethical and legal responsibility of the producers and health regulators.

◆ Warning Labels on all imported products where Australian authorities have not ensured compliance eg "CAUTION: The standards and contents of this product have not been verified to comply with strict Australian standards".

There are many common sense initiatives that need to be addressed by experts, not bureaucratic fumblers and this is where your Local come Federal House of Representatives Members helps us get issues addressed in a reasonable timeframe.

Australian Securities & Investment Commission (ASIC)

ASIC IS AN independent agency (independent of government ie the people) which has been delegated the government's responsibility for the vital government function of regulating companies and security investments. This merely demonstrates government ministers of every political persuasion wanting to be removed from responsibility, and to be above reproach in their knowledge of corruption within their own ranks and with the corporate world.

ASIC is the only "**National Corporate Watch Dog**" but having the government provided monopoly ASIC is a law unto itself and no one is watching over them. ASIC charges A$212 per annum for your company registration and if you are late you can pay up to 100% of that fee in fines. The A$212 is not a cost to administer your company, their computer issues the annual notice and you return it, there may be some changes in address or other details but that's it!

It's just one more cost of doing business – paying for ASIC. If you fail to renew within their further prescribed time, your company is de-registered and you must pay back the annual fees for the years of de-registration (as if it has been a cost to ASIC) to have the company re-instated to the ASIC register or you can apply to the Supreme Court which costs A$1,250 for the application plus any legal representation. If you want to change the name of your company, they wack you A$320 for a job that takes a clerk less than 5 minutes with some small cost to send you a computer generated change of name, giving approx A$300 net profit to ASIC. Is this extortion, profiteering at the expense of small business? A government service, or is this more unaccountable exploitation?

ASIC has stood by and seen many major corporate players over the past few years fall down taking the hard-earned money of individuals with them. Directors of public companies – including banks – are only accountable for managing the company and its assets, while mismanagement has not been deemed a crime unless it is proven to be fraud. If personal guarantees from the directors of the board were obtained for their performance, as is expected of the directors of their customer borrowers, the level of effort, commitment and performance in achieving reasonable goals would no doubt improve. Ensuring there would be less defunct companies and far less costs and losses to the taxpayer who is often the investor.

◆ When a person takes on a high profile, exorbitantly paid position, the onus of a personal guarantee is the least that could be imposed and accepted by him.

The de-regulation of Superannuation funds has seen many more fraudulent operators sting the "mum and dad retirement savers" and superannuation investors. Every other day we hear of operators with their schemes ripping off people but by the time it is reported to ASIC and only IF ASIC decides to intervene, it is usually too late, the horse has bolted, assets stripped and documents destroyed or "lost". The fraudsters have absconded with the loot or concealed it! You can then join the 40,000 plus people each year who lodge complaints to ASIC and only if the culprit is high profile enough and only "if there is a chance of money at the end of the day" may ASIC agree to conduct an investigation or fund a liquidator to carry out investigations and prosecutions.

That is, if it is seen that media coverage would be damning should ASIC remain inactive and appear not to be doing their job. Thousands of fraudsters abscond each year while ASIC does very little to apprehend or prosecute. The best you will get for your complaint is standard letter number one (in part): *"After careful consideration ASIC has decided that we will not take any further action into the issues you have raised . . . . In determining which matters we will select for further action, consideration is given to a range of factors, including the likely regulatory effect of any available action . . . . we will keep your complaint on file for future reference"* and they may list your complaint in the "Scam Section" on their website, but that's it, and the worst part is, we are paying for this corrupt Government conduct! But what is actually being said or interpreted in the standard response is: regardless of fraud and breaches of corporation's laws, unless there is sure money at the end of the day for ASIC, forget it, we're not interested in dipping into our cash-cow, and regarding the "regulatory effect" – we may very well have stuffed up in de-regulating an industry and could be held liable for the damages, or at best we might have to change our rules to re-regulate an industry but in the meantime, if (ASIC) has de-regulated an industry, there is probably no means of recourse against any operator within that industry, even for ASIC. It is mandatory for responsible government to ensure:

◆ ASIC to install a strict code of conduct for all company directors, as provided by the Senate and provide sufficient information and education as to the ramifications and minimum sentences attached to fraud etc before allowing persons to become directors. There is good incentive for everyone to act properly in all dealings and this will prevent losses and reduce frauds against innocent people and the expensive demand on our legal and government resources.

◆ ASIC must be a direct government function, answerable and accountable to the House of Representatives under the same guise as ACCPC and ITSA as determined by the Senate's Constitutional directives.

◆ Re-regulate all industries by legislation as determined by the independent Senate to ensure all codes of trade practices are adhered to in providing responsible government. This would include banks, insurance companies, investment and financial fund managers.

By government (both parties) & ASIC's failure to regulate, it has enabled financial planners and finance brokers to receive commissions both from their investor client as well as those who entice the financial planner with lucrative secret commissions. That is, clients are deceptively misled irrespective of grave risk or lack of security. If the investor(s) with the finance planner or the borrower(s) with the finance broker are unaware of the secret commission their broker is receiving for the services they have paid for this is clearly fraud, as it is:

1. A conflict of interest, in
2. Obtaining "Secret Commissions" by deceptive conduct.

All too often the financial product has a high risk and the higher the risk the higher the secret commission. The investor goes broke, along with the risky business but the financial planner currently has not liability, just double payments. Why have governments allowed this to go on for years? You're still judging, and is this is a government for the people or for the profits from the people also a conflict of interest and thus a breach of our national constitution.

All business names, partnerships and sole traders need to be the sole responsibility of one national government regulated agency not State Fair Trading Offices. That is, ASIC would be the national authority for registering a company, business or trading name and ought not to be independent of our government.

◆ Every company offering investment opportunities to the public must be supported or underwritten by an "insurer". If insurance coverage for losses to investors from validated projections is not provided by the entity, then ASIC would not grant consent to offer any investment product by way of a prospectus to investors. That is, not worthy of insurance coverage not worthy of investment, resulting in minimum risk to all of us. Simply, if it's not insurable it's not saleable or worthy of investment. Hefty fines, jail or community sentences for directors or individuals who fail to provide a copy of insurance before taking investments.

◆ Introduce an insurance for investors who invest into public companies; similar to the redundancy scheme with premium payments applicable to all companies based on turnover. The onus would be on the insurer to pursue directors if there has been fraud but compensation would be paid to investors who would not need to rely on class actions by victims.

High flying craftily astute business people hide behind the corporate cloak of what appears to be "solid" investments. "Firepower" with projects and projections (promises) to perform and provide a good return. These misrepresentations to investors to gain trust in them are perhaps inadvertently backed up by ASIC in granting or consenting to their prospectus in going out and seeking investors. Hundreds of retirees and aged persons in a class action against "Fincorp Investments" (Slater and Gordon) which purported to have 10 property developments, but there were none. "Firefox", "HIH" and the list goes on with very few of the thousands of crooks ever exposed to the public as ASIC works to fob off the 40,000 plus complaints each year and hasn't realised yet that prevention is the best cure rather than continue in seeking A\$212 pa for company's annual registration with penalties for late lodgement, this is not a service industry, it is a government function.

Why would ASIC spend money on investigations or change corporate requirements to increase the responsibilities of their independent corporate watchdog monopoly? Its interests centre on preserving its cash cow empire not guaranteeing and protecting the Australian public.

The most salient cause of the "World Financial Crisis" was not a downturn in business; this was merely the effect of government allowing deregulation of the financial industry through their delegated corporate regulators. This was aided by sloppy accounting practises which concealed or prevented full transparency as to the *actual* position of a public corporation, thus causing mum and dad investors to lose small fortunes.

Creative accounting and shoddy auditing standards can demonstrate a healthy surplus or profit when the opposite may be the true position. Accounting and auditing of companies is not for legal and accounting expert's benefit, it is and imperative reliance to everyone. Superannuation funds were designed to finance our retirement and thus to entice us into investing into shares in listed companies and the banking system, but this cannot exist safely if we do not have sound accounting and legal methods, or trust those empowered to protect us.

Strategies of withholding the true position of public companies have been allowed to be carried on and only through banning these known complex accounting strategies can this be prevented. This has included the overvaluing of assets and subsequent losses to so many by deceptive, although currently legal methods. In years gone by, when people lived in a true economy of money only being worth what you could buy with it, Auditors signed Balance Sheets demonstrating "a true and fair view" of a company and could be relied on. This justified the criteria of a lending bank but with creative accounting which changes the financial events nationally and internationally, it proves how little this Statement now means, or rather that it cannot be relied on.

◆ New methods need to be developed by regulators and implemented by the proposed National Senate in respective constitutional reform, to include:

Non-trading assets in a company's accounts need to be regularly re-valued to reflect current market values. That is, when assets cannot be sold immediately they have to be re-valued and perhaps de-valued by Certified Valuers for the Balance Sheet and the true (profit or loss) position shown. This can cause a company to be in breach of its loan agreements with its lenders, who could force liquidation or rather they would be compelled to rely on legislated punitive action to save the entity and minimise investors losses. Otherwise, if an asset is re-valued upwards or maintains its unrealisable value or an unachievable projected profit is shown on the Balance Sheets, dividends are paid when there is no profit causing the entity into financial demise but this too can be a great tool for marketing for new investors to get the company's directors out of the proverbial (no different to a Ponzi Scheme but legal) and this is common with many property investment companies and the major cause of many investors losses.

"Contingent Liabilities" or events which could go off the rails in the future but have not yet, are not necessarily signed off on the Balance Sheet and are often difficult to quantify accurately, so companies enter into alternative contracts to transfer any risk to others assuming that the other party could meet the risk. This gives the impression that the directors have been diligent in their duties.

This is why the US government revived IAG for had they not, many companies around the world would have had to meet these liabilities which they had no provision for and the banks could not even estimate how much that would have been. There is no control over "Hedge Funds" and with very aggressive short selling they have the power to manipulate markets and drive down shares to levels where breaches of loans occur and cause liquidations. Then the assets are picked up cheap by profiteers.

Corrupt company directors paying corrupt "Ratings Agencies" that is, those who are supposed to give a true rating of companies for the market and investors to rely on, have cost Australians $2 billion in recent times for wrongly granting AAA ratings and they together with the company directors ought to bear all responsibility for compensation.

Ever wonder about the deceitful pursuit of money over people? What or rather who is really behind it? We all are! Think of it in this example; A company is formed – it could be any of the banks, a mining or electrical power company, Coles or Woolies but for this example, let's say Telstra. Telstra sells shares to shareholders (many through superannuation fund managers) and pays a return to the shareholders of about 5%pa to warrant massive wages to their executives. To achieve these massive wages and dividends to shareholders, it raises the costs and charges to their customer base, some can afford it and some cannot. Now, you are the customer and you are the shareholder – you've paid very high costs on one hand as the customer to receive the service, yet on the other, you receive a dividend in your superannuation or share portfolio, nullifying any real return, but the main beneficiaries are the executives and those who allow them to overcharge us all as customers. Another example? The 9% pa superannuation (and rising) which government dictated you must pay into, because you cannot be trusted to handle the money you have earned, ends up in a mining company, together with the government's contribution (versus paying you a pension or reducing taxation). This gives you a return, on average after fees to the fund manger of say 5% pa (a bit more than CPI) which you cannot access, while you are paying more than 7% on your home mortgage, for the home which gives you 10% pa capital gains and eventually be able to live rent/mortgage free. Then government applies higher taxes on the mining company you hold shares in (as an election stunt) appearing to give you a better superannuation return but it also goes back into the mining company who have just had an increase in taxation (more tax but more investment) and thus dividends to investors are reduced! Government looks like a hero, but the super paid to us is nothing compared to the extra revenue swiped by government to spend on eg UN Treaty Agreements etc and we look like mugs, losing money both in the inability to reduce our mortgage and compulsorily paying into a poor return investment.

The Australian Stock Exchange requires continuous disclosure and for directors to report on potential problems which may negatively impact on a company. Such publication, be it in annual reports or through regular reporting or other means of potential problems or losses in the value of a company or to its shares would immediately have a negative impact on the value of business. If the company wasn't in serious trouble it most certainly would become and perhaps cause total collapse and prevent the ability of getting fresh blooded investors in. This would prevent the renewal of loans and see the directors denied their hefty pay packets and benefits, so these ways of non-disclosure through creative accounting diminish exposing this requirement.

◆ Independent supervision of the Stock Exchange must be exercised by ASIC as a not for profit government function.

◆ Auditors, directors and valuers must be personally liable for inaccuracies once new banking standards are introduced and they must provide their Professional Indemnity insurance to ASIC to regulate for investors.

◆ ATO to amend the above and other pertinent accounting practices in closing loop-holes and non-disclosure and in providing a simple, honest and transparent system for ASIC to monitor.

Jeffrey Lucy, Chairman of ASIC stated in May 2006 *"ASIC receives more than 40,000 complaints a year"* why? Because this cumbersome system has allowed white collar crime to flourish, as this corporate watch-dog is only interested in pursuing and prosecuting easy targets with a high return or where the exposure in the media will be too embarrassing to ASIC and the government if no pursuit is perceived to be attempted.

I have personally witnessed the complacency to investigate by ASIC, or any government authority from the highest government ministers of both State and Federal and from both sides of the parliamentary tables. They are just not interested in what would appear to be nothing able to further government or their agency's agenda. Prima facie proof on hand, transcripts from public examinations held by a court appointed liquidator, as to persons purporting to be directors while they were trading in a deregistered company for over three years; and then trading insolvent in an associated company, and then trading in that company after it had been placed into liquidation; and then by a Phoenix company in the issuing of worthless trade fund vouchers (counterfeit). More than A$15 million dollars had been issued and no authority steps in!

In spite of numerous complaints by many who had been defrauded in this matter, these complaints were just dismissed by ASIC. The matter was also referred to ASIC by no less than three liquidators of six known companies in liquidation due to this fraud, all to no avail or interest to ASIC. Proof on hand but no investigation or funds provided to the liquidator to continue prosecutions to recover more than A$8 million for defrauded creditors. From 2005 communications were sent to the most senior politicians, State Labor, Federal Liberal and to both oppositions at the respective times; to State and Federal attorneys general; the ACCC; the NSW Police who referred and recommended the matter to the NSW Fraud Department, who then recommended to ASIC to pursue it under the Corporations Act, rather than the police under the Crimes Act, but this request by the NSW Police was dismissed by this Federal Government – appointed corporate watchdog ASIC's response: *"barter schemes have been de-regulated by ASIC in 1999".*

Is this complacency due to ASIC's inadvertent or deliberate decision to de-regulate an industry? Giving ASIC the out not to investigate – that is ASIC has no longer a *"regulatory effect"* after having de-regulated this industry in 1999 or is it just perceived, that there is no money in it for ASIC, so why would ASIC bother spending money, just to put crooks in jail? But this complaint about a de-regulated industry pertained to the most serious breaches of the Corporations Act, no de-regulating that!

The allegations in many complaints were supported by the Affidavits of 10 others, many of whom have also provided official complaints to ASIC and everyone got the same **Standard Letter Number 1.** (In part): with the usual thanks for your complaint, and *"Although we have decided not to investigate your complaint at this time, this does not prevent you from pursuing any civil remedies otherwise available to you . . . . To pursue this matter privately, but you should please note that we have recorded* *the information you have provided in our confidential database. This information will assist us if we receive further similar complaints . . ."*

As a response to a request for assistance, there was a letter dated 14 January 2009 from the Minister for Corporations, Nick Sherry: *". . . In relation to bringing the matter to the attention of the ASIC, I would point out that ASIC is an independent statutory authority. As such the conduct of its investigations and enforcement cases is generally a matter for its discretion. I am precluded from giving ASIC a direction about its policies or priorities in relation to a specific case. One of the reasons that ASIC was established as an independent body was to ensure its decisions and actions are, and are seen to be, independent of the political process".* That is, the respective **Corporations Minister advises the he cannot give a directive to ASIC** and yet it is purported that he represents and protect us as the Corporations Minister! The greatest cop out of all time, the only corporate watchdog unanswerable and unaccountable to the government, appears to be providing the greatest relief to the Minster for Corporations and the government of the day, both Liberal and Labor who have initiated and have allowed this to continue. Millions of Australians continue to beg for help from government and unless their plight is juicy enough to be taken up by current affairs programs, they go begging, with their life often left in ruins.

Have you suffered with these sorts of problems? Tell us about it at the website <www.aussieswannakiss.com> "Tell us your story" because under the current disguise of "Confidentiality Laws" you and I cannot know about each other's issues. This is a ploy to keep people with grievances divided in not knowing the massive extent of problems and the cause of complaints and thus providing government with an excuse for no accountability – problems? What problems?

The liquidator of the companies in the above matter has been self-funded for the past three years, that is without ASIC providing any assistance whatsoever in conducting public examinations or towards the legal costs. There have been some outstanding people, legal professionals, who have given of their time to assist the liquidator, just to be able to help the decent individuals who have been abused by these crooks. The liquidator received from ASIC the same standard letter No. 1 in February 2008 as to his complaint regarding the destruction of pertinent company documents. **No different to the Heiner Affair but where Corporations Laws specify that directors are responsible for maintaining all company records and accounts while the Criminal Code provides for the destruction of evidence:** *"Any person who knowing that any book, document, or other thing of any kind, is or may be required in evidence in a judicial proceeding, wilfully destroys it or renders it illegible or undecipherable or incapable of identification, with intent thereby to prevent it from being used in evidence, is guilty of a misdemeanour and is liable to imprisonment with hard Labor for three years."* The liquidator of those companies had lodged a complaint with ASIC regarding the destruction of company records and on 25 Feb 2008 ASIC advises the liquidator *". . . After careful consideration* (as if) *ASIC had decided that we will not take any further action into the issue you have raised at this time, bla bla blaaaa*

(the usual jargon about how ASIC assess every complaint and this does not prevent you from pursuing any civil remedies . . .)"

There is more than sufficient evidence for ASIC to prosecute and the crooks have recoverable assets for the creditors, but for reasons of complacency, incompetence or sheer absence of responsibility by ASIC, they have made those involved in this scam seem to be above the law with ASIC taking no interest or action, irrespective of evidence of breaches to the corporations act; trading insolvent, trading in deregistered companies, trading in a Phoenix operation (ie taking the assets of a company and trading on while leaving the creditors with nothing) and other corporate crimes. How far does it have to go to become worth investigating by a no care, no consideration detached government agency?

In the above matter it was all just falling on deaf ears until in late 2008 when for fear of prosecution by the liquidator for their part in this fraudulent operation, one of the victims (after having received several death threats at gun point) suffered with his business being burnt to the ground – but still no intervention by the police or ASIC! Evidence, provided to Mr Turnbull, the then leader of the Federal Opposition and that which has been advised on many occasions is available for easy determination, but no police and no ASIC On 14 Sept 2009 a letter was received from the **Parliamentary Secretary for NSW Police containing a blatant lie "... the matter has been thoroughly investigated and there is no evidence to support your fraud allegations involving .... (company)"** This response was but a mere attempt to appear as if to be doing the job of good governance when the opposite is the truth. This is just tantamount of the ineptness of the NSW State government but a false and misleading lie from one of the highest offices in this country, yet this will not be pursued by Ms Keneally or any subsequent Premier in spite of her office's undertakings. Ms Keneally has greater concerns for the effects of adverse media coverage with a coming election and the allegation that yet another of her MPs got caught with their hand in the community chest. Ms Angela D'Amore and her electorate staff are being investigated by the Independent Commission against Corruption for having allegedly rorted (defrauded) the same parliamentary allowances as the MP for Penrith Karyn Paluzzano, who was forced to resign. There may be *"no evidence to support allegations of fraud"* by Ms D'Amore but there is certainly evidence of her failure to investigate counterfeit and fraud.

Summary: Federal governments distanced themselves from accountability for regulating business trading while their agency ASIC de-regulates industries = no one is accountable or responsible. Businesses and taxpayers are paying to support a watchdog who rarely growls or bites, apparently disinterested in justice or fair dealings. It's like putting members of Alcoholics Anonymous in charge of the Distillery industry. Oh, but government is quite happy if individuals want to pay for their own investigations and legal actions, but after being ripped off, what chances do they have of that!

Due to the lack of interest by the respective authorities, one of the creditors adhered to the *"civil"* legal system thanks to the decency and generosity of her legal representatives, which many of her counterparts could ill afford. The matter was the subject of "barter funds" being issued in a deregistered company. She won that case in 2006 in the Supreme Court against the purchaser of a home as the judge deemed that the company was deregistered at the time of the sale. That is, the bogus bucks were worthless. You would imagine that ASIC would be pro-active in seeking out judgements in an effort to prosecute those who have breeched corporation's laws, but no! So ASIC was advised of this judgement, but no, still no investigation or prosecution. It was also revealed that the person who bought the house was neither a member of this barter scheme nor did he have A$510,000 available to him, but together with his solicitor and the director of the bogus barter scheme, they were able to trick the vendors solicitor and complete a bodgie sale. But the appeal was lost by the vendor, as in the initial hearing there was no need to provide evidence of fraud (which was also not available at that time) and by the time the appeal came around, no "new evidence" to demonstrate fraud, was able to be submitted in the appeal process.

So you're damned if you do and you're damned if you don't, it was a case of **"court procedures outweighing facts or justice"** demonstrating that our justice system is not one based on justice, but procedures. Help was begged for from State and Federal members to get ASIC to support the liquidator in pursuing these crooks, but again, it was not on their radar.

This is a matter of a major fraud involving many innocent individuals who had been misled with deceptive misrepresentations by dishonest persons and their legal representatives, into providing goods, services and property while these crooks continue to trade on today, ripping off others and living off their ill gotten gains, without any government intervention.

Fraud, Ponzi and Pyramid Schemes come and go taking with them the hard earned money of innocent people because of the lack of regulating and the failure of government functions, and this greatly contributes toward the 40% plus of bankruptcy due to "Economic Conditions" and excessive interest. It is imperative that:

◆ All industry must be regulated by Senate constitutions and maintenance of these constitutions delegated to ASIC who is answerable and accountable to Federal House of Representative for accountability to the people.

A plumber would not go into his own business unless he had completed a plumbing apprenticeship or a brain surgeon would not participate in surgery without full qualifications, but have either of these trades been educated in the running of a company or aware of their responsibilities as company directors? How many new Australians start new companies and cannot speak the lingo, let-alone understand their corporate and legal responsibilities as they start trading and building up their debts to creditors and then just leave the country with full pockets?

◆ It should be mandatory that all persons complete an ASIC approved business course before they make mistakes that would cost them and others everything. Information and access to all organisations and associations to assist them in every facet of the business must be provided by ASIC as a Business Advisory Service of ASIC and the business monitored to ensure trading is positive, not dissimilar to a trust account inspector or those who provide the annual return are held liable for misleading information that allows crooks to trade on insolvent. This is the security anyone would expect from an Australian Securities (and Investment) Commission.

◆ No person ought to be allowed to become a Company Director unless they can speak English, posses good written skills and have completed a short course provided by ASIC (at a not for profit cost) as to their responsibilities and in providing undertakings for their performance and compliance as a director to the ASIC rules, regulations and accountability process.

◆ All current company directors of small and medium business must also undertake the same Company Directors course to ensure compliance and prevent future losses. This would not put a dint in the ASIC massive profit, in fact it could probably save money for ASIC and Australians over time with a reduced complaints department and losses minimised.

ASIC regulated business laws must prohibit and prevent "White Collar Criminals" from being company directors but wishy-washy suspension from being a company director for a specified period of time, say 5 or even 10 years won't stop them. These disqualified directors just set up another company in the name of another person, their wife or their father and they then just become a de facto director, unless they are both caught. In this case of aiding the disqualified director, the assets and income of any persons who have aided this criminal should be taken in retribution for the victims of the initial and subsequent crime for repayment.

◆ Harsher laws for these types of "White Collar Criminals" to include working until the debts are repaid for whatever time it takes even if it means for the duration of their natural life. The greater the crime, the greater the time, the greater the chances of reducing encumbrances on society! Needless to say, that "Plea Bargains" should not be entertained in this arena, or any other.

My warning to everyone is to be diligent, very diligent, with everyone you do business with. Don't be shy to ask for credentials and proof of every representation as not everyone is as honest and trustworthy as you are, or you would like everyone to be. While we should not judge anyone unfavourably, we must **"Respect and Suspect"** treating those you have just met with suspicion until you have proof that they can be trusted. Do your own company and personal searches, never just accept what you are told and always make sure your legal and professional representatives are fully qualified in the areas of law and commerce you require, and that they approve of everything you do. They have professional indemnity insurance if they make a mistake, but you don't! Make sure that all of your instructions are in writing so there can be no confusion or misunderstanding and also to provide you with any comeback if need be and to prevent costly errors or poor judgement.

National Taxation and Treasury

THE MAY 2009 Federal Budget was purported to be a very harsh budget to bring the deficit back into line but as we know this has blown out to the highest level this country has every know. Irrespective of the budget, the government found A$500 million required for new embassies in Jakarta and south east Asia and also for Mr Rudd's increased private army to 601 persons, and to support Mr Peter Garret's A$250,000 overseas trip, and infrastructure projects such as A$3.75m for the Albury Fruit Fly Circus. These "essentials" were to see reduced contributions to the cost of cataract surgery in aged people and reduced health care rebates and the imposition of A$30 towards doctor consultations; reduced government superannuation contributions and reduced pensions by lifting the eligible pension age from 65 to 67. This budget and the undisclosed expenditure and donations, certainly demonstrates the inability to manage the financial affairs of this country. It is no different to putting our national purse into the hands of the Milky-Bar kid who was sent to buy meat and vegies but he ends up in the lolly shop and comes home with nothing for dinner. It is also why the Liberal party obtained external verification as to its budget estimates prior the 2010 election.

Currently our three tiers of "white collar" government takers are dipping into our pockets to fund three tiers of administration and three opportunities to waste money. Unqualified financial determination by unskilled ministers is the root cause of quadruplicated inquiries causing national inefficiency and losses to most facets of our communal lives and infrastructures. Under our current Local, State and Federal political system we can never harness the opportunities to maximise every tax dollar as the "party" resistance would never allow it.

Putting all of our tax eggs into one basket would provide the greatest scales of economy this country has ever seen, but this can only work if we have a cohesive, non party aligned government. Where money is allocated to Resources Ministries as approved by The House of Representatives, being those who not driven by diverse party or personal motifs, but focused on supporting the Resources Ministries with all of the correct checks and balances.

With the exception of local council rates, all of our tax revenue from every source, together with income streams from e.g. national road revenue, to national public transport fares, to national government agencies such as ASIC, to State government and other payment sources would be paid into the one National (ATO) Treasury as "Consolidated Revenue". This would ensure that all government agencies, utility providers and Resources Ministries are managed with solid and accountable income and expenditure statements and that the costs to the public reflect fair market prices to sustain and improve government functions. Departments could actually be accountable for real budgets versus productivity.

All income derived and expenditure made by the National (ATO) Treasury would be audited externally together with all income and payments from every agency and Resources Ministry to ensure all funds have been managed well and have been dedicated to the function they had been approved and budged for. That is, no siphoning off of funds to meet any "other costs", no unwarranted expenditure, no granting of favourable contracts to pals and no blowing out of projections or budgets without disclosed scrutiny. Annual reports would be available to the public at large through the National (ATO) Treasury's website reports.

◆ As mentioned, the costs to support the Local/Federal Member of the House of Representative from the Local Council government facility would be borne by the local constituents as part of the local administrative cost derived from local rates. This is saving the collective taxpayer the total cost of two tiers of government, ie the current State and Federal governments and their oppositions, although replaced by the Resources Ministries.

Most Resources Ministries and their subordinate boards would derive little or limited income from sources other than government, particularly health, with Medicare as the income to meet the expenditure to Hospitals, Doctors, Pharmaceutical, Ambulance Services, Dental, Optical and so forth. Allocations to meet the cost of education, defence (all services including police), Welfare and aged care, Business and Foreign Affairs, the High Court, the Senate and government agencies including ITSA, ICAC, ASIC, ACCPC etc.

The Judiciary would have a source of income based on user pays, as does the National Roads and Transport systems, National Planning and Infrastructure, ASIC etc. based on the costs of operating each of these Portfolio Ministries. That is, these are primary government functions, provided to the taxpayer, they were never deemed or intended to be cash-cows or profit generators.

Wages and all benefits to all government ministers and employees would be subject to appropriate determination and conform with new national industry standards and capped.

The Local Council would have representation from the various Resources Ministries for easy access by constituents. The role of Local councils would alter:

◆ Local Councils would determine and collect the appropriate local rates based on their current and projected costs of providing services and for the administration of their Local/Federal Ministry, only.

◆ All planning matters assigned to the National Planning and Infrastructure Department with payments to the National (ATO) Treasury for investment as determined by National Planning & Infrastructure department. The National Planning Ministry is one portfolio which would definitely have offices at local level with its share of costs and rent, contributed to the local council.

◆ Similarly, all revenue from parking fees and other fines would be paid to the National (ATO) Treasury for the benefit of the National Roads and Transport Ministry with expenditure towards maintenance and improvements and not greedily grabbed by local councils through their aggressive subcontractor ranger brigades.

The National (ATO) Treasury would work with all Resources Ministries, as it would work in consultation with National Planning, National Roads and Local Governments in determining short, medium and long term maintenance and improvement planning based on consumer demands and priorities being met. This overcomes the current Constitutional hurdles in Federal government's inability to make payments to any respective Local Council without the interference of obsolete State government and with these amendments to the National Constitutions provided by the Senate. This is why it is imperative to revert to and amend our Constitution of 1901 – abandoning legislation that does not conform.

We are one country, the sooner we start acting like it, the sooner we will fix most of our problems and then have a greater capacity to help others, particularly our descendants.

The Banking Industry

"Money is not the root of all evil – people who handle it wrongly are"

DURING MY YEARS in business I have encountered numerous operators of small, medium and relatively large business (including many distraught farmers) who have suffered at the hands of their unscrupulous banks and who were left legless by the legal system. Through an association formed with others in 1993 I gained success for many people in re-negotiating for them with their bank and bringing to the public foreground the many inequalities of bargaining power between large and small business. I felt deeply, the frustration of trying to navigate around the impenetrable government bureaucracy which appeared as an underlying conspiracy to undermine small business, coupled with incompetence and indifference to the needs of the "small, insignificant Australian" by those on a higher level in the food chain.

Government saw fit to de-regulate banks forgetting that their very job is to "regulate and administer" particularly industry practices and thus ensuring each Australian is treated fairly and ensuring the Federal Constitution is upheld. This is not the case especially since deregulation. The scapegoat was *"competition will keep them* (the banks) *competitive"* but the banks' objective is to produce high returns for their shareholders and high incomes for their executives as their primary objective. Do banks collude with each other to maximise their returns and ensure their competitors do not disadvantage themselves let-alone each other? While this has little chance of ever being proven by an inquiry, the proof that this happens is pretty obvious!

De-regulation has enabled every successive government to enjoy the ability to shrug off any responsibility, for example: Banks failure to comply with Reserve bank interest rate reduction recommendations. No matter how much a government minister wants to escape responsibility, responsibility remains with the Federal government as economic conditions are the result of government performance. Aussies have been let down badly in their expectations of their democratically elected politicians who do not want to accept this responsibility or accountability. Failure to provide protective legislation or rather have allowed adverse legislation and unfair practices to be made in favour of big banking business with big tax benefits to government as well as big political party financial support or donations, which is the price we the taxpayer and customer pay for poor or inadequate governmental management.

Good government regulation and fair practises are the very essence of a good economy but this has not transpired and we have been left to be exploited. With poor international investments and bad priorities a prosperous country can turn into a third world cesspool. The "theory" of de-regulation has failed as does the RBA's ability to impose interest rate cuts onto an industry which self regulates.

In early 2008 the Reserve Bank of Australia raised interest rates several times as the *economy was going too well* so government instigated an adverse means of maintaining inflation in forcing us to slash or **"STOP SPENDING"**. The "experts" at the RBA increased the interest rates on mortgages and in doing so, penalised us for spending and then for their perceived efforts of slowing down spending and the CPI, banks and government were rewarded with higher returns. The economy did slow down to a degree warranting government concern in undoing **what they had done!** Within months and purportedly due to the greatest world stock market calamity since the great depression, which any expert ought to have foreseen, the Reserve Bank dropped the rates by 1% followed by a further ¾% and a further 1% in February 2009 to a 3% low, being the lowest level in 45 years but do the banks immediately drop the full rate as fast as they imposed the increases? Then in each consecutive month September, October and November 2009 the Reserve Bank lifts the interest rates. In November the Reserve deemed an increase of .25% but most banks almost immediately lifted it by .4% warranting billions of more profit dollars to their bottom line and in sheer defiance of the RBA with their no means of remedy (by government) but to "name and shame" as if banks care while they are counting the extra revenue. This is the cost of our not stopping government deregulating the banking industry.

In fact it was established that many banks only passed on part of the reduced interest to mortgagors while they increased rates on business loans. Thus the employer has the onus of passing on these costs to their customers as part of their expenditure, resulting in reduced business and increasing unemployment while the banks appear blameless. And these increases and then reductions work to our detriment! Then not only does the RBA drop the rates (which should never have been raised) government compounds the problem by giving out or back, heaps of cash as incentives to get us spending again and to win over the donkey voters. While the US, New Zealand and others still pay less than 2% the Reserve Bank of Australia, with no excuse of inflation to rely on (housing industry is down, retail is poor), increases interest by a further .25% to 4% and again in April a further .25% to 4.25% *and again in May a third increase to 4.50%* (ie home loans start at 7%). Note: **As at March 2010 New Zealand homebuyers pay 2.5%, Europe 1%, UK 0.5%, the USA 0.25%, Canada 0.25%. Australian banks borrow money at less than these rates but we continue to be ripped off with Government punishing home buyers while rental vacancies are at 1% and international buyers are buying up the very limited supply and pushing up prices.** If Australia weathered the storm as reported and if we're doing so very well in times of a "World

Financial Crisis", why are Australian homebuyers being penalised by the RBA with undue increased with more increases threatened during the coming year, founded on no inflation to cool and a very unstable world market. Perhaps part of the increase in interest is passed onto those fortunate enough to be able to save money but the majority are penalised for having a home loan.

Offers of tax breaks are given and then they're dropped and the grand-daddy of them all would be the introduction of new limitless ETS tax destined to be the biggest tax windfall for government this country has ever seen. Concessions or rebates are initially offered to lower income earners (more white collar jobs) to gain support, but these will be taken away and it flies in the face of those who will no longer be able to save money as they will have to meet the cost of the new tax or banks will need to borrow more from overseas lenders. Allowing this is not reliable or diligent measures of skilled ministers, it is just the lack of focus on sound long term financial planning of major primary Australian interests. Reliance on the RBA with their crystal balls in lowering and raising interest without concern for the damage to those who have lost or will lose their jobs and homes due to their inability to maintain higher than was necessary interest, is not the way to harness inflation but to increase revenue.

If a person were to have been affected by the irrational decision of the RBA and had lost the family home, would it not be conceivable to challenge the board of the RBA for losses and damage in a class action? Sounds unreasonable? If a person were then declared a bankrupt as a consequence of *"Economic Conditions"* would that person also be seeking to hold those who maintain the economic purse strings responsible? In any other commercial dealing, there would certainly be a case for harsh and unconscionable conduct, for the inflicting of loss and damage!

Playing with interest rates by banks, the Reserve Bank of Australia and government is playing with people's lives. The RBA may appear to be independent of government but as government does not intervene to protect people from their own action of deregulating banks, this in itself seems misleading and a conflict of interest. Reducing interest does not legitimately increase spending. Spending can appear to have increased but this is more than often due to the increased costs of petrol and thus food prices, giving a false perception, which "experts" ought to be able to recognise. In other works, interest is inappropriately increased based on our blowing our dough on unnecessary commodities but actually it is spent in meeting the inflated costs of living. Increasing interest just compounds the family's inability to put food on the table and a roof over the family's head and greatly contributes to a family becoming dysfunctional with undue imposed financial and emotional poverty. It is overdue that government stops penalising people with increased interest, a short term fix-it weapon, when experts ought to know that a sound comprehensive long term plan will provide a structure to accommodate all financial levels of society, now and for the future.

Individually if we allow our expenditure to greatly exceed our income we are living beyond our known means and on credit. We have no guarantee that we will be working in three years to meet the original debt (plus the exorbitant interest rates) we created today and this is our own financial mismanagement into "things" we can live without. It is no different to investing in the "futures market" of, say, a wheat crop to be grown in three years but for drought changing those great projections and plans. If we make bad investments, we bear the burden of our poor decisions and cannot hold anyone else accountable but if we allow bad managers to manage for us, we are as responsible for the losses as they are. Short term unskilled government ministers on both sides of the table will be long gone when the realisation of a much more than A\$300 billion government deficit will be unrealisable and unsustainable with fewer farmers, less productivity from the little industry left in Australia and the mining industry is owned by overseas interests.

"Buying a loan" to buy a house is the only product in the world which changes in price for years after you have bought that product which can make the contract inequitable. A contract is a contract and any change needs agreement by *both* parties.

With variable interest, that is able to be increased, it can blow out personal budgetary scope beyond any agreement. Often this then provides an inability to maintain, or at best place undue financial pressure on would-be home owners. When interest rates are high, property market values are then affected and have the potential to change our financial worth and our ability to maintain financial commitments to repayments. The Federal government opened the flood gates to overseas property purchasers and while this will see our property values rise, it will place home ownership out of the scope of most first home buyers, and in many instances it has reduced rental accommodation availability. Many overseas investors are cashed up and their demand is not met by our limited supply, so prices are artificially inflated. Most Aussie home buyers are not cashed up and so we have to pay the artificially higher price for a property and take a higher earthquake prone loan, or go without. This doesn't happen with any other product or commodity be it a car on fixed interest, or any other commodity you may have purchased for cash or at fixed interest rates.

Then when the "owner of the loan" the bank, declares a 8.5% "earthquake" interest rise, this increases your purchase price or the cost of your home loan and you cannot afford the house any longer, irrespective of how much you have paid, the bank moves in and takes over and you and your family are out on the street. If the trend of default accelerates, mortgagee sales increase and the value of all properties reduces, unless they are quickly picked up by cashed up overseas buyers – sounds like a plot! In the USA some properties have lost more than 60% of their market value while the mortgage then exceeding the value of the house by as much as 100% of the new value. This diminishes the overall investment of principal and negates the interest paid to nothing more than a bad investment. Thousands of Australians each year lose their homes to their mortgagors, families are left homeless and millions of Australians cannot afford the most basic needs in life.

Capital gains for the home owner is a myth: Whatever was paid for your house 20 years ago say A$300,000 (unimproved) if sold today for say A$900,000 – try and buy a comparable property to the one you just sold for less than A$900,000 You will pay about the same amount as you got for the one you just sold, so where's the capital gains? The only time this works is if you're moving to an area where the values are less than in the area you sold, or if you have improved the property you sold, and bought another unimproved or downgrading from say a house to a unit. Also, the house you bought at A$300,000 actually cost you at least A$600,000 with interest.

Very few people earn enough to buy a house outright so we all need to borrow at least 50% to 80% of the purchase price of the day. In the 1960s the price of a home was the equivalent of three years wages while today it is almost 10 years wages. It is clear that we are financially worse off today than we were 50 years ago and the burden of stress associated with financial difficulties and frustration are great contributors to the 50% of marriages ending in divorce "when money goes out the window, love goes out the door" too much pressure for any mortal to withstand. It certainly is a time for Australia to consolidate and this would start with reassessing our income to our cost of living – by skills and demographically.

The de-regulated banks get the windfall of higher interest rates and fees, posting billions of dollars profit in times of a "World Financial Crisis" and then they are bailed out when they make poor international investments, but the mortgagor suffers the inability to keep up home repayments. A fairer and more prudent, common sense method for the purchase price of the money is based on fixed interest:

◆ Interest charged on bank loans must be reflective of the fixed cost of the money borrowed. That is, the interest amount paid to investors e.g. today 3% plus the competitiveness between banks being dependant on the margin the bank wants to achieve for itself, usually 1.5% to 2% to a total fixed rate of say 5% for the duration of the loan. This how to "keep them honest"

If the RBA deems 3% interest is paid to savers/investors and the bank get up to 2% as its margin, there is no reason why all home loans are not fixed loans at say 5% for the duration of the loan. This is honest business, able to be committed to without stress to the borrower.

Greed has been clearly demonstrated in hefty fixed interest rates being applicable if you want to safeguard your interest rate. That is, the bank doesn't want to miss out on any increase in rates during the term of your loan so they slug you an extra few percentage points, just in case rates go up and they should miss out. On the other hand, you try to minimise your interest so you don't go for the higher fixed rate, but the bank wins every time.

◆ Government re-regulating banks with Senate provided trade practises, including the fixing of home loans and the ACCC limiting the rates, fees and charges by imposing a maximum percentage on the cost of services provided to prevent exploitation. This is crucial while interest rates are low and sustainable and should ensure that no loan agreement can be amended or altered during the term of the agreement, unless agreed by both parties and to their mutual benefit.

When was the last time you picked up the daily newspapers to check the Court Listings? Most people thankfully don't have to, but on any average day you'll note the massive percentage of all litigation involves the major banks. You will also note that only the highest profile commercial solicitors and barristers act for the banks against their lesser experienced counterpart legal practitioners. Imagine all of those unlimited funds to fight disputes with their bank's customers. Imagine how hard it is to find say A$300.00 plus an hour for your solicitor when things are not going well for you, while the bank dishes out more than A$800.00 an hour to its legal team.

De-regulation coupled with inept legislation and one sided loan contracts have caused the massive disparity of fairness and inequality. This is now further feathered with government guaranteeing banks performance. That is, government has a vested interest to protect the bank, or payout (taxpayer's money)! There are many basic fundamentals which must be amended in regulated banking legislation and adhered to:

The following has been extracted from a submission presented to the *Federal Governments Finding a Balance of Fair Trading in Australia, Published in 1997 ~* which would remedy many of the problems society encounters due to greed and unfair dealings. While some of the initiatives have been taken up, they need to be standardised and regulated by a Senate directive:

Finding a Balance of Fair Banking

L OANS ARE ONLY ever taken by a customer out of the need to grow or develop personal and business assets for a financial gain. A loan is only ever granted by the bank for financial gains but provided that the bank is satisfied that adequate security and serviceability are available. This ensures the bank is secure in every respect for the limited risk they are taking (generally less than 80% of the value of the security), but the customer has little if any security in the event that the bank does not maintain the terms and conditions of the original agreement ie if the bank resorts to harsh and unconscionable conduct by instigating high interest or terms that may differ with the advent of changes in bank policy or preferred lending directives pertaining to any industry sector.

◆ This is an inequality of bargaining power. In many instances business loans ought to be considered a joint venture or bilateral deal, where both parties have entered into an agreement to share in the profit whilst not subject to economic trading conditions. Consideration as to other options for business loans based on either a fixed interest rate or an agreed percentage of the audited profits, would certainly open up many new doors for opportunity to grow Australian business with the sharing of risk.

◆ Customers must receive copies of every document signed and there must be a total elimination of any "Authority to fill in the blank spaces" by a bank, as it can leave the customer unwittingly exposed.

◆ On application for a loan, the bank must supply the customer with a copy of the government's ACCC regulatory body's approved Code of Conduct and Ethics and Standard Practices Procedure for Banks and Financial Institutions, including Senate approved comprehensive, plain English definition of the terms of the proposed loan, as to :

a) When and how much the interest will be and the banks margin (fixed or variable to be agreed and included into the loan agreement).

b) When and how much the fees will be and if or how they will be charged (regulated).

c)   Advice that the customer will be notified if there are any changes to the initial offer and acceptance. The bank would require the customers' consent to accept amendments or increases, thus allowing the customer to make alternative arrangements if this is not suitable or acceptable, at no penalty or break clause to be imposed if the client leaves due to the bank change in terms.

d)   An agreement by both parties to accept the outcome of a mandatory arbitration in the event that the Banking Ombudsman cannot resolve the complaint within 60 days of lodgement of a complaint.

     An arbitrator ought to have the power to direct the instigation of amended terms if it is found that the terms are unconscionable.

e)   Personal Guarantees must be limited by an amount agreed to by the customer, based on the principle amount only. That is, it is unconscionable to have unlimited guarantees particularly if these be third party loans supporting an initial advance for a business loan plus interest and penalty rates.

f)   Cross collateralisation of loans with securities can create the means for the bank to cause a default or take securities for other loans, not intended to be extended by the guarantor. Security must be limited to specific loan account(s) with the customer and the guarantors consent.

g)   Banks disclosure of customers' information – both locally and to overseas entities is a contravention of privacy laws. No authority consenting to the sharing of information should be placed on a customer, this is intimidation.

There are many levels of damage that can be created in sharing or providing customers information. Customers may be exposed to damage, eg a personality conflict between the customer and a particular bank officer, who may make adverse personal comments about a customer in the bank's file provided to credit agencies, banks and others lenders.

h)   Under the Freedom of Information Act the customer must has the ability to see his or her file. Many complaints have been received advising that the bank has told the customer that their file is "lost" or cannot be located, rather than disclose the contents if it is adverse to the bank.

i)   An obligation that the bank in giving an opinion is accountable to the customer as to the information supplied with a copy provided to the customer to determine the accuracy and seek amendment if inaccurate. If a customer is planning to leave his bank, comments could be made to the new bank which may be misleading, defamatory and thus damaging in an attempt to prevent the move. I suppose even if the information is accurate, it could be construed as defamatory in which case, no opinion should be provided and this would be up to the customer to consent to or reject the supply of same or the proposed bank accept the customer on face value, security and serviceability.

Often a customer shops around for the best deal available to him. In this process, he provides an application for finance to one or more lending institutions who may all conduct a Credit Reference Association check, but all inquires are registered on the customer's file. Often the customer may choose not to take up an offer but the fact that an inquiry has been made is often misinterpreted by another lending institutions, as a refusal of credit. It may also give the lending institution an edge, knowing whom the customer has approached and this may be damaging to the customer's negotiations. Therefore, only when a loan is accepted and processed towards settlement should a credit check be conducted. That, is the loan would be subject to a credit check as a final stage of completing the loan and therefore only one entry to appear on the customer's credit record, for an undisclosed amount.

Bank Interest and Fees – Currently, fees and variable interest rates are totally dependent on the bank's policy of the day, their compulsion to "appear" to be competitive to potential investors and in determining how much profit they want to make in a specified period. A decision of the Reserve Bank to drop rates is never readily accepted by the banks but quickly grasped when rates go up. Very few major banks pass on saving immediately, rather they defer for days and weeks with many only passing on a percentage of the RBA decided reduction and often they raise fees on commercial dealings to craftily compensate themselves for interest reductions on other mortgage products.

Amounts are taken from the customer's account with and without the customers' knowledge and consent. Most customers believe that banks are not trustworthy and are seeking to obtain the maximum financial advantage for themselves. That is, for their executives and their shareholders. Remember, you may be both the shareholder and the customer – work out per dollar, which of you earns or pays more?

Currently tricks are used to get you in: Example "Current Affairs" program on Channel 9 on Tuesday August 27th – Anne Lampe of the Sydney Morning Herald highlighted her understanding of the costs involved in maintaining her personal cheque account ie No cost up to 40 cheques and a small fee for 41+ cheques, yet at 43 cheques she realised that she was charged for all 43 cheques. Too easy to overlook and be ripped off!

Standardisation of maximum fees must be applicable, enforced and monitored by a bank watch authority as part of the ACCC or rather the ACCPC. Currently the banks are **profiteering from confusion and tricks** and the realisation that a sensible customer will not waste the time required to report "errors" to the Banking Ombudsman or the Consumer Affairs as it is not commercially viable. In fact it would cost more than what, in most cases would be recouped from overcharges. The introduction of a 100% fine paid plus the overcharge to the customer would ensure these errors are remedied.

j)   Currently banks use customer's credit balances in their cheque accounts, free of interest to the customer. That is, obtaining a financial benefit for the bank but none for the customer whose money has been lent on the short term money market but the bank imposes account keeping fees and charges for the banks further benefit. Interest must be paid to customers on all credit balances in any type of bank or cheque account, just as fees and charges are applicable on accounts, especially when the account goes into overdraft. Alternatively, no interest would warrant, no account keeping fees and charges.

k) This is a "Service Industry". In all service industries, tax invoices are provided for services rendered. **No service provider has access to his customer's money** and the bank is no different to say the plumber or the accountant etc. Fees and charges are currently deducted from the customer's account, yet no "tax invoices" for services are currently provided.

On current profits the banks are posting, the ACCPC should question how a service provider can achieve profits greater than BHP for the costs of providing no product and a minimum service for maximum profit. To charge for services we would anticipate receiving same at a true commercial rate. Again, this requires regulation to ensure there is no exploitation, with maximum margins to be instigated based on the true cost of the service.

l) Dishonour Fees – ought to be borne by the payer not the payee. The rate charged to the payer ought to be the actual cost of this transaction (with the maximum margin). Some banks charge up to A$38.00 on each dishonoured cheque and receive an account keeping fee, whilst not paying interest on any credit balances.

m) Currently customers do not receive compensation for their investigation costs in determining bank errors, nor are penalty rates paid to the customer for bank errors. Again, this comes down to the inequality of bargaining power between the customer and the bank. The imposition of fines on banks must be commensurate with the value of the customer's time lost.

n) The big question is, where does the money go and who gets the interest for the current three days required to clear a cheque when clear funds have left the payees account? Surely with our technology, there is no reason why cheques are not cleared immediately on depositing, if clear funds were in the payees account. Either the money is in the payee's account or it isn't. Where does it go and who earns the interest on these multi millions of dollars daily? This certainly warrants an ACCPC investigation and regulating.

Dispute Resolution (further to National Judiciary Ministry) – It has been suggested that the Banking Industry Ombudsman's jurisdiction ought to come under the powers of the ACCPC. This would be the first step in addressing complaints, followed by prompt mediation or arbitration. Generally customers who think they can afford litigation, resolve themselves to this measure but they do not realise that most cases run for several years in the court system and after years, find they can ill afford the unanticipated escalated costs, the time away from productive income and the stress on the family unit. This is even more apparent when a customer wins a claim and then must fund an appeal by the bank. So a customer can lose even if he wins. Litigation is both disruptive, counterproductive and no one wins.

The introduction of a compulsory alternative dispute resolution system administered by the ACCPC through the National Judiciary could be fully funded by imposing a 0.05% premium on all new loans. This could be held in a government fund for this specific purpose with the premium adjusted if held funds become excessive and based on demand.

In general, the complaints received from customers encompass: Overcharging interest, imposing penalty rates and fees to obtain an unfair advantage for the bank and causing loss and damage to the customer. Tampering with documentation to protect a bank officer who may have had the need to rectify his errors/mistakes or non-authorised dealings, or to get out of an agreement, or provide the ability to call in loans or security due to policy changes towards an industry sector or a speculated non-apparent problem with a loan.

The banks entertain litigation, in purporting to *"appear to be doing the right thing by its shareholders"* and currently rely on the legal system, as these costs are tax deductions to the bank but are not to private individuals. That is, legal fees are paid to the legal firms and then claimed as expenditure in running the business. More than often the end result for the bank from a successful litigation is that the legal costs and judgement debts are unrecoverable which may then be treated as tax deductions by the bank – that is no loss either way you look at it, win or lose! The same applies for a commercial decision in business in writing off a bad debt. If it can be proven that the debt is unrecoverable, it's a tax deduction but the same is not so for the private individual – a gross miscarriage of justice as this is inequality.

Through a litigation funding scheme, arbitration would provide a level playing field, a prompt and effective method of enabling everyone to move on, rather than expending vast sums on litigation. With a bit of lateral thinking: If banks directed the funds that had been earmarked for litigation were utilised in debt or interest reduction in rewriting loans it would provide the same tax deductions to the bank, again no loss. A positive result for both the bank and the customer could be achieved through an independent arbitrator, who would be able to see outside of the square to what is fair and reasonable for the two parties as both parties had entered into a business relationship anyway you look at it.

Through equality we can eliminate litigation, and litigation is eliminated so is aggression and animosities, allowing all sides to get on with constructive business, while instilling a national culture of equality and fairness. This will also defeat exploitation.

The Bank of Australia

O NE OF THE greatest potentials for money making in any country lies with the banks and the greatest cause of international debt is the banks. For reasons unknown to most level-headed people, the governments of the 1990s decided to get out of the Commonwealth Bank of Australia and the State Bank of NSW Both of these institutions served the people of Australia very well but they were sold off for a pittance and have left a void for patriotic investment while we owe a rapidly growing debt to foreign banks.

At no time were the Australian people asked nor did they agree to the sell off of government owned and operated banks. It is proposed to establish a new national Australian banking entity, particularly for the investment of superannuation funds to protect our money from being invested overseas and provide local funding for rural, infrastructure and development of new business resources.

In the midst of a "World Financial Crisis" and on the day after the Labor government posted its May budget (while international banks were trading in the negative) the Commonwealth Bank of Australia posted billions of dollars in profit. This seriously questions why any government would have firstly sold us out and more so, today, why there is not at least some rhetoric in establishing a new Bank of Australia. This could happen within the existing structure of the Reserve Bank of Australia, to a more commercial entity with branches servicing Australians.

The nonsense of investing our money internationally as a preference to within Australia firstly, is worse than our selling primary products to overseas markets and then buying them back processed but after having provided profits, improving industry and providing jobs to other countries to our financial destabilisation and demise. That is, we invest money with say an investment manager who lends it to say the Bank of America, who lends it to where it can get the best return, often under secured. More than often overseas banks lend it back to Australian borrowers at much higher margins or because of the way it is adversely handled it may be lost as was the case with Local Councils, Charities and Local Superannuation Fund Manager who blew some A$1 billion.

That is not to mention the many white collar fingers who take a share along the way; the initial investor gets say 3% for investing "the raw (money) product" and the brokers along the way get more than but say 3% in wholesale margins. Our local business enterprises borrow it back at more than 6% penalising both individuals here and our businesses as excessive costs restrict and prevent growth. Now if that investment manager is a superannuation fund he will also take say .5% in fees from your 3% return when through the Bank of Australia, we could receive a flat 3.5% return without fees to brokers (ie say 1% more) and our businesses could borrow for say 5% saving 1% and providing a 1.5% gross profit for the Bank of Australia to meet overheads and for reinvestment into developing Australian business.

Kevin Rudd (12 May 2006 when wearing a different hat), puts this spin on the situation (syn) "*Under Mark Vaile as Trade Minister, Australia has suffered four consecutive years of trade deficits, a record current account deficiency and foreign debt that has now reached half a trillion dollars*". In addition he stated, "*Mr Vaile has no plan for reversing Australia's trade performance, no new initiatives for Australian exports in the budget released this week*". Mr Rudd went on to confirm that he believes the banks are to blame for the growing account deficit, for the chronic trade deficit being one of the largest in the developing world with foreign debt about to break the A$500 billion mark. That was just four years ago and many countries are suffering the effects of the worst downturn since the 1930s yet Mr Rudd after 2 years as PM offered no remedy for his having worsened our international debt, matters he accused Mr Vale of failing to address, other than to rely on *mining the hell out of our country*, with China now one of the greatest beneficiaries and land owners in our country.

Remember, so far there are only "signs" things may be getting better although unemployment continues to grow and construction is shrinking. Western governments are investing money back into propping up the high end of town rather than into initiatives to build solid new business, not just short term infrastructure improvements but into establishing Australian grown and made products that will pay for the overdue infrastructural needs of a growing nation. The May 2009 Federal Budget did not demonstrate one initiative to improve productivity in Australia, just a reduction in both the government contribution towards the 30% private health care cover and government superannuation contribution.

Money from what was a surplus, due to excessive taxes of the previous Federal Liberal government, was thrown at us to win our support for the Federal Labor government, while they digressed from imperative issues, swept under the rug, rather than putting solid plans for our future in place. A commercial person realizes that band aid fixes are more costly than addressing, rectifying and planning for the long term, up front.

If the initiatives in this book are taken up, the national saving would be enormous and this money together with Australians investing into Australian Bonds through the Bank of Australia could reinvent our secondary manufacturing industries. Private enterprise could be both assisted by government grants, or government takes the initiative of establishing new business venture assets. Government loves selling off our assets, so government ought to grab the opportunity of creating new business and then selling newly established business together with fair goodwill consideration to Australian business entrepreneurs, be they individuals, consortiums or public companies. Let's take an example of how this national overall scenario would work:

1. Through the National Planning and Infrastructure Department an area is focused on e.g. Orange or Lithgow in NSW where local business has been suffering, where house prices are reasonable but there is a declining population due to lack of industry and thus diminished infrastructure.
2. The National Planning & Infrastructure portfolio "NP&I" determines suitability of this area as viable for say the establishment of a new version of the Pacific Brands clothing manufacturing industry. The new factory would be based on all renewable energy utilisation and practises.
3. Plans are established to improve road and rail transport to and from the closest main centre, in this case Sydney for local and international distribution. Determine how many jobs will be provided and ensure adequate housing, medical, educational and recreational facilities are in place to accommodate the influx of new residents.
4. Nationally promoted opportunities for a cost effective clean life style are offered, particularly to the unemployed and the 680,000 homeless. Wages would be determined based on the cost of living, see section on Employment, Industry and Business. It may be possible that once a new business is up and running that the employees get together and buy the business and hold shares. That is, it may be a co-op of workers or consortium who chooses to establish the new operation and share in the profit.

It is proposed under reformed taxation, that higher tariffs be imposed on imported products and this would certainly make locally manufactured superior quality products e.g. wool and cotton garments far more attractive both to our local market and internationally. That greater emphasis is placed on forests to produce timber and paper products, reducing our reliance on plastics and petroleum products (this will certainly achieve reductions in pollution). Replicate this 1,000 times and into every sector of industry from primary and processed foods, to all forms of manufactured items and we become self sustaining in every aspect of our lives. It would create hundreds of thousands of jobs, billions of dollars in tax revenue to sustain ourselves, our national cohesive infrastructure and ensure equality for every Australian.

With the establishment of the "Bank of Australia" and the shareholders being every Australian, we would all benefit from the billions of dollars in profits made and kept here rather than gone to overseas lenders and enterprise. **It's time, time we thought locally first!** I would dare say that with a better level of customer service, better investment products and more competitive fees and charges than the "Big Four Banks" competition in banking will improve and achieve self funded retirees. There would be more industry confidence and better security in placing our saving, superannuation funds and in buying Australian bonds.

Like it or not, money makes the world go around. We do not need to be dictated to in regards to a limitless tax disguised as an ETS in helping third world countries. If our economy is strong we are able to help turn these countries' economies around to becoming self sustaining nations with loans and education. Repayable loans, not gifts but fixed interest accruing repayable loans from a new economy able to repay one day. This will provide attractive incentives to any country to give enough to provide the much need hand-up, not limitless hand-out. Loans to citizens, not gifts to corrupt governments, in meeting the costs of regulated systems of education, agriculture, irrigation, infrastructure advancements and in providing a solid government structure to get those economies in order. *"Give a man a fish and you feed him for a day, teach him to fish and you feed him for life".* The greater the (strictly accountable) financial support, the greater the financial and moral return will be to the investing country, its individuals and to the beneficiaries forever.

Superannuation and an Aging Population

*Superannuation is a luxury while many cannot afford
to keep a roof over their heads, yet they are forced to pay into it.*

THE AUSTRALIAN GOVERN-
MENT introduced compulsory su-
perannuation contributions to ensure retirees are not dependant on the aged pension
and thus save the taxpayer the cost of supporting a purportedly "rapidly increasing
aging population". These super fund contributions are withheld by employers and
contributed to super fund's managers and only recently have these funds been paid
to fund managers of "our choice" as long as it's a government recognised fund. But
we still have no control as to where the recognised fund manager invests our money
eg sub-prime lenders! Government recognised could become government directed,
if government were to demand these funds to meet the government deficit or other
expenditure.

Access to trillions of dollars without the consent of the contributor could
see government enforce a lower rate of return, giving little if anything to the
superannuation investor and currently we can't do a thing to prevent this. In fact
research has shown that people investing into superannuation funds feel that this is
no longer their money no different to just another tax. Currently over **A$12 billion
sits in unclaimed superannuation funds** waiting to be claimed and the owners
do not realise their funds are being held. If unclaimed, who will get this money? This
would be **great seed capital for the Bank of Australia,** until owners claim their
money.

With a "full documentary" loan relied on by banks, the 9% contribution
to superannuation funds is not considered as accessible income in determining
serviceability for a home loan, and can put a young home buying couple out of the
market for their own home. If the household income is say A$80,000 less tax and the
regulated 9% pa is contributed to a super fund, which is subjected to many contributing
factors in the hands of who (some receiving secret commissions from investment
banks?), our return can and has produced poor results, particularly reducing our
borrowing and loan servicing capacity. Imagine if a government dictated increasing
the superannuation contribution to 12 or 14% how many more families would be out
in the street? They might have super when they retire, but probably not enough to

live on and no home to live in at 70 Forced savings, negatively impacts on the "plan" of being able to sustain ourselves in later years let-a-lone diminishes our ability to sustain a mortgage, keep a roof over our families heads and develop equity.

Superannuation contributions are kept from us for our later years, which sounds great but what about making ends meet to get to those years? And what about the shortfall in the mortgage interest repayments (without fixed interest rates) and the escalating cost of living, and will the super funds be adequate enough to afford retirement? No. While we have the freedom to select a superannuation fund, **what could be more prudent than investing our super into our own home, with the same government super contribution in paying off loans sooner, reducing interest and then using the equity (to acquire more investments) in becoming self funded retirees, not dependant on a pension? The more people putting money into their home/super fund, the less pensioners and the less cost to government! Make sense?** Of course safe guards need to be established to protect the home super fund. I have several ideas but this is better handled by those skilled in that area. With only one third of Australians having their own home and vacancy rates at 1% – the objective must be to get more Australians into their own homes – a roof over their head and financial security.

If these super contributions and tax benefits were directed into reducing the principal off our home mortgages each year, such as a self-funded super scheme, it would, perhaps be to the dismay of banks but it would save every family in interest for the term of the loan. It would enable the earlier repayment of the loan and provide security to enable families to build wealth through the development of other securities, say government bonds through our own bank which could guarantee a non reliance on an aged pension. Now why hasn't this been done? Of course there would have to be conditions, including if the property were sold, the total of the super contribution over the years must be re-invested into another home or properties or perhaps the tax benefit is forfeited and repayable.

America has massive current concerns associated with supporting an aging population with an unsustainable 2% birth rate and more than 280 million people. If the US assessment, by those qualified to determine the required resources to sustain the elderly can be relied on, they project that 100% of all of the tax revenue within the next 40 years will be totally directed by the US government towards welfare and Medicare for the over 65 year olds.

By comparison: **In 1988 we had 1.8 million people over 65 years old, that is, 11% of the then 16.6 million population and in 2008 we had 2.8 million people over 65 years old, that is 13% of our 21.5 million population – up by only 2% compared with 20 years ago. While the population increased by 5 million over 20 years, the over 65s group represented an increase of 2% hardly worth the massive government propaganda when there are more than 300,000 migrants coming in, each year. Just excuses for higher taxes, digression and hype to divert attention away from e.g. the cost and failure of**

Floppenhagan, being ripped off with the cost of school buildings, the pink batts and other waste in governments failure as to community concerns and needs. That is, emphasis is wrongly placed on "an aging population" rather than on developing new business, hence new jobs and new taxpayers.

As the population increases, so does the number in the workforce, if we still have industry, and this should be the concern of responsible government. Over the past 10 years our governments have been creating an unsubstantiated urgent panic or scare mongering, merely trying to shed the responsibility for caring for the aged and getting money turning over. This is nothing more than a means of reducing responsibility for our aged, those who have worked and who have built this country. They have the right to expect the next generations will want to show their thanks by supporting them (if it is needed) and be given the opportunity to say thanks, remembering that they will also be aged one day and will expect the same treatment as they give. Governments want everyone to be proactive about compulsory saving. The compulsion of both Liberal and Labor Federal government's for compulsory superannuation, many taxes and high interest has seen many families now feeling the financial pinch which greatly impacts and destroys lives.

Referring to the Population Chart in Section 1.: In 2005 our population was 20.3 million and in 2008 it was 21.5 million. Currently the largest sector of our community is between 35 and 49 years of age equating to approximately 22% of the population, together with the 50 to 64 year olds 17% ie 39% are currently supporting the less than 13% over 65s (although many people continue working into their 70s). It will be the survivors of 17% (50 to 64 year old Baby Boomers) who will progressively get to 65 all in the next 15 years and chances are by that time there will be very few of the current 13% still alive and therefore in say 15 years we will still have around 13-14% over 65 years of age (of the suggested 35 million population) who will be supported by the currently 0 to 34 years olds ie 47% of the current population, so the imminent financial drain on society regarding proper support for "the aging population" is rubbish, government fear tactics used to justify tax hikes and compulsory savings. What is warranted is better care and a higher quality of life and better investment opportunities for our savings!

Increasing the eligible age for pensions from 65 to 67 years of age is not unreasonable given the better medical resources and longevity created, but providing a lousy extra A$32.50 for a single pensioner is nothing short of rorting those we have a responsibility to support with dignity. There would have been a massive outcry of resistance from Ministers in accepting anything less than the 3% increase in the salaries they awarded themselves, with a second increase in 2009, but it is expected that our senior citizens just cop it sweet, when a minimum of A$400pw for a single person would have been more in order. But for those who are reliant on government housing, the increase has been negated with the NSW State Government imposing higher rents on public housing properties. It was as if the NSW Labor government had a windfall with the extra A$33 to grab.

The May 2009 Federal Budget is quite a contradiction in its financial priorities; While government expects penny strapped elderly persons to work longer and be self sufficient, government itself wastes billions on non priority international interests and rewards their own members. One of the clearest examples of the hundreds of millions of dollars wasted by short term unskilled ministers:

Liberal governments provides incentives to Australians to have their own superannuation and medical insurance with rebates of 30% yet Labor, renowned for wasting money and clocking up huge debts for the country, would scab on these rebates, opting to reduce superannuation and health care subsidies than to scrutinize their expenditure and curb their waste. This is no different to the US experts dishing out billions of taxpayers dollars to bankers who awarded themselves bonus salaries, then government trying to get the money back. The difference being, that this has been at the hand of two short term governments in meeting their two differentiating short term agendas.

The short-sightedness and waste of the Federal Labor government is clearly demonstrated in their failed attempt to cut the Medicare rebate in half for Cataract surgery from A$630 to just A$312. Time and money wasted by government in trying to reduce the subsidy, while professional doctors try to maintain the subsidy. This service is priceless when it comes to restoring the sight of 98% of the 140,000 patients each year to normal vision. This improved vision provides improved quality of life, improved ability to continue in being self sustaining, continue to work, be able to read, to drive, to shop, to feed themselves, maintain a healthy mental state and self esteem. Without this surgery it impacts drastically far more on the taxpayer's pocket than could ever be saved from scabbing on this surgery. Risk of falls and hip fractures in the elderly are a consequence of poor vision. Premature detrimental effects of poor vision on the elderly causes early retirement and it also greatly impacts on their families and results in the greater demand for government subsidises to nursing homes for fear of the adversities associated with living with blindness.

This is an **essential surgery** which must be available to every Australian. Someone dropped the beans they were counting in Canberra with this one, as Cataract surgery is a cost cutting exercise if one were to consider the overall cost of hip replacements, hospitalisation for all forms of accidents, carer costs and nursing homes. **With the reduced burocracy as covered so far, there would be no more waste by unskilled politicians, while with experts running this Health Resources Ministry there would be more than sufficient funds to pay 100% of the cost of this surgery for every Australian, if and when needed.** When heavily challenged by the aged and concerned groups over removing subsidies for cataract surgery, Labor back-peddled, etching its way around the issue by introducing a separate Medicare item number, to appear as some kind of concession, but maintaining its objective (to save their hide) of reducing the subsidy by 10% to the elderly of this most imperative need. It wasn't worth the time government invested for the meagre detrimental result.

Not all elderly people are retirees or pensioners. Many still maintain their financial investments, pay tax, live comfortably and provide for their own nursing home costs at the appropriate time but there are many pensioners who for whatever reason never had the ability to save or accumulate superannuation but many in this category own their own home.

Many pensioners in their own homes receive the full pension and take advantage of reverse mortgages or sell equity in their home for interest free loans, repayable on their demise. This provides a bit of extra money over and above the government pension. Many pensioners (who own their home) are remiss to draw on the equity and would rather struggle and juggle to live on the meagre pension existence just to be able to leave a larger inheritance to their kids. While other pensioners in rental accommodation have to find the rent as well as struggle to survive and they do not have the ability to gain any extra in making ends meet. Many live unbearable lives, a living hell of daily watching their very few pennies. In this scenario it is only fair that the pensioner be means tested into two groups;

1. A pensioner who has no property or equity to draw on and who needs the equivalent of the minimum basic wage say A$18,000pa for a single or say A$30,000 for a married couple to live a decent standard or diverted to a nursing home for full (better) care at the appropriate time.
2. A pensioner who has a fully owned home over the value of say A$500,000 ought to be treated as if this is the retiree's superannuation fund, able to draw on the equity to survive at home or until their placement into a retirement home or demise. That is, the pension ought to be repaid to the government from the sale of the property at the time of the demise of the person, with the surplus, above the pension, paid to nominated beneficiaries of the estate. If there is a deficiency, it would be written off, as per category one above. If this pensioner is placed into a cared facility, the property would be leased by the government or next of kin with rent received as a credit towards the costs of the care facility/pension cost, or the property is sold when the person leaves it and the money invested and accounted for to the beneficiaries after the minimum of say A$18,000pa is deducted for the term of care. There is of course the option that family members take care of the person and they receive the full benefit of the rental or pension or equity equal to the pension, rather than a carer's payment.

Naturally both groups would receive free public health care benefits; free government travel and other pensioner discount benefits.

The above is indicative only, but the proposal is for the home to become the superannuation (if no other asset has been achieved over the years) for those paying off their home today, and by those who have paid off their home yesterday, with the elderly not being a *purported* encumbrance on the financial aspects of society and while we are able to provide the best quality of life. In effect, a system where beneficiaries to a property do not benefit at the cost to the taxpayer and where retirees are self sufficient, which appears to have been the objective of government but in an ill conceived method – what can you expect from (too many) drongos?

Amending payments by implementing (2) above would reduce government pension spending and enable greater government financial resources to provide for those who need assistance, particularly our aging and younger population. It would mean that in retirement the retiree would be expected to either draw against a reverse mortgage for living costs, or down size their living requirements and invest the money to provide interest in meeting living expenses or sell a percentage of the house which maybe a more secure return than unskilled investing into the Stock Exchange or receive the repayable but interest free pension.

Many elderly live a lonely existence and many need home care but eventually we will all have to have some sort of care facility or retirement living. There is a greater demand for care facilities but neither local, State or Federal governments have protected the vulnerable in providing adequate facilities. This is where the National Planning and Infrastructure Department would assess every area and based on the demographic requirements, would ensure sufficient facilities are installed giving the best aged care, managed by Local government (if not privately owned). We have witnessed horror stories, such as an 89 year old veteran who woke to find his face being gnawed by mice, substandard food, insufficient staff numbers, poor health standards and care. These issues must be addressed together with sufficient facilities which should be on par with at least a three star hotel and nothing less. Public and Private Nursing Homes must continually prove that they provide a standard of care as stipulated in strict guidelines and monitored regularly to ensure this code is adhered to. It is all too easy to forget that it was the older generation who have given us the wonderful inheritance of this country and how we treat them is how our kids will treat us.

Taxation Reform

GOVERNMENT IN THE first part of the 20th century had achieved more with less. If all of the economies of scale are taken into account; re-defining all government infrastructures are implemented at all levels and a simple formula for tax payments are relied on, then we would achieve double that which we current achieve. The most efficient way to collect the appropriate amount of taxes is just as important as to how it is expended by responsible and accountable government and these are the keys to all of our individual and collective financial success.

We have gone from a one tax system of Colonial days to today where we have income tax; payroll tax; sales tax; company tax; GST with its senseless input credits and debits; land tax; water taxes; stamp duties; fringe benefits tax, to name but a few. Mr Howard's initial election promise was that there would be *"No GST"* then he back-tracked as politicians do well and perhaps that was a good move, although the GST job remains incomplete. At the inception of GST it was promised that the GST would be the tax to replace all taxes. GST was intended to defeat tax avoidance in the cash economy and this may have had some impact but GST hasn't minimised this problem rather it is just one more tax to slug us with.

Government at all levels rely on imposing extra taxes disguised as punishments. The Alcopops tax can do nothing to reduce teenage binge drinking. Since the prices increased kids have moved onto other more potent alcohol choices. Exorbitant taxes on tobacco products for those who are hooked on nicotine and the chemicals governments have allows to be used in these products, is knowing that these people will find the money to buy tobacco products even if it means going without a nutritional diet. Tax penalties are not solutions to problems, its just greedy money grabbing.

Hundreds of millions of tax payer dollars are spent each year in determining and collecting taxation due to the complexities of the tax system. This is also one of the greatest time wasting and costly exercises to firstly each individual, the private and public business sectors and by government taxation employees. From scaled up taxation for higher income earners to tax rebates for dependants, child care, draught relief, medical insurance, superannuation etc; from rebates on various business tax deductible items to depreciation of assets; from company tax to GST; from tax on banking and other transactions to import tax and sales tax; from higher tax on alcohol, fuel and tobacco products to no tax on essential food items; from land tax to stamp duty, it is a maze of complexities where, ultimately, any increased revenue is depleted in the administration process. This lends so well now to a simple system, able to achieve a greater return from both a lesser income, and a lesser expenditure into human resources, particularly the public. That is, rather than increasing company or any other tax, in deceptively appearing as if government has effectively reduced the deficit, change the system.

The Housing Industry Association (HIA) has condemned State and Territory governments in a report confirming Australia is one of the highest taxed developed nations when it comes to property rates and having the highest reliance on transaction taxes, including stamp duty with most of these taxes levied by State and Territory governments and total up to 3% of gross domestic product, the seventh highest in the OECD. Dr Ron Silberberg, the Managing Director of HIA said that *"State governments use property (transactions) as a gold mine to fund their budgets with home owners subsidising State revenue to the tune of billions of dollars through transaction charges and bloated mortgages. In 2003-4 the States and territories collected more than A\$10.47 billion in stamp duty and more than A\$3.059 billion in land tax"* and *"The current practice used to collect stamp duty on new housing involves triple counting, is inequitable and amounts to nothing more than a State government revenue rort as the Warburton and Hendy Report shows"*. This clearly shows the 50% discount begrudgingly extended off stamp duty by the NSW State Government was nothing more than a marketing or public relations ploy.

We have been subjected to years of excessive taxes through interest, petrol and the many taxes imposed by the three levels of government, yet it took a purported "Recession" for government to reduce mortgage interest and give stimulus band-aids. There has never been real government intervention or a permanent remedy, rather continued political deception through an intricate, excessive and confusing taxation system.

In their report, Peter Hendy and Dick Warburton also found that Australia was the eighth lowest taxed country overall of 30 industrialised countries in the OECD, with relatively low taxes on individuals and GST. So what we have is an imbalance between property and transaction taxes (State imposed) versus income and GST (Federal). You remember how GST was sold to us, *"the tax to replace all other taxes"*. The big question begging to be asked – would any State government ever agree to giving up their gold mine? What this means is that the Federal government collect most of the revenue and drips it out ever so slowly, so State governments impose their own taxes, with 40% collected to feed their own burocracy – doesn't this now justify the abolition of State governments and its taxes, for a national transparent approach by expert Resources Ministers?

The administration of taxes and accountability need not be as costly and time consuming an exercise and nightmare for business as it is. Currently the cost of running the ATO alone is enough to run the administration of a small country and for the small to medium business person, it can involve up to 20 hours a week to administer together with the payroll, workers comp and other insurances, superannuation and long service payments etc. Twenty hours means an additional staff member to a business owner or he or she does this unpaid work for no additional financial benefit and costs must be increased to what may become non competitive rates.

Unions seek *"secure jobs with secure income and secure benefits for their members"* but this is absolutely 100% reliant on security for the business owner, who is in business not just for these benefits to his employees but his financial commitments to his lenders, all of his overheads and his family, before he sees one red cent. These government and union encumbrances and demands have seen the pendulum swing too far to one side; see section on Employment, Industry and Business. There is a simple solution, which requires minimum effort with maximum results and a fair deal to all Australians based on our individual level of income and expenditure.

During the 11 year reign of the Liberal Federal Government, our high collective taxes and the sale of assets such as Telstra together with low expenditure on maintenance and improvements to infrastructures has undisputedly eliminated the massive national debt inherited from the previous Federal Labor government, and provided more than A$15 billion in surplus, that was before Labor got their mitts on it. By the same token the NSW Labor State government has also reaped in a fortune from selling off valuable assets over the corresponding 12 year period and has resulted in a State in undeclared bankruptcy.

Prior to the 2006 Federal budget Peter Costello was boasting of an anticipated A$10 billion surplus but when a Treasurer projects a A$10 billion surplus and then proudly announces a A$15 billion surplus, this is no great success for him and his party as purported. It just means they didn't have a clue as to the validity of their projections and had over taxed many sectors of the country and failed to invest into infrastructure to achieve this unanticipated surplus, purported as an outstanding result.

Our tax system is complex, expensive and untenable to maintain, it needs to be simplified and not be made more complex or take years to implement.

The Henry Tax Review, which cost taxpayers millions of dollars has hundreds of complex recommendations and is reflective of the desires of the convener of the report, the Labor governments. But like the "2020 (Public Relations) Summit", Labor will determine only those few recommendations which best suit their propaganda machine, especially in an election year. This will be yet another report to sit on the shelves of taxpayer funded reports. The best Labor will be able to come up with would be the "Ruddin Hood Scheme", that is, take from the rich and appear to be giving to the poor majority. A short-sighted, socialistic approach in taking from the rich which only reduces the rich's ability to provide jobs and benefits to those less well off. Imposing harsh taxation only reduces business and increases the majority of subjective welfare recipients. The stimulus (free lunches) handout payments and wasted money, including all consultants reports, will now be pursued for pay back, but how at how many times over?

We need the best road and transport systems; the best comprehensive health care; the best educational opportunities for our kids; the best of everything but with only 22 million people in a land so vast, it is difficult to achieve these objectives immediately and without better and fairer methods of achieving our urgent short and long term objectives. The sooner changes are implemented, the sooner we can all reap the benefits.

Consider a decisive consolidated plan of all Resources Ministries creating a deficit over the next 10 years to 2020 of say two trillion dollars. This may seem insurmountable but keep reading into the National Planning and Water sections and remember the objectives of the new Bank of Australia. The proceeding 10 years to say 2030 given an increased population and productivity through taxes (and savings from not delaying expenditure into new industry) this deficit would not reach such a level. It would have reduced rapidly over those years, funded by the increase in Australians paying tax during these 20 years and in growing into new rural infrastructure. That is, with the infrastructure plans and budgeted costs in place at 2010 prices the savings will have been greatly reduced on the same plans and spending requirements (if they were to be planned and carried out by 2020). The same example applies if you were to have built a house in 1980 for $150,000 and today it would cost you $450,000.

Within the next 15 to 20 years we would achieve and sustain our most extensive national objectives through re-assessing our national tax and revenue income simply and fairly.

I would propose that all taxes be reduced to three. The amounts here are indicative only and need to be determined from the current income levels of each sector, the anticipated increase to the work force from new business and the collective ability to meet our national costs, including Medicare and all Portfolios. A redefined National (ATO) Treasury will know concise expenditure and more concise income revenue derived from the three forms of tax. The expenditure costs will be less than are currently as the 3 levels of handling would be reduced to one and provide for greater expenditure;

1. "Income Tax" and "Company tax"
2. "Expenditure Tax" or "E-tax" replacing the "GST" (fresh produce exempt)
3. "Import Tariffs"

1. Income Tax and Company Tax

A tax free threshold of say A$18,000 should inspire people to get a job rather than collect unemployment benefits. Assistance with relocation costs and housing would help in taking whatever jobs are on offer irrespective of where the job maybe, or discontinue the welfare. There are thousands of jobs but it may require people to move to the job and not wait for a job to come to them.

Assuming we rely on the same income tax scale method as is currently relied on, rebates would reduce the income tax based on the number of dependants. Rebates that are currently paid in the form of family assistance, child care and maternity leave through a very expensive administration rather than a reduction in taxation. Similarly a decrease in company tax to eliminate depreciation and other tax rebates as well as a higher scale of taxation as companies reach higher profits. This would save on all double handling in government collections and then payments. It would ensure mum and dad business pays a lower rate of company tax (say 25%) than would say a mining, banking or international corporation (say 45% on profits over A$500 million).

a) With the proposed school admission age reduced to three years of age, see section on Education, child care subsidies would be eliminated. Government currently funds public and part of the private school costs based on a per child basis and the current child care subsidies plus the cost of administering would cover the reduced aged students.
b) All costs of health care provided under an improved public health care system paid by Medicare, see section on Health.

Should *all company profits remain in Australia?* Radical you say? I don't think so. Countries such as South Africa will not allow people to take valuable assets or excessive amounts of money out of their economy, yet we do. We have inadvertently allowed our governments to sell off assets and Australians businesses, with the profits moved overseas providing minimal, if any, benefit to this country. The mining industry takes raw minerals overseas to process, resulting in the value of the processed goods escalating over there, not here and the profits going elsewhere but minimised tax on raw stock. Australians want these assets and those profits back. If international corporations are not happy to allow the profits to stay and work here, sell the asset back to Australians. This is a major part of insulating or quarantining ourselves for financial independence and sustainability. Put it to a vote?

Should employees be treated with more accountability than business? Currently, based on government determination, employers withhold a percentage of the wages for holiday and sick pay as well as super etc. This has not aided productivity ie if you don't take the sickie, you don't get paid for it. Assuming all employees were treated as subcontractors, paid their entire hourly rate, productivity can be improved and employees can benefit from paying their holiday pay and self governed superannuation into say their mortgage to reduce interest, redraw on when holidays are taken, see sections on Superannuation and Industrial Relations.

To reduce government administration, means and identity testing and the cumbersome requirements of the Centrelink system, family allowances and assistance based on the number of dependants in a household would be provided through tax reductions rather than paid as welfare benefits, unless the income is less than the tax free threshold.

As nonsensical, complex and a waste of time as the bureaucracy involved in charging farmers for water licenses on one hand, while determining welfare for them on the other – is granting tax concessions or negative gearing for property investment on one hand while charging stamp duty, land tax and then capital gains tax on the other. Also, allowing GST and depreciation concessions on equipment purchased to run a business, when equipment purchases ought to be considered as expenditure necessary to run the business and simply claiming the purchase price as expenditure – the monetary differences are neither here nor there.

No industry in Australia should be penalised over any other or have greater benefits than another. In this vein, those making greater profits ought to be taxed under a scale not dissimilar to income tax. For example, as a guide only: A company tax free threshold under say A$20,000: 25% tax applicable on profits under A$5m: 35% between A$5m and $10m: 40% between A$10m and A$50m and 50% of all profits when a company achieves above say A$50m.

Similarly but say monthly the employer business lodges the company or business tax return without consideration for depreciation but comprising of the total gross incomes from sales less expenditure associated with running the business and together with the E-tax (if applicable ie an end seller) paid as the monthly taxable profit or tax loss (to be adjusted in the following months with tax losses carried forward, if applicable). The two taxes are determined and provided directly to the National (ATO) monthly with one annual summary.

2. **Expenditure Tax or "E-tax" replacing the "GST" – Applicable to the end user only, which we all are:**

Only business providing goods and services to the end user would collects say 11% (1% for replaced health fund premiums and no tax on fresh produce) on top of the end sale price of the goods and services.

The GST debit and credit system produces encumbrances on business and government, a great liability which reduces revenue. Revenue can be increased not just by savings, but with a better system. Here is an example:

Let's say a manufacture sells his widgets for A$1 per kilo and adds 10c for GST but he deducts the GST he has paid on cost of goods and other operational costs, say 5c of 50c that is, he pays **5c GST**. Then the wholesaler buys the widgets for $1.10 and when he sells them for $2.20 he deducts his operational costs, say 10c on A$1 that is he pays **10c GST**. Then the retailer buys the widgets for A$2.20 and sells them for A$4.40 assuming his operational costs are A$2 his offset credit is 20c and so he pays **.20c GST** to the ATO. That is, the total from the manufacturer to the consumer to the ATO is **.35c GST** If the E-tax would be applicable to the end consumer only on the A$4.40 the tax, based on 10% this would be **.40c GST**.

That is, a **.5c higher return to the ATO** and no difference or extra cost to the consumer while saving time and money to all business' and the ATO along the way. This will also prevent the massive cost and workload for the ATO with refunds and the financial distress to businesses, some desperately waiting for GST credit refunds cheques.

It is proposed that those who are exempt from charging the E-tax are the providers of goods and services to other business whether they are primary or manufactured goods as the input debit and credit system writes off most of the government benefit along the way anyway, it just creates a mass of extra time and costs with the end user still paying the currently 10% on cost. Exceptions would include tradesmen working on construction for a builder, with the builder charging the 11% to the end buyer; farmers or manufacturers selling to wholesalers would not pay the E-tax but the retailers then impose the 11% to the end consumer. All paid weekly or monthly to the National ATO thus improving government cash flow while reducing government costs of administering with the B-pay system. The Australian Business Number "ABN" to replace the company tax file number and extended a similar numbering system to all sole traders and partnerships, ensuring all business complies with weekly payments.

There would be no adjustments for capital purchases or input credits just a flat and fixed one tax replacing all others. That is, replace State and Federal imposed stamp duties on property purchases, capital gains tax, land tax and all other forms of tax imposition with one E-tax on all transactions on all end sales.

This would be paid weekly or monthly (to minimise potential loss to the ATO) into the National ATO on all "Sales Transactions" (not on the sale of private second hand goods) be it the sale of a house (at the time of sale), car, boat, food, clothing, holiday accommodation, travel, alcopops, petrol and tobacco products, service and tradesmen will only charge the expenditure tax to the end user for every service and commodity. Note: 11% being say 1% towards Medicare in lieu of payments to private health insurance see section on Health.

For a computerised business, say Coles, it would be less than one hour per week for the business to administer and pay the say 11% off all income and paid directly into the ATO account. Non computerised business would not be disadvantaged ie total the income and draw a cheque for the 11% and post with the summary of sales. Standard issue ATO software provided at no cost or hard copy for non computerized business.

Just imagine what the small business owner can do with those extra hours, work a bit more, play a bit more, spend more quality time helping mum with the kids and their home work or just enjoying life with the family that might otherwise have fallen apart or led to problems with their kids, from unintentional neglect. Most ATO staff could be transformed from collectors of income to administrators of Resource's Ministries income and expenditure and perhaps ATO services could be extended to perhaps new Federal initiatives. This could include assisting families with a lack of budgeting skills in determining better ways of achieving their financial goals without risk or any stress and assisting other government functions and agencies to meet the additional staffing requirements of the hospital and medical system.

3. Import Tariffs

Many countries, with responsible government, maintain the imposition of high tariffs on all imported goods to ensure their local industry is protected. Australia also had tariffs but these have been removed under free trade agreements and UN treaties, proving to have been the most inept decisions and the greatest liability to this country. The removal of tariffs contributed to the demise of our manufacturing industry and Government have an obligation to re-impose tariffs on a scale that would ensure current and new Australian manufacturing initiatives can be competitive with imported goods.

Government has always sought ways of imposing higher taxation and financial impositions on higher income earners, but this together with increased interest on home mortgages as a means of "slowing (retail) spending to curb inflation" have penalised everyone.

Imposing tariffs particularly on luxury items or items that are not life sustaining, is the fairest way and it also provides a level competitive playing field for local manufacturing, thus more jobs. There is no doubt retail spending may slow down temporarily, that is, until competitive Australian manufactured goods can be provided at a similar price to imported goods but the financial benefits are insurmountable for all local business. Gone may be the days of high turnover with minimum profits, but better to obtain a real profit from the real value of competitive goods. As well as the tariffs in providing new jobs, that is new taxpayers we have the ability to repay the national debt in our becoming self sustaining in all facets of our lives. We will also have set the scene for productivity and security for families and provide incentives for an increased population of new taxpayers in decentralised areas. This is but a datum point for specialists from economic and financial fields but they must not be hindered with political agendas.

◆　Imposing tariffs on all imported goods is not unlike that which is charged on goods imported into many countries. That is, if you can afford these goods you can afford the extra tax, this is called fair! Increased tariffs will create greater competitiveness with Australian primary and manufactured goods.

A simpler, fairer and cost effective tax will improve our quality of life by providing better benefits to all of us. The only other taxes would be from the imposition of local council and water rates, in accordance with Senate governed costs determination.

SECTION 3

The Business of the Country

National Planning & Infrastructure "NP&I" – Regional Development

IN MY OPINION and I'm sure Bob Katter, Independent Member for Kennedy would agree, that a **"National Planning & Infrastructure Ministry"** ought to be relied on by every **"Local come Federal Ministry"** individually and collectively and every **"Federal Resources Ministry".** This ministry would be the backbone of moving Australia forward, **"it's all in the planning".** The National Planning Ministry would provide the framework and the ability to prevent duplication or rather triplication and procrastination while maximising national resources in the networking of Resource's Ministries in-tune with the requirements of all local municipalities to a national consistency with maximum benefits to all Australians.

Through the new Bank of Australia, if say, a trillion dollars were to be invested from Australians savings, superannuation investments (with new regulations imposed, stipulating that all Australian super investments must be invested in Australia), taxation revenue including the national savings from reduced bureaucracy were to be made into Australian bonds over say, the next 10 years, the bank would be able to "self-fund" new Australian industry, infrastructure and the urgent need to provide housing while providing a safe return to investors, us, not international sub-prime or other lenders.

The Bank of Australia's investment into short and long term business and housing developments in rural areas and centres would be repaid from interest and profit share generated from the profits received by new industry and improved industry. Increased business means increased taxation revenue from productivity, not based on increased tax from imposing new taxes e.g. Carbon Emissions Trading. New factories with new technology to ensure emissions are reduced and profit is taxed in the normal course of good business. Of course in meeting renewable energy sources, if there needs to be a financial void filled, there is our proposed E-tax for short or long term adjustment.

Expenditure into revitalising ailing semi rural and rural areas in Australia, and also into new areas zoned for development, is the surest way of repaying any government deficit and justifies money invested into improved infrastructure, nationally. Infrastructure improvements are currently and totally dependent on the assumption that the world economy will recover and business will resume to where it was previously. Assumption is very expensive and provides no guarantees for ordinary Australians but new and improved business does! As the saying goes, when you "assume" you make an ass out of you + me. Ordinary Aussies deserve guaranteed jobs and improvement, not possibilities pegged on the promise of foreign events.

At tremendous cost, local councils have been bickering with developers and residents for many decades. Councillors in their current roles are no different from the other two levels of government, holding onto and protecting their own agendas and seeking revenue at every opportunity, in their also relatively short tenure in office. Developments are often approved, by local ministers who hold no more expertise than any ordinary Australian, even when the development is not suitable, or is not in the long term interest of the local community. The case of the Wollongong Councillor's cash for favours to ensure the developer's development application was approved, is only one case which highlights both corruption and a conflict of interest towards the job entrusted and it is needless to reiterate the State Government's conflict of interests in schemes which lead to litigation at the rate-payers' expense.

One case involving the development of Rose Bay and Double Bay marinas highlighted the council's investment of A$700,000 into its legal bill. Even though this was a success for the council and the residents, it came at a cost that could have been alleviated if the appropriate planning was as stipulated under a National Planning Authority. Also, a culture has developed with residents, known as the "NIMBY" (or Not In My Back Yard), with local resident protesters of proposed projects, seeing the project not to be in "their interests". I have known of residents who objected to the internal design of a small new house, advising the owners of how they should plan it and further objecting to the removal of sick old trees which gave them a "view" so rather than plant their own, they just objected to the plans. The approval process ought to take no more than a few days but it is often dragged into months at the cost of the owner in interest and more consultants' fees to get the approval sought. Government incentives with reduced stamp duty provided to home builders is then negated with the struggle to get through the barrage of council costs and bureaucracy to get approvals to build their home.

Woollahra Council is certainly not isolated as an example of forging forward with planning issue litigation at the expense of the community. In the Wentworth Courier 19 Nov 2008: "*Woollahra Council has spent almost $1.4m defending 49 planning decisions in the NSW Land and Environment Court since July 2007 – but has won only eight outright*" and "*between July and October 2008 the council scored just one outright win in 13 cases*" and Cr Petrie of Woollahra said, "*I'm not sure that the Land and Environment Court and its commissioners, in many cases understand our concerns and needs. I'm not sure they don't just say Pennant Hills can have this sort of development, so Woollahra can too*" and Cr Petrie would be absolutely and undisputedly right.

What is suitable and needed in one demographic area may not be suitable for another, but what expertise is relied on to make this most fundamental determination?

A body stuck in its own area, with its own motives and limited focus, or officers of the court, or a body with a total overall national picture, able to determine unified guidelines to specific areas. A body having the ability to compare and enforce standards respective to similar demographic areas, say Woollahra to Toorak or Studley Park, Bondi to Manly, Northcote to Redfern and so on. On a comparable national scale this will bring about consistency and meet the requirements for the short and long term growth, ensuring adequate infrastructure is in place for parking, water, power, aged and child care, schools, hospitals etc. rather than place greater demands on these very stretched resources in densely populated urban areas.

If millions of dollars of ratepayer's money is spent each year in court battles it's not being spent on services, improvements and the needs of the ratepayer. Frustration, costs, losses of opportunity, resentment and litigation on all sides can be prevented when everyone knows the guidelines and acceptable limits and usage for all respective areas on a national basis. But inconsistency between council planning, resources and requirements in differing locales remains an issue to residents. It is to the detriment of maximising or even providing the benefits of sufficient schools, hospitals, aged and child care, shopping centres, roads etc. To achieve this we need to provide a superior level of understanding which can only be provided with an educated cohesive effort by those specialised and able to provide a national overview in determining suitability for housing, agriculture, mining, manufacturing etc. and what is required to achieve this in all areas by ensuring there is sufficient water and new dams, rail lines etc. while not being hindered by petty Local or State agendas.

We only have to look at the difference between how the city of Sydney just grew with limited planning from 1788 and the problems encountered with the need for growth in the 21st century. Compare Sydney with a city like Canberra, which was largely planned from the ground up and able to facilitate growth. Sydney has industry along-side residential areas, while Canberra has designated areas for residential, for commercial and industrial, with easy access between all areas on good road systems.

Erratic re-zoning of areas and approval of projects or industry is not restricted to local council, no sir – when there's the mighty buck involved the State Labor Government is there. Farmers are rightfully up in arms over the NSW State government's plans to allow the mining of the NSW food bowl and the potential destruction of the underground water system, which has the potential to annihilate farming in favour of mining interests. If global warming (or rather, due to the exposure of this scam) now climate change, is a Federal Labor issue, this is a clear contradiction by the State Labor government to their Federal counterparts proposed Carbon Emissions tax, or perhaps more appropriately, another major ETS tax contributor.

Re-addressing rural and urban areas with a national overall view would provide new opportunities and justify much needed infrastructure. The installation of alternative power sources to meet the decrease in emissions, a national integrated road and rail infrastructure, a system of new dams to service new and existing centres in overcoming water shortages where towns are struggling to retain people who are leaving for the lack of work and facilities. These are the issues that are currently held tightly by Local and State Government but greatly neglected with no solutions. New towns would be developed based on the National Planning and Infrastructure Department determination of appropriate new industry, specific to each area's suitability and provide a massive increase in jobs associated with farming and manufacturing for local and export markets. It would create incentives for decentralisation into rural areas, taking the pressure off the infrastructure in cities and suburban areas and improve everyone's lifestyle.

Our cities, especially Melbourne and Sydney, are like whirlpools that draw people in because they're hunting for new or better jobs. Sydney is expanding rapidly, particularly in the north-west region, yet there is no public transport and no motorway to service the area suffering with a congested road system. State government sought A$4 billion from Infrastructure Australia to meet this cost, but was refused as it appeared obvious, that this was a crisis management plan approved by State government before the costs were factual or accurate, and synonymous with the history of mismanagement of other roads system. While people are moving to the cities, this process has bled rural centres, so these centres have lost more vital services, like doctors and work. Some towns have sold town blocks for a song, just to get people to move there. There is a real logic to maintaining and strengthening rural centres and improving transport links to these centres. Otherwise, we're adding to the chaos of burgeoning cities and their transport chaos.

In short, our national priorities are all wrong. We've lost sight of how to manage rural Australia just ask Senator Barnaby Joyce one man who has a grip on our national requirements. A key reason is that we're looking at its issues in penny packets rather than big slices.

◆ It is proposed that the entire country, as one unit and crossing all borders as if they do not exist, be broken up into areas most suitable for; mining, forests and forestry industry, manufacturing, light and heavy industry, dams and irrigation, various agricultural activities, urban and semi urban areas.

◆ Areas along the coast and in the north of the country would be tapped into for water harvesting, particularly flood prone areas. This would provide piped water to dams for irrigation of arable land west of the Great Divide and establishing new industry. Similarly, relocating areas for manufacturing and commercial usage from urban areas to less expensive rural to reduce overheads and make industries more competitive – this, with the proposed new tax system, beats moving to China!

◆ There would be stipulated "National Guidelines", pertinent and specific to all and every area nationally, that cannot be overridden by any developer, council or complainant for their own personal benefit. That is, if a person wants to buy into any area, they can check the localised guidelines as to what can and cannot be constructed, rather than challenge the National Planning and Infrastructure Department. This negates the need for any Land and Environment Court challenges. As all Resources Ministries the NP & I would be governed by the Senate legislator and decisions can be challenged, firstly to the House of Representatives and then to the High Court if there be a need.

Just as there are now "Model Rules" online for groups to establish nationally consistent constitutions, there should be online national guidelines which recommend guidelines for optimal town planning.

For example, many classical church designs create single-use buildings. More modern designs can create spaces which are churches at weekends and may reserve certain spaces for a permanent chapel but could be built close to aged care facilities for recreations use. They could also be hired out for other appropriate activities (activities which themselves only require temporary use of the space, not 24/7 occupation). Model town planning guidelines could recommend much better use of space, increasing utility and consuming fewer resources.

◆ All new and existing industry and residential developments would have alternative energy sources subsidised or funded by government with favourable interest and terms from the Bank of Australia or other banks. This would provide Australian and international manufacturers the opportunity to reconsider Australia, as the costs of business would be greatly reduced.

◆ The NP&I department would employ "Certifiers" who are not independent of the NP&I for approval and completion certification, paid for from the development application costs.

◆ The NP & I through the National Office of Fair Trading would ensure that all faulty building works, as covered by the builder's warranty insurance, are pursued by the NP & I (Fair Trading) for the owner, with the NP & I providing prompt authorisation and payment for the rectification of incomplete or faulty work. The NP & I would pursue the builder, no longer reliant on owner(s). This would require building contracts to be amended advising both the builder and the owner of this facility and the agreement of the builder to reimburse the NP & I.

◆ Section 94 contributions currently paid to local councils for improvements to local infrastructure would be paid to the NP&I who would ensure these funds are dedicated to the respective area's prioritised needs, if supported by the local constituents.

The "NP&I" would publish, for access to all architects and individuals, the online guidelines of what can and cannot be constructed in each and every area of the country. Issues such as the footprint of a development, the height restrictions, approved use and all pertinent environmental issues would be subject to the approved local SEP encompassing the specific demographic stipulations for that area. This would ensure that no sand mine would be built in an area such as Swansea or within 200m of a public school, or that 10 storey buildings are not approved in a single occupancy area or where the area is over-developed and it cannot currently sustain the local demands for say, parking or traffic flow.

This may mean, in some instances that the NP & I determinates the need to buy properties for local councils to develop "user pays" (ie self-funding) car parks to service the areas demand. Or, that car parks are built underneath local parks in providing sustainable living options to the residents who currently pay daily fines for double parking or parking illegally overnight, just to be able to park in close proximity to their home. Local councils are far too inept to focus on solutions to parking problems rather they employ or subcontract the services of unscrupulous rangers in blatant revenue raising activities from people just wanting to park near their home. People in the Waverley Municipality, for example, would be more than willing to pay for weekly parking close to their home. Residents detest local government for its lack of utility and money grubbing in lieu of a council providing adequate planning. Based on history, adequate planning is something councils and State governments are ill equipped to provide.

◆ When a new plan and development application is submitted, it would only require a local officer of the NP&I to ensure that the development conforms to the established national precedents. Then the application is either rejected for amendment and resubmitted or alternatively approved, all within, say 2 days and not (as is currently experienced with some applications) taking up to 6 months for an approval and many ending up in the Land and Environment Court. Development application fees would be paid to NP& I not the local council in meeting the costs of the services provided in approval and certifications.

This entire process of approval of developments would be **removed from Local council and State governments** although the current councils Building Department persons would perhaps be adopted by the NP&I. Reducing overheads for all concerned with rent and administrative costs paid by the NP & I to councils, rather than wear stand-alone costs. In this scenario, the NP&I would be able to relay between the council, the constituents and the NP&I for the common good of each respective area. The entire cost of the NP&I would be carried by private and government Development Applications, paid for on approval.

Again, government functions need not be profit generators but rather facilitate the country's requirements as its priority. Transparent annual income and expenditure would be provided to the National (ATO) Treasury to ensure the costs of the expenditure are met. It would also ensure planned improvements to parks, roads, hospitals, schools, social and sporting venues are budgeted for in all short and long term objectives from the revenue raised from development applications and development contributions from multi home and commercial developers.

Roads and rail systems must belong to all Australians and are essential national transport routes. It is nonsense that they be divided by State borders, attracting inconsistent administrative costs and maintenance by each State. Add to this the inability in many instances to come to agreements, often relied on as an excuse not to proceed with constructive initiatives. Once again, this is money better spent on maintenance and improvements as derived from the National Roads & Rail revenue sources.

The National Treasury (ATO) would get the national income from roads, fines and registration costs. It would determine the expenditure for improvements based on educated and factual submissions from the National Transport Ministry with their short and long term objectives, based on demographic demand and safety requirements. There would be no chance of the approval of say, a three lane motorway between Perth and Broome in 2010 but you would expect a minimum of a four lane motorway on all main arterial roads into all major cities where the use determines the requirement. If there need be a toll to repay for that investment, the charge could be attached to the vehicle's registration and paid say, monthly to the National Transport Ministry. Refusal to pay would equal termination of the vehicle's registration until repaid with a small administration cost for reinstatement but there would be no additional fines for none or late payment, this is extortion as is pre-paying for tolls which may never be used. When that motorway has been repaid, the toll would be reduced to meet maintenance costs only, or simply removed, not retained at a higher level as a windfall directed to "other use" by any authority. If the funds for the new motorway were borrowed from say, the Bank of Australia, it would be repaid principal and interest to the investors.

The ability for the Australian government to provide a transport system for tomorrow's 50 million people needs and requires a long term solution today. You don't have to be a genius to realise that a three lane freeway costs more than a two lane freeway but the cost of construction of a three lane freeway tomorrow will be more than triple the costs today.

Nathan Rees conceded that there is no money to add an extra lane to the M2 and M5 freeways but in comparison to today's costs, it would have been a small price to pay when those main arterial roads were initially constructed. These additional lanes would have been paid for with the savings in lost work hours due to traffic jams and so forth. The investment today for an infrastructure that won't be maximised for years would seem to be excessive expenditure, but it can be justified in the long term savings and the reduced loss of lives through reduced road fatalities.

This is merely one example of where over expenditure to the point of excessive borrowing makes sense but only if there is long term work and business opportunities to counter-balance the investment. Otherwise, we are building new suburbs for people who can't afford them because business opportunity has been priced out of existence and there are no jobs, or few jobs. There should be incentives for decentralisation, particularly to those who just cannot afford to own their home in major cities but must commute to work. This includes skilled and unskilled migrants who would move to new areas for new employment opportunities, rather than remain unemployed and unable to secure their own home in densely populated areas. Better incentives for a safe and affordable lifestyle cannot be questioned.

Real national leadership on transport would begin the work to introduce high-speed trains. Suddenly, centres such as Moss Vale would be a short commute away (no worse, and probably faster, than a Campbelltown to Central run today). The objective of this example at this point is to merely demonstrate that spending now is in fact a saving later, with the benefits now and later. Better to **grow into an infrastructure than burst out of one**, with our kids realising in 2030 that our current attempts at saving money today was in fact at their expense. Better that our kids will be able to look back with pride at the inheritance we have left them.

But this also shows why "real" leadership is needed on transport, with a commitment to timeframes regardless of election timetables. Currently, there is no conception of national planning and only erratic localised planning begins when there is no choice for government to succumb to demands. Under the current 3 tier political system, national planning would be yet another disaster in the making. Australia needs real planning which builds based on co-ordinated, national requirements, not on the short-term whims of political expediency.

Redefining Responsibility

MR RUDD PROPOSED tax reductions for those who move to rural areas but there would be no tax for them, as currently rural and semi-rural jobs are drying up fast, and it would rather that the taxpayer would be providing more welfare.

To safely increase decentralisation, first we must decentralise existing industry and develop new eco-friendly industry supported with a strong infrastructure and competitive wages. This will provide the balance needed to justify new infrastructure. New business investments will provide new jobs and additional taxation paid from the newly created jobs. Fast train systems would enable people to live in areas they can afford and safely commute to work without the need for more congested highways.

Today we have no mechanism – other than a futile public outcry of disapproval – in trying to stop governments selling off our assets and utilities. And who knows, tomorrow, maybe it'll be our national parks and beaches! I'm sure the NSW State Government has considered selling Bondi Beach! With disbanding State governments, local government would adapt to new responsibilities:

◆ All parks, beaches, schools, State and Federally owned property must be returned to the local government and administered for the benefit of the local constituents and visitors and not to be dealt with in any joint venture or sold off.

Responsibilities of local government must be re-defined to include the administration of public facilities and in working with respective National Portfolios, including but not limited to:

◆ Parks, beaches, local schools, rubbish, community centres including aged care and child care facilities, local business networking and education, social activities by local council. A front office representation for all Federal government portfolios would also be housed by local councils, although funds contributed by each Resources Ministry as part of their expenditure. All costs of the Local/ Federal Ministers Office would be funded from the revenue as currently received in local rates and subsidised by each Resources Ministry, also reducing the cost of their independent local representations. That is maximising the resources and minimising expenditure. Rates, together with income from user pays child and aged care, would be based on the cost of operation and maintenance and all would be audited by National Treasury (ATO) auditors who would set the level of rates based on the required expenditure.

Again, to be too specific, the establishment and maintenance of say, a school or hospital does not come under the administration cost of the Local/Federal Government, rather pertinent to their respective portfolio(s).

Government aged care and child care facilities are local community issues and need to be worked by local council together with the respective National Health Ministry's National Aged Care sub-portfolio. Same as the National Education Ministry would work with local government for, not just child care but early education or the first stage of integration into the school system. These functions are vital to a stable community and need localised administration by council in working in and with the community to provide the best facilities for both the frail aged and to nurture the very young. While Federal government may assume these responsibilities, currently they are State government responsibilities, albeit in very poor condition for Federal government pulling the purse strings – it's a no win for every Australian and currently neither State nor Federal have been able to provide these two primary areas with good governance. Again, State government is redundant. There is nothing State government can achieve that a consortium of local governments cannot, but without the 40% of revenue to pay them.

Unless a facility has been established by a local council, there is no current responsibility for councils in these areas. Often responsibility is shrugging off for the overall welfare of their community, where less than favourable consideration is given towards the aged and child care in lieu of over development in an area already strangled and struggling with inadequate infrastructure. Residents in densely populated urban areas are suffering the effects of over population and **poor long term planning and maintenance by councils and State governments.** The lack of maintenance is deeply felt on local infrastructure which is more than apparent with the serious collapse of the wall along Cooper Park in Bellevue Hill. This was due to Sydney Water failing to maintain and repair leaking old water pipes which finally burst in Northern Sydney suburbs, Bellevue Hill, Carlingford, Moore Park and other locations resulting in some dime witted politician suggesting that State government reduce the water pressure and this is the best bandaid plan rather than fix old pipes and implement a better system of checking and replacement. Millions of litres of sewage runs into our ocean, promised to have been fixed 20 years ago, remain a problem. Years of State governments failing to maintain water and drainage, where 6% of water is lost due to leaking pipe and other infrastructure become dilapidated and inner city congested developments continue, yet in times of draught rangers cruise the streets to impose fines on water wasters! This is no different to the weeks of known gas leaks in San Franciso which resulted in exploding gas pipes destroying homes and killing more than 20 people.

Residents and politicians of any persuasion are not skilled planning experts and while councils engage experts, they more than often do not accept the recommendations, if the advice does not conform to the councillors' agenda (same as on all 3 levels of government). Self-importance, which comes with being elected and the false egotistical belief that they understand the planning process better than trained staff or that they have access to superior planning determinations than a National body can provide, will give rise to rebuking any national approach that will improve life for all of us.

Waverley Council is heavily involved in the current debacle over the Benevolent Society's aged care and child care facilities in Bondi. This is a huge, prime piece of real estate with a magnificent heritage protected house and established fig trees – a property which was so very generously bequeathed by a generous benefactor for the benefit of the local community, then State entrusted to the Benevolent Society for a token payment, to ensure this objective was achieved and maintained. Now the Benevolent Society seeks to over develop the site for its financial gain and no doubt this includes to the benevolence of its board of directors (certainly this is worthy of a government inquiry). Around 2006 the Benevolent Society closed its doors to the aged with the two levels of self contained units (40) standing empty for four years. The grounds are no longer enjoyed by the many local aged people who once lived in the centres retirement village and nursing home facility, and its much needed child care facility is gone as well. Plans are being pushed by the Benevolent Society for the over-development of the site with a tiered ten story apartment building. Sources say that the plans include a 40% odd allocation of units to be dedicated back to the care of the aged (the rest sold commercially), but that is approximately what the current premises house today, without overdeveloping this local asset. No one can imagine how an old person could get out of an inappropriate housing situation on say, the sixth floor in any emergency or if the lifts are out of order. This can only be classified as yet another *"profit before people"* project and while not very benevolent to the aged or the young or the local community, it results in much infighting between the developers, the Council and the locals.

It would seem that the Benevolent Society may have has lost their understanding of what "benevolence" truly means and has "replaced benevolence with profit". While the local council knows that the developer has the resources to keep fighting until they win, and the locals will be the losers once again, unless a National Planning & Infrastructure authority were to intervene and determine to either retain the current approved zoning and usage and height restrictions. What appears to be happening seems no different to people donating money to a church for distribution to the poor or improvements to their church but the church then assumes the money and the property for itself and its own business and other benefits.

I believe, in all fairness that the NP&I Department or the Land and Environment Court, under these circumstances would deem that this property should be sold by the Benevolent Society to Waverley Council at a fair land value (ensuring the proceeds of the sale are directly to the benefit of those in need, not re-invested) based on its current use as a retirement home and child care facility. That is not based on a value as would be determined as a development site. In fact, as this property was a donation to the community, it should be taken over by the council for the intended use as determined by the benefactor and not sold to council in this money grabbing exercise by a "charity!" Two more levels could easily be added, with elevator access and without affecting the environment or the security of the elderly. This would double the occupancy of the aged and come a little closer to the under provided demand of the Waverley area.

Retaining assets for our kids must always be our primary concern. Roads and rail lines are national assets irrespective of which States, towns and suburbs they run through. The improvements and maintenance are also national issues by a National Road and Rail Portfolio Ministry and

◆ National roads need to be administered nationally to reduce duplication in administration costs and by doing this, alone, it will increase available funds for upgrading and maintenance.

◆ No government should have the ability to sell off or go into any joint venture partnership deal involving our roads, rail or other assets. This is a conflict of interest by the government and is not in the interest of the people. These assets belong to our "common-wealth".

The clearest example of this conflict of interest was between NSW State Government and the operators of the Cross City Tunnel, this is just not in the interest of the public at large particularly in perpetuity. There is sufficient current and projected income from registrations, infringements and transport fares to meet the cost of upgrading and maintaining of our road and rail system, providing all of this revenue is not sidetracked for other purposes including an over employed bureaucracy, extreme bureaucratic encumbrances and thus mismanagement.

New road, rail, dams, rural and urban development's would be mapped out in conjunction with the respective Portfolio Ministries in determining requirements for existing and new facilities, in accordance with the future demand in each specific area, with urgent consideration for the more than 680,000 homeless people to cater to at this stage. Local council would confer with the National Planning and Infrastructure Department to ensure the requirements of their local constituents are met.

◆ Road tolls should be operated as a *"user pays system"* but **all** revenue belongs to Australians with every cent derived from tolls, fines, parking meters, fares, vehicle registrations and driving licenses should be re-invested into the transport system. All revenue going back into the cost of improvements and repairs to the national roads and rail network, not into State treasury coffers to meet other bureaucratic costs and mismanagement.

◆ Payments of tolls could be automatically charged to a vehicle's registration and paid monthly in arrears with a twelfth of the vehicle's annual registration. That is, no payment equals no rego! This does not require any third party to collect or account for our funds or impose penalties with "interest". A fine is a penalty, not a loan requiring any interest, this is extortion.

◆ A transparent annual National Roads Revenue Report in plain English should be published advising of all income and expenditure, together with projected income and expenditure for the preceding year. This would form part of a 5 and 10 year plan with annual monitoring of projections scrutinised by the independent members of the National House of Representatives and the public with recommendations taken into consideration before acceptance.

There are many other benefits of this national approach, including the reduction in crime, which in itself would save on police and all other resources:

◆ It is proposed that all vehicles would be fitted with a unique, non removable detection device, for charging tolls, tracking and immobilising stolen vehicles, nationally. This would certainly greatly reduce, if not extinguish car theft and the massive costs to the public, insurance companies and owners.

◆ Standardising road rules and road systems would save lives by reducing confusion. The NSW government has introduced a T-way lane at Blacktown and with no warning you can find yourself in the wrong lane and "entrapped by the very lengthy median strip" and then expected to wear three demerit points and a A$220 fine, if you have never encountered one of these before. This T-way system has been a tremendous waste of revenue with few buses using these exclusive lanes, while traffic builds up on congested lanes. This is yet another example of inept decisions by those unskilled to make them, their only goal being revenue raising and appearing to be doing the right thing.

Consistency through national road rules and systems standardisation is pure common sense and would provide a cost effective and compassionate method of saving lives. Commercially, it will also reduce hospital, medical and other costs.

"If we fail to plan, we're planning to fail"

Water, The Environment & Natural Resources

After people our second greatest resource is water
but without water there is no life, no people . . .

IN THE 1960S the world population was 3 billion and in 1999 it was 6 billion. It is projected that in 2050 there will be 9 billion inhabitants living on this planet. Each year, there are 1.4 million children around the world dying as a result of drinking polluted water. In China half of their 21,000 chemical plants are located near two of the country's largest rivers, posing a major threat of pollution.

With looming water and fuel shortages and concerns for greenhouse gases and climate change, the world is waking up to the inability of many countries to feed themselves and survive. While global warming and the hype over carbon emissions are hot topics internationally, there is very little consideration given to the fact that global changes maybe beyond our control. That is, had we lived at the end of the "Ice Age" we would have had just as great a concern then, as we do today for global warming. What were once lush rainforests are now deserts, with the remnants of the vegetation, transformed into "fossil fuel" beneath the arid desert sands. Where once vast inland oceans existed, deserts now exist. Our global landscape continues to change, and mankind must make concessions or changes in where and how we live, and how we conduct life in accommodating our world, and not to the contrary. No technology or Emission tax will cool the Earth, only nature and our ability to conform to nature. Scientists warn of massive deaths from famine, unless there is equitable rationing of the world's remaining reserves of fossil fuels, and the capacity to feed the world may be reduced to 2 billion, so on our current course, which 7 billion will be sacrificed or be the victims of unskilled bureaucratic bungling?

The option for governments to consider the introduction of a one-child family policy has proven to be to those nations detriment (see adversities in China and Spain with static and negative population growths). Water purification is very problematic in developing countries where more than 80% of sewage flows into rivers and underwater reservoirs without first undergoing any treatment, irrespective of whether the water is reused. In some developed countries varying levels of wastewater treatment is relied on. In Turkey, 3.6% of sewage water is recycled compared to 90% in Germany. Such a growth in population would require a billion hectares of natural ecosystems to be cleared to grow food, thus depriving the world further of the services these systems provide.

Deforestation, "the lungs of the world", the only natural combatant to global climate change which thrives of CO2 (carbon) to date has left these reduced systems struggling to absorb the abundance of growing carbon dioxide in our atmosphere and thus reducing the oxygen output we need for healthier lives. Further clearances would hasten the extinction rate of other species, and cause human beings trying to survive to regress in every facet of our lives. Hollywood has done a great job in portraying this scenario and I don't want to go into the ramifications of this sort of catastrophe, but we can appreciate why government is spending A$35 million of our money on building a bunker under Parliament House, in protecting themselves and maybe it will be from us! Unfortunately if we do not get pro-active with addressing every issue in this book, "Food will never be so cheap again".

Ambrose Evans-Pritchard wrote on 25 Oct 2009: *"The world's grain stocks have dropped from 4 to 2.6 months cover since 2000, despite two bumper harvests in North America. China's inventories are at a 30-year low. Asian rice stocks are near danger level. Wheat has crashed 70pc from early 2008. Corn has halved. The "Ags" have mostly drifted sideways over the last six months.*

The US is the agricultural superpower. Foes will discover why that matters. The world population is adding "another Britain" every year. This will continue until mid-century. By then we will have an extra 2.4 billion mouths to feed. China and Southeast Asia are switching to animal-protein diets as they grow wealthy and as the Koreans did before them. It takes roughly 3-5kgs of animal feed from grains to produce 1kg of meat.

A report by Standard Chartered, the End of Cheap Food, said North Africa and the Middle East have already hit the buffers. The region imports 71pc of its rice and 58pc of its corn. It lacks water to boost output. The population is growing fast. It will have to import, and cross fingers. The UN says global farm yields must rise 77% which means redoubling Norman Borlaug's "green revolution". It will not be easy. China's trend growth in crops yields has slipped from 3.1pc a year in the early 1960s to 0.9pc over the last decade

We've all heard the stark anecdotes: precious topsoil weakened by over-farming, dust clouds darkening the Asian (and Australian) skies, parched land becoming desert and rivers running dry," said Mr. Grice.

Since 2000, China has lost nearly 1,400 square miles each year to desert. Urban sprawl is paving over fertile land in the East. Water supply from Himalayan glaciers is ebbing. The Yellow River has been reduced to "an agonizing trickle". It no longer reaches the sea for 200 days a year. Farmers are draining the aquifers. Environmentalist Ma Jun says in China's Water Crisis that they are drilling as deep as 1,000 meters into non-replenishable reserves. The grain region of the Hai River Basin relies on groundwater for 70% of irrigation. China's water troubles are not unique, North India lives off Himalayan snows as well. Nor can we take fertilizer supply for granted any longer since "peak phosphates" threatens.

One can be Malthusian about this. Grizzled commodity guru Jim Rogers certainly is. "The world is going to have a period when we cannot get food at any price, in some parts." He advises youth to opt for a farm degree rather than an MBA, if they want to make serious money. Mr. Grice remains an optimist, believing that human ingenuity will rescue us. You can trade the "Ag" rally by investing in exchange traded funds (ETFs), but this amounts to speculation on food. There are ancient taboos against this practice or you can invest in the bio-tech, fertilizer, and land services companies that will both make money and help to solve the problem.

Strictly speaking, the world has enough land to feed everybody. The Soviet Union farmed 240m hectares in Khrushchev's era. The same territory now farms 207m hectares. Troika says crop yields could be doubled in Russia, and tripled in the Ukraine using modern know-how. Africa's farms could come alive with land registers, allowing villagers to use property as collateral for credit.

None of this can be done with a flick of the fingers. What seems certain is that the terms of trade between country and city will revert to the norms of the Middle Ages. Landowners will be barons again".

Of course, Government Ministers have the resources of expert consultants and engage them in providing experts reports but they are also able to dismiss expert advice, if it does not conform to other party priorities! They are not specific portfolio or resources experts, amongst experts, working to provide us with dedicated, educated and focused attention and solutions to our real issues and objectives. This focused objectivity and independent determination is 100 times better than relying on politicians with their diverse political objectives or various States or local ministers agendas. They all simultaneously wear the uneducated hats of many Ministries, and stand in our way, not just of expediting positive results but many unknowingly or uncaringly, are uncompromisingly adverse to the sustenance of society.

So where are we currently with State or even national water planning? The States and Federal Government after 100 years had *"agreed to agree"* on a plan of water sharing but there is no plan agreed to as yet! Under the current legislative and constitutional diversified powers, it could take another 100 years for non skilled politicians to come up with a plan that would work, let-alone implement it. By then it will be too late for our children's children, but unfortunately, this agreement just to agree has now fallen by the wayside once again.

The Australian on 6 March 2009 reports, *"Kevin Rudd's A$13 billion deal to rescue the Murray-Darling river system imploded as South Australia threatened to go to the High Court to force States upstream to release water and pay damages."* And *"Martin Hinton QC, the (SA) State's Solicitor-General will lead a legal team consisting of top constitutional law experts and private practitioners to further develop South Australia's case. Money spent on lawyers in the High Court would be better spent on projects that create new water for the Murray".* Mr Brumby said, *"The SA Government knows full well that removing all the water trading barriers immediately would not provide enough water".* So now the taxpayer will pay for litigation to test the constitutional rights of the States by top charging lawyers. And we don't get a single drop of water for our trouble.

Plans to revive our biggest river system have failed again, due to extended infighting of State governments over the Murray-Darling Basin. NSW has banned a buyout on a 240 billion litre water sale and Victoria won't go along with the Federal Government's A$3.1 billion water buy up for the environment. NSW is now considering joining South Australia in its High Court action, freezing the whole deal. **Farmers around Deniliquin, desperate for water are even more desperate for the money to feed their families, they are ready to sell A$70 million in water rights to the government, then take this money and whatever they get for their land as well as the A$170,000 from the governments Centrelink "Exit Strategy Plan" and run! They will leave the land to those who will benefit – the "Landowner Barons" and miners who will grab these opportunities.**

Of water, Professor Mick Young said, *"If we don't fix it quickly, we are going to be the laughing stock of the world and have a river which we couldn't manage. It's bad for the environment, bad for the farmers who need the cash" and it's bad for the whole country"*. While Senator Nick Xenophon said, *"the States had shown they couldn't be trusted to run the basin"* and he called on the Federal Government to take over.

The Opposition Water spokesman Greg Hunt said, *"the Federal government's plan to save the basin was a shambles"* while Federal Water Minister Penny Wong gives her *skilled* opinion saying she's *"not happy with what occurred"* and that *"the Federal government did not want to buy into a long legal dispute with the States"*. Once farmers are cashed up, do you think they will hang around till the money runs out or sell up, cut their losses and move to the city? And then who will be left to feed us? Maybe the oligopoly supermarkets will pick up the farms cheap, or just increase imported foods and government can dig more mines? With cheaper imports and screwing the farmer on prices, currently we are paying for groceries more than 40% over the cost of similar items in New York or Paris or London. Eventually, the price of international produce will increase due to limited water and if our duopolies or other commodities traders become the growers, there will be no option but to pay whatever they want to charge for food.

Water is the single most prominent example of damage to the country from negligence and contempt by all State and Federal governments, who cannot fix these problems. Rather than challenge and changing it by putting a referendum before the Australian people, it is left a hindrance to progress, for diverse ulterior motifs. Designers of the constitution in 1901 did not foresee mans ultra egotistical objectives outweighing the interests of the governed. A select few in each generation, who are constitutionally provided with the ability to continue jeopardizing the very life blood of this country" the "primary issue preventing and constraining Advancing Australia.

In this context, and to reiterate, what chances do we have of the current political (Westminster) system of government which is now dictated to us by the UN under the numerous adverse treaties our politicians have unconstitutionally signed us up to, in being able to address any of our most imperative national issues of health, peace, education, security and sustainability, while the most basic lack of water starves the entire country from survival.

The fault no longer belongs to those who framed our Constitution. It is our fault. It is our fault, if we don't have the courage to reframe the Constitution and our government's structure so our current circumstances are dealt with. Our forefathers knew a land of "drought and flooding rains" but more and more it seems the flooding rains are limited to North-East and Northern Australia while everywhere else gets drought. They knew droughts, certainly, but not where a record decade-long drought could go back to back with the prospect of another decade of draught. If this were deemed man-made, it would only be for the creating of an imbalance for the lack of forests and opting for plastics over forestry industries.

Our future is much too much important to be left alone in the company of politicians and academics with a single world order agenda. To reiterate: While the 108 year old Constitution gives States the power to run the Murray-Darling, the Federal government takes power when it suites it and colludes with the States to steal water rights, putting a cap on usage to send farmers to the wall.

The lucky country is bloody dry out back, most of the time and getting drier closer to home! Massive dust storms are the result of topsoil erosion, the result of draught with irrigation and vegetation the only combatant. The dams were way down in 2008 and still are – and there is no guarantee that they will ever be full again or back to a comfortable level, even after much rainfall in April 2009, Warragamba Dam still sits at 60% odd capacity. By mid 2009, Canberra, our planned city, had missed much of its autumn rain and faces summer with close to 40% of its water capacity. That in itself is also a classic example of bad planning and failing to build for the future. The ACT is now planning to massively increase the dam height for its main water storage, but has already missed the many years of better rain that might have filled it. Another example of short term planning without consideration for long term savings and benefits, by those with short term tenures of office but with long term pension schemes.

There's speculation of environmentally unfriendly desalination plants; talk, talk and more talk of water harvesting for urban areas and recycling of sewage, all good initiatives subject to the specific requirement for the water and the impact on the environment and subject to taking these national initiatives to fruition. Water is our greatest natural resource – let's face it – we can't live without it! If we farmed water and channelled "*grey water*" sewerage for irrigation, as well as harvesting it from the lush northern river system to the outback, we could be totally sufficient in feeding ourselves for generations to come. Local and export trade from the increased fresh and canned produce to trade, particularly with third world countries, would make Australia one of the most profitable counties with, the best lifestyle for every Australian.

We would employ more Aussies, welcome more migrants into primary and new processed agricultural industries and in developing manufacturing in rural areas where there is just no hope today. The Fitzroy River near Rockhampton sees 95% of its water wasted, Grafton has 5 dams and no algae or regular flow, yet billions of dollars are spent year after year on drought relief which could be eliminated if water were channelled to where it is needed.

Water is a national issue and we are all affected if one State or another suffers from drought, floods, fires, or from natural and man-made inflictions. Farmers are not only disheartened, but continually year by year many farmers stay on trying to save their properties and require government subsidies to stay on the land. Taxpayer funded subsidies that ultimately could easily be eliminated by increasing the valuations of properties to a level that disqualifies welfare recipients, rather than directing relief into maintenance and improvements to inland irrigation and water supplies. This would benefit us all in a relatively short 10 year term, for tens of generations to follow us.

All of the issues pertinent to one State affects us all nationally and must be gathered under one umbrella to maximise the benefits of income, expenditure and benefits. The development and management of water resources is the most crucial aspect to our lives, now, and it is our future. With no State governments to block or resist the way of a national focus, an appointed expert National Water Ministry is mandatory in achieving maximum national benefits. With the greatest of respect, neither, Malcolm Turnbull, Penny Wong or any other politician has the qualifications to wear the hat of Minister of Water & Natural Resources. Mr Turnbull is a successful barrister and a merchant banker, and while he gave a shot at being a Federal Opposition Leader of Parliament, he knows as much about water management as any unqualified individual Australian, when it comes to this issue or the communications industry. Efficient and rational decisions are encumbered as no politician has the credentials required to make the best non political decisions. Even if they could, these decisions are hijacked or intercepted by their party's agenda and political philosophies.

◆ We need a skilled National Water & Natural Resources Ministry (like all Ministries) to work with the National Planning and Infrastructure Department, board members who are able to produce a plan and sound costing within, say, six months.

Why six months and not 100 years? Because, you can be very sure that most of the **experts in every respective field, from transport, to health, to education, to water etc. have provided submissions, have lobbied governments and have participated in the research in those costly reports, which just sit on "those shelves!" These experts are passionate for their field of expertise, as**

they live and breathe the answers to our problems. They're out there, just dying to roll up their sleeves and get stuck into it! Only they can implement urgent short, medium and long term plans to be tabled by their Resources Ministry to a new non-party aligned National House of Representatives, those with no other agenda but our best interests! With genuinely dedicated and audited costs signed off, work could commence quickly, without the hindrance of the would be do-gooders, who do nothing but stop progress for what is best for the country, and who pose a threat to our mere survival and the survival of many of our native species.

The Resources Ministries, being made up of people with the most superior education and knowledge in their specialised fields would not be burdened with inflated egos, but would grab international success stories in dealing in water solutions, particularly from Israel. Israel (while under great adversity from its neighbours for the past 60 years), transformed the desert into lush agricultural enterprises and does not suffer from a lack of water. I am fortunate to know such an expert, who would have the highest credentials in the country, Dr Aharon B.Sc (Geology), M.App.Sc. (Hydrogeology & Engineering Geology), Ph.D. (Chemistry). Dr Aharon is a member of the Australian Institute of Mining and Metallurgy, a member of the Geological Society of Australia and has been a professional geologist and hydro geologist for more than 25 years. He has consulted too many mining projects nationally, mostly in hydrogeology, locating groundwater in all types of geological environments. He has also had many years in academia following a research path in chemical oceanography and hydro-metallurgy and tutoring in geology and chemistry. He recently published several papers describing and analysing the groundwater resources of an area of central NSW (sleeved rolled up and dying to get into it!).

Dr Aharon participated in a conference which Mr Turnbull convened when water was the hottest topic on the political agenda. He submitted a letter to Malcolm Turnbull but the response from Mr Turnbull was standard letter number one *"thanks but no thanks"* – no different to fobbing off the concerns of any single constituent who has been wronged by a government department. I have asked Dr Aharon Aharon PhD to contribute to this book:

"Water is one of the most important resources needed to support a growing nation. Primary resources are desperate for water, secondary resources demand water and the population centres are all surviving with water restrictions. When is the government going to develop better water management? Practically, that is, not just lip service. At the moment water issues are a political football with no affirmative action.

With the imposition of water restrictions, rural and urban, what are Australian governments going to do to supply sufficient water to a growing nation, to farmers, industries and the towns and cities?

Dams in NSW are at their lowest levels, ever. There are no plans in NSW to build another dam in another catchment to harness water. One of the best areas, the Colo River, has sufficient water to supply Sydney. It is time to start NOW as it will take 20 years from inception to operation. There will be years of planning and greenies and environmentalists *to hurdle. The environmentalists will find a rare bird, a rare ecology or some other creature "near extinction" to support their fight against supplying Sydney with enough water for 2025. Meanwhile, Sydney will have increased water restrictions such that people may be forced to have showers using bottled water at $5 per litre!*

Other ways of dealing with this finite resource is to recycle water. Discussions about desalination are financially far too high when considering other alternatives. Desalination should only be used as a last resort.

Recycling sewage water has an ugly stigma about it. So much so, that as successful as the treatment process is, it should only be "grey water" for industrial purposes, agriculture parks and gardens.

Storm water comes off roofs, pavements and roads. Some storm events turn the roads into rivers, yet we let it flow straight to the ocean. Contaminants in storm water are carried into the storm water drains in the first few minutes. The "first flow" of storm water can be either treated or passed to the ocean. After the roofs and roads have been washed clean, the water would need minimal treatment before pumping it into reservoir storage.

Looking at Google Earth, an approximate visual assessment of the roof and pavement areas of residential areas varies between 60% in the densely populated areas to 10% in garden suburbs. Storm water running off roofs and pavements is wasted water. It could be collected, treated then piped back to water reservoirs around Sydney. Currently, all storm water goes straight to the ocean. Storm water is relatively clean and would need minimum treatment before piping it to storage reservoirs ready for supplying consumers. This would be a far more cost effective way of collecting water.

Cities along the eastern seaboard are high rainfall areas. It would be a shame not to capture this valuable resource. Sydney itself is a huge catchment area. A rough calculation of catchment area in Sydney ~ about 20% is roof, pavement and road surfaces. Let us harness this resource without more procrastination and excuses.

◆ Recycled water is essential. Spend a hundred billion dollars or more over the next 1 – 15 years to harvest coastal storm water and channel it out west, or east if you live in Perth.

◆ Irrigate the land and particularly boost the rivers to revive the environment and develop the most competitive primary Australian produce for local and export industry in the world.

◆ Harvesting and purifying storm-water and sewerage into city tanks for urban areas is the least costly, producing the best result for the most environmentally friendly means of collecting water.

◆ Desalination and irrigation of the inland would enable greater produce for local and export markets; and increase the sustainable living area to accommodate a growing population. With an increase in irrigated area, the best agricultural initiative is for the production of Ethanol. Our tropical regions are ideal for this agricultural purpose.

This alcohol fuel would ensure we are no longer dependent on fossil fuels, creating excellent opportunities to sustain satellite towns and to break the poverty cycle, provide migrants to these newly opened areas with opportunities while reducing pollutants in the urban areas and avoiding continued dependence on costly imported fuel. It is a proven success in Brazil and is in greater demand in developed countries as the alternative fuel. Flexi fuel motor vehicles are produced in Australia and are bought and run on Ethanol in Brazil, so why are we not using it in our own flexi-cars (those able to use both fuels and a mixture of) here and now if not for the taxes on imported fossil fuels. As mentioned earlier the Hy-wire salt solution vehicle that could power our homes is the most superior option. In five years we could be less than 50% reliant on fossil fuels and have created an excellent export market for this green initiative.

Recently both sides of Federal parliament scoffed at the Green's suggestion of discontinuing coal exploration and export. The thrust was based on the loss of thousands of jobs in the mining industry, but there was no thought for loss of life due to the catastrophes the mining industry presents, and the thousands of litres of water required for each ton of coal extracted and cleaned. For example, the millions of tons of coal extracted from the earth and the connection to the Newcastle earthquake of 1998. Not all mining firms like the expense of refilling a void with overburden and there have been many natural catastrophes around the world with the voids underground created from the extraction of fuels. The sooner we eliminate fossil fuels in all of their forms, the safer the world will be. The sooner we harness wind, solar, hy-wire, Ethanol and Geothermal power, the more jobs will be diverted from the mining industry into cleaner renewable fuels and the exportation of our regenerated agricultural industry both as primary produce and processed produce. To achieve this, we need commitment by specialised persons with the financial resources to back them and to see that they are not hindered in achieving their objectives by those who would destroy our economy under the UN Agenda 21 and other treaties.

As drought spreads, farmers leave and if it rains, without new dams, the water dissipates to no Australians advantage. Imports have risen and local production has declined and continues to decline. According to the Australian Quarantine Inspection Service, between 1 January 2008 and 31 May 2009 more than 4200 tonnes of prawns were imported from China into Australia. This was in addition to 153 tonnes of frozen broccoli and cauliflower, 65 tonnes of fresh apples, 95 tonnes of fresh pears, 325 tonnes of garlic, 72 tonnes of peas and 4292 tonnes of peanuts and peanut butter. Last year, imports of Chinese vegetables rose by 35% from 2007, making it the second-biggest importer, behind New Zealand and these imports have increased during 2009

Just days (7 Dec 2009) after his ousting from the leadership of the Liberal Party, Malcolm Turnbull stated, *"First, let's get this straight. You cannot cut emissions without a cost. To replace dirty coal fired power stations with cleaner gas fired ones, or renewable energy like wind let alone nuclear power or even coal fired power with carbon capture and storage, it is all going to cost money"* and *"To get farmers to change the way they manage their land, or plant trees and vegetation, it all costs money. Somebody has to pay."* Australians are truly overpaying for good government, overpaying to greedy duopolies but with that remedied it would fix all of these problems. That is, with focused expert administration of our resources and departments, abandoning international treaties, investing into our agricultural and secondary industries we would have more, and it would cost less.

All State and Federal governments have dissimilarly failed the Australian people. Liberal achieved a surplus of A$15 billion and rather than irrigate and increase productivity, governments would rather reap the cheap land grab for mining and the interests of monopolies but more so for other major world governments. Now, the Federal Labor government is extending a carrot to farmers as an, "Exceptional Circumstances Exit package of A$150,000 (taxable)" to be paid to those who leave their farm, plus A$20,000 for relocating and retraining into no doubt, additional white collar jobs or welfare recipients, in the land of Pacifica and earning an honorary membership in the First World Government. Desperate farmers have no choice but to take the money and run, a well contrived scheme over many years from Liberal to Labor. Is the destabilising of the Australian agricultural industry sheer incompetence or corruption, or is it in conforming to some other agenda?

Carbon is the single greatest fertilizer the world has, and its absorption is reliant on vegetation, no tax can achieve this. Australia's 1% of the world carbon is not nearly enough to fertilise the outback with the proposed water initiatives. Reforestation and increased agricultural activities with improved quality of soil, coupled with alternative fuels for industry is what is urgently needed. Forests are our world's lungs and are our best natural resource for construction and other purposes. There are so many opportunities in the forestry industry just waiting for the taking that will replace our dependence on fossil by-products!

With water diverted to those currently arid but arable lands of ours, no more will we need to rely on importing inferior fruit. Nationally we will be able to produce seasonal fruit all year round and safely transport it and the newly manufactured goods on new roads and significantly improved rail systems from revitalised rural and industrial areas. These would be built relying on alternative power sources and then we will be totally self-sufficient as a nation, providing unionists can see how their future can grow as the nation changes.

Feed and fuel the Nation efficiently & economically
and we secure our future and the environment.

Kevin Mitchell, Coordinator One Nation Farmer Ethanol Awareness Campaign 2010 provides the following for every Australian to seriously consider and support: *Unfortunately over zealous profit driven egos of both political and corporate circle have proven that they cannot and must not be allowed to control Ethanol. If oil companies take control of our emerging Australian Bio-fuels Industry they will continue to adversely affect the unregulated price of fuel as they do with fossil fuels. This affects the price of our food and all of our daily needs, driving our currently depleted economy into complete meltdown, yielding chaos and subservience to anyone with a handout. Remember, increased prices are falsely relied on by government to depict an overly healthy economy to justify a (fake) need to increase mortgage interest rates."*

Farmers have been pushed to the wall, many on welfare due to governments failure to remedy our water problems; the introduction and support of FREE Trade and low or no tariffs; allowing an inequality of bargaining power with no protection against exploitation; an over indulgence in burocractical hurdles and land-use rights taken away from them without as much as their Constitutionally due compensation. Farmers must be given this great opportunity to be the AUSTRALIAN ETHANOL INDUSTY. Not just grow the crops for a few pennies but to produce Ethanol and this is urgent – any delay will ensure companies such as Ethtec, Bio-Energy, BP Exxon Mobil, Caltex and chemical companies like Monsanto will close them out, permanently, with us all being subservient to corporate giants who support government parties with millions of dollars in political donations.

This initiative will not be a first for Australia. It is up and running and healthily in America. It is backed up first by the backbone and grass roots of this industry the non-profit Org. "ACE" (The American Coalition for Ethanol) which supports them in every way! Govt support comes from the US Department of Energy & US Department of Agriculture with reports that there are well over 2,000 and climbing, US Farmers Cooperatives. The majority of farmers, being members of "ACE" all having the ability to fuel and feed their nation and to reduce the effects of fossil fuels on our environment. Imagine if Australians had the opportunity to invest their superannuation into this industry through the proposed Bank of Australia, a true peoples bank owned and operated by them, the dividends are insurmountable, with government concerns for an aging population, extinguished. "CELLULOSES BIOFUELS" is now a reality. CELLULOSES can and will replace toxic oils. It is no longer about "Fuel versus Food". No more excuses. Our farmers also have a new alternative crop? One that reproduces itself up to ten times its weight, daily! ALGAE TO BIODIESEL that farmers can produce to power the nations heavy transport industry.

Because of Australia's vast rural and vegetated landscape, it has the chance to become the farmer led CELLULOSES BIOFUEL CAPITOL of the world. We are currently on the ground floor and with our desperate national need we must get up and get to work while the opportunity presents itself and before it is again taken from us. Our farmers can and must play the vital pivotal role in this for us all, and not foreign oil magnates.

Robert Zubrin a celebrated Author, Aerospace Engineer & President of Pioneer Astronautics research and development) wrote in his riveting book "THE ENERGY VICTORY Breaking the OPEC CHAINS" of how to do this by using the one and most prolific material mass on the planet! **Organic WASTE**! Beginning with our farming waste which the farmer leaves behind after harvesting to rot on the ground and other waste that we continue to send to land fill? All our green waste is delivered to rubbish tips all over the world, with all of the inherent environmental problems and associated costs of this! Waste that mostly and simply falls to the ground left to decay! Yet one that in reality is a most valuable resource that we have simply failed to recognize or utilize! One which has been proven has the way and wherefore to enable us to the break away from the many corrupt influences of fossil fuel that has seen our world economies in decline and millions poisoned! 2000 Australians die every year from fossil fuel exhaust inhalation, while our organic and human waste dwarfs against the mass amount of fossil fuel taken from the ground! One measured in billions of metric tons and not just gallons or liters of toxicity!

Fossil fuel is a costly privilege that is ever rising in dollars not cents or sense! One that sees us enslaved to it and willing to patronize it even to our total economic peril! If the price of fossil fuel were dictated to be A$10 a liter tomorrow, we will whine and groan but we will have to find it and we will. We may have to nick it from our kid's savings or their dinner plate – we will do anything to find it, from anywhere. If we do not move in this positive Ethanol direction, fossil fuels will be one that we will seemingly be willing to blindly accept, offering up as a sacrifice, the lives of millions of us without so much as a whimper, while allowing the destruction of our entire way of life! Now the chance to end this hazardous threat forever is here! Don't take my word for it, read about it yourself and let the significance of this major issue sink in!

I recall what Robert Zubrin had to say back in 2007 and the article he wrote over three years ago and what he foresaw has now become reality: *"The time has come for change. To liberate ourselves from the threat of foreign economic domination, to destroy the economic power of the terrorist's financiers and to give ourselves the free hand necessary to deal forcefully with them, we must devalue their resources and increase the value of our own. We can do this by taking the world off the petroleum standard and putting it on an alcohol standard. Only fractions of the plants that farmers grow are actually sold as commercial crops. Large quantities of vegetative material, such as the stems, roots, and leaves of corn plants, for example, are left to waste. This is also true of tree leaves that are discarded in the fall, and vast quantities of grasses and weeds that grow, yellow, and fade every year without being eaten or otherwise used by man or animal. In 2005 the US Environmental Protection Agency calculated that smoke, soot, and other particulate pollution from cars currently causes approximately 40,000 American deaths per year from lung cancer and other ailments! Alcohol fuels do not produce smoke, soot, or particulates when burned in internal combustion engines and neither methanol nor ethanol causes cancer or mutations".*

In these three years, technology has seen Zubrin's words transform into practice with the recent revolutionary announcement and release by US private owned car manufacturer "VERDE" of their amazing new invention in the 400 HP V8 HP2g EPA approved "Revenge Verde" Super car with its amazing engine that uses only Eth. 85% to power its engine, how? By producing at or near the point of combustion, an electro – magnetic pulse that produces a type of hydrogen power blast which ignites the HP elements that then propel this amazing car along under normal driving at an unbelievable 110 MPG in fuel economy! It is now accepted that through celluloses all our human waste can be turned into a fuel (makes sense that Canberra has a major plant to handle the mass of output) that will allow us to take back control of our economies. This is how far technology has come, yet it's just the beginning and Bio-fuels need our Australian farmers as much as our farmers need Bio-fuels. Robert Zubrin says: *"The prize for embracing this will soon improve radically our economies and the many health problems of the world!"* Read the full text by Robert Zubrin **"The Energy Victory"** Australians farmers have the technology available to them now but they need to step up to the plate and follow their US cousins to achieve these new processes, as detailed and documents in the US Department of Agriculture and Energy files plus the articles from the US Farmers coops themselves, we invite you now to go to the ACE interactive website and to personally accept their invitation to interact and take part in its amazing factual and current way of dispensing the truth, where it will dispel any misconceptions you may have of its benefits to mankind! Environmentally, medically, financially and socially: www.ethanolfactor.org

The benefits of farmers owning this industry include, not just an environmentally friendly and health friendly fuel; national reduced fuel costs; minimum cost and effects of transporting fuel and the profits going to our farmers and investors, but that the bi-products can be used as fertilizer to replenish the trace elements desperately missing from our farms and it will also feed livestock in a land thirsty for every drop of water, not to mention, that there will be no loss in taxes which belong to every Australian citizen. Unfortunately, there is no way our current political party system of governments would ever transgress from their ulterior agendas or aspire to supporting our farmers with such an innovation. Rather, get the farmers off the land "cheap" so it can be dug up for mining or sold off to the oil companies for their financial and other benefits which is not in anyway to the benefit of 22 come 35 million Australians. I draw you to the proposed restructure of government as contained in this book, as it is only this non-party system which is prescribed to in our 1901 Constitution which can provide and assist not just our farmers, but every Australian in thinking and acting locally, firstly!

Currently there are more than 75% or approx 16.5 million of our national population living in major cities, leaving less than 25% on the land to feed us all and to be able to provide sufficient produce for export on a very competitive market. This is not sustainable in the long term, particularly with so many farmers having to rely on social welfare to support themselves and so many moving away. With imported cheap fresh produce grown under inferior health standards (adversely effecting our health) we have

to consider that, unless more of our country is worked efficiently, adverse weather, coupled with less available water at increased prices we will see a future where our shrinking crops are totally priced off the shelf and we could be left with little if any agricultural industry and then paying more to those we become reliant on for food.

If this happens, our standard of living will decrease as we will not be able to afford the luxury of an apple. We could become a very poor country dependent on what will be very expensive imports – as the cost of goods from overseas will also rise as international water resources dry up. The costs of produce will be determined by the growing world population's demand versus the limited and shrinking supply. That is, if less is produced it will cost more to buy from anywhere it can be grown.

Oligopoly supermarket chains dictate to the farmers how much they will be paid for their produce and for fear of not making a sale our farmers are subservient to their retail masters. Orange growers receive as little as .8c a kilo for oranges while the supermarkets sell them for more than A$3.50 a kilo. What a margin! But one bad season can see the farmer go under, his livelihood destroyed, often his family broken into pieces and his property up for grabs at bottom dollar. Many farmers cannot get pickers and currently we are importing Pacific Islanders to harvest seasonal crops as we cannot entice local unskilled pickers, or the unemployed to productive work.

This makes way for someone to capitalise on this disaster and more conglomerates buy up this land for, say, mining. With this small return to farmers is it any wonder they do not have the financial resources to replace trace minerals into the soil, those which would ensure the nutritional value of the produce is high and the farmer fails to rest the land every few years to enable it to recoup from exploitation. The replacement of trace minerals into the soil is what causes us to have to rely on vitamin pills. Better we pay a few cents more per kilo on fresh produce and save on vitamins.

◆ Growers markets bring fresh produce from the farm to the end buyer and should be supported at every opportunity and the ACCC must ensure neither the farmer nor the consumer are exploited.

Prior to the 1960s fish and chips were considered a part of our healthy nutritional diet and one of the only takeaway foods available at that time. Deep sea fish was deep fried in peanut oil and we never heard of a need to take Omega-3 supplements, as brain function was just fine. Fish was cheap and everyone loved it, but today fish is dearer than meat. Chicken was considered a luxury in the 1950s as they grew free range, eating natural grain to their full term, but today with supplementing growth hormones to animals to expedite sales we have compromised the health of people once again for profit, so fish was the go at least twice a week and it remains the stable diet of those in many nations.

Our oceans are becoming depleted of fish and the ecology of the ocean is not weathering well as the polar caps melt and ocean currents alter. As our world population grows, so does the demand to fish our oceans, hence Indonesian and 'flag of convenience' fishermen illegally fishing here out of their necessity to survive but the

◆ The implementation of more fish farms to repopulate the oceans would cater to the current and growing demand. It would reinstate to a healthy level, the various ocean fish life. Everyone has a right to eat, repopulating the ocean will help feed our neighbours and keep our boarders secure. This is what is required to work in harmony with our environment.

And on the flip side, while illegal fishing activities of mass proportion are going on, illogical bureaucracy imposes on anyone who wants to drop a line in the water for some recreational fishing the need for a licence. Worse, this provides just another bureaucratic job in taking and administering licence fees but fishing authorities allow ruthless fishermen to dragnet the bottom of the ocean destroying turtles, the ocean bed and all in its way and more prudent to prevent than penny pinching from what has been allowed unlicensed, since man first stepped on the surface of the planet.

We farm oysters and need to turn ocean fishermen into fixed fish farmers. Fresh water trout farming is a successful inland industry and there is no reason why certain sectors of our coastline are not netted to farm many varieties of fish for the local and export markets, including to our neighbours in Indonesia. That is, in selling fish to Indonesia it would reduce our costs to our coastguard and other services while increasing our export revenue. With increased supply and reduced costs, we can achieve a more competitive price putting fish on our tri-weekly menu and it will alleviate the illegal fishing trade and allow our oceans to repopulate. Whatever we do, we need a plan that is internationally known and professionally enforced because when other countries allow their fishermen to wipe out their own fish reserves, those fishermen must look to our side of the Exclusive Economic Zone if for no reason other than feeding their families.

Over the next few years we could see our country divided into two groups, opposing each other; The Climate Change Sceptics and those wanting to do more to stop Climate Change. Greenhouse gases or rather pollutants can be reduced and this may have some effect on climate change. One thing is for sure, trading in Carbon Credits will not help either group.

Humanity has treated the world, its resources and the environment abominably, tearing down rainforests, polluting the atmosphere, dumping toxic waste, tipping rubbish into the oceans, diverting water flows and killing off species and each other.

Australians have never desisted from any sensible call to arms. When there was water shortage, we all became pro-active in being conservative. Given multi-coloured recycle wheelie-bins we separate and recycle and we are aware not to litter. If given a choice of glass over plastic for milk and other products, we take the glass. Creating compost heaps, turning off lights, changing to cost effective light globes etc. Whatever it takes, Australians conform when government gives positive initiatives but we need more and we need to be more vigilant.

The indestructible plastic bag is responsible for the destruction of so many species. It is overdue that we change our priorities and directions, including:

◆ Biting the bullet and banning the (plastic) bag nationally. Paper bags are from renewable sources and are biodegradable. Be pro-active in abandoning as many forms of plastics as possible, with alternatives.

We have so much in metals already extracted and in use in many forms and that which is the major contributor to pollution but if we

◆ Recycle everything from sewage and forest debris for fertilisers to plastics, metals, clothing etc and then the Earth can heal and we can improve our quality of life and offer a better world to our great grandchildren.

We are here to make good use of the world's resources – not to use them up or abuse the earth. In repopulating the oceans and assisting the fishing industry, fish would no longer be a luxury food and this is perhaps the greatest way of assisting to feed developing nations.

Financially, Australia makes just as much money from our agricultural resources as we do from our mining resources. Water to support our current and new agricultural industry is vital, not just to us, but to the ecology of the world and all of its inhabitants. Agriculture doesn't deplete the Earth of its resources or cause meteorological catastrophes. Agriculture is the future in developing our primary resource and then into secondary industries, we create real jobs and feed the world while mining creates pollution, environmental hazards and deserts.

There are so many options for the production of energy to replace fossil fuels. One most logical comes in the provision of Geothermal Energy and it must be owned and operated by the people, as a not for profit operation. Again, this can only be achieved by a government with the interests of Australians as their only objective. Geothermal Energy is from the Greek word *geo* meaning earth and *thermos* meaning heat. It is power extracted from heat stored in the earth. This geothermal energy originates from the original formation of the planet, from radioactive decay of minerals and from solar energy absorbed at the surface. It has been used for bathing since Paleolithic times and for space heating since ancient Roman times but is now better known for generating electricity. Worldwide, about 10,715 megawatts of geothermal power is online in 24 countries. Geothermal power is cost effective, reliable, sustainable, and environmentally friendly but has historically been limited to areas near tectonic plate boundaries. Recent technological advances have dramatically expanded the range and size of viable resources, especially for applications such as home heating, opening a potential for widespread exploitation. Geothermal wells release greenhouse gases trapped deep within the earth but these emissions are much lower per energy unit than those of fossil fuels. As a result, *"Geothermal power has the potential to help mitigate* **global warming** *if widely deployed in place of fossil fuels"*.

In 2010 the United States led the world in geothermal electricity production with 3,086 MW of installed capacity from 77 power plants. The largest group of geothermal power plants in the world is located at The Geysers, a geothermal field in California. The Philippines is the second highest producer, with 1,904 MW of capacity online with Geothermal power making up approximately 18% of the country's electricity generation. Other demonstration projects are under construction in Australia, the United Kingdom, and the United States of America. If the ground is hot but dry, as is certainly the case in the Australian outback, earth tubes or down-hole heat exchangers can collect the heat and provide clean power for new industry in planned areas. But even in areas where the ground is colder than room temperature, heat can still be extracted with a geothermal heat pump more cost-effectively and cleanly than by conventional furnaces. These devices draw on much shallower and colder resources than traditional geothermal techniques and they frequently combine a variety of functions, including air conditioning, seasonal energy storage, solar energy collection, and electric heating. District heating applications use networks of piped hot water to heat many buildings across entire communities. In Reykjavík, Iceland, spent water from the district heating system is piped below pavement and sidewalks to melt snow. Geothermal has minimal land and freshwater requirements. Geothermal plants use 3.5 square kilometres (1.4 sq mi) per gigawatt of electrical production (not capacity) versus 32 and 12 square kilometres (4.6 sq mi) for coal facilities and wind farms respectively. They use 20 litres (5.3 US gal) of freshwater per MW·h versus over 1,000 litres (260 US gal) per MW·h for nuclear, coal or oil. **Geothermal power requires no fuel (except for pumps) and is therefore immune to fuel cost fluctuations** but capital costs are significant. Direct heating applications can use much shallower wells with lower temperatures, so smaller systems with lower costs and risks are feasible. Residential geothermal heat pumps with a capacity of 10 kilowatt (kW) are routinely installed for around US$1 – 3,000 per kilowatt. District heating systems may benefit from economies of scale if demand is geographically dense, as in cities, but otherwise piping installation dominates capital costs. Geothermal power is highly scalable: from a rural village to an entire city.

A geothermal heat pump can extract enough heat from shallow ground anywhere in the world to provide home heating but industrial applications need the higher temperatures of deep resources. The thermal efficiency and profitability of electricity generation is particularly sensitive to temperature. Geothermal power is considered to be sustainable because any projected heat extraction is small compared to the Earth's heat content. The Earth's geothermal resources are more than adequate to supply humanity's energy needs for more than 4,000 years of power, harnessed from Geothermal renewable energy all without any Carbon Tax and providing an environmentally friendly, reduced cost of living.

In treating our world with care and respect, we can provide a sustainable and safe environment for all of the world's inhabitants. It all starts on the land and with skilled government, not hindered or dictated to by any alien government with an alternative agenda.

Security and Defence

AUSTRALIANS BY AND large, are probably one of the most charitable nations in the world. We give billions in aid from government, corporate and individuals to under-privileged countries and to those who have suffered tremendous loss due to acts of nature, poor economic conditions and apathetic governments. The A$1 billion assistance given by our government to the Tsunami appeal in 2004 only highlights the extreme lengths we go to in being generous to all mankind.

Equal in ranking to generosity, is national security. The introduction of a multicultural society has provided more benefits than adversities but we are experiencing problems with racial unrest, which has been suffered in many other countries but this is now fought here. Problems which stem from race hate and perceived inequality culminate in terror attacks and it's a whole new ball game for our mindset of peace and security.

There have always been and continue to be wars and now we have the "War on Terror" being fought in Afghanistan and Iraq and no doubt this will extend to Iran unless some very gutsy country takes the initiative for us all to stop an imminent nuclear war. Civil wars in Timor and Fiji are examples of the sort of "moral depravity" going on all around the world. I say moral depravity because many nations, and certainly their leaders, have chosen quick fixes to improve their lot. Australia has enjoyed the benefits of being a democracy because our forebears, and us, have worked hard to have those benefits and defend them. But some nations seem to think that democracy and its benefits can be shipped by container, or that it falls from the sky. Fiji doesn't extend equal rights to its Indian citizens. Every time a majority Indian led government has been rightfully elected there, a coup has ensued. Yet its Indian citizens are the core of Fiji's entrepreneurial spirit, if they all left then some people wouldn't be surprised to see native Fijians lying around waiting for coconuts to fall and expecting tourists to make their own breakfast and clean their own rooms.

Around the world, corrupt leaders are embezzling aid money and visiting their constituents in their armoured Mercedes' to explain why money is so short. Sadly, the generosity of many charitable westerners are paying for the butter for many nations, allowing their governments to buy guns, while the intended beneficiaries starve and our government fails to ensure these funds are provided to the intended but in conforming with adverse international treaties.

While witnessing the emergence and growing unrest in Australia, we are stretching police resources beyond the capability of suppression. In all wars prior 9/11, Australians participated in wars on foreign soil but never here. If riots, unrest and fighting were on foreign soil, our soldiers fully armed would go in, shoot and kill the enemy but the enemy here is like no other. Terrorism lives and breeds amongst us with motives based on religious radical fundamentalism, as well as mental instability caused by mind altering drugs and alcohol abuse. Crimes that provide profit from dealing in drugs, to crimes associated with joblessness and misguided beliefs.

Federal and State Governments take initiatives in establishing anti-terrorist groups to assist in the defence of our country, while other government decisions fob-off the security of our major civilian and military installations to unskilled security officers. ICAC may investigate how people were able to "buy" security licenses but an inquiry into who made these irresponsible decisions and the motivation to farm out the responsibility of government would be more prudent. Security of our country is best returned in all forms to those best equipped to do the job, our defence and police forces and not unskilled or even skilled, private enterprise or government ministers.

Unfortunately we have reached a point where our enemy is not only not obvious, but very well concealed. When United States Army Major Hasan opened fire at Fort Hood in Texas, which is one of the Americas largest military bases and he killed 13 of his own, questions must be raised as to just who is on whose side in the fight against terrorism and how do we define or divide the would-be terrorist from his victims. This was not an isolated US incident. How do we prevent it? What should the punishment be? We cannot rehabilitate those who have been brain washed. We cannot alter ingrained and continually reinforced perverse mindsets which are based on unjustified murderous causes, with words of goodness and kindness or pamper them in our prison system. We delude ourselves that everyone has the same love and caring traits that we do and while our laws are not reflective of the crimes, we stand to be annihilated at home or succumb to their causes.

Drugs and alcohol have the same impact on our society, destroying those who have been caught up in it. We all have a part to play in the effort to protect ourselves and each other to stop alcohol and drug related violence, racial violence and acts of terrorism from the damages of loss of life and the costs to our society. ICE and other drug dealers and those who wilfully or not, take innocent lives and those who destroy property in arson attacks are destroying our peaceful society, and they are no different to any common terrorist. There is only one way to fight this enemy and that is to take a strong stance with the full wrath of more appropriate sentences, this is both a serious deterrent to crime and also fair punishment, both which a peaceful society is entitled to.

Internal Police Forces – The most prominent day to day defence forces the public encounter are the police, who have the most difficult job of all. Nationally we have fewer than 2,000 Federal Police including those involved in the crime commission and we have fewer than 60,000 police for our 22 million people. Over the past 5 years, as many police have joined the force as have left, thus police numbers are almost static in spite of spiralling crime.

Unfortunately police departments are also hamstrung by the disparities between States governance and by inept ministers. Police work under the most extreme level of difficulty coupled with contentious political interference and lack of support for what is required in bringing peace, security and stability back into society. I'm not suggesting marshal law be instigated, to the contrary, but police must be supported better than they have been. More administrative staff, quicker turnarounds for court hearings and judgements more appropriate or befitting crimes. Police contend with repeat law breakers from small crimes by juveniles who under legislations slip through the net of conviction until they become adults and hardened criminals. Adequate legal measures would deter crime and ensure police would be able to function in the vein they were intended, rather than have to fight their way through our legal system and in being treated with contempt from unlawful persons.

It was reported that some 270 men and women police officers resign from the police force each month, that's over 3,000 in any year who leave their chosen careers after being provided with costly training. Leaving for reasons which include job dissatisfaction and others take sick leave suffering depression and stress with many resorting to long term pensions. Thousands of lost hours paid out in sick leave each month. Job dissatisfaction suffered by police is both costing us a fortune and allowing criminals to flourish in our society.

There have been cases where persons who criminally injure a police officer, are themselves hurt and receives more care and consideration than the injured police officer. What message does this send throughout the police force? Police also spend large numbers of hours investigating issues and making arrests, only to see offenders released on technicalities or given a slap on the wrist. The net result is that many police take the view that many misdemeanours and some crimes are "not worth police time", and again the public suffers.

There is a story (possibly an urban legend) about a bloke who rang police to report a prowler in his yard. The police asked numerous questions and were clearly disinterested in taking action especially as, to that point, only trespass had been committed. *"No police are in your area."* So the bloke starts audibly rattling through some drawers while still talking and finally says, *"Look, don't worry, I've found my shotgun and I'll fix this myself"* and with the sound of something metallic clicking together, he sets down the phone. Four minutes later there are three squad cars on the bloke's lawn and the prowler caught. The bloke takes aim at the prowler – with his camera and newly fitted lens. *"I thought there were no police available in my area?"* he comments. *"Did I say shotgun? I meant I'd found my Canon."*

Redeployed State government employees would provide more police back up staff in assisting police with reporting and administrative rolls and would enable police to carry out the job of policing, not to be bogged down in anything other than police work. At the same time, more practical and legal training is needed for police prosecutors so fewer cases fail for technical reasons.

◆ Senate and judicial national review of minimum criminal sentences is the only assurance police can have in obtaining the respect they rightfully deserve and in giving police the ability to carry out their job to full determination and satisfaction. To reiterate, this would include juveniles because if they're *"old enough to do the crime, old enough to do the time"*. Penalties and sentences would warrant respect for the law and what it can do if you break it or fail to give respect to those who implement the law for all of our safety.

◆ A life sentence must be for the term of the person's natural life, if the crime warrants and not in a summer camp with luxuries to boot, hard Labor with earned financial recompense paid to victims or society. I believe, particularly in these times and under special circumstances, we need to reconsider under a referendum, Capital Punishment?

◆ Establishing and educating society as to the minimum sentences appropriate to crimes is a greater deterrent than educating kids in how to escape responsibility.

Legislative definition as to what constitutes a terrorist, to say – "Any person(s) who plans or participates in the destruction of life or property; and any person(s) who takes away the civil liberties of another; or any person(s) who incites civil unrest; and any person(s) who is aware of these plans and actions and fails to prevent it by informing authorities"

◆ There would be no statute of limitation for prosecution to apply in regards to crimes against humanity.

◆ Penalties for lack of respect toward police to be imposed if and when appropriate. This would ensure better behaviour and taught in the national school system under the Code of Conduct.

Society is founded on respect. Light and generous sentences by the judiciary assume that the offender is a relatively reasonable individual who demonstrates respect in their life. That is, a show of respect before the court, supported by friends to achieve a minimum sentence, this is not respect, but only demonstrates contempt. How is respect taught today and does it really exist?

The lack of respect is the resultant of over bearing civil libertarian bureaucrats. It may not have been the intention but this is what has been produced; contempt for parents, teachers and key authority figures in the lives of children and young adults, who perceive authority as impotent, powerless and are therefore, ridiculed.

So the question remains, who is teaching our young people to be respectful, or to even, respect themselves? As far as I can see, the answer is a resounding "no-one" except for the parents prepared to take the risk and care enough to invest the time into their kids.

Our Defence Forces – Fewer than 3.5% of our population are employed by our collective Army, Navy, Air forces and Coastguard and while government advertises for recruits, these forces remain understaffed while offering wonderful opportunities for training in various trades. Not every person wants or needs a university degree or even the Higher School Certificate in following a career of their choice, or what they have an aptitude for. When a 15 to 25 year old cannot make up their mind as to what they want to do in life or when they leave school, there must be four options proposed for their choice, as unemployment benefits should not be provided to healthy young people:

1. Find a Job, wherever or whatever is offered, or
2. Continue studying at TAFE or University and then find a job, or
3. Undertake an apprenticeship either with private enterprise or with one of the government defence services or with the police force; coast guard; ambulance; Emergency Services; Fire Fighters etc., or
4. Join one of the regular defence services for, say, three years until one of the above is decided on and then perhaps continue to serve as a reservist for a prescribed time.

There is no such thing as unemployment, particularly for our youth unless they are suffering with a crippling, debilitating disability. Without a daily purpose, responsibility and commitment there is no reason to get up in the morning. Depression, anxiety and mental disorders can set in and destroy self esteem and good personal choices, making the long term unemployed, unemployable. It would be interesting to note how many of the recent drunken riots involve the unemployed.

Millions of dollars are spent enticing young people to join our defence forces and hundreds of millions of dollars are spent each year on welfare payments for youth who laze around with no direction in life. Many just fill in their Centrelink form to demonstrate attempts at getting a job, but they never do. No ambitions, no goals and little if any self esteem to satisfy their self created egos, which is often developed to conceal their feeling of inferiority or inadequacy – so they hit the bottle or get into drugs to finish the job. Again, it requires society to step in to rectify these problems of antisocial behaviour with assertive directives. Ultimately this will produce a satisfied member of society with new skills and a sense of worth and belonging, where today no level of government has achieved any advancement or remedy for these issues.

Consider it in terms of respect. People who bludge on society, or exploit its generosity as if it was a weakness, are not showing our society respect. **A fair go means making a real contribution and getting a fair go**! A fair go does not mean you have a right to sit on your backside and spend your sit-down money because society owes you a living. No society in the world is expected to give payment, benefits and equality without a fair return.

◆ The army or one of our defence forces offers great options and also for unruly juvenile criminals or bullies in teaching them how to be a part of society and in learning new skills. It is not suggested that the armed forces be a police or jail authority. Rather for those who have committed crimes and would appear not to be a threat to society who we can provide with the opportunities they may not have at home or in their community, although initially resistance maybe demonstrated. In addition, why should society pay to keep them either on welfare or in jail when they can work, learn and earning skills as a form of redemption through honest work and in building their lives.

Wars of the 21ˢᵗ Century – The Many Evil Faces of Terrorism

THE PERCEPTION OF a terrorist – is of some dope who straps a bomb to his body and blows himself to hell, together with buildings, planes, buses, trains and innocent people or who openly shoots, just to kill for some fanatical cult type of cause. This is only *one* form of terrorism which gets our attention. Terrorists come in many forms and they have many different objectives. In defining a terrorist: Generally it would be those who seek to wreak havoc and destruction, in satisfying their sick need for recognition or claim to some perverted fame for themselves or the retarded glory of their cause and objectives. This also applies to arsonists and others.

Cyber Wars – Cyber-crime was once just limited to very cleaver hackers who robbed our information to access our bank accounts and rip us off, but now millions of people's details are being sold for as little as A$5 per person by well orchestrated criminal organisations. Three billion dollars per year is currently being extracted from Australians' bank accounts and we pay the price of this in many ways. Although e-banking is very convenient, 20% of Australians are currently defrauded in identity theft and it would seem the old way of paying by cheque is currently the only guaranteed way of defeating this fraud.

Cyber-crime can lead to Cyber-war which is not just an act of terrorism but the most effective war of the 21ˢᵗ century after a nuclear bomb. With almost every facet of our lives governed by computers, we are increasingly vulnerable to computer viruses which have doubled in the past year. The designers of these viruses are able to take down an entire city or an entire country, as Russia did to Estonia. Russia and now China are the world leaders in their ability to steal secret government, corporate or personal documents and are able to plan and carry out Cyber attacks with little to protect us. It is the replacement of the cold war with its spies and espionage specialist. Well executed, a Cyber-war against say, Australia could leave us without power, water, all essential services, particularly communications which would leave all of our defence forces unable to even communicate with each other. Our emergency resources could not handle the havoc and damage that would be created and therefore it is only common sense that, all government security data must not be on-line and more security resources need to be invested to protect us individually and nationally.

Propaganda and Supremacy: We accept too readily what we see on TV, hear on the radio and other forms of media as factual reporting, when more often than, its not. More than often we are fed contrived digressions from the truth and more than often we get opinions, rather than facts, as much of the media reporting is based on "theatre" and "ratings" than accuracy or relevance. Opinions often formed and presented under the auspice of a country or cause including false accusation, are then relied on and wrongly believed. For example, News reporters demonstrating abuse of Arabs living on the Gaza Strip when this was but the purported victims putting on a show for the media in gaining sympathy while condemning Israel, after their daily bombing of Israel for months. Fact is there was more carnage caused by our allied forces in bombing Iraqi and Afghanistan citizen, but no condemnation there! In World War II more Germans were killed than British and Americans combined, but there is no doubt in anyone's mind that the war was caused by Germany's aggression. And in response to the German blitz on London, the British wiped out the entire city of Dresden, burning to death more German civilians than the number of people killed in Hiroshima and in 1944, when the R.A.F. tried to bomb the Gestapo Headquarters in Copenhagen, some of the bombs missed their target and fell on a Danish children's hospital, killing 83 little children.

Media reporting on the use of red pens by teachers in schools and the blame game in politics versus real issues like the pursuit of The Heiner Affair or of our sabotaged Federal Constitution, or Agenda 21, or the Lima Declaration, or the Kyoto Protocol and other adverse UN treaties which have required our conforming to these retarded treaties, go unreported to keep us in the dark but suffering the consequences, individually and collectively. This is propaganda by stealth (sneakily withholding).

If you haven't realised it yet, **we are already well into WW3** the difference is we have not dealt with the enemy appropriately. Do you know who they are? Think about it! *Those who seek to wreak havoc and destruction, in satisfying their sick need for recognition or claim to some perverted fame for themselves or the retarded glory of their "cause" and objectives.*

In recognition of who they are, there are two groups with the same objectives:

1. The Radical Religious Fundamentalist who wants the world to convert to Islam or die, and
2. Those who adhere to philosophies adverse to our way of democratic life and the civil rights our forebears fought and died for. Those who under the UN pursue tyrannous rule and who have taken hold over us, but most of us haven't woken up to the socialistic impediments on us yet.

In effect, the majority of UN nations seeking recompense for developing nations are Muslim nations, so 2. above seeks to support 1. above, making them one and the same. Fundamentalist numbers are vast and growing and there is little we can do to stop this, but to be vigilant in protecting our Constitutional Rights and taking the harshest measures against anyone who abuses these rights and thus revisit the truest intent of our Constitution. This has been a slow moving war which stated in England several hundred years ago and accelerated since 1975 with only the final touches to be put in place with the One World Government Treaty. You must really be thinking this woman is a crack-pot – do your own research, I have and I can assure you, it has taken all my guts to write the things I have, as I am not into conspiracies.

Unfortunately as **the first victim of war is the truth**, we must be more vigilant in questioning media reports for accuracy and relevance to what could really be the truth. Ask your politicians to explain to you the UN Treaties, if they cannot, you know you have a problem. If you don't have proof, consider anything else to be lies. Be aware that there are those who misrepresent and are misleading us with downright lies, but these lies always have a way of leading to conflicts of massive proportions eg the ETS Cap-and-trade scam. We are also at a great disadvantage, not knowing a country's true political agenda or the objectives (not even our own) of their propaganda machine.

Propaganda is the greatest weapon of any "party" those with their own agenda, no different to all the spies who ran around in the 50s and 60s with the Cold War between Russia and USA, or Hitler in the 1930s and many others. Most countries have their own propaganda machine, able to withhold the truth from their people and able to create illusions to gain support and even go to war. It's not "the people" who make war but political groups, activists, parties and governments.

John Loftus, a former US Justice Department Prosecutor, states that, *"After WW2 the USA employed Nazis in their CIA. From 1945 to 1948 the British Secret Service protected every Arab Nazi it could but still failed to squash the State of Israel. Then the British sold the Arab Nazi agency to the US predecessor of what became the CIA. This Egyptian Muslim Nazi unit was deployed by the USA to Afghanistan as a counterweight against Arab Communism and to take on the Russians who funded Arab communists. The USA called this unit the MAK, which from 1979 was run by an Arab by the name of Azzam and his assistant Osama bin Laden."* One of many questions begging an answer – why within 24 hours of 9/11 did President George Bush expedite the deportation of more than 20 of Bin Laden's relatives from the USA?

The Taliban is now funded and supported with hundreds of millions of Saudi dollars each year (from our petrol dollars) to go inflict terror anywhere, except in Saudi Arabia. Hence 9/11 and our war against terror begins in the west, yet, it was the west who created one of its own worst enemies of the 21st century. If you should want to read more on this, go online and type in the words "banna" and then "Nazi" there are articles about these goings-on. You can also see the effects of dangerous political propaganda with the unforeseen ramifications of counterproductive "white collar" workers seeking to justify their existence by exploiting all of us, and providing proof that "whatever we do (good and bad), we do to ourselves". No different to the Italians in Afghanistan paying the Taliban not to shoot them. When they left the region and the French moved in, 10 French soldiers were massacred as the Italians failed to tell the French about their 'deal' with the Taliban.

White collar egocentric politicians continue with deceptive spy games, now to a level that only revolt by citizens of democratic countries may alleviate, with "Tea Parties" by citizens now underway. The US government has established a "Shadow US Government" which operates out of two secret bunkers in the USA (in anticipation of an International Treaty). Bureaucrats are scrambling to finalize the installation while the majority of the world's people are oblivious to what is to befall them. Americans are starting to fully appreciate that Obama is but an actor and it is only a matter of time before he and his colleagues instigate more adverse changes towards their citizens who do not conform or comply with "The Single World Order". Also worth reading, the Wild Lands Project in the US <www.propertyrightsresearch.org/articles2/wildlands_project_and_un_convent.htm>

Propaganda begets paranoia. Paranoia sets governments into a tailspin with a perceived need to overindulge into many security agencies, which results in, conflicts between these agencies. There was enough information before the well planned terrorist attacks of September 11th 2001 American security agencies knew prior the events but failed to act. Although 9/11 was the single most horrific act on American soil, it opened for US politicians the war-gate to the rich oil fields of Iraq and the expensive war effort. Why didn't US security agencies act to prevent 9/11? Was it perhaps just a case of not knowing which agency should be acting or not wanting to share or relinquish "control" to any other "competitor" agency, and so no affirmative preventative action was taken by any agency, in preventing the loss of 3,000 innocent lives. This is the result of having too many agencies and too many organisations all running their own race in keeping their bureaucratic butts in jobs (like 3 levels of government for 22 million people). This is the arrogant result of overzealous micro-management by government. Then shrugging off responsibility inappropriately to a myriad of agencies, is short-changing the country of a cohesive agency, for the excessive and irresponsible expenditure. It is imperative for any country that:

◆ A single cohesive defence ministry for our total security needs be handled by skilled military personal, not to be subverted by any government or minister, which could see this organisation compromised in its function for the pursuit of any "higher government objective" or unwarranted extending into our rights to privacy, freedom and legal redress. For this reason, ASIO and the police would form part of the National Defence Portfolio under a constitution provided by the Senate.

Tolerance & Religious Fundamentalism – My grandfather fought for Australia in WWI, in France as did many of our forefathers. He and most of our diggers fought wars during the 20th century with many paying the ultimate price with their lives, for our right to live in peace and freedom, a safe and happy life. Now we confront a greater threat and from within our borders from those who are born here and those who are influenced by a mass international radical religious fundamentalist movement. For the first time, from new and relatively new migrants, minority groups seek to see us compromise our standards and beliefs in wanting to change our way of life in our succumbing to their demands for our social and religious reform or else, we should suffer the consequences.

Australia should never be a place for race hatred but we have seen personal attacks, sexual assaults and demonstrations of bad attitudes and contempt for young Australian girls, referred to as less than human. Girls blamed by some "clergymen" for inciting sex attacks because they put out as "cat-meat". Race and gang wars are mounting through Sydney and Melbourne based on perverse teachings and by those who deplore them for this. While some Middle-Eastern and other youth have brought their conflicts and infused culture to our country, many now born here have been indoctrinated by their parents' radical teachings. It's just not what our diggers intended for us, nor is it what the majority of Australians want. There are no remedies offered by any government or civil rights groups, just lame laws and in these circumstances, **I would squarely put the blame for broken laws associated with adverse racial behaviour on the parents and clerics of these criminals, if any awareness can be established or proven.** That is, share the consequences of penalties and sentences for their teachings and for their failure to prevent by altering authorities. If they are found guilty, they ought to be deported back to where they came from. How can we blame someone else for another's behaviour? Example: Mrs Skaf sat through the trial of her sons – she heard the graphic descriptions of what her darling boys did and why they received 35 and 55 years in jail for their crimes against Australian girls. Crimes which would never have been done to Muslim girls! Then outside the court, Mrs Skaf insulted these victims calling them *"sluts"* and here is the "proof of the pudding" as to who are their teachers, to share in the conviction for fostering this behaviour. **This behaviour is not inherent it is taught rigorously,** and doubtful if it were in our public school system.

Then there were the 5 blokes who were planning terrorist attacks and got sentences of 20 years plus, yet surely as the equipment was found in their homes, their families were aware of the plans but they failed to alert authorities or intervene, harbouring these criminals, yet no prosecution for what could have been mass murder.

Yet to be "politically correct" we succumb to seemingly harmless intimidating methods as employed by some minority groups in gaining support and sympathy. Suggesting sufferance from "oppression" as their best defence in offending others, with accusations of "*Islamophobia*" in gaining the upper hand to gain submission, for fear of not wanting to project or be considered discriminatory or politically incorrect. Islam is not the problem, it's the preachers of hate and division, the loudmouthed lieutenants and their hypnotised converts who have opted to believe that subversion, assaults and even open rebellion are justified. Those seeking to convert the world to their beliefs in validating same, is no different to any form of party ideology, be they communist, or whatever. Muslims or anyone who share a love for Australia and seek to share its bounty equally, respecting a fair go for all, are welcome here, those who don't, need to go home. No legal return allowed. Doing this isn't intolerant on our part, it's common sense, you don't allow a rabid dog into your house and then feed it, that is simply stupid.

Race hatred, intolerance and change to a culture starts out small. It's like cancer. How many shopping complexes in our major cities no longer play Christmas carols at Christmas because of pressure from Muslim interest groups? No fair dinkum Aussie of any background or belief is prepared to allow Australia to follow in the path and subsequent social and economical demise as has been experienced by some European nations. Countries such as France, England, Germany, Holland (which now seeks to ban Islamic law as contained in the Koran) or Spain which were all once buoyant economic and cultural societies but where some sections are now turning into criminally overrun slums and potentially third world countries. Enough political correctness: Justice H.H.J. Collins of the Central London County Court lifted a ban on the British National Party "BNP" in a court case http://mybnp.co.uk/newsletter/ehrc.pdf Speaking after being given his party membership card, Mr Singh said he was determined to ensure that the BNP's message was heard without distortions and lies. *"Only BNP Can Save Britain from the "Terror" of Islamist Colonisation and Protect British Identity"* says first Sikh Member. *"All of the other parties follow policies which will result in the Islamification of Britain,"* Mr Singh said. *"Already there are over 85 sharia law courts operating in Britain, all with legal force and recognised by the State. Sharia law is becoming entrenched in financial institutions as well. This is the direct result of the policies followed by Labour, Conservative and Lib-Democrats who have encouraged Islamic immigration,"* Mr Singh said. *"I know first-hand the results of Islamist colonisation. I saw what happened to my homeland when it was overrun by Islamists and I do not want that horror visited upon Britain".* Remember, we are under the sovereignty of the Great British Empire, whose laws are decaying from within with Sharia Law courts and Sharia Banking spreading. Great Britain as with many countries in the European Union are fast becoming third world countries and these are some of the reasons for my advocating to insulate our country.

It should be noted right here, that I know many, many good Australian Muslims who have integrated very well into our society and they do not expect us to convert or die or change our culture to suit them. The following pertains to others. This is one of those times when it is good that Australia is so far removed geographically from Europe and is relatively young in our history, to be able to observe and appreciate the ramifications of poor short term decisions and take preventative measures to ensure

RACHEL EMMES

we do not suffer the same consequences. It has been suggested that Australia could be rushing towards the same problems as Denmark as *"once our Muslim population gets to 2% we will face the same threats"*.Susan MacAllen suggests that Canada, Australia & the US could learn a lot from Denmark who she suggests have a very logical immigration system, as what happened there could very well happen here and no doubt this has contributed to Rev Fred Nile proposing a 10 year moratorium on Muslim immigration. A contributing editor for "Salute the Danish Flag – it's a Symbol of Western Freedom" by Susan MacAllen: *"In 1978-9 I was living and studying in Denmark. But in 1978 – even in Copenhagen, one didn't see Muslim immigrants. The Danish population embraced visitors, celebrated the exotic and, went out of its way to protect each of its citizens. It was proud of its new brand of socialist liberalism won in development since the conservatives had lost power in 1929 – a system where no worker had to struggle to survive, where one ultimately could count upon the State as in, perhaps, no other western nation at the time.*

The rest of Europe saw the Scandinavians as free-thinking, progressive and infinitely generous in their welfare policies. Denmark boasted low crime rates, devotion to the environment, a superior educational system and a history of humanitarianism.

Denmark was also most generous in its immigration policies – it offered the best welcome in Europe to the new immigrant: generous welfare payments from first arrival plus additional perks in transportation, housing and education. It was determined to set a world example for inclusiveness and multiculturalism. How could it have predicted that one day in 2005 a series of political cartoons in a newspaper would spark violence that would leave dozens dead in the streets – all because its commitment to multiculturalism would come back to bite?

By the 1990's the growing urban Muslim population was obvious – and its unwillingness to integrate into Danish society was obvious. Years of immigrants had settled into Muslim-exclusive enclaves. As the Muslim leadership became more vocal about what they considered the decadence of Denmark's liberal way of life, the Danes – once so welcoming – began to feel slighted. Many Danes had begun to see Islam as incompatible with their long-standing values: belief in personal liberty and free speech, in equality for women, in tolerance for other ethnic groups, and a deep pride in Danish heritage and history.

An article by Daniel Pipes and Lars Hedegaard, in which they forecasted accurately that the growing immigrant problem in Denmark would explode, in the article they reported:

'Muslim immigrants constitute 5% of the population but consume upwards of 40% of the welfare spending. "Muslims are only 4% of Denmark's 5.4 million people but make up a majority of the country's convicted rapists, an especially combustible issue given that practically all the female victims are non-Muslim. Similar, if lesser, disproportions are found in other crimes.' 'Over time, as Muslim immigrants increase in numbers, they wish less to mix with the indigenous population. A recent survey finds that only 5% of young Muslim immigrants would readily marry a Dane.'

'Forced marriages – promising a newborn daughter in Denmark to a male cousin in the home country, then compelling her to marry him, sometimes on pain of death – are one problem. Muslim leaders openly declare their goal of introducing Islamic law once Denmark's

Muslim population grows large enough – a not-that-remote prospect. If present trends persist, one sociologist estimates, every third inhabitant of Denmark in 40 years will be Muslim.

It is easy to understand why a growing number of Danes would feel that Muslim immigrants show little respect for Danish values and laws. An example is the phenomenon common to other European countries and Canada: some Muslims in Denmark who opted to leave the Muslim faith have been murdered in the name of Islam, while others hide in fear for their lives. Jews are also threatened and harassed openly by Muslim leaders in Denmark, a country where once Christian citizens worked to smuggle out nearly all of their 7,000 Jews by night to Sweden – before the Nazis could invade. I think of my Danish friend Elsa – who as a teenager had dreaded crossing the street to the bakery every morning under the eyes of occupying Nazi soldiers – and I wonder what she would say today.

In 2001, Denmark elected the most conservative government in some 70 years – one that had some decidedly non-generous ideas about liberal unfettered immigration. Today Denmark has the strictest immigration policies in Europe. (Its effort to protect itself has been met with accusations of 'racism' by liberal media across Europe – even as other governments struggle to right the social problems wrought by years of too-lax immigration.)

If you wish to become Danish, you must attend three years of language classes. You must pass a test on Denmark's history, culture, and a Danish language test: You must live in Denmark for 7 years before applying for citizenship. You must demonstrate intent to work and have a job waiting. If you wish to bring a spouse into Denmark, you must both be over 24 years of age and you won't find it so easy anymore to move your friends and family to Denmark with you. You will not be allowed to build a mosque in Copenhagen. Although your children have a choice of some 30 Arabic culture and language schools in Denmark, they will be strongly encouraged to assimilate to Danish society in ways that past immigrants weren't. In 2006, the Danish minister for employment, Claus Hjort Frederiksen, spoke publicly of the burden of Muslim immigrants on the Danish welfare system and it was horrifying: the government's welfare committee had calculated that if immigration from Third World countries were blocked, 75% of the cuts needed to sustain the huge welfare system in coming decades would be unnecessary. In other words, **the welfare system as it existed was being exploited by immigrants to the point of eventually bankrupting the government. We are simply forced to adopt a new policy on immigration.** The calculations of the welfare committee are terrifying and show how unsuccessful the integration of immigrants has been up to now,' he said. A large thorn in the side of Denmark's imams is the Minister of Immigration and Integration, Rikke Hvilshoj. She makes no bones about the new policy toward immigration, 'The number of foreigners coming to the country makes a difference,' Hvilshoj says, 'There is an inverse correlation between how many come here and how well we can receive the foreigners that come and on Muslim immigrants needing to demonstrate a willingness to blend in. In my view, Denmark should be a country with room for different cultures and religions. Some values, however, are more important than others. We refuse to question democracy, equal rights, and freedom of speech.'

Hvilshoj has paid a price for her show of backbone. Perhaps to test her resolve, the leading radical imam in Denmark, Ahmed Abdel Rahman Abu Laban, demanded that the *government pay blood money to the family of a Muslim who was murdered in a suburb of Copenhagen, stating that the family's thirst for revenge could be thwarted for money. When Hvilshoj dismissed his demand, he argued that in Muslim culture the payment of retribution money was common, to which Hvilshoj replied that what is done in a Muslim country is not necessarily what is done in Denmark.*

*The Muslim reply came soon after: her house was torched while she, her husband and children slept. All managed to escape unharmed, but she and her family were moved to a secret location and she and other ministers were assigned bodyguards for the first time, in a country where such murderous violence was once so scarce. Her government has slid to the right and her borders have tightened. Many believe that what happens in the next decade will determine whether Denmark survives as a bastion of good living, humane thinking and social responsibility, or whether it becomes a nation at civil war with supporters of Sharia law. And meanwhile, Canadians clamor for stricter immigration policies and demand an end to State welfare programs that allow many immigrants to live on the public dole. As we in Australia and in Canada and in the US look at the enclaves of Muslims amongst us, **and see those who enter our shores too easily, dare live on our taxes, yet refuse to embrace our culture, respect our traditions, participate in our legal system, obey our laws, speak our language, appreciate our history . . . We would do well to look to Denmark, and say a prayer for her future and for our own."***

Failure to instigate serious measures in a National Code of Conduct, taught to all citizens and migrants could breed just the contempt required to undermine our lifestyle, our values, and our religious and political freedoms. It would ultimately change what this country was built on and our future direction. Australia has been extremely generous to all migrants, particularly in providing substantial financial and other benefits and there have been many resentful jokes to reflect Australians' contempt for abuse of our hospitality. Australia does not enforce or pressure migrants to participate in the Australian way of life but the general consensus of Australians is unilateral: Australians are not prepared to be tolerant of those who are intolerant of their host country, those who do not tolerate fair and good values and our laws. Rather than subvert our standards, let these people go somewhere else, somewhere where they are able to subvert that country's standards, in many cases, to where they came from and where their true allegiances lie.

From world adversities and terrorist atrocities demonstrated by extremists in London, New York, Israel, India, Bali and other countries, we have learnt a host of lessons. We have come to the one and only very positive conclusion, the acknowledgement and appreciation of the need to express and enforce our culture and standards. Our freedom of religious faith, our generosity, our civil rights, liberties and our way of life are only ours as long as we protect them with the greatest forces we have, from those who would encroach or impose their oppressive beliefs and murderous acts upon us and this is *"true political correctness!"* This is the meaning of *"true blue multicultural Australianism"*

Australians are very aware that inequality in any aspect of society and the failure to recognise the demands of the majority, for fear of retribution by any minority is the greatest form of political incorrectness, causing the most dangerous injustice to us all. In saying this, we must be pro-active in picking up our own personal game or level of behaviour and acceptance of what is acceptable behaviour. Without a good standard from ourselves we have no ability or right to demand this of others.

The war between East (Islam) and West (non Islamic "Infidels") has gone on for centuries but it took 9/11 to kick us into gear. This one single act of war has changed the world as we have known it. We acknowledge the threat of Muslim radicals, their ability to infiltrate our borders, live among us like any Joe Blow and kill us at the drop of a hat. We innocently live under the illusion that all people are peace loving, as we are and are as caring of each other, as we are but the individual psychological makeup of people is as different as apples are to bananas. Diversification is only good when we all have the same values and virtues. That we share the same love of life and of each other and the same Code of Conduct, but sadly this is not the case when it comes to any group who have "*self supremacy issues*". No decent Australian would compromise the life, lifestyle or security of one single Australian, for anyone.

The proposed solutions may be to the dismay of naïve civil libertarians, with their misguided belief of true political correctness. What may appear as cruelty to a minority may very well be kindness to the majority. Many civil do-gooders unfortunately fuel the problems in society based on their misconstrued views or lack of full comprehension of the very adverse mindsets and objectives of those who do not conform to the overall requirements of a cohesive society, and thus they too become the enemy, intolerant or discriminatory against the majority.

There are groups of Muslim radicals who live in other parts of the world including those just outside of our border calling for Jihad, the ones who treat Australians with contempt at every opportunity. We are free to travel to their countries as tourists, spend our holidays there, spend our hard earned money in their countries and to our horror, get blown up and have poison served at local bars, like in Bali. Although we don't have capital punishment here, I doubt one Australian shed a tear when the Indonesian courts executed the Bali Bombers, no one asked, where are the civil libertarians? Why aren't they intervening?

The Australian government works hard at maintaining relations with, and supporting Indonesia. Simple arithmetic demonstrates how Muslim contempt by our neighbours could skyrocket with the successful election of a radical fundamentalist. Indonesia has more than 220,000,000 people with approx 87% followers of the Islamic faith. It is one of the largest Muslim populations outside of Arab countries where radical self declared supremacists are living in a land of only 1,919,443 sq kilometres. Compare this to our 22,000,000 people (10% of Indonesia's population) with approx 87% of the Christian faith who live in a land of 7,682,300 sq kilometres (almost 4 times larger than Indonesia). They break our boards to fish our waters with contempt for our laws, while the Indonesia government fails to stop them or the boat loads of people leaving from their shores for Australia. Then, rather than turn them around and send them back to Indonesia, we extend the hand of friendship in starting a new life here, rather than in Indonesia? If 500 boats simultaneously left from Indonesia or Asia for Australia, we do not have the resources to stop them. They would just arrive on our shores – do we take them in, or turn them around, or stop them on out to sea with any measure?

Australians have always been good neighbours in rushing to every cause. Providing emergency relief and funding when needed as we did after the disastrous effect of the 2004 Tsunami but did we provide help to the helpless or did we aid political motifs in giving money to the Indonesian government? Was A$1 billion intended to enforce good relations, able to provide Australia with some sort of good working relationship with Indonesia eg prisoner exchanges? If it were A$10 billion it could never guarantee compromise or a promise of peace. It would do no more than a piece of paper called a "*Peace Agreement*" did for Israel in giving up land to people who call themselves Palestinians. A worthless piece of paper supported with broken promises to live in peace. Reciprocated respect and tolerance between nations is all that is needed to maintain peace but supremacists, fundamentalist groups and dictator governments have celebrated successes for thousands of years because all it takes "*For evil to win is for good people to do nothing*" and succumb to those who can achieve subservience from weak governments.

If ever there would be support by an America, Australia or any democratic country's government for the likes of Iran over any other democracy, it would be the ultimate appeasement of terrorism and the ultimate demise of democracy. It would be the final victory of fundamental terrorism that would see society return to barbarism.

The following has been provided by a very dear person who wishes to remain anonymous. The objective of this story is to highlight how easy it is for peaceful people to live in denial or just turn off until their very existence is in peril, and how any minority group or party can grow and become a most dynamic adversarial power against peace and the right to life. Whether it be by one of the many white supremacists groups or religious fundamentalists or by political groups, who seek to gain power by controlling the minds (or purse) of others. They purport to provide unification and create patriotism where it is greatly needed, in the ranks of the either financially or otherwise suppressed, or those who do not have adequate or compassionate leadership. People look to those who "appear" to offer the shortcomings they want and often need, but for leaders with tyrannous motives who are equipped to create the most devastating destruction of life and civility:

I used to know a man whose family were German aristocracy prior to World War II. They owned a number of large industries and estates. I asked him how many German people were true Nazis and the answer he gave has stuck with me and guided my attitude toward fanaticism or "parties" of any kind ever since. *"Very few people were true Nazis," he said, "but many enjoyed the return of German pride, and many more were too busy to care* (too involved in their day to day lives, with the media feeding them what they want them to know, sound familiar?). *I was one of those who just thought the Nazis were a bunch of fools. So, the majority just sat back and let it all happen. Then, before we knew it, they owned us, and we had lost control, and the end of the world had come. My family lost everything I ended up in a concentration camp and the Allies destroyed my factories."*

We are told again and again by "experts" and "talking heads" that Islam is the religion of peace, and that the vast majority of Muslims just want to live in peace. Although this unqualified assertion may be true, it is entirely irrelevant. It is meaningless fluff, meant to make us feel better, and meant to somehow diminish the spectre of fanatics rampaging across the globe in the name of Islam. The fact is that the fanatics rule Islam at this moment in history. It is the fanatics who march. It is the fanatics who wage any one of 50 shooting wars worldwide. It is the fanatics who systematically slaughter Christian or tribal groups throughout Africa and are gradually taking over the entire continent in an Islamic wave. It is the fanatics who homicide-bomb, behead, murder, or honour kill. It is the fanatics who take over mosque after mosque. It is the fanatics who zealously spread the stoning and hanging of rape victims and homosexuals. The hard quantifiable fact is that the "peaceful majority" is the "silent majority" and it is cowed and extraneous.

Communist Russia comprised Russians who just wanted to live in peace, yet the Russian Communists were responsible for the murder of about 20 million people. The peaceful majority were irrelevant. China's huge population was peaceful as well, but Chinese Communists managed to kill a staggering 70 million people. The average Japanese individual prior to World War 2 was not a warmongering sadist. Yet, Japan murdered and slaughtered its way across South East Asia in an orgy of killing that included the systematic murder of 12 million Chinese civilians; most killed by sword, shovel, and bayonet. And, who can forget Rwanda, which collapsed into butchery. Could it not be said that the majority of Rwandans were "peace loving"?

History lessons are often incredibly simple and blunt, yet for all our powers of reason, we often miss the most basic and uncomplicated of points that, peace-loving Muslims have been made irrelevant, by their silence. Peace-loving Muslims will become our enemy if they don't speak up, because, like my friend from Germany, they will awaken one day and find that the fanatics own them and the end of their world will have begun. Peace-loving Germans, Japanese, Chinese, Russians, Rwandans, Serbs, Afghans, Iraqis, Palestinians, Somalis, Nigerians, Algerians, and many others have died because the peaceful majority did not speak up until it was too late. As for us, who watch it all unfold; we must pay attention to the only group that counts; the fanatics who threaten our way of life.

Lastly: At the risk of offending someone, I sincerely think that anyone who rejects this as just another political rant, or doubts the seriousness of this issue, is part of the problem.

Many young first generation Australians of Middle-Eastern heritage live here with some deluded, romantic notions that the place of their ancestry and their religious beliefs gives them superiority to that of Australians. They are more patriotic to their heritage than to their place of birth. Collectively this creates unity (which they are not getting as Australians – feeling apart from not a part of, with no guidance as to what is acceptable to be inclusive) with others in forming "the pack" or "the brotherhood" mentality.

Truth be known, it is only their parents who can teach them that had the place of their ancestry been half decent or provided the benefits of peace and opportunity, their parents would never have given up what they had to come here, leaving family and friends behind to make the journey to an unknown place. The pack, gang or brotherhood mentality, are problems taught by fanatical fundamental clerics and are often influences (again) learnt in their homes and communities. Often their attitudes are as a result of unemployment or a perceived lack of purpose, self esteem or feelings of inferiority. These causes create the inability to integrate into society and assimilate peacefully. Young men in particular are yet to learn that all Australians are free to worship in their own way, while working and playing with others from every corner of the earth with respect, peace and love. If we harness and address the problem to work in the interest of the majority now, the problem can go away in the next generation or two.

Australian citizenship is a privilege not a right and every migrant must accept the repercussions for their non conformity to our laws and proposed Code of Conduct. If a young person is up to no good or mixing with gangs with anti-Australian motives, the parent(s) must seek government assistance to overcome the problem or be held accountable. More than often it will save the life of their own child in the long run and reduce hate crimes. Both positive and negative cultures, customs, beliefs and attitudes are developed and nurtured in the family home firstly and then taken to the streets. If these attitudes and behaviour are detrimental to our society, those who embedded them or reinforce them must bear responsibility. Parents should not feel that if their child runs off the rails that it is a reflection of poor parenting, rather it's a crime not to call out for help. It is this failure to act by parents that they should be held accountable for. While many young thugs may have little regard for themselves or the consequences to themselves, they hold their family in the highest regard and therefore,

◆ After accurate determination, or as a result of a hearing, if it is found that the family has influenced or failed to notify authorities – they must be held responsible for the actions of their young person's antisocial behaviour, as if the family had committed the crime. Imbedding antisocial beliefs or failure to take assertive action should also bear the consequences of revoking citizenship and deportation, with any assets taken in lieu of prosecution costs and damage, if applicable.

◆ Incitement of racial or religious bigotry or prejudice should not be tolerated under any circumstances and treated as seriously as physical abuse. Violence as a result of this sort of behaviour should be treated in the harshest sentencing our courts must administer. Lengthy jail sentences with hard Labor for payment to victims and society, a deterrent and fair retribution.

◆ Any act of terrorism or attempted act of terrorism should be deemed to be an act of attempted murder, with the criminal's citizenship revoked after serving the appropriate sentence and deported back to where they came from or the country to where their allegiances lie.

Unreasonable you might say, but the loss of life and token penalties and sentences is what is unreasonable. We must stop deluding ourselves that everyone has the same basic good intentions and mindset towards each other. We must acknowledge that terrorism in any form is a war like we have never seen and it can spread. Zero tolerance is the only remedy. We must bear in mind that many fundamentalists are not concerned for themselves but fear retaliation by the Australian community against their family. This is a greater concern than any penalty we could impose on the terrorist personally and only this will eliminate the majority of threats against our society.

Very few terrorist acts, or planned acts, are not known to close family members and friends, who could and should seek to prevent crime against Australian society. The ramifications for breach of our proposed Code of Conduct must be encompassed in the pledge of allegiance and should be accepted by all new Australians in their citizenship and visa terms and perhaps as one of the very few times an interpreter would be required to explaining and having signed that the person understands and agrees to these terms.

I suggest reading or watching the interview **"The Psychology Behind Homicide/Suicide Bombings"** with Pierre Rehov, Documentary Filmmaker. MSNBC's "Connected" program discussed the July 7th London attacks with Pierre Rehov, a French film maker who has filmed six documentaries on the Intifada by going undercover in the Palestinian areas. Pierre's film, "Suicide Killers," is based on interviews he conducted with the families of homicide bombers and would-be bombers in an attempt to find out why they do it. The line of questioning is extensive, but here just are a few questions and answers:

Q: What socio-economic forces support the perpetuation of suicide bombings? A: Muslim charity is usually a cover for supporting terrorist organizations. But one has also to look at countries like Pakistan (where we outsource call centre work), *Saudi Arabia and Iran, which are also supporting the same organizations through different networks. The ironic thing in the case of Palestinian suicide bombers is that most of the money comes through financial support from the Occidental world, donated to a culture that utterly hates and rejects the West, mainly symbolized by Israel and the USA.*

Q: What role does the UN play in the terrorist equation? A: The United Nations is in the hands of Arab countries and third world or ex-communist countries. The UN has *condemned Israel more than any other country in the world, including the regime of Castro, Idi Amin or Kaddafi. By behaving this way, the UN leaves a door open by not openly condemning terrorist organizations. In addition, through UNRWA, the UN is directly tied to terror organisations such as Hamas, representing 65 percent of their apparatus in the so-called Palestinian refugee camps. As a support to Arab countries, the UN has maintained Palestinians in camps with the hope to "return" into Israel for more than 50 years, therefore making it impossible to settle those populations, which still live in deplorable conditions. US$400 million is spent every year, mainly financed by US taxes, to support 23,000 employees of UNRWA, many of whom belong to terrorist organisations (see Congressman Eric Cantor on this subject, and in my film "Hostages of Hatred").*

***Q: How can we put an end to the madness of suicide bombings and terrorism in general?** A: Stop being politically correct and stop believing that this culture is a victim of ours. Radical Islamism today is nothing but a new form of Nazism. Nobody was trying to justify or excuse Hitler in the 1930s. We had to defeat him in order to make peace one day with the German people.*

***Q: Are these men travelling outside their native areas in large numbers? Based on your research, would you predict that we are beginning to see a new wave of suicide bombings outside the Middle East?** A: Every successful terror attack is considered a victory by the radical Islamists. Everywhere Islam expands there is regional conflict. Right now, there are thousands of candidates for martyrdom lining up in training camps in Bosnia, Afghanistan and Pakistan. Inside Europe, hundreds of illegal mosques are preparing the next step of brain washing to lost young men who cannot find a satisfying identity in the Occidental world. Israel is much more prepared for this than the rest of the world will ever be. Yes, there will be more suicide killings in Europe and the US. Sadly, this is only the beginning.*

Note: **The UN with its adverse treaties and designs on a one world government is in the hands of Muslim countries** and there are nearing 500,000 Muslims in Australia, making our Muslim population almost on par with our Aboriginal population. Muslims are no longer a minority group warranting any special treatment and are able to conform to the culture of their host nation. In the USA Muslim recruits are picked up in jails, and thus making up almost 25% of the US population. There are more than 30 Islamic camps throughout the US where recruits train. Jihad will not come from outside of US borders but from within, see the website "The Third Jihad". The term *"Suicide Bomber"* must be replaced with *"Homicide Bomber"* in all forms of media, by governments and by ourselves. In this context, "suicide" portrays an individual in a selfless act of dedication, an absolute sacrifice to his or her cause and gaining the status of martyrdom. It does not truly describe the criminal act of homicide, the murdering of innocent people. Homicide reduces this to an inferior senseless, cowardice crime thus defeating the status of martyrdom and any glory.

Juval Aviv was the Israeli Agent upon whom the movie 'Munich' was based. He was Golda Meir's bodyguard and she appointed him to track down and bring to justice the Muslim terrorists who took the Israeli athletes hostage and killed them during the Munich Olympic Games. Juval shares some advice: Forget hijacking airplanes, because he says terrorists will never try and hijack a plane again as they know the people onboard will never go down quietly again. Aviv believes our airport security is a joke – that we have been *reactionary* rather than proactive in developing strategies that are truly effective. For example:

1. Our airport technology is outdated. We look for metal, while the new explosives are made of plastic.
2. He talked about how some idiot who tried to light his shoe on fire. Because of that, now everyone has to take off their shoes. A group of idiots tried to bring aboard liquid explosives. Now we can't bring liquids on board. He says he's waiting for some suicidal maniac to pour liquid explosive on his underwear; at which point, security will have us all traveling naked! Every strategy we have is *reactionary*.
3. We only focus on security when people are heading to the gates. Aviv says that if a terrorist attack targets airports in the future, they will target busy times on the front-end of the airport when/where people are checking in. It would be easy for someone to take two suitcases of explosives, walk up to a busy check-in line, ask a person next to them to watch their bags for a minute while they run to the restroom or get a drink, and then detonate the bags BEFORE security even gets involved. In Israel, security checks bags BEFORE people can even ENTER the airport.

Aviv says the next terrorist attack in America is imminent and will involve suicide bombers and non-suicide bombers in places where large groups of people congregate. (ie Disneyland, Las Vegas casinos, big cities (New York, San Francisco, Chicago, etc.) and that it will also include shopping malls, subways in rush hour, train stations, etc., as well as, rural America this time. The attack will be characterized by simultaneous detonations around the country (terrorists like big impact), involving at least 5-8 cities, including rural areas. Aviv says terrorists won't need to use suicide bombers in many of the larger cities, because at places like the MGM Grand in Las Vegas, they can simply valet park a car loaded with explosives and walk away.

Aviv says all of the above is well known in intelligence circles, but that the US Government does not want to 'alarm American citizens' with the facts. Thousands of terrorists are entering the US illegally and many purport to be asylum seekers. The world is quickly going to become 'a different place', and issues like 'global warming' and political correctness will become totally irrelevant. On an encouraging note, he says that Americans don't have to be concerned about being nuked. Aviv says the terrorists who want to destroy America will not use sophisticated weapons. They like to use suicide as a front-line approach. It's cheap, it's easy, it's effective and they have an infinite abundance of young militants more than willing to 'meet their destiny'. He also says the next level of terrorists, which America should be most concerned, will not be coming from abroad. But will be, instead, 'homegrown', having attended and been educated in our own schools and universities right here in the US He says to look for 'students' who frequently travel back and forth to the Middle East. These young terrorists will be most dangerous because they will know our language and will fully understand the habits of Americans; but that Americans won't know/ understand a thing about them. Aviv says that, as a people, Americans are unaware and uneducated about the terrorist threats inevitably to be faced. America still has only a handful of Arabic and Farsi speaking people in its intelligence networks, and Aviv says it is critical that we change that fact SOON.

So, what can we do to protect ourselves? From an intelligence perspective, Aviv says the US needs to stop relying on satellites and technology for intelligence. We need to, instead, follow Israel's, Ireland's and England's hands-on examples of human intelligence, both from an infiltration perspective as well as to pay attention to and trust 'aware' citizens to help. We need to engage and educate ourselves as citizens; however, most western governments continue to treat its citizens, 'like babies'. Our government thinks we 'can't handle the truth' and are concerned that we'll panic if we understand the realities of terrorism. Aviv says this is a deadly mistake.

Aviv recently created/executed a security test for US Congress, by placing an empty briefcase in five well-traveled spots in five major cities. The results? Not one person called 911 or sought a policeman to check it out. In fact, in Chicago, someone tried to steal the briefcase! In comparison, Aviv says that citizens of Israel are so well 'trained' that an unattended bag or package would be reported in seconds by citizen(s) who know to publicly shout, 'Unattended Bag!' The area would be quickly & calmly cleared by the citizens themselves.

Unfortunately, America, Australia and others haven't been 'hurt enough' yet by terrorism for their government to fully understand the need to educate its citizens or for the government to understand that it's their citizens who are, inevitably, the best first-line of defense against terrorism. Aviv was also concerned about the high number of children in America who were in preschool and kindergarten after 9/11, who were 'lost' without parents being able to pick them up and about our schools that had no plan in place to best care for the students until parents could get there. (In New York City, this was days, in some cases!). He stresses the importance of having a plan, that's agreed upon within your family, of how to respond in the event of a terrorist emergency. He urges parents to contact their children's schools and demand that the schools too, develop plans of actions, just as they do in Israel. Does your family know what to do if you can't contact one another by phone? Where would you gather in an emergency? He says we should all have a plan that is easy enough for even our youngest children to remember and follow.

Aviv says that the US government has in force a plan, that in the event of another terrorist attack, <u>EVERYONE's</u> ability to use cell phones, blackberries, etc., will immediately be cut-off, as this is the preferred communication source used by terrorists and is often the way that their bombs are detonated. How will you communicate with your loved ones in the event you cannot speak to each other? You need to have a plan. If you understand and believe what you have just read, then you must feel compelled to send this to every concerned parent, guardian, grandparents, uncles, aunts, whomever. Don't stop there. In addition to sharing this via e-mail, contact and discuss this information with whomever it makes sense to. Make contingency plans with those you care about. Better that you have plans in place, and never have to use them, than to have no plans in place, and find you needed them. If you choose not to share this, or not to have a plan in place, and nothing ever occurs – good for you! However, in the event something does happen, and even moreso, if it directly affects your loved ones, this message may haunt you forever. Telling yourself after the fact, "I should have told everyone I know about this" plus, "I just didn't believe it", will not change anything. You were alerted, had the chance to do something and instead of erring on the side of caution, you chose to disregard the warning.

Few of us have heard of another recent trend, "Sharia Lending". Sharia law is the common day law derived from principles of Islamic faith. The majority of Canadian Muslims already use conventional mortgages but there is a growing market for Sharia-compliant mortgages. Under Sharia law, institutions are not permitted to charge interest on loans. However, deals are usually structured so the homeowner leases to own the property, basically paying rent instead of interest. So, those mortgages end up costing owners the equivalent of an extra percentage point or more. Canada's own Muslim congress is concerned that the lenders are taking advantage of disadvantaged people, using religion to prey on a vulnerable market. Sharia banking is widely available in the United Kingdom and is offered by some US banks that see a major financial opportunity. The global market for Islamic finance has grown more than 20% annually since 2001 and is currently the **fastest growing segment of the financial services industry**. Hang on a moment. Wasn't it banking greed that took advantage of bubble loans to prey on poor people who got dream loans to buy houses? Is the money industry allowed to continue playing fast and loose again, this time threatening to prey on Muslim poor? Muslim poor who have cousins abroad with nuclear weapons? But that's not all. We need to consider what additional leverage may be placed on the assets assembled by Sharia loans and whether these funds are being used to finance extremist Islamic causes. Sharia loans are hard to spot now, because they may not occur within the banking system. That makes it doubly difficult to track any outgoing sums.

Arson, Drugs and Alcohol Abuse – A terrorist can be an arsonist whose calculated actions kill humans, fauna, property and the environment. This terrorist can destroy quietly, without too much attention, just like any drug dealer, selling drugs (particularly bad drugs) to our young and vulnerable, that is, destroy them but for profit.

Without national zero tolerance, we are as much a part of the problem as dealers are, as our laws and sentencing do not conform to the severity of the crimes. The growing drug, alcohol and gang violence problems are not confined to the individual's self-affliction. It affects the entire community, and is perhaps of greater and more insidious danger than any damage a hijack terrorist can do. Today drugs are sold by children to children in primary schools, while everyone looks to be politically correct when dealing with children. This is not kindness or caring for kids, it's a disaster just waiting to happen to them and to us. Our communal level of tolerance is our worst enemy and poses the greatest threat to Australians society. If we continue to tolerate and respond to the many forms of terrorism with compassion or consideration for any individuals circumstances over the carnage they intend or have done, we are a part of the problem and simply risk our own destruction.

Although not openly acknowledged in this context, drugs and alcohol abuse are a form of destruction of society, or if you like "terrorism" living and growing in our midst. Not one with guns and bombs but with needles and pills. ICE has been tried by more than 5% of Australians who have then suffered schizophrenia. They not only put themselves at great peril but those who must treat them and those who love and live with them. They place a tremendous drain on our medical resources and destroy family's lives with the abuse and loss of loved ones.

Babies born to addict mothers are diagnosed as addicts, destroying these totally innocent new lives. How much more so will the effects of ICE and other harmful drugs be on future generations. Imagine if at any one time, say, 1% of Australians were given a very bad batch of ICE on one night that killed them all. That would be more than 200,000 people dead without a bullet fired and they would have paid the enemy very handsomely when buying these drugs. If you were just a little sceptical, you could see the importers and dealers as a force working not just to make massive profits but to eradicate or destroy our people in a fashion that achieves the same results as a terrorist in action. These are not soldiers in a war, who if taken as prisoner would be covered under the Geneva Convention for war crimes, these are murderers no different to homicide bombers killing the innocent in times of peace. Yet IF caught, they are not tried as murderers but convicted of having goods in possession and for dealing in drugs, receiving a lesser jail sentence and let out early on parole, while their victims and their families receive a life sentence.

These enemies of our society are cowardice predators, killing innocent people for profit and are able to escape our lame legal system as it is near impossible to tie a death back to any particular dealer.

Arsonists are no different as they go about lighting fires to destroy life and property in their quest to satisfy their desire to obtain a moment's media glory in the knowledge that they are responsible for this disaster.

◆ To alleviate the practice of drug dealing or unwitting attempted murder for profit, the legal system must be acting more appropriately in convicting drug dealers, arsonists and would-be terrorists of any description with the crime of attempted murder, warranting a sentence befitting these heinous crimes. Imposing hard labour and a starting sentence of 20 years, upping the sentence based on the size of the deals and the extent of the human and other damage.

This would certainly put fear of trafficking and death from drugs and by arson into these would be murderers. If it can be established that any person or persons aided directly in these dealings or concealed their knowledge by failing to inform authorities, they should also receive a sentence for aiding in the dealings with hard Labor for the term of their natural life. This is real justice, this is what the parents of children who have died unnecessarily expect and not any less, and this is the only deterrent that means anything.

◆ Again, a **"Life Sentence" should be defined as "for the remaining term of the natural life of the offender" and not less.** The ability to rely on an abusive childhood, or mental disorder, is not an acceptable defence. It is just an excuse used for minimising or excusing a sentence. This is where it is imperative that a responsible parent is able to evaluate potential antisocial behaviour in their children and why it is important for the parent to seek help, not wait and hope that nothing will happen or that it is a stage that will pass. This is where educating everyone as to a National Code of Conduct and ramifications for non compliance can leave no room for excuses.

If a crime is committed because of any mental disorder:

◆ It is obvious that the offender needs to be committed to a mental institution, and not be allowed to live in society. He or she is a threat to others and perhaps himself. We have farmed out mentally ill persons to live at home, visited by nursing staff to supervise medication but there are those who need to be confined to institutions which have all but been closed by cost cutting incompetent governments.

Dr. Gilbert Whitton, addiction specialist with South Sydney Area Health Services, states: *"90% of people use alcohol, 40% use nicotine, 20% cannabis, 10% use other illicit drugs and 3.3% prescribed psychoactive drugs".* On 14 Jan 2009 it was reported, *"The number of arrests for using and possessing ecstasy has skyrocketed in the past two years, with figures from the NSW Bureau of Crime Statistics and Research showing an increase of more than 55%. The report also revealed arrests for cocaine had jumped by almost 40% and that cannabis arrests were up by almost 20% over the same period."* All Australians are paying heavily in so many forms, from the cost of violence, to the cost of medical and hospital requirements, to the cost of the penal and court system, to the loss of lives and the denigration of our overall personal and communal development.

Financial desperation has caused some pensioners go "doctor shopping" – that is, from one doctor to another obtaining subsidised prescriptions, which they on-sell to drug addicts, making a huge profit for the pensioner while facilitating the drug addict, who becomes unemployable. We all know that drug dependency needs a lot of money to feed the habit, which leads to a life of crime and destruction. Good personality traits and the freedom to make good choices and decisions are altered, taking away this freedom with the overwhelming desire to satisfy the destructive cravings. The result is the ultimate destruction of the individual, the family and impacts on the whole community.

◆ Medicare tracking of prescription purchases, particularly those with a healthcare card must be high on the agenda of the Health Ministry with action against perpetrators would certainly reduce this activity and the various costs to society.

Over the past year, doctors have prescribed for children they diagnosed with Attention Deficit Disorder "ADD" 264,000 prescriptions of Ritalin and other mind altering drugs to treat children with this, in many cases, perceived disorder. This is up from 11,000 prescriptions over the previous year. It is now being discovered that once these children grow up and are taken off these prescribed drugs, which have done the job of altering the mind, these young adults feel the need to find other drugs as they just cannot cope with life without drug dependence. So before filling a prescription for "*Mind Altering Drugs*" – which may give short term peace and quiet to pursue "other" interests, think about the long term brain damage and the graduation to hard drugs which could destroy your child's future. Be sure that the Attention Deficient Disorder is not the kids.

The widespread progression and use of hard drugs is up there with the greatest problems our society faces. If one were into conspiracy theories, it could be speculated that this would be the best way our enemies could win a war against our society without firing one single bullet. That is, in providing drugs like ICE, our enemies get rich at the loss of our kids and our future society. The only answer is to keep our kids physically and mentally active and as parents, not to be a mentally or physically absent. It is our choice to be preoccupied with our kids rather than pursue other personal and business interests. After all, it was our choice to have the kids, our responsibility to be accountable for their behaviour and it is our responsibility to ensure they are healthy, mentally and physically! There is no money in the world that can compensate for the loss of a child at any age.

While we all have freedom of choice in how we behave, growing drinking problems, particularly with young adults, is often the result of poor community priorities. Getting very drunk, is a means (or excuse) of escape from the realities of life, from problems in society together with the need to vent frustrations from no work, to no meaningful purpose in life, to lack of self esteem. With no other apparent means of escape, kids go to their drinking holes looking for "a good time" and often end up dead, or killing someone else in a drunken rage or trading their healthy lives for an AA membership. There can be no excuse for antisocial behaviour but government has facilitated business in "profits before people" with extended trading hours until the early hours. They have chosen to be blind to the very expensive adverse costs to the community in providing the opportunity for kids to denigrate their standards, attitudes and to the demise of a generation with the destruction of life and property. It's a great drain on society, to police, hospital resources stretched to the limit and to reiterate, to where Councils now seek to take from State Government their responsibility to:

◆ Cut trading hours back till 12am and hold those responsible financially accountable for all damage and costs associated with their drunken violence, see earlier recommendations regarding appropriate sentencing. This is the real deterrent particularly for parents of dependant young persons.

Where 60% of homicides are due to intoxication, it is no longer the freedom of the individual that must have priority but the safety of our society and intoxication must to be treated as if it will lead to a potential homicide.

It is only with strictness that kindness can replace the problems we have allowed to transgress into society. This is not the denial of freedom, or rights but the freedom of the entire society to live in peace, see section on Attitudes and Priorities Create our Environment.

National Healthcare –
Doctors; Hospitals; Medication; Optical and Dental

THE MENTAL AND physical health of our society is as important as water – not an issue to be squabbled over in the division of powers, not a privileged for our people but the right of all Australians to have the best health support available. In spite of a booming economy over the past decade, our health system is in crisis as it is mismanaged or dictated to by non-medically skilled politicians who are further encumbered by their party's alternative agendas, no different to every other portfolio of national relevance. **In early 2010 we endured a debate between the then PM Kevin Rudd and the Opposition Leader Tony Abbott over the future of the Health System, both men having been failed Health Ministers, yet both wanting to determine the future direction of the entire country's health system and relying on our memories being short.** Of course the States will not readily give up anything, even though the national proposal is based on the States getting into a mess with health. Again, a national approach is the best option but not under the current political party system. Adopting Rudd's plan will only see his government gain more control for more stuff ups, more losses, more incompetence, more burocracy. Rudd threatened a referendum to take over national control. Again, this would be great but not under the current party system, while currently we have to either live with the States continued incompetence or we go with the Federal incompetence, you're judging here? There are arguments that *"you don't have to be educated in any specific portfolio to do a good job of it, you just need good advisors"* but the current system does not demand that good advisors proposals and advice be accepted and actioned and in most cases it is not, especially if the party has other objectives.

Until 2008, we could not fill the abundance of vacant positions for nurses and now nurses are being let go and hospital beds are closing down while the system's experts are cry out for more beds, more nurses and doctors and better facilities. This is no different to the education system and all other systems. There cannot be true empathy unless you walk in the shoes of experts.

Despite more than one third of all Australians living in NSW in its state of financial devastation, the NSW government in August 2009 owed overdue hospital creditors more than A$140 million and I dare say with current creditors, placing our hospital system in dire straits. Resources are stretched to the limit in rural areas with hospitals unable to pay basic costs of food provisions, morphine and basic medical requirements for patients, let alone the unpaid wages of doctors and hospital staff. This is certainly not restricted to NSW it is seriously endured in the Queensland health system, with their best offer being one free cup of coffee and advice to seek help from the Salvos, rather than give them their due wages to pay their living expenses and stop the mortgagee taking possession of their homes. Again, for any business this is blatantly "trading while insolvent" a criminal offence under the Corporations Act, if not for the paramount concern of health care for our people.

Due to the negligent decay of rural infrastructures and rural business, people have moved to city areas and doctors don't want to move to these rural areas. Interns are compelled to complete a 6 month internship in a rural area to be able to obtain their qualifications, as a means of getting medical help to rural areas. Waiting lists for surgery run for more than a year and to cover up this disgrace some bright spark thought of a great ploy! Do not allow waiting lists to exceed 1 year, so the real figures are concealed. While patents sit in ambulances waiting to see which hospital has a bed for them, women who are ignored in emergency rooms deliver babies in toilets. Seriously ill patients are sent home and the list of medical atrocities grows, while the grievances of skilled hospital administrators, doctors and nurses, their plans and remedies, fall on the unskilled deaf ears of government ministries. Politicians over the years have created this situation and add to the confusion, in a system they arrogantly cannot rectify or give it over to those who can.

To save Labors State and Federal government faces and win votes, Rudd proposed to take over the national health system. Keneally and others appeared to drive a hard bargain to retain the GST, that is, to get extra money in bailing them out, but what a relief it will be to both the NSW State government to give-over the liability it created in the hospital system and for the Labor government in harnessing more power for the UN World Heath Organisation. A national hospital system which has no endorsement or support from the medical profession while almost 70% of Australians (surveyed) are supportive of National Health but what's the plan? This may very well be yet **another excellent strategic public relations scheme by the Labor cohorts.** Alternatively, we are stuck with the redundant, cash strapped, mismanagement of State governments, particularly the crisis in the Health system. What choice do Australians have? This is my argument for Independents without party objectives in making up a National House of Representatives, as well as Resources Ministries made up of experts in their respective fields, common sense?

Rudd seemingly became desperate, bribing the State Premiers with billions of dollars of borrowed money, showing how desperate he had become to be seen to be 'doing something' so desperately needed. He knew his political career was over if he didn't push this Bill through. He had been exposed for being an all-talk, no action Prime Minister. In the two years of his tenure as Prime Minister, Rudd had become a Hollow Man who hadn't achieved anything worthwhile for Australia, rather to our detriment. Kevin Rudd's report card shows everything that he has done has been intangible or a shocking waste of money that has plunged Australia into unprecedented debt. The amount of money Rudd sought to throw at the States is breathtaking especially as there are no details. Amounts which sound like they've been plucked from thin air, all the while the taxpayer funded Henry Tax Review was kept a secret from the public, to be used at the most beneficial time in providing Rudd with just the right propaganda to secure votes. We are right to be very wary of unskilled government's health schemes because the devil is in the detail – and details are very sparse to say the least.

It is interesting to note that there has been no mention in the Labor proposed health plan to include issues such as optical, dental and mental health care, albeit by the "Greens".

There are 650,000 Australians waiting up to three years for dental treatment. There are thousands of people in real pain and suffering who feel helpless and have nowhere to turn. Dentistry is subsidised by health insurers but only to the health insurer's nominated portion of the total account. This is the amount health insurers allow to be claimed to enable them to still make a profit. How many Australians can afford health insurance and then pay "the gap" left after the health insurers kick in a small portion? Premiums are set to rise but there is no guarantee of more benefits paid. An interesting comparison – if you smashed up your car, would your insurer limit your claim to exclude say, the boot or one rear door?

Without health insurance there is very limited dental attention available to the community as public Dental Hospitals are overrun and booked out for years and there are concerns as to inferior treatment in these under resourced facilities. There have been suggestions of imposing a new levy on income earners (an extra tax) which has been deemed nonsense by Neil Hewson of the Dental Association. That is, if income earners have a higher tax imposed on them, then why wouldn't they also be entitled to full dental cover, no different to any non-income earner who they are subsidising in this extra tax? With the amended to governments and with the GST turned into an e-tax, (applicable to the end user only), I defy anyone to prove that there would be a need for more money to provide for the following proposals:

◆ Dental: Medicare would pay for all annual checkups and preventative treatment for all Australians. Then allow for a set annual amount for extractions, fillings and dentures, a realistic amount to be determined by the respective National Health Portfolio Ministry with participating dentists advised of the annual limits.

One of our greatest examples of government mismanagement was in the establishment of the Medicare claim system. Thousands of Australians sat and waited every day to have a claim processed at Medicare and at other health insurers. Tens of thousands of unproductive work hours lost waiting to process claims and get money back. This together with the thousands of staff in hundreds of offices with all of the overhead costs of office rent, computers, phones and all other overheads needed to maintain these offices. Costs all forming part of the cost of Medicare when bulk billing by hospitals and doctors would provide hundreds of millions of dollars to the forefront in rectifying the hospitals crisis and

◆ Redeploy office staff into the medical system, filling the urgent need for nursing aids, thus enabling nurses to focus on their specific job without the stress currently endured. This and inadequate resources has caused many to leave the profession. Administrative staff able to be retrained into productive "*blue collar*" hospital staff. Sufficient nurse's aids would be able to work towards combating diseases most prevalent in hospitals, such as Golden Staph. That is, in retraining we have reduced the overheads of administering the system, facilitated the urgent "blue collar" need in our hospitals, reduced hospital damages claims (with over 4,000 negligence claims per year), reduced the lost time and frustration of Australians, with no loss of employment and produced a financial remedy for an ailing hospital system.

Federal government (June 2009) introduced billing of Medicare by doctors and hospitals to reduce the above costs but will these employees be retrenched or retrained to where they are needed? Will these expensive overheads cease in the closing of excessive offices or be retained as a continued drain on our community purse? Will these savings be vested back into the health system or diverted to other government nominated areas such as new government offices, politicians pay increases and travel scams?

The Liberal Government tried to shove off the pension with compulsory superannuation and encouraged Australians to take up health care cover, providing a 30% subsidy. The Labor government would snitch that back as a cost cutting method (recouping stimulus payments in giving with one hand and taking it and more back with the other). Millions of dollars were spent by Liberal in researching and implementing the medical insurance rebates system, then to be foisted with a change in government. In spite of pre-election promises to fix the problem, nothing has transpired over 2 years from Mr Fix-it (Queensland Health) and he cannot achieve success during his leadership, while Mr Abbott (having been the Minister for Health and producing nothing) is partially right in local management administration, but better this be under the auspice of an organisation such as the **"Australian Medical Association"** as the **"Australian Health Resources Ministry".**

Alleviating Medicare fraud with hundreds of millions of dollars lost every year with the illegal use of Medicare cards by visitors to our country. With the instigation of an Australian Security Card and a thumb print required rather than a signature the Medicare system would not be as susceptible to these fraudulent claims. Also, deregistering a doctor for aiding in any medical fraud would severely reduce any attempts at fraud, as the risk to the doctor would be too high. There are many other cost cutting, common sense reductions to be made, while increasing health services:

1. Treat people at home where possible using ambulance services or enhanced district nursing services. Hospital emergency departments are inundated with people having to wait for more than five hours for attention. It has been suggested that the emergency department should be put on wheels ie a doctor in a small van be fully equipped and sent out as a home doctor service as it used to be provided. This is a great idea and not unlike community based "First Medical Responders" which are voluntary community services albeit trained by the State ambulance service. The fact is, ambulances are already fully equipped and have an infrastructure that could accommodate such a service with minimal improvements. However, district nurses are an alternative and if they were co-located with ambulance or local medical facilities (GPs, pathology services or super clinic complexes), their travel times would be shorter and more responsive.

2. To reiterate: Charge all of the cost of medical attention to those who incite drug and alcohol related violence or the parents of delinquent minor children. If these accounts are not paid, they are to be treated as unpaid creditors with community service to the value of the account. This will encourage individuals to sort out these problems and not encumber society.

3. Under the National Planning & Infrastructure Ministry, consolidate the resources of rural hospitals with some becoming Super Clinics with medical, dental and optical (part time if required) centres based on the demographic requirements needed today with the ability to extend the services as an area grows (subject to National Planning) but to include:

♦ An ambulance able to drive up to say 150K or 1½ hrs from the centre for emergency purposes.
♦ A dentist who visits the centre with pre-arranged weekly appointments for one or two days per week.
♦ Same as dentist, for optometrist.
♦ The Medical Centre to be equipped with x-ray and diagnostic equipment.
♦ Ability to perform day surgery and minor surgery without referral to hospitals.
♦ Many surgical procedures can be performed in day surgery conditions and where the surgery becomes an overnight ward, to be attended by a nurse for short hospital stays by a small number of patients as required.

The best example of this type of operation that I have known is the Alpine Medical Centre in Jindabyne. Got a suspect melanoma, administer a local injection, cut it out, stitch it up – all within half an hour, send it off to pathology to see what it WAS rather than what it *is* and then determine what to do. Do it, sort it out and charge it once to Medicare (credit given to a experienced doctor for his education decision). Compare this with seeing the doctor and getting a referral to a specialist, charging Medicare; attending the specialist and charging Medicare again as appropriate or the health insurer for a small portion back. Bear the balance or if no insurance wears the whole cost; book the hospital and undergo the expense of surgery and charge Medicare and the health insurer and bear "the gap" ie three charges to Medicare versus one.

Most of our social and political problems have been created by an over indulgence in bureaucrats and burocractical procedures, rather than pursing effective solutions by those skilled in every portfolio. Imagine a system where you had to get a doctors prescription for Codeine or Aspro, it would ruin Medicare and place the demand on doctors and patients to the point of chaos.

One third of Australian kids need glasses and while we donate used frames from old glasses to third world countries, these frames only need cleaning and new suitable lenses installed for our kids or any person needing glasses. A simple cost effective method of reusing frames under Medicare, would fix this problem at a fraction of the cost. Poor eyesight is a problem which leads to the inability of children to learn and concentrate and then the frustration associated with this is demonstrated in bad behaviour.

4.   The cost of a pair of glasses for a person would be based on eye testing which is currently covered by Medicare, the cost of the lenses including fitting them into the reused frames, no more than $100 per recipient each year.

One of the biggest businesses on this planet today is the pharmaceutical industry which produces medications at a fraction of the prices charged. Government provides subsidies for our pharmaceutical needs and to pensioners but for many this isn't enough and life saving drugs can cost the earth – or you just die. What is astounding is that we pay 15 times more than the British for many pharmaceutical drugs and yet our government doesn't question the suppliers . . . . hmmmm?

5.   Government needs to be more proactive in seeking means of reducing the cost of pharmaceutical products to its citizens, ensuring there is a set maximum price for all prescribed drugs and ensuring drugs are not over-prescribed.
6.   Pharmacists are usually better informed about some prescribed medications than many doctors. In an effort to reduce the demand on doctors and Medicare costs, pharmacists should dispense prescriptions for Codeine, common antibiotics, pain relief and other common ailments which account for many unnecessary visits to the doctor and costs to Medicare. But there needs to be a prohibition on drug companies providing any form of incentives to doctors and pharmacists for prescribing their products.

Prevention has always been better and cheaper than cures. For every one of the 55,000 odd heart-attacks each year, it costs the taxpayer A$281,000 Taxpayers also foot the massive bill for mammograms and government seeks to increase the age for this imperative detection in an attempt to reduce the cost. Colonoscopies, x-rays and other tests are paid for by taxpayers Medicare and it makes for common sense to have a consolidated early detection of:

7. MRI scans every 10 years for the over 20's and every 5 years for the over 40's paid by Medicare.

The cost of this early detection consolidated scan would see savings in the current numerous x-rays and tests, reduced medical and hospital costs. It would prevent many deaths and suffering from diseases now only found when it's too late.

Contributions to health care insurers have not provided patients with full hospital, full medical, full dental, full optical or full pharmaceutical cover. Payments or rather subsidies of these vital services are determined at the discretion of the insurer to ensure that they can provide a profit after all of their overheads. Medical insurers such as MBF, HCF, NIB and all others are in the business of making a profit for their company. Millions of dollars each year are expended by health insurers on their overheads and millions of dollars are spent on advertising to attract membership premiums and subsequently increasing their profit. Sure, they offer incentives and benefits like A$150pa for acupuncture, massage, running shoes, aromatherapy, and so on but how many people want acupuncture or even claim those benefits? Services not wanted and not taken up are of no benefit or saving whatsoever to the member when he has to meet the "gap" in the payment to his dentist. Better these billions of dollars in overheads and profits currently paid to health insurers are vested in Medicare, making Medicare a first-class health care system for all Australians.

The average medical insurance premium for a family is more than A$2,000pa with many not making any claim in a given year. Rudd approved a 6% increase to annual premiums which is more than 5 times CPI and cannot be justified. Then, unless you pay an extra premium not to have an excess applicable to your hospital stay, you could be up for a large sum of money before you see any benefit whatsoever. It is far better that we, as a nation, eliminate medical insurance premiums (enriching private business when our health system needs funding for improvements) by the taxpayer and

◆ **Abandon Health Insurances and introduce a full-on, first class comprehensive Public Health care system available to all Australians through Medicare**. Dispense with health insurance premiums which only make for profits to the insurers, and only if needed, replace the health insurance premium with say a 1% increase to the e-tax.

All claims would be by the hospital or the doctor via bulk billing, consider the savings: Closed Medicare offices with all practitioners and hospitals directly claiming on-line, that is a greatly reduced cost in Medicare overheads. Medicare staff retrained in our hospital system, to remedy understaffed hospitals and of course the reduction in Medicare fraud. We would be replacing the cumbersome infrastructure costs of Medicare's administration and the premiums to health insurers, directed directly to the front line. The saving of billions of tax dollars would be there to meet our national health care needs, including pharmaceutical and all optical and costs, to where real **services can be provided**.

Health Insurance should be a personal choice. The only time private health insurance may be required is if people wish to have private hospital facilities or a dearer pair of glasses or cosmetic or other elective surgery. These are luxury items, not a "need" and if wanted, you pay for it, but health, education and security are government functions to provide.

◆ The appointment of skilled members of a new National Health Resources Ministry would work in conjunction with the National Planning and Infrastructure department and in consultation with local governments and others. They would determine the national demographic health requirements, be it for full hospital facilities or Medical Centres who provide home care services. The Health Ministry would comprise of experts in each of the health portfolio's sub-portfolios of pharmaceutical; dental; optical; medical; ambulance services; flying doctor service etc. It would determine what is required in improving existing facilities, reduce or increase facilities in line with the per capita ratio of demographic areas and in conjunction with other Resources Ministries with consideration for planned new industry and housing.

Like all National Resources Ministries, determine urgent short term, medium and long term objectives supported with accurate expenditure. There is no doubt that the National (ATO) Treasury would need to provide a very serious injection of funds into hospitals to rectify decades of mismanagement. With streamlining of system in skilled hands; national scales of economy taken into consideration and with the above savings, any initial injection of funds would be remedied while ensuring we have the best health system in the world. Then we would be much better placed to assist those in countries needing our help as well.

There would be no more changing from one unskilled politician to another who is governed by his party's agenda and this massive burst of expenditure to the frontline would create new jobs from retrain redundant office workers who would otherwise be seeking unemployment benefits. This is true nationally focused stimulus.

As a civilised society we have a moral and financial responsibility to care for each other and especially our aged, our physically and mentally handicapped and with the highest level of dignity and respect they rightfully deserve.

Currently there are insufficient and inadequate facilities for all of the various forms of mental and physical disabilities. Often young, disabled persons are placed into nursing homes with the aged. This would have to be cruel to both. The elderly are not mentally or physical disabled and the disabled need specific care requirements.

The elderly have given to society over their lives. They have worked, paid taxes, produced and educated the current generations, made innovative decisions and many having fought for Australia. There would not be a decent person who does not believe that they are entitled to be cared for in the best possible way. If family members of aged or disabled persons are unable to provide in-home care for their relatives needs, government homes and institutions must be fully funded by government. Again, the Health Resources Ministry would work with the NP & I in determining local demographic requirements for Local government's administration.

There is no sound reason as to why Australians do not have the best medical and care resources nationally but for the fact that currently this portfolio is handled by three levels of unskilled persons in these very skilled required area. With more than 50% of the income currently paid to these levels of burocracy almost extinguished and those funds properly directed, cost is not a factor.

National Education

"Education is the seeking of human growth and potential."

OUR KIDS ARE our future and we all bear the responsibility to give them the best education in equipping them to succeed in every facet of their lives. A child starts to learn from the time he or she is born and by the age of three the child has learnt 80% of all of his or her physical skills of walking, communicating, toilet training etc. but Australia ranks 27th of 42 countries in relation to early childhood development. Contributing factors to this low standard include, whether the child receives fresh food or processed foods (often with excessive salt, sugar and chemical additives), whether the child has been affected in its development by parental drug or alcohol, whether the child comes from a safe functional family and whether the mother is full time with the child, or alternatively who she leaves the child in the care of, to nurture. So, when should school or pre-school start? General consensus is three years of age as this is an age when the child's inquisitive mind is at its most open to new ideas of behaviour, concepts of how to learn and learning.

Teaching our children is the most privileged of occupations. There is no higher worthy goal in life than to impart wisdom and learning through nurturing each other, especially children, and nothing more precious than imparting knowledge to young influential minds. It is this influence that shapes lives and sets them on the path of self sufficiency – or adversely, with complacency or abuse, it can destroy lives. It can give both the teacher and the student the opportunity to learn and enjoy exchanges with each other. One where teachers are an extension of the parents, able to provide a positive experience to their students, a second tier of support, a trusted person where a child ought to be able to turn in times of confusion or problems. Where a child learns and enjoys trust and confidence in others. All research has proven that a child learns more in a warm, positive, nurturing, fun environment, than in a cold, strictly disciplined place. Lack of co operations from kids (who know their rights out weight their teachers) can cause teachers to become only interested in pursuing their monetary need for "the job". This can lead to teachers holding "contempt for their "brat students" and this negative attitude will detrimentally shape personal development and attitudes and the future of our society.

Society has bred Civil Libertarians who are aided by overzealous political legislators in seeking to micromanage yet another facet of government. The word "Libertarian" says it all – *"one who maintains the doctrine (teaching a particular system or beliefs) of the freedom of the will, one who advocates liberty with regard to thought and conduct".* These libertarians are persons whose own will is to enforce their particular beliefs on our young developing minds. Children, not yet at an age able to make valuable life altering decisions for themselves are taught "their rights" with many becoming rebellious in the pursuit of selfish beliefs. Parents who feed, educate, love and provide all of life's sustenance are prevented from necessary reprimand (a major part of parenting) are often then frowned on for their juvenile delinquents poor behaviour and the damage some cause, as many kids have not been taught how to behave and conform to conducive conduct. Teaching kids their rights before the rights of others only leads to selfish acts of eg drunken violence and the ultimate destruction of their own lives and that of their loved ones.

Civil Libertarians are not held responsible for having conveyed very confusing messages of defiance and lack of accountability for the tender years of children, who go on to suffer because they lack the kindness of consistency, routine and discipline children need and enjoy in the security this provides. They are also not held accountable for the negative attitudes and damage this has yielded, to kids, their family and their teachers. Attitudes are contagious, and the wrong attitude (including, disrespect and self interest, above all else) is dangerous to individuals and to society.

With minimal means of reprimand available to teachers and parents as a result of this "political correctness", not all children prosper in this environment. The rights of responsible adults rank behind the rights of children, allowing the problems in society to escalate and this can lead to complacency by some teachers towards kids. With the wrong messages, often children become uncontrollable bullies, with bullying one of the greatest problems suffered by teachers, let alone their victims. Sadly, bullying can beget bullying. The bullied become the bully be it from behaviour seen or suffered at home or if a child has had minimal parental attention. Often bullying is the result of sufferance from a lack of self esteem, often demonstrated in attention seeking to gain control or power in the playground. It is this very same vein of contempt and unreasonable rights of ill-informed children that creates disrespect for authority, vandalism, anti-social behaviour, crime and rebelliousness. That, in turn often leads to valuable members of the police force abandoning their jobs for lack of job satisfaction or the ability to perform their job and to enable them to maintain their own health and sanity. Often inadequate parenting and the inability to reprimand can result in sufferance by the whole family and our entire society, as *"Whatever we do, we do to ourselves"* individually and collectively. **Common sense and common decency would dictate that teaching kids "Ethics, Morals and Virtues" will pay hansom dividends eg "Respect for others" would see bullying as a problem of the past! Virtues such as helping others would see crime reduce and morals could see less broken families, a good start?**

Methods of liberal discipline in school generally require several things at the same time. These are skilled teachers who are enthusiastic and engaging. It requires students to be intelligently and emotionally engaged with their education. It requires methods of removing unruly children from classroom groups but not beyond supervision and activity. If any of these things are not available in constant supply, there is a risk that some children will be alienated from learning and their experiences may become progressively negative. However, the most obvious statement is that not all children cope with a free liberal education environment. Some need stronger direction and close supervision, but this isn't achievable in a one-size-fits-all approach to children and their rights. Education seems to work on the principle that it is better that there are education casualties, and bullies and their victims, than ensuring the education suits the child. Discipline is today a very dirty word, mostly because people confuse it with punishment.

It is only through the closeness and friendship of a teacher with a child that a teacher is able to detect a dysfunctional family and can suggest family assistance in overcoming these problems. This often overturns the bullying problems and subsequent anti-social problems in society but it can only be achieved with mature clarity.

Just as not everyone is cut out to be a police officer, a doctor or plumber, neither are many of those teaching our kids, cut out to be teachers. Teaching is often a final option as a career path, not a first choice. Aptitude testing must be conducted throughout school years as the child develops with an interview to determine a child's interests, skills and capacity. This is done in many schools but how much input helps the child to get to the next stage of their education or into a career? If a child's interests are towards a trade, they should be encouraged and assisted to get into that trade sooner rather than later, but no child should be allowed to leave school without having a plan in place to commence immediately. A teacher must have the ability to be strict while kind and have the aptitude for teaching before being allowed to become a teacher and, through incentives, be rewarded for their good results with kids.

The Bush administration's education reform act stated that *"No Child is Left Behind"*. It set expectations, but fell short on funding, earning scorn from teachers and parents alike. Now the Obama administration seeks to set the US education system on a strong path. Arne Duncan, the new Secretary of Education in the US government, who sorted out and reformed the Chicago's troubled school system, is now poised to oversee the largest US Federal investment in education since the GI Bill with about $100 billion available to invest in, as he says, "what works." He wants better teaching for more students – not just those living in affluent suburbs – ensuring more students have the preparation they need to enter and succeed in college. Here's the plan: Ensure access to good teaching; provide better quality teachers; reward talented teachers; move out bad teachers; and pay teachers more to take on tough assignments. Central to knowing "what works" is collecting good information, and resistance to this is inevitable. Duncan wants to instigate comprehensive data systems that track student performance from kindergarten through high school, which tracks student performance back to teachers and ultimately to schools of education.

The most fundamental ability for a teacher to be able to teach is his or her ability to nurture, to inspire the student and to be able to open the student's mind. This can only be done if the student respects the teacher. Then the teacher is able to inspire the student to "want to learn". There is a story of a teacher who always opened his lessons with a joke and when everyone was laughing he knew they were happy; he had come close to them and that their minds were in an open and positive State for him to be able to teach effectively.

There is no doubt that for effective consistency, we need a National Educational approach and curriculum, under the same guise as all proposed National Portfolio Ministries and to be incorporated into this approach, the following is proposed:

◆ Appointment of teachers aids, say one aid to two or three teachers for all preparation work and to assist with playground rosters etc. Also, in extending school hours to incorporate extracurricular activities and homework. The aids would be sourced from redundant State government positions and this would enable teachers to spend more quality teaching time with students, rather than in preparation etc. and students are able to spend quality time with family, rather than on homework.

Before and after school care is a very important issue to working parents. This cost reduces the family income, even after taxpayer subsidies and reduces the ability and incentive to work. Alternatively, many kids are left to their own non-constructive devices until parents come home. There are also issues of homework and extracurricular activities which can be incorporated into the school day that would add to the quality of life for our children.

How many millions of dollars were wasted on advertising of kids on lounge chairs being thrown into a swimming pool, when that money ought to have been invested into after school sports and other developmental activities? It's no secret that in keeping kids fit and healthy both physically and mentally, they get filled with confidence and there is no room for self doubt or negative attitudes or attributes. Building healthy competitive spirits and strengthening relationships between kids and teachers in its self brings about a level of respect and co operation in the classroom.

◆ Redefining pre-school and school hours from 8.30am till 5.00pm would ensure time is spent on physical activities; learning Australian civil issues of History, Geography, Code of Conduct and Politics, as well as Social Skills (yes, manners). This would incorporate home work, thus ensuring that when kids are at home with their parents, they are able to spend quality time together in helping get the dinner ready and having dinner together and talking.

It would not be unreasonable that teachers work from 8.30 till 5.00pm with one hour for lunch and morning tea and still enjoy a 37.5 hr week with 3 terms allowing 2 weeks for May and Sept holidays and 6 weeks at end of year. That is, 10 weeks of holidays compared to all other industry standards of just 4 and ensuring kids learning routines are not disrupted every 8 or 9 weeks.

Not one of us is born with genetically ingrained morals, manners and virtues. The best we can expect is to be born with a kind nature, but all skills and behaviour must be taught, if they are to be upheld and in providing a better quality of life for all of us. If we want our young girls to be treated with respect, able to elevate their own standards in making their own choices and not feel pressured to succumb to sex or bear guilt in deciding to abstain, then it is our responsibility to give our girls the opportunity to aspire to wonderful examples of woman-hood like our own great role model Princess Mary or the late Princess Diana.

Our girls and boys need to be given every opportunity, including the opportunity to be taught from a very young age: **how to learn,** this is a skill, not to be assumed that all people know how to learn. Learn about the benefits of humility, modestly, dignity and discipline. How to develop and refine their character and improve their standard of living and thus their quality of life, not needing drugs and alcohol to escape their reality. Unfortunately many kids in our communities are denied these lessons. This is not old fashioned – it's the basis of a Code of Conduct for a safe and peaceful society, where kids are able to reap the rewards from how they are treated, with respect and particularly girls. Girls who grow up in this sort of environment are less likely to binge drink or act in a way that some would consider them to be *"fly-blown meat . . . . asking for it!"*

Every child is a source of pride but more than ever, kids need an education in how boozing-up or bashing each other is not the Australian way, rather they learn how to resolve conflict without their fists in being real men and women. We can teach a child that drugs and alcohol are dangerous but to teach them how and why they deserve better in their lives and how this can be achieved, this is the objective. As compulsory a subject as English and more so than trigonometry for many, the following social skills need to be introduced into early childhood development to have any impression on our kids in breaking bad habits of the past few generations and in developing long term healthy skills in providing every opportunity to excel:

1. **Etiquette** – which would include everything from the correct use of cutlery for various courses right through to good manners e.g. opening the door for a lady especially mum or someone elderly. Etiquette and good manners are the essence of good behaviour and sets a national standard rather than be confronted with a situation where they wish they knew how to behave.

2. **Elocution** – Aussie slang is great but listen to our kids, do they know how to speak correctly? There are many benefits to speaking well, in using the English

language proficiently and in developing a strong vocabulary and there is plenty of room in, say, extended school days activities for at least one hour a week of etiquette and elocution lessons. To be taught the art of good conversation and debating. There is no reason why elocution and etiquette are not taught from pre-school in developing good life long habits. In fact from the survey at our website, there has not been one person who does not agree with this.

I must pass on one small tip for improving kid's vocabularies without it seeming like a chore: I have my daughter learn a new word from the dictionary (almost) every morning while she's getting dressed for school. She then comes to me, says the word, spells it and tells me what it means. It takes two minutes but that's more than 200 new words every year. It is also a small but real demonstration that I want a role in making a difference in her education. The expansion into of "Spelling Bees" into the school system, making it extremely competitive would certainly pick up kids' vocabulary and communication skills and replace the generic all encompassing "f**k" in its forms of noun, verbs, adjectives etc in being the excuse word for the lack of a good vocabulary.

3. **Deportment and Dress Sense** – *"Clothes Make the Man"* and of course this applies more so to women. First impressions count and once the initial impression is made, it's hard to change the mindset of others. We are always on our best behaviour and dress well for a job interview or a bank loan – that's called respect for others and us. Unfortunately this is something often lacking in daily lives.

We have gone from the smart and elegant dress sense prior the 1950s to having far too much emphasis placed on sex appeal, looking "sexy". Fact is, elegant is sexier than too much tit'n bum, we've all got them, but flaunting them only demonstrates that's all you've got! How many teenage and prepubescent girls have you seen lately, dressed like whores? Kids need to be taught the benefits of self preservation and of their personal appearance out weighing looking sexy, and why defacing the body with tattoos is so dumb.

We don't have to go back to Victorian times, but how we act and how we dress is how we are perceived and treated – that will never change. Self esteem is a reflection of self dignity, good dress sense and elocution. A smart vocabulary warrants the respect of others or adversely, look and act like a "bush pig" and you'll be treated like one. Much of this is dependent on how mum and dad conduct themselves. Ear-rings have been around for thousands of years but earrings in the eye brow or through the nose or in the stomach or on the tongue, sorry this is not fashion – it's self mutilation. It's a poor excuse for attention seeking and just plain ugly. It's like saying "Look – I'm an individual, like thousands of others mindlessly following this unhealthy trend."

◆ As a National Education initiative, perhaps the renowned June Daly-Watkins or Pat Woodley could be commissioned to design and implement a course in Etiquette, Elocution, Deportment and Dress Sense. This would have far more reaching results, together with an "Active Kids" programme in overcoming Obesity and mental disorders, increasingly suffered by many kids today.

Kids should not be left to their own devices with technology, hanging out around the streets, causing millions in the removal of graffiti, or vegging-out in front of the TV, or just plain getting into all sorts of trouble. No amount of TV advertising of lounge chairs throwing kids into the pool will work, only a regulated format by the respective parents, together with initiatives by government organisations. Admit it or not, kids may rebel but they do like a routine that gives them a sense of security and life lessons on how to manage their time in maximizing every opportunity they wish to pursue.

Remember the Scout movement's motto *"Be Prepared"* – something generally our kids today, are not. Not prepared with survival skills; not prepared with social skills and not prepared to accept authority~ good old fashioned back to basics skills and life lessons in building and developing young minds to become confident individuals. We have allowed kids to be lazy, self absorbed and self indulgent, spending too much time in "draining the brain" in front of TV or the computer, eating heaps of sugar and salt products. Especially during school holidays when, say, summer camps for 2 or 3 weeks in January till school resumes could provided co-ordinated programs similar to those in America and again, overcome obesity and mental shortcomings.

Responsible parenting requires kids being taught (initially at home) how to behave, allowing teachers to give their undivided attention to educating them. Unfortunately, teachers have had to bear the burden of some parent's failure to teach their kids basic behavioural skills or for having taught them bad behaviour. Given the current out-of-hand circumstances and the damage not just to children but to society, it is the government through the proposed National Education Resources Ministry's responsibility to take this initiative to rectify with strict focus on real education and no peripherals such as sex.

Until the late 1950s the age of consent was 21 and most of society's problems of dysfunctional families, single teenage mothers rarely existed. From the early 1960s sex, promiscuity and violence have been flaunted to death on TV and our social standards have dropped so low that we are trying to convince ourselves that this is acceptable behaviour or our democratic freedom. Ms Bishop, as the then Federal Minister for Education said *"It should be a matter for school communities to decide on the nature and extent of sex education offered in their school"*. Imagine the country's standards if every school community varied the levels of acceptable sex education, we'd go from no sex education to, an anything goes standard and this great advice from an unskilled education, Federal Minister!

Labor MP Tanya Plibersek stated, *"50% of all year 12 students have had sex and about 25% of year 10 students".* She went on to say that *"the Federal budget includes A$500,000 for developing educational resources for students on the financial issues of teen parenting and the government was not targeting the area that required most attention".* Yet on the ABCs Q & A Show on Mon Feb 22, 2010 when asked about her discussions with her child about sex she stated, *"that's private between me and my child"* as it ought to be in functional homes, not a school subject. Areas not included, but more appropriate include understanding how not to get into these situations, respecting ourselves and expecting respect for our choice not to participate in sex, and the benefits of sexual abstinence and what consensual sex really means. As a society we have gone from frowning on unwed teen pregnancies to financing and rewarding single children having children. A child parent, with no parenting skills and a child, two kids who then grow up together with no mature guidance of a functional family, one an ill equipped parent who eventually sees no light at the end of the tunnel, resorting to alcohol and addictive drugs, to abusive behaviour, and a child who faces a disastrous future. Is it any wonder education levels are dropping, when government helps kids to focus on sex, drugs and rock 'n roll.

Responsible sex education is best handled by responsible parents or in segregated community sessions and many responsible parents do not want the government to intervene but in public schools there is no option offered. If this is a concern to you, take the initiative and petition your State and Federal government's education departments starting with your children's school – that other than in the course of reproduction in biology classes and incorporated into moral and social behaviour education, the benefits of abstaining from sex and drug be limited to the ill effects, with a focus as to the severe emotional, physiological and physical ramifications.

Focused education should be teaching kids budgeting skills in avoiding a life of misery from financially over exposing themselves and in developing their positive physical and mental skills. Advise the school that you will discuss and provide sex and drug education with your children in the privacy of your own home and you will explain the benefits of reframing, so that the focus of schools is to be on education and healthy activities. There are plenty of good books to assist you in discussing these delicate subjects and these discussions should help to broaden the bond between you with your kids, so that they feel they can discuss anything and everything with you.

Teaching 7 year olds about sex in schools and especially in a mixed group, is both ridiculous and entices promiscuity. Better for kids to be taught that sex is the culmination of a loving permanent relationship, not the foundation of a relationship because if it is, then there is no real loving relationship at all. Also, that the ability to abstain until the appropriate commitment, is the truest test of love which goes beyond sex to a long and meaningful marriage. That sex is a means of fulfilling love and not the objective.

Kids need to be kept very busy and taught relevant topics and interests that will enhance their lives. Love is the objective kids are really looking for and perhaps it is the replacement for attention and affection they can't get anywhere else and thus sex gets confused with love. Better the opportunities to teach our children are directed to areas of real importance in their lives. Many people can all look back on early school years and ask *"... why wasn't I taught about the pitfall of business; personal and small business financial planning and how to avoid mistakes when I was at school ...."* and *"... what does the Constitution offer me ...."* and *"... how does the government operate, where do I go for help ...."* As a society, we have been placing too much emphasis on sex and drug education, *"forbidden fruit"* which will always only seem sweeter. Focusing on forbidden fruit and stimulating our kids in this direction, diverts their interest from emphasis on the curriculum, on subjects and development of personal self esteem, confidence and helping them seek out their most appropriate skills, talents and interests in determining their best suitability for their future work.

Removing kids from forbidden fruits are no different to removing them from a dangerous environment. It's really one thing for a parent to say "I love my kids" but it's quite another to actually do something positive to help them. Parental behaviour and participation in their kids' lives, is the greatest example kids learn from and it is imperative that all examples and role models are what we want kids to aspire to. The most basic example is in accepting a **zero tolerance of vulgarity, promiscuity or profanities** in the home or anywhere else. We once lived well enough without the crime and drain on society, these poor attributes provide and we can once again. Let it be well known that this is just not on and you will not tolerate it any more. Don't allow violence or bad behaviour into your home, especially through the TV in any form as this is what leads to hate, violence and anger which affects attitudes and good choices. Monkey-see, monkey-do and we must accept responsibility for our kids if we have failed in our homes.

The Federal Government purported to take a positive stance in raising the school leaving age to 18. This is not in the interest of every child, particularly those who want to pursue a trade career, or have never had an aptitude for learning. This is an obvious means of artificially keeping them off social welfare and more importantly from a political stance, to project a false lower unemployment rate. If the top end of education is of benefit to the child, then it is the bottom end that is in need of addressing:

◆ Lower the age for kids starting school to three years old. This is when behavioural skills are developed and if before five yeas of age, children can be taught how to learn. They will be inclined to improve their scholastic results and social skills and perhaps stay in the educations system past 16 years of age.

Nationally, we have more than 1,200,000 kids who are under four years of age. The mind of a young child is like a sponge, absorbing everything at a faster rate than at any age. Currently, the opportunities to maximize early childhood development appear to be negated, due to national inconsistency of educational standards and more appropriate lessons. Kids need Humpty Dumpty and to use their imagination in being creative but they can be taught so much more and with the initiative to incorporate 3½ year olds into the school system, many of the issues adverse to the child and to society can be overcome.

We have the encumbrance of very expensive bureaucratic paper shuffling in administering early child care, subsidies to eligible recipients, but not to all. Complex tax rebate systems which are, in most cases, both insufficient to provide adequate assistance to the family, or to the learning centres. The most effective method and in the best interests of the family is, for mothers to nurture their children till aged three, if she is able to and then send them into the public or private school system. There are many benefits to the community, particularly to the mother and her children and the costs would probably be absorbed with the replacement of:

◆ Government administration staff currently employed to administer child care subsidies could be retrained as child care workers and teacher's aides within the public and private school systems.

Teachers Colleges could then boost professional standards with courses for one to two days weekly over, say a 4 year period for teacher's aids wanting to become teachers and participating in job sharing. This could also facilitate existing teachers who want to improve their teaching skills. This would not be full time college, as the current four teachers college course to be a teacher, also is not.

◆ Child care subsidies and tax rebates would no longer be required as those funds would be vested into the National Education Ministry to meet these costs, same as the National Health Ministry.

Mr Abbott recently advocated for 6 months parental maternity leave at the cost of big business but how dumb is that! Big business will only increase costs passed onto consumers to cover their costs. Families have been seeking Maternity Leave payments for 18 weeks leave but this is not enough time for either the mother or her baby and 12 months is far too long for an employer to keep a job open, let alone contribute for no productivity. There is a perception that the cost of having children is a cost that ought to be met by the government. No government can afford to maintain all families through this time. This is a cost that a family must be prepared to bear when making the decision to have children and how many. There must be assistance offered in repayable loans and it is perhaps a time for families to consider and evaluate their priorities in life for what they need and where they want to live to achieve this.

For example: When a family lives in an area where the mortgage or rent for a home is less than 30% of the husbands income, mothers are not financially pressured to have to go to work and often this is a decision that needs to be made by mum and dad. It comes down to living within one's means and where a move to a more affordable area can provide a better lifestyle or, if not, they should be prepared to get into debt and depend on the wife's income. Perhaps as an alternative family assistance offer:

◆ Government would provide the proven net income for three years, based on the previous three years of taxable income of the full time carer. This would be, say an interest free loan paid monthly over the three years and then would need to be repaid over the next, say, 10 years when mum is back at work and the child is in school and while dad also claims her and the children as his dependants.

◆ Unemployment benefits for persons staying at home to look after children after the child turns 3½ should cease. With free education and medical treatments, there is no reason why even a single mother cannot get a 30 hour a week job which would give her more than double what she receives in unemployment payments and this would save the national purse a small fortune. Dispel the concept of relying on society for financial support!

No child should be allowed to leave school under 16 years of age and not before successfully completing a proficiency test in all fundamental subjects. The exception would be serious juvenile offenders who should enter "boot camp" style tough-love training camps and also receive remedial education and training. To allow such children to end up mixing with jailed criminals is to ensure they graduate as criminals and are lost to society.

It would be up to the proposed National Planning & Infrastructure Ministry to work with the National Industrial Relations, the National Education Ministry etc. to determine each area's current and future projected needs in relation to each respective skill. Then, based on skills requirements the National Education Ministry would work with schools and their students in determining aptitudes and abilities in pursuing jobs and opportunities both for their financial and personal needs. This will help kids find a most appropriate, for them, trade or skill and job satisfaction.

◆ Australian children must be guaranteed positions in colleges and universities as a priority over children from other countries, irrespective of the financial advantages. Our children must be afforded every means of financing their education independent of their family's ability to repay. HEX or similar should be extended to every child who wants to further their education. This is clearly our responsibility as a nation and to all of our benefit.

In developing new business and increasing all trades activities nationally, there will be many new opportunities to train our children into fields they have the best aptitude for but those best to teach and direct them are firstly those educated in the highly skilled field of eduction. **Those best equipped to head our National Education Resources Ministry are teachers, not hindered by politicians or civil libertarians** for their own objectives. Teachers given a mandate from our proposed national Senate and based on what the nation determines should have educational priorities.

National Industrial Relations
and Building Business

THOUSANDS OF MIGRANTS arrived in Australia since the 1950s, grateful to be able to work hard in peace and safety. They never whined or complained as they struggled and juggled to make a new life here and in their gratitude they have helped mould Australia into what it is today. From all corners of the globe they came, including those from war torn Europe, many having been victims of torture, starvation, loss of loved ones, homeless, abused and deprived of the most basic of human rights. Having suffered the worst deprivations at the hand of in-humanity, they arrived, not knowing what to expect or what was awaiting them in starting a new life. Australia extended an outstretched arm and an open hand to many who had nothing to offer but a promise to work hard and to contribute to being a part of this great new country, and they did.

Many arrived with limited education and a very limited command of English but with a keen need and want to learn and work attitude. They had strong work commitments, moral ethics, determination, good will, manners and human values and they worked very hard. Refugees who played their part in helping this wonderful country grow and who brought with them and shared their rich customs, cuisines and characters. Not all Aussies welcomed these new Australians, nor did they want to understand or empathise with these downtrodden souls, often called "Refo's" (refugees); Dago's and WOGS. So new adverse challenges had to be overcome as they were abused and accused of taking jobs from Aussies where, in fact, many of these jobs were the jobs Aussies didn't want to do. Through their hard work, these new Aussies created more jobs, more growth, more opportunities and they participated in creating the wealth Australia enjoys today. Many of these migrants excelled to the greatest heights of Australian business and created millions of jobs for Australians.

In appreciation for new beginnings, the freedom to worship in accordance with their own religious convictions and the ability to retain their customs in peace, thousands of migrants have eagerly grasped the "Fair go" Aussie culture, with common sense and a caring attitude towards every other Aussie. Proud to be Australians who have truly integrated peacefully and to them we owe a debt of gratitude, not for making Australia into a segmented multicultural society but a cohesive culture of **"True Blue Australianism".**

Australia has a wealth of diversity in its people and their multitude of skills and talents with the *"will and a drive"* to work hard and enjoy the fruits of their Labor. The Italian bricklayer who toiled hard under our extreme weather conditions, the Greek greengrocer who goes to the markets at 3am to give us the best produce he can, all working hard alongside each other. Thousands of migrants came here to help build the Snowy Hydro Scheme and have added to the Australian flavour, that without, we would have a pretty boring place. There was no such thing as a job not suitable for anyone who wanted a job – it was a case of take anything on offer and being very grateful for the opportunity. Today those Dagos and Wogs are well established builders, developers and so on and they provide many jobs for others. Their kids and their grandkids have been educated here and are Aussies who have grown up with an appreciation for the personal sacrifices their parents have made for them and their country. They are proud family-oriented people, who still work together, often still within the family business and together with every other Australian, they continue to help each other, a real credit to them and to us all.

They worked hard and often for less than their worth with an attitude of, "I am grateful, I have a job, I can feed and house my family" and it was not so much of an issue as to how much you earned, but what you could buy or afford to buy without debt. It was a perceived value for money. If a person lives in a less affluent area or a regional area, the mortgage is less and basic priorities take precedent in providing a quality of life and this is no different today. Migrants worked and they saved, never living beyond their means and they ensured their kids were well educated and their kids are the employers today.

As a nation of individuals we excel in almost every field, from sporting heroes to medical research. Per capita, as a nation have one of the world's highest rates of achievers in all fields, but we export our raw products and buy it back manufactured, at more than 500% of our primary product selling price. We deny ourselves job opportunities for a perceived inability to be competitive. We impose insignificant (if any) tariffs on imported products, compared to what is charged by other countries on imports. The Labor component of other countries coupled with minimum tariffs does not encourage us to buy Australian products. We are not competitive on the world market and we continue to buy our processed resources back rather than develop those industries here. More often than not, we buy back our own inventions and initiatives which were taken up and developed by overseas corporations, picked up for not much more than a song. Australia has a proud history of great ideas and inventions, but an appalling record of funding those ideas to ensure we benefit locally and internationally, exponentially.

More than 800,000 small businesses are relying on their ability to do an honest day's work for an honest day's pay but they are caught up in bureaucracy that prevents expansion and lateral thinking. Financial Institutions will only lend secured

"Risk Free" money at double the security of the loan amount required. No security, means no business expansion or working capital and if you fail, you lose everything and often you are never able to get up again, yet many innovative people can be saved and prosper, with the right sort of people running government. Most business people will work at their business, free enterprise not free trade, for many years with little if any form of pay or reward for their efforts in their attempt to reap the long term rewards. Some succeed, some plod along and many fall by the wayside losing their many years invested, their assets, their self esteem and becoming a liability to the community at large. This system is not forgiving to the victims of "economic conditions" and employers do not have unions to protect their interests as their worker members do.

The Federal Government – after the May 2009 Budget – claims that export sales are up but this is false reporting, as the truth is disguised in convoluted accounting. Export turnover figures may appear to be up, but this was based on selling more produce at lower prices to achieve the same financial return. That is, produce and manufacturing sales are way down to our farmers and small business but replaced and appearing increased by the massive coal and iron exports, owned by monopolies. The international debt is not down, and retail sales are not up but for a massive increase to mining interests. We are now in a time of dire need to refine all of our resources, cut backs and mergers and the removal of duplication, and getting back to where:

"Money is the means of <u>achieving</u> the objective, it should not be the objective.
Our objectives as a community must be to improve the lives of
all Australians with money earned and spent here.
In building and owning our assets and utilities"

The National Business Resource Ministry must be made up of experts in business, legal and financial matters and should be proactive with access and assistance to all businesses with plans to support expansion and development, forecast difficulties and ways of overcoming them.

The National Industrial Relations Ministry must work arm in arm with the National Business Resources Ministry to set "minimum wages only" with all wages above this level to be negotiated between employer and employee and subject to the cost of living in specific urban and regional demographics. This will achieve competitiveness and create jobs here not overseas. This would also alleviate the hundreds of awards and the confusion created. If the employer doesn't pay enough above the award, he or she will not have the workers needed to get jobs done, this is **real Work Choices, real Enterprise Bargaining.**

It is imperative that the new trade practices be established to give a balance to protect small business. New and improved trading standards between the ACC(P)C and the National Industrial Relations to ensure there is a fair balance for the employer and the employee and this will ensure ownership of Aussie business is strong and we can afford to keep it here. These initiatives would include:

◆ Setting *maximum* mark-up percentage margins on goods and services from the manufacturer or importer, to the wholesalers, to the retailers, to the consumer ensuring inflation is contained and not requiring interest hikes which only hurt people and present a false accounting of increased sales. This would create the competitiveness purportedly sought by government in deregulating industry and ensure consumers and their businesses are not exploited.

◆ Determine national minimum standardised wages across every industry. This would alleviate the hundreds of wage awards and add-ons in defining e.g. 1. Unskilled Labor; 2. Basic skills; 3. Skilled Labor; 4. Advanced skilled and trades; 5. Professionals and 6. Advanced professionals. These categories should be graded to cater to the various costs of living in urban or rural situations.

For example: A minimum wage for, say, a call centre person (basic skilled) in Orange would vary to say the same job in Sydney, just as the cost of living also varies greatly but both able to achieve a sustainable lifestyle. The gauge could be the ability to purchase a home for, say, the current 10 years of wages. When unions fought for equal pay it was also at a time when the price of an Australian home was based on 3 years income. All wages must be reworked to determine the actual cost of living where a house is again the equivalent of say 5 years wages, not 10 or more. Living in rural areas where the cost of living is less than in the city, it is reasonable that the wages can reflect the cost of living: Example: A young family with a mortgage in the city needs at least A$1,500pw or $43ph. But, in a rural home, the same family can live very comfortably on less than A$1,000pw or $28.50ph providing adequate work and a solid infrastructure of schools, medical and social resources are provided in the same ratio achieved in the city. It's a fallacy to think that moving to the city enables people to earn more money because it also costs more to live in the city, negating any financial advantage but compromising quality of lifestyle offered in urban areas.

The National Business Resource Ministry would incorporate the Industrial Relations, perhaps headed by Alan Fels who would determine these minimum wages awards based on the cost of living in rural areas, compared to living in an urban area and taking into consideration the skills levels in both scenarios. After this determination, it would be up to the employer to provide above awards and incentives.

These wage demographic differential are what has affect our ability to be price competitive both nationally and internationally and our ability to grow and provide more jobs. This initiative would provide the competitive edge, which was not provided and resulted in taking away or outsourcing call centre work to Pakistan and

India. Job that unemployed Aussies would have grabbed at lesser remuneration in rural areas, given the opportunity and without union intervention.

◆ All executives of public companies should have salary caps. Based on performance, the Managing Director of a national bank would receive the award for "Advanced Professional" with incentives based on performance. That is, for providing a profit after efficiently running a business, for investors and shareholders.

◆ The same would be determined for every function of government, based on experience and educational standards attained. No overtime penalty rates for government employees, rather job sharing if the need is there and in overcoming more than 100% on top of some government employee's wages.

The administrative workload encumbering business causes operational costs to escalate. These costs are either absorbed reducing profit or are added to operating costs, often making the business less competitive. These are not the costs of invoicing, banking and paying suppliers but the costs in maintaining employees which is enough to turn anyone off employing staff with the various wages, holiday and sick pays, training and tool allowances, the PAYG tax, payroll tax, workers compensation, work redundancy, superannuation contributions etcetera, etcetera and etcetera. **The greatest assistance we (government) can give, particularly to small business and all employees, would be to treat employees as if they are self employed, responsible to meet their own commitments.** This, rather than as if employees are stupid and are incapable of administering our own affairs of setting aside holiday pay or whether to invest superannuation it into the mortgage, until we take holidays. From biblical times, a worker worked for a day and got paid every cent for that day.

For example: Once the gross wage for the week and for the respective skills level plus employer incentives is determined, there need only be 3 payments:

1. The income tax as a fixed percentage of the gross wages paid to the National (ATO) Treasury, subject to dependant rebates.
2. A fixed percentage for redundancy, sickness and accident insurance, workers compensation premiums etc. is paid to the nominated insurer for the employee,
3. The net amount to the employee including their superannuation, holiday pay and the weekly percentage of the accumulated long service payments.

Long gone are the days when we cannot be trusted to handle all of our own money be it superannuation, long service or holiday pay, which should be included as part of the hourly gross income and paid after 1 and 2 above. Education as to budgetary skills need addressing together with information as to what can be achieved from work and saving versus being frivolous. Our income ought to be paid to us weekly and up to us to determine how and when we need to spend or save it. Weekly wages because there are savings which can be obtained in weekly mortgage payments versus monthly. In this day and age, these funds could save our home or at the least reduce our interest costs on a mortgage account in providing earlier ownership.

This would also ensure *"sickies"* are not abused. Currently if you don't take them, you don't get paid for them and this system would be a deterrent to that, while increasing our total annual national productivity. There has been talk of a tax free threshold of say A$18,000 to inspire people to get a job rather than collect Centrelink payments. This should be supported in taking whatever jobs are on offer, irrespective of where the job maybe. Perhaps assistance with relocation, if required, could be made from the long term welfare savings.

If the employee is a member of a union, he would make these payments directly, no different to paying a gas or electricity account and business can get back to the basics of making money and not having to be the government appointed administrator or the trustee of the employee.

Multicultural or Multinational Australians

AUSTRALIANS HAVE BEEN arriving by boat for the past 220 years. After WW2 Frank Lowy, Harry Triguboff together with thousands of other refugees or displaced people, arrived and accepted any (menial) work offered, immediately. There were no (endless) government handouts – people were brought into hostels, found accommodation and work and they moved on making new lives for themselves. My father arrived in 1949 on a Wednesday and the following Monday he started work cleaning trains at Central railway in Sydney, no welfare for him, his parents or his siblings and none of them have ever received any welfare or pension in the past 61 years. The contribution from migrants has Australia the lucky country that it is today.

Asylum seekers or refugees are those who are supposed to be seeking a safe haven or sanctuary from persecution in their homeland. It is understandable that those truly escaping persecution would look to any country able to offer a new life. Most countries are bound by the **United Nations Convention Relating to the Status of Refugees** to extended asylum and **we have a moral, humane RESPONSIBILITY to help all of mankind, but we have an absolute OBLIGATION to protect our citizens, our culture and our economy firstly.**

It has been suggested that there may be terrorists among groups of asylum seekers and this suggestion has created furore within our political circles, but among the hysterics, there is truth. Many asylum seekers arrive in Australia with no identification or papers making it almost impossible to determine who they really are, or where their political or other affiliations lie. We have no idea what their activities have been prior to their arrival in Australia. Many have come from countries where animosities are held towards Australian soldiers fighting in their homeland and there is no way of accurately gauging what their true intentions are for coming here, versus accepting asylum in any of the countries they passed through on their way here.

Although not widely reported in the Australian press (as it would have exposed Mr Rudd to ridicule) on 21 October 2009, a New Zealand Afghan refugee's appeal to have a police search of his home declared unlawful was denied by the NZ Court of Appeal. He is now considering taking the case to the NZ Supreme Court. The refugee arrived in NZ from Afghanistan in 1995 and was granted refugee status, claiming he'd be killed if he was sent back and that his wife and children had been killed. When the NZ Police raided his Mt Albert (Auckland) home, they found it had been converted into a virtual command centre. There was evidence of a clandestine cell of refugees who had been granted NZ residency. The Police found evidence of a conspiracy to attack the Lucas Heights Reactor during the 2000 Olympics, including a Sydney street map with access routes highlighted. The Police said the cell they uncovered consisted of about 20 mainly Afghani refugees in Auckland, who had been familiarising themselves with the Western way of doing things. They found strong indications that at least some had military training from photographs of the refugees – New Zealand residents brandishing AK-47s – who were engaged in armed conflicts. Officers believed some of the refugees had fought in hotspots such as Afghanistan, Iraq, Iran, Bosnia, Chechnya, Somalia and Sri Lanka.

Delving deeper into the cell's affairs, detectives began to suspect some newcomers were using the relative obscurity and remoteness of New Zealand as a launching pad for more sinister activities. So not only is Australia at risk from the illegal arrivals via boats, but also from those using our neighbours as a stepping stone. This has been widely reported in the NZ press and certainly confirms that Wilson Tuckey's point.

Alarm bells are ringing but unfortunately we have no option, we are stuck with a government who adapts to adverse or rather "no real" boarder policies. Ministers who have no idea how to protect Australians and are far too arrogant to accept what worked in the Howard policies. Effectively, Kevin Rudd distanced himself from what he's done in opening our borders to whoever can afford to pay the smugglers thousands of dollars to get to Australia. How many bona fide refugees have access to thousands of dollars to pay the smugglers? Not Kevin Rudd or any government, guarantee Australians that there are no potential terrorists among refugees in light of the NZ experience? Can he guarantee Australians that the thousands coming here on work permits (paid well below our wages and who cannot understand a word of English to pass tests to get green cards but work on dangerous construction sites) or permanent residency visas will ever be going home?

When confronted on this issue, Kevin Rudd utilised tactics of *"the best defence being offence"* that is, ridiculing any opposition or contradiction to his purported "superior" determination and stingingly criticised Mr Tuckey. This should have been seen for what it was, a blatant attempt to protect his backside. In one fell swoop, Kevin Rudd has undone all the systems the Howard Government put in place to protect Australia from the risk of people who may have deliberately destroyed their paperwork to be able to arrive in our waters to further their mandate. There have been other despicable acts from those purporting to be genuinely intent on being Australians, such as the Cleric who wrote disgusting letters to the widows of Australians who have died – our war heroes. We can never be sure of every person's true motives, but as stated, **Australian Citizenship is a privilege, not a right**. We need to be able to withdraw citizenship from offenders who break our laws and who refuse to adhere to decent standards. The threat of deportation for failure to comply would make Australian Citizenship a valuable reward, rather than just a key to our very generous social security. Issues that need to be addressed by immigration authorities to determine if:

1. There still persecution in the country of origin? That is, can they return when civility is regained?
2. Those leaving countries such as Sri Lanka, Iran or Afghanistan travel through Pakistan, then India or China, then Burma then Thailand to reach Malaysia and then Indonesia before they set sail for Australia, but they do not seek asylum along the way. Why not, if they were purely and genuinely seeking asylum from adversity?

Does Indonesia and Malaysia fail to accept them and fail to stop breaches of their own border security? No, because they are aware that the destination is Australia? This being the case, these countries in effect have aided in the crossing of our borders, also demonstrated in Indonesia and Malaysia's failure to prosecute people smugglers. Asylum seekers are able to take asylum in any of these countries, but they persist in risking their lives to get to Australia – the land of great welfare and benefits. They jump the queue ahead of those who wait patiently for their right to migrate and negate our ability to stop them, with Christmas Island overflowing and more people arriving weekly due to weak government. Thousands of new Labor voters, who will show their gratitude to their benefactor Rudd or his successor Labor PM at election time and those who will continue to allow them to bring their relos over on the Family Reunion Program. What happens to the boats after they have delivered their human cargo to Christmas Island?

Irrespective of age or circumstance, it should be mandatory for those currently living here to learn English. New migrants (over 5 years of age) should learn English within the first 6 months of arriving but preferably during the period before immigration, as a show of good faith and sincerity towards their host country. Work and accommodation must also be provided and accepted. This is also a means of showing a true intention to integrate and contribute. If there is reluctance, perhaps there is no real or true intention?

This would save the new Australians and us a fortune in the costs of interpreters and translations into various languages, for every service from telecommunications companies to government. It would prevent harm and losses made by those not skilled in the English language for their failure to understand what is happening in the work place, in our government offices, banking, in schools, news etc. It's fine to have signs in ethnic languages providing that the majority of signage is in English. Try shopping in suburbs such as Ashfield without an interpreter.

◆ It is not politically correct for Australians to offer services and information in other languages. It costs us a fortune to provide these services as these costs are passed onto all users and taxpayers.

◆ Learning our history, our proposed Charter of Rights and Code of Conduct should be required in for those obtaining (work permits) permanent residency and citizenship. This will reduce misunderstandings and excuses for failing to co operate. This, also enable migrants to demonstrate where and how they can make a difference in improving their lives and the Australians who are sharing their country with them.

◆ The best form of integration is through honest work. It is imperative that asylum seekers commence work quickly to both reduce resentment of those who would take advantage of our welfare and to demonstrate a true intent to be a participating Australian.

It cannot be assumed that everyone living or wanting to live in Australia would know our "Code of Conduct", our core values, or Charter of Rights for a fair dinkum AUSTRALIANISM (that is, the cultural makeup that we want to achieve and maintain). We cannot afford to assume issues of such significance and gravity are just known or are just common sense – common sense, as we know, is not so common. These codes and expectations may not have formed part of the culture of a country from where the migrant has come from. To reiterate due to the gravity of this, the Code of Conduct and Charter of Rights would spelt out in plain English and be taught with continued reinforcement to everyone to ensure there are no misunderstandings or excuses for failure to comply. The serious ramifications for breaches of conduct must also be explained.

Immigration currently account for approximately 1% of our annual growth rate and in spite of an almost 6% unemployment rate, we are still seeking skilled and unskilled Labor, all around the country. There are thousands of able-bodied persons who can fill those jobs and immigration preferences should give to our current and future requirements, in all specific areas:

◆ A National Industrial Relations Ministry would be able to assess with the National Planning & Infrastructure Ministry, where the growth is and will be, and what Labor requirements will be required in every specific industry and all demographic areas for at least the proceeding 10 years. This would be published and circulated to the Education and the Immigration Ministries to work at filling these requirements.

Skilled and unskilled labour requirements determined and designated job opportunities would be provided before arrival, and to the migrants who now live very comfortably on unemployment benefits. Older persons could undertake trade apprenticeships and work in a trade as an assistant or as unskilled labour and this must also be pursued versus receiving unemployment benefits, indefinitely. There is no such thing as a free lunch and too many migrants claiming to be seeking asylum have chosen Australia for their economic benefit in being welfare and benefits recipients. Refugees must be prepared to integrate, work and accept housing in areas where they will be beneficial to the country and themselves, if not, they are not refugees but bludgers and we don't need them here. In simple terms, our way or the highway back to where you came.

With a national focus on new industry there would be the renewal of hundreds of existing satellite townships in rural and semi-rural areas. Then government would be able to provide housing and work opportunities. A refugee or a migrant must find it financially attractive to be given work and a workable home mortgage for repayment over, say 20 years. This should be appreciated as a more favourable option than welfare benefits, which have put a huge drain on our society, anything else is abuse of the host country.

At March 2010 with softened boarder protection laws, Christmas Island was overflowing with people living in tents with 4100 new arrivals. Based on these figures at a conservative cost of A$80,000 per new arrival, these people alone have cost the Australian taxpayer A$328 million.

Over the 2 years the Rudd government was in power and policies changed, taxpayers have paid out A$628 million to asylum seekers in: aged pensions, disability support pensions, Austudy, Newstart Youth Allowances and A$21.6 million in Baby Bonus payments. Payments they would never have received if asylum was sought in Indonesia or any of the other countries they passed through on their way to Australia? Barnaby Joyce refers to some are "economic migrants" – those selecting their best option rather than grateful to whoever takes them in. This does not constitute being a refugee, nor an asylum seeker.

Once migrants are established here, of course their relatives can seek migration based on family reunion policies. It doesn't take long to learn "all the tricks of the trade". If this continues and as our population grows, Australia will become a welfare country with substandard conditions and the inability to provide anything for anyone.

A Federal government report stated that there is a **growing welfare dependency:** *"Since 1974 the proportion of working age Australians receiving an income support payment has risen from a modest 5% to around 20% today. Around 2.6 million working age Australians currently receive some welfare payment".* Add to this, aged pension, growing refugee migrant payments, child care support etc and we exceed 40% – yet there are thousands of people around the world who have skills and financial resources who want to help build this country but are refused migration due to ridiculous issues.

The clearest examples are white South Africans who live in fear for their lives every time they leave the fortress they call home but cannot come here because they do not hold the required points in a stupid system. Examples: A retired lady in South Africa who is quite comfortable and able to support herself wants to move to Australia. She has two sons in Canada and one daughter in Australia but because the majority of her family is not here, she is not allowed to migrate. The Australian government requires similar would-be migrants to have A$500,000 in the bank as a bond and they have no ability to make any claim for any assistance (many cannot claim Medicare) for ten years. If we are to take in more refugees we need more migrants to bring their resources, set up new businesses to employ these refugees and our own welfare recipients.

Another example is the doctor and his wife (a teacher) with their family who cannot come to Australia unless he signs a contract that he will work in rural Australia for 5 years. Unfortunately rural Australia cannot provide for his religious observance and religious school attendance required for his children. There are thousands of people living here and working under visas, because we need their skills, but they cannot obtain Medicare, yet asylum seekers are given red carpet treatment. This once again demonstrates how damaging it is to have complex legislation and rules instigated by short term Ministers. This area alone can create the greatest imbalance to the future of our economy and our way of life. Australia requires common sense, sound legislation and equality for the long term in all areas.

◆ We should be placing migrants into their own home, with work on arrival and aiding migrants who are now living in government housing or are receiving rental assistance. Immediate efforts need to be made to provide their own home and work in semi rural and rural areas. Repayable loans provided for the purchase of the house from the government, with the suggested free health and education benefits as proposed for all Australians. The only cost of living would then be the repayment of the non urban home, food, clothing and sundry. This will quickly turn refugee welfare recipients into productive members of our society and improve our unskilled employment, or if this is not acceptable, leave. Of course this is subject to the new business initiatives by skilled government.

This comes back to who is qualified to make these decisions and where is the balance of fairness? There can be absolutely no incentive for a refugee to work, if welfare and benefits outweigh an earned income.

◆ Benefits of unemployment must be restricted to 6 months at the same rate our pensioners receive. Work offered nationally must be accepted or benefits terminated.

◆ If proven that poor cultural attitudes and customs are developed in the home and transgressed into our society, the migrant parents must accept responsibility for their kid being involved in these gangs. In the most serve cases, deported for their failure to intervene by seeking police or government assistance, before acts of violence or crime erupt.

With the proposed planned relocation of factories and new industry, as suggested, towns that have been bribing people to move there would have an abundance of new residents and work for the town and its new and existing citizens. There is a commonality between people of the same race or religion, that we respect, but it would not be right for people of the same nationality to "*take over*" a suburb or a town. This raises incidents of discrimination which more than often leads to the lack of integration and resentment on all sides.

As immigration increases, it is the challenge of the 21st century in learning and teaching tolerance. The trick is that people should be able to integrate and work with others of many nationalities and cultures while practicing and marrying persons of their belief or faith, if they choose.

The following is an extract from the book *Life Is No Rehearsal* due to be released in 2011 – check the <www.aussieswannakiss.com> website for info. The book is based on equality and how individually and thus collectively, we can improve our quality of life and achieve happiness which doesn't cost a cent.

SECTION 4

"Life is No Rehearsal"

Breaking The Cycle of Poverty

Feed ourselves and we feed the world

I T'S AS IMPERATIVE to fix our political system as it is to fix our social standards. Australia needs more productive Australians, more good people to enjoy our common wealth and to enrich all of our lives. We need to populate Australia with Australians to meet the financial and cultural demands of our society. To provide the long term infrastructural requirements of this still young and developing nation. There are many ways to attract contributing immigrants while we continuing to take in refugees, those who have passed the strictest scrutiny of security checks and motives for wanting to live in Australia. We are not an inhumane society – we offer people living in depravity, the opportunity to come and live here in peace and to enjoy this wonderful country. There are ways they can help combat the costs of their absorption into our society and ways in which we should insist upon be accepted as reasonable, for genuine migrants.

In times of war and depression, diamonds have been given for a loaf of bread, proving bread is of greater value than any diamond. The value of any product is only based on the supply able to meet the demand in creating the perceived value. If there is an oversupply, the value diminishes and an undersupply pushes up the value. There are many ways society can change the perception of value and ways of thinking, way *"outside of the square"* that we can consider. An example: In Holland, where most of the population ride bicycles as their main mode of transport, there are more than 160,000 reports of stolen bicycles every year. This costs the Dutch government authorities and the police in time/wages and administration more than the cost of say a A$200 bicycle or A$32 million per annum. If say, when a child turns 10, the Dutch government gave every child and adult wanting one, a bicycle, (say 20,000 bicycles per year) it would cost the government A$4 million a year. Compare this with the conservative cost of the police administration at say A$300 per stolen bicycle report, for 160,000 reports, a cost to the Dutch taxpayer of more than A$48 million – the value of bicycles would be completely diminished, and so would theft. The Dutch government would save A$44 million per year, police resources would be freed up and channelled into other areas or even reduced. There would be far reaching other positive results, including reduction in fuel needs, reducing environmental impact, the need for extending road capacity, costs of insurance and the cost of accidents, thus hospital costs would also reduce. This is placing people before profits, to yield greater overall benefits for every facet of society. This example is extreme but it demonstrates the ability for good government to be able to turn a struggling society into a wondrous place where everyone lives in peace and happiness. Where everyone has enough without exorbitant government costs, where taxes can either be reduced or directed to greater advancements, rather than continually attempting to fix otherwise unfixable problems:

Nothing breeds contempt and hatred more than poverty. Nothing breeds more disharmony and crime in any community, than poverty. Nothing breeds intolerance more than poverty and the lack of ability for people to live in peace more than inequality, injustice and supremacist egos.

For decades, Federal and State governments have been claiming to be combating unemployment, but government deregulation of industries and alternative agendas does not afford the ability to overturn poor short term decisions made over the decades. Promises of retraining but with no solid jobs offered and hundreds of people every day losing their jobs (except for extra Xmas staff), these promises are just mere rhetoric by spin doctors. Today, youth unemployed is so high in some areas with no prospects on the horizon and many contemplating moving interstate for perhaps better opportunities than NSW offers.

We must consider the obvious: Over the past 50 years, both primary and secondary manufacturing has been all but destroyed. Other than short term injections into long overdue infrastructure, long term business opportunities must be created in regional areas where work and housing can be provided. There is no reason why every Australian should not own a home, have a job and live a quality life in accordance with demographically capacity. There is just no excuse for any poverty in Australia today, if the right people are doing the jobs to create this.

Like it or not, there are "financial classes" in all societies and there are major differences in the standards of living. It's easy for the knockers to criticise the wealthy, but being mindful that without the wealthy, there can be no wealth shared around in spending and no jobs created if the wealthy do not spend or invest. Thus, rightfully, the wealthy deserve respect and appreciation. Our affluent society are a minority and reducing while the majority today are middle class, although struggling to stay that way, but there are far too many Australians who are unemployed and homeless needing urgent help. In breaking the cycle of poverty we will improve all of our standards of living and Advance Australia. **This can only be achieved with kindness and strictness to the adherence of a proposed Code of Conduct and a People before Profits attitude and by installing a transparent political system, which has no agenda other than the best interests of its citizens.** In this, we will reduce crime; improve productivity, reduce demand on police, courts, hospitals, doctors and nurses, mental illness and create unity with no division, discrimination or contempt.

To achieve this and just like the "out of the square proposal for Holland", we must give to get! No indiscriminate waste e.g. throwing money at people in financial handouts but in giving hand-ups – free education from 3 years of age, free health, free business support, government loans with competitive terms, equality at every corner. We do not need to spend another A$1 billion on consultants in the next two years for politicians to reject experts advice. We need a competitive Australian owned bank where Australians invest into a national programme of planning and for Australians to be able to work at these new opportunities and pay back to those who have invested in them, simple? Through the proposed Bank of Australia, investment into government bonds to set up new manufacturing and agricultural businesses can be made. For example; Process produce into more and competitive frozen, canned and dried produce for the local and export markets. This will require people to move to these areas and they will reap the rewards.

Our unions and IR laws have priced us out of many markets – turn this around and demand, call centre business by banks, telecommunications companies and others be moved back where this business belongs, here, for those who would gladly do those jobs and for a lower wage. People in our country areas, whose cost of living is much less than their counterparts in our cities, can afford to earn less and they want these opportunities to be able to continue living in outer regions of Australia, but currently have no choice as these jobs do not exist to them as they are not afforded these opportunities.

There is a school of thought that says, *"more trade fosters good international relations"*. This is only the first half of the sentence the balance is this, *"providing there is a reasonable balance of trade"*. In the case of China and others, we export raw materials to them on terms which those countries generally dictate, having the greater bargaining power. Then we buy back value-added goods (phones, stereos, TVs, etc) at exorbitant prices when those goods can be made here. If that is hard to understand, consider why Farmers Markets are becoming more and more popular – farmers meet customers face to face and get feedback which major supermarket chains may either charge them for, or not provide. Customers get goods directly at cheaper prices than the supermarket, but the farmer makes 100% of the sale price, even if the sale price is half the supermarket chain store price. If we replace the word "farmer" with "Australian business" and "supermarket chain" with "large international monopolistic firm" then you can understand what is happening to us at a global level.

Unions Fees are supposed to reflect a *"not for profit"* ie not for profit to donate to party politics and with some 1.9 million union members, the fees should be reduced to reflect the cost of overheads only and a projected income for specific union activities with transparent accounts to their members, naturally. It is only reasonable that all unions consolidate for the common good of workers entitlements and sound working conditions. Currently the many unions and their priorities are as diversified as the political parties and their respective agendas.

The extent of union involvement in politics ought to be confined to working with the Business Resources Ministry.

◆ Representation of the consolidated union would form part of the IR Business Ministry to ensure fair trading with employees is achieved for all demographic areas and in relation to each specific skills category, to provide harmony and a fair balance in the workplace.

Fair consideration needs to be made for the disparity of living costs. Consider, for example, a worker in, say, Walgett, NSW who wants to sew piece work in a new local Australian manufacturing factory, or at home. They agree to be paid by the piece – that is (after all) the business of the worker and his employer. Why should an employer be penalised by a slow worker and a fast worker penalised for the extra effort? Similarly, if a group of women want to get together in Cloncurry, Queensland and set up a call centre to bid for work currently outsourced to Pakistan and they are happy to earn A$10ph as their cost of living even if it is by far less than their city counterparts – that too is their business.

This is free trade and fair competition. Not in an international sense, when cheap goods come in without tariffs and destroy our local industries, that free trade is far too expensive. A worker will only accept the job if they are happy to accept the offered income, governed by the set minimum IR laws. If the employer wants to get the job done, he will pay a rate not less than the government published rate for minimum sustainability or by the piece if manufacturing and he may offer incentives for meeting deadlines or minimum quotas.

We have the space and we have failing towns screaming out for work and enterprise. **STOP national division and adverse political agendas, STOP unskilled persons running our imperative portfolios, STOP the demise of Australian society, STOP the destruction of families due to financial pressure, STOP inequality at all levels of society, STOP our towns dying, STOP sending call centre work to Pakistan, India and other countries, STOP sending our agricultural and manufacturing industries overseas.** We can allow our people to work cheaper – lower living cost warrant lower income rather than earning nothing, or worse, depending on social security payments

Charity begins at home in Australia, and we must fix up our own home so we can help fix others in other countries. The world is going in a misguided direction in seeking a global economy. There are far too many international disparities which have shown to be detrimental. For example, a worker in China can earn US$6 per day and save a few dollars each week, while in Australia we cannot save at A$20 per hour. We must think and act locally, firstly!

◆ Relocate the homeless and those who want a break, and the unemployed willing to move, with a home in towns begging for citizens. Given jobs currently being outsourced overseas and in new business to improve all of our lives and our environment.

Relocating and helping homeless families to move into their own home from government housing, with these proposed newly created work opportunities, with greater export opportunities and with more space for more new Australians – the cycle can grow within this plan that provides for growth, and not a system which currently we have outgrown.

◆ New and revived towns will provide opportunities for struggling business' and trades people to move to regional areas and overcome the obstacles of excessive competition. Overcome the demise of their lives, their assets, and their family's mental and physical health. New industry will improve with new green initiatives to clean up the world without an ETS. Currently we struggle to get professionals and tradespeople into the country areas, but with the establishment of new business, doctors, carpenters, plumbers, electricians and others who are currently reluctant to live in rural areas would seriously consider the benefits. Those who are relucent to decentralise, are only relucent because of the current lack of business, opportunities, infrastructure and facilities.

A home with a loan and work would also be a great incentive for young Australian families who would like to take up this offer. With lower living costs in rural areas than in densely populated, high demand and thus high cost urban areas, it stands to reason that a lesser income can sustain a less costly family budget. It could also ensure if mum wants to stay at home, she can rear her family without the cost of after school care and that marriages have a better chance of survival and for families to be truly functional. It also allows the family to be proactive in the community and to further their interests and education, individually and as a family. Rural areas often have less pollution, are safer and healthier. Work isn't far from home, so parents spend more time with their kids. Who needs a gang when competing activities include horse riding or riding quad bikes, weekend local bushwalks in a clean environment away from the Big Smoke!

To reiterate, I believe one of the best ways to populate Australia with Australians is by opening the flood gates to the world's homeless children and all the while lifting spending in every industry sector, particularly employment.

In the plan to decentralise, it provides a quality of life which comes with the opportunity to rebuild the nation "On the sheep's back" Ausbuy: "KEEPING JOBS HERE – If Australians spent A$25 pw week on 100% Australian owned and made goods, we would reduce our foreign debt by A$25 billion a year. That is why Ausbuy says "Buy Australian Owned and Made" and Ausbuy guarantees that the decisions, the profits and the jobs stay here. The anger against Pacific Brands is misguided – they did not want to make 1,800 people redundant, these are the consequences of government policies with cheap imports *and low wages overseas. Pacific Brands are Australian owned by Australian shareholders and forcing them out of business just means all those iconic Australian brands like Berlei, Holeproof and Bonds, will be bought by foreigners and then we lose all the jobs. Profits and decisions about the business being made overseas. We do not want to be a branch office of overseas. Already too many quality Australian Brands have been lost – Dairy Farmers, Golden Circle, Arnotts.*

Wake up Australia and support our own companies, whether they produce goods or sell services and no matter what size they are – conglomerates or one person operations they are employing Australians and Australian families. Already 4 in 10 people get some form of government support. Do we want more people relying on handouts? We only want a fair go and we have not been having that for decades. We need to work together to safeguard our future and stop falling for the gloom and doomsayers. We are better than that!"

Breaking the cycle of poverty will reduce crime and demands on every sector of our society. It will create unity, individual and national prosperity and it will give a quality of life, second to none, to those who are suffering. Effectively, government would be diverting what is currently spent on social security into productivity investments. It's the chicken who lays the egg and not vice versa. Build the new business and the egg will hatch! A *chain is only as strong as its weakest link* – good government is only as good as its individual and collective priorities. Ensuring equality, transparency and that every sector of the country and every portfolio is successful, and only then can the choices for the people be easy, effective and good.

Poverty is real and a burden, causing sufferance to the whole of our society and as a caring society we have an obligation to help those who are suffering to improve their circumstances, firstly. With a positive "people before profits" attitude and efforts, we can achieve more and it will not cost more. As a community, we all have the responsibility to reshape and improve each others lives. In doing this we improve our own life, it is purely a matter of choice by each of us individually without self or party interests or egos.

Egos cause financial stress for "things" and this can cause obsessive greed, for more; a bigger house, a boat, expensive furniture, a better car, even an affair on the side, if for no other reason but to cover up insecurities and inadequacies. This is all just building and supporting an ultra ego to the point where it is a matter of whose ego has priority for the space in any relationship, business, government and particularly, in a marriage. George Carlin was a comedian in the 1970s and 1980s and he wrote a very appropriate message which is too important not to share: "*The paradox of our time in history is that we have taller buildings but shorter tempers; wider freeways but narrower viewpoints; we spend more but have less; we buy more but enjoy less; we have bigger houses and smaller families; we have more conveniences but less time; we have more degrees but less sense; more knowledge but less good judgment; more experts yet more problems; more medicine but less wellness. We drink and smoke too much, spend too recklessly; laugh too little and drive too fast; get too angry; stay up too late and get up too tired; we read too little and watch too much TV and we pray too seldom. We have multiplied our possessions but reduced values; we talk too much, love too seldom and hate too often.*

We've cleaned up the air but polluted our souls; we've conquered the atom but not our prejudices; we write more but learn less; we plan more but accomplish less; we've learned to rush but not to wait; we build more computers to hold more information, to produce more copies than ever but we communicate less. These are the times of fast foods and slow digestion, big men and small characters; steep profits and shallow relationships; two incomes but more divorces; fancier houses but broken homes.

These are the days of quick trips, disposable diapers, throwaway morality, one night stands, overweight bodies and pills that do everything from cheer you up, calm you down to killing you.

Remember; spend some time with your loved ones, because they are not going to be around forever. Say a kind word to someone who looks up to you in awe, because that little person soon will grow up and leave your side. Remember, to give a warm hug to the one next to you, because that is the only treasure you can give with your heart and it doesn't cost a cent.

Remember to say "I love you" to your partner and your loved ones, but most of all mean it. A kiss and a cuddle will mend hurt when it comes from deep inside of you. Remember to hold hands and cherish the moment for someday that person will not be there anymore. Give time to love, to speak, to listen and to share the precious thoughts in your mind and remember life is not measured by the number of breaths we take, but by the moments that take our breath away".

The richest person is not the one who has the most, but the one who needs the least!

According to the renowned Professor Ron Penny, *"Mental illness is the fastest growing disease in Australia, outranking certain cancers"*. Drugs are given, therapists talk patients up and down, but the best cure for depression and anxiety is in our own heads and in our loving, caring attitude to those closest to us who need our help. We can succumb or give into our problems, our depression and allow this mental condition to take control of our lives. We can be consumed with worry and allow our perceived negativity to conquer us and push us down into the dungeon of depression, the chamber of misery and to allow ourselves to be enslaved by defeat and negativity, but this is just in our own mind.

A new mental condition called *"Motivation Dysfunctional Disorder* (MDD)" has been recently classified in an attempt to explain or help understand Bipolar disorders, ADHD and other conduct dysfunctional disorders. "MDD" in its mildest form can be as simple as the complacency to get out of bed on a Monday morning through to lazing around all day and not having *"the energy to get up and go"* and it is believed that this can lead to anxiety and depression with life threatening health issues as the end result, which ranges from Obesity through to the will to no longer want to breathe.

Far too often we focus on the solution and not the problem which makes matters worse, rather we resolve the "Causes" diminishing the "Effects":

There has been a tremendous world success in the *"Secret"* book, lectures and video series. It tells the audience to seek and *"ask from the universe what you want and you'll get it!"* but we must be convinced that we'll not only get it but we've got it already! In thinking, speaking and subsequently acting with a **POSITIVE ATTITUDE**, even in times of adversity it gives us the greatest opportunities of changing and in achieving positive results. Many call this "praying to God", while others might call it faith, and some would say it is a call to the forces of nature. It's just a choice of what language suits you best.

The essence of true love and happiness is the acceptance of all that is, has been, will be and will not be. Life is not about how we survive the storm but how we dance in the rain, it's the journey, not the grave: **Happiness comes from within, from making good life choices and with contentment for whatever we have. Success and Happiness are a state of mind – an attitude based on our healthy perception of ourselves, and is not based on what we have or who we can impress.** We can only achieve true "Happiness" from within ourselves and the best way for us to be happy is to make others happy. This comes from changing the direction of our thoughts from wasting valuable energy in worrying to using the abundance of powerful energy we have towards finding and working on solutions and from negative speech to positive options. If you're still thinking that you've got nothing to be happy about, then just act happy and you'll be happy after-all – *"It costs the same price to be happy as it does to be miserable"* Rachel Emmes.

As we are should be compassionate towards our family and friends, so must we be for every member of our society and we must ensure our government is just as compassionate about every single Australian, individually and collectively. Ensuring there is equality through the rank and file to every facet of our country. This is the cycle from emotional and financial poverty to prosperity that we all so badly want and the only cycle that counts.

With the culmination of all of the above, the implementation of concepts after refinement and if voted by the majority of Australians in supporting improvements in favour of the people are put into action – we will get the results we all deserve. Where we as a society may one day again, be able to allow our children to play in the streets without fear; where we can again sleep with our doors unlocked, without fear of unwelcome intruders; that our values and relationships are placed higher than that of worthless things. Where government becomes the servant once again and we as a nation of healthy and positive individuals can focus on positive advancements and personal improvements as all of the mundane fundamentals of life have been catered to by those who do not have any other objectives or agendas, than our well being. When we have delved deep into our soul for our personal refinement, then go back to Chapter 1 and demand the *"common sense changes".*

I do not believe we were intended to be on the face of this beautiful world for 70 odd years and wander aimlessly from day to day, nor are we here for our self gratification. The realisation of our specific purpose in life is not so well disguised if we use our specific skills and talents – **our mission in life will become obvious**. We all have the opportunity to make a difference to our own life and the lives of each other and this is the secret to a long, happy and stress free, thus healthy life.

Life is a challenge but the best part of the way in meeting its challenges, is through the strength of community. Through the skills we bring and share in achieving, **True Blue Australianism – the patriotic and peaceful unification of a diverse multi-faith society, striving for a unified culture.** In meeting the challenges ahead we need to do more sharing and rely less on our individualism, because it really is a case of united we stand and prosper, divided we fall and lose everything. I'd really like to hear your constructive comments at <info@aussieswannakiss.com> and in finishing for now I'd like to share this story with you:

The Spoons

A MAN WAS HAVING a conversation with God one day and he said, "*God, I would like to know what Heaven and Hell are like*" so God led the man to two doors. He opened one of the doors and the man looked in.

In the middle of the room was a large round table. In the middle of the table was a large pot of stew which smelled delicious and made the man's mouth water. The people sitting around the table were thin and sickly, they appeared to be famished. They were holding spoons with very long handles that were strapped to their arms and each found it impossible, after reaching into the pot of stew, to put the spoonful in his mouth because the handle was longer than their arm.

The man shuddered at the sight of their misery and suffering and God said, "*You have seen Hell.*" They went to the next room and opened the door. It was exactly the same as the first one. There was the large round table with the large pot of stew which made the man's mouth water. The people were equipped with the same long-handled spoons, but here the people were well nourished and plump, laughing and talking.

The man said, "*I don't understand*". "*It's simple,*" said God, "*It requires but one skill. You see, they have learned to feed each other, while the greedy think only of themselves.*"

The great adversity of the Victorian Bush Fires in February 2009 and the floods that devastated northern Australia gave Australians the opportunity to band together in caring and with the compassion Australians know best. Raising over A$150 million in such a very short period of time: food, clothes, household items and other goods came pouring in from the furthest ends of our country, in nothing less than the Australian way – an outpouring of love, caring and kindness for others. People who didn't know each other sent help just because Australians are naturally kind and generous, especially in times of tragedy. Just imagine for one moment, what we can do as a nation and for our own long, healthy and happy lives, if this kind of love and caring for each other can be our goal, not just in times of tragedy but always, in everything we do. This must be the objective from a new non political party government, to our youngest and newest citizens. For Australia to achieve stress free, this culture it must be instilled in our young and it's our responsibility to ensure they are educated in every good facet of life. Our survey and petition at <www.aussieswannakiss.com> gives us collectively the opportunity to take back that which is rightfully ours, the direction and priorities of government in providing each of us with the opportunity to get on with the job, with equality and caring for all – *This is the meaning of a fair go, worth documenting and worth teaching to our kids, as this is the culture of true blue Australianism!*